THE HOUSE OF

GUCCI

THE HOUSE OF

GUCCI

A Sensational Story

of Murder, Madness,

Glamour, and Greed

by Sara Gay Forden

WILLIAM MORROW

An Imprint of HarperCollins*Publishers*

HarperCollins books may be purchased for educational, business, or sales promotional use. For information please write: Special Markets Department, HarperCollins Publishers Inc., 10 East 53rd Street, New York, NY 10022.

FIRST EDITION

Designed by Nicola Ferguson

Printed on acid-free paper

Library of Congress Cataloging-in-Publication Data

Forden, Sara Gay.
The house of Gucci: a sensational story of murder, madness, glamour, and greed / by Sara Gay Forden.
p.   cm.
Includes bibliographical references and index.
ISBN 0-688-16313-0 (hardcover : alk. paper)
1. Gucci (Firm) 2. Gucci, Maurizio, 1948–1955. 3. Business men—Italy—Biography. 4. Clothing trade—Italy. 5. Trials (Murder)—Italy. I. Title.

HD9940.I84 G84 2000
364.15'23'094521—dc21   00-040954

00 01 02 03 04 QW 10 9 8 7 6 5 4 3 2 1

For Julia

Contents

Acknowledgments

Many people shared with me their experiences with the Gucci company and the Gucci family. I value their trust in me, for their associations with Gucci inevitably provoked deep emotions and lasting impressions. Key people who contributed to this book include Gucci's CEO Domenico De Sole and creative director Tom Ford, who granted repeated interviews between 1998 and 2000. Former Gucci creative director Dawn Mello also spent hours with me between New York, Milan, and Paris, describing her work alongside Maurizio Gucci. Andrea Morante offered a wealth of information and unusual insights into the personalities of the players. Investcorp chairman Nemir Kirdar recounted his own dramatic story, how he came to underwrite Maurizio's vision for Gucci, and how he painfully realized all hope was gone for achieving that dream together. Former Investcorp executive Bill Flanz also gave generously of his own experience, time, and contacts, helping me reach a broad range of people who in turn added their own dimensions to this story. Rick Swanson, currently at Gucci and formerly at Investcorp, painted vivid pictures of Investcorp's experiences with Maurizio Gucci, mixing priceless anecdotes with concrete facts and figures. Gucci's CFO, Robert Singer, described the adventure of taking Gucci public. Among other former Investcorp executives who helped are Paul Dimitruk, Bob Glaser, Elias Hallak, Johannes Huth, and Sencar Toker. Thanks also to Larry Kessler, Jo Crossland, and their staff.

In Florence, fashion historian Aurora Fiorentini's painstaking research to piece together the Gucci archive has been invaluable. Fiorentini shared her discoveries—from official documents unearthed from state archives to historic bags collected one by one from previous customers, to accounts from local artisans. Gucci's press offices around the world under the supervision of Giulia Masla cheerfully and efficiently helped me locate printed and photographic material and coordinate a daunting series of interviews. Claudio Degl'Innocenti shared his idiosyncratic view of Gucci's production and manufacturing side, while Dante Ferrari helped take me back to what it was like in the old days. Many others, not all of whose names appear in the pages of this book, also recounted their unique experiences.

Roberto Gucci deserves particular thanks for his gracious cooperation—even though there are large parts of the Gucci story he would much rather forget. Giorgio Gucci provided me with printed material about the family business and his father, Aldo, while Paolo Gucci's daughter Patrizia helped answer some of my questions.

Although Italian penitentiary officials denied my requests to interview Patrizia Reggiani Martinelli in Milan's San Vittore prison, she corresponded with me from her cell, while her mother, Silvana, tirelessly answered my questions. Paola Franchi also invited me to her home several times to recall her years with Maurizio.

Some of the most valuable recollections came from Maurizio's loyal assistant, Liliana Colombo, and his driver, Luigi Pirovano, remarkable people who became a kind of protective family for Maurizio. Maurizio's lawyer, Fabio Franchini made available precisely recorded information and helped me know the passionate yet vulnerable Maurizio he had grown fond of and tried to help. Severin Wunderman recounted stories for hours, enabling me to enrich my portrait of him, Aldo, and others. Logan Bentley Lessona, Aldo Gucci's first public relations professional, opened her memories and her files.

Enrica Pirri shared treasured memories of her more than twenty years with the Gucci family, with whom her ties still run deep.

With respect to the murder investigation and trial of Patrizia Reggiani, former Criminalpol chief Filippo Ninni, prosecutor Carlo Nocerino, Giancarlo Togliatti, and Judge Renato Lodovici Samek helped me retrace the story and understand the complexities of the Italian judicial system, while my friend and colleague Damiano Iovino became an invaluable and entertaining bench-mate during the long hours of testimony.

None of these experiences would have ever found their way into a book if not for my agent, Ellen Levine, and my editor, Betty Kelly, two remarkable women who spotted the appeal of the Gucci story. Their interest and support along the way were invaluable.

I want to thank my parents, David Forden and Sally Carson, for their constant encouragement, including my mother's editorial advice. My appreciation also to my husband, Camillo Franchi Scarselli, who urged me to take the leap into writing this book and supported my efforts. Our daughter, Julia, learned to accept my commitment with grace.

My good friend Alessandro Grassi gave me a congenial office "home" in which to write the book. I owe special thanks to friends and colleagues around the world who put me up during my interviewing trips to different cities: in New York, Eileen Daspin and Marina Luri; in London, Anne and Guy Collins, Constance Klein, Karen Joyce, and Marco Frattini; in Paris, Janet Ozzard, Gregory Viscusi, and Penny Horner. Thanks also to Teri Agins, Lisa Anderson, Stefano and LeeAnn Bortolussi, Frank Brooks, Aurelia Forden, and Thomas Moran, for help and encouragement along the way, as well as to my assistants, Chiara Barbieri and Marzia Tisio, who transcribed miles of interview tapes. In Rome, AP bureau chief Dennis Redmont and Sen. Francesca Scopelliti did all they could to help me try to get an interview with Patrizia Reggiani. In Paris, Marie-France Pochna offered brilliant insights on two French businessmen: Bernard Arnault and François Pinault. Thanks to Patrick McCarthy and Fairchild Publications, my former employers, for giving me the leave of absence that permitted me to write the book, and in particular to Melissa Comito and Gloria Spriggs for quick and cheerful photo and archive research. Finally, thanks to some unforgettable mentors from my Mount Holyoke College days, where I realized that writing could become a way of life: Caroline Collette, Richard Johnson, Mark Kramer, and Mary Young.

Interviews:

Carlo Bacci
Alberta Ballerini
David Bamber
Silvana Barbieri Reggiani
Sergio Bassi
Aureliano Benedetti
Logan Bentley Lessona
Patrizio Bertelli
Carlo Bonini
George Borababy
Armando Branchini
Carlo Bruno
Richard Buckley
Roberta Cassol
Rita Cimino
Liliana Colombo
Aldo Coppola
Pilar Crespi
Enrico Cucchiani
Antonietta Cuomo
Vittorio D'Aiello
Gianni Dedola
Claudio Degl'Innocenti
Rafaelle Della Valle
Domenico De Sole
Paul Dimitruk
Lisa Fatland
Franco Fieramosca
Aurora Fiorentini
Stefania Fiorentini
Dante Ferrari
Nicole Fischelis
William Flanz
Tom Ford
Paola Franchi
Fabio Franchini
Carmine Gallo

Francesco Gittardi
Bob Glaser
Pierre Godé
Giorgio Gucci
Guccio Gucci
Patrizia Gucci
Roberto Gucci
Orietta Gucci
Junichi Hakamaki
Elias Hallak
Johannes Huth
Joan Kaner
Claire Kent
Nemir Kirdar
Richard Lambertson
Concietta Lanciaux
Eleanore Leavitt
Carlo Magello
Cedric Magnelia
Maria Mannetti Farrow
Mario Massetti
Dawn Mello
Suzy Menkes
Nando Miglio
Andrea Morante
Alberto Morini
Filippo Ninni
Carlo Nocerino
Giuseppe Onorato
Carlo Orsi
Luigi Pagano
Gaetano Pecorella
Anita Pensotti
Gian Vittorio Pillone
Franca Pinzauti
Enrica Pirri
Gail Pisano

Luigi Pirovano

Carmello Pistone

Marie-France Pochna

Patrizia Reggiani Martinelli

Dante Razzano

Renato Ricci

Renato Lodovici Samek

Franco Savorelli

Robert Singer

Chantal Skibinska

Amy Spindler

John Studzinsky

Cristina Subert

Rick Swanson

Burt Tansky

Salvo Testa

Giancarlo Togliatti

Sencar Toker

Pietro Traini

Paolo Trofino

Allan Tuttle

Franco Uggeri

Dominique Vananty

Serge Weinberg

Severin Wunderman

Michael Zaoui

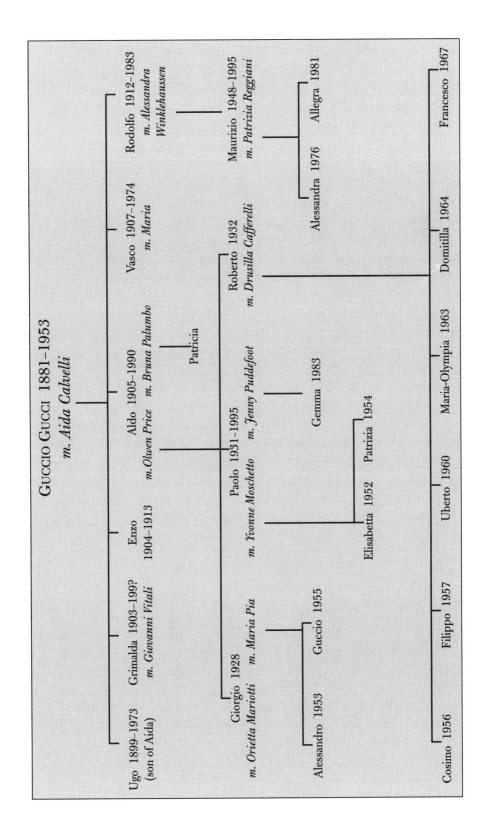

GUCCIO GUCCI 1881–1953
m. Aida Calvelli

Ugo 1899–1973
(son of Aida)

Grimalda 1903–199?
m. Giovanni Vitali

Enzo
1904–1913

Aldo 1905–1990
m. Olwen Price   *m. Bruna Palumbo*

Vasco 1907–1974
m. Maria

Rodolfo 1912–1983
*m. Alessandra
Winklehaussen*

Giorgio 1928
m. Orietta Mariotti   *m. Maria Pia*

Guccio 1955

Patricia

Paolo 1931–1995
m. Yvonne Moschetto   *m. Jenny Puddefoot*

Roberto 1932
m. Drusilla Cafferelli

Maurizio 1948–1995
m. Patrizia Reggiani

Alessandro 1953

Elisabetta 1952   Patrizia 1954

Gemma 1983

Cosimo 1956   Filippo 1957   Uberto 1960   Maria-Olympia 1963   Domitilla 1964   Francesco 1967

Alessandra 1976   Allegra 1981

1

A DEATH

A t 8:30 A.M. on Monday, March 27, 1995, Giuseppe Onorato was sweeping up the leaves that had blown into the entryway of the building where he worked. He had arrived at eight o'clock that morning, as he did every weekday, his first task being to swing open the two great wooden doors of the building at Via Palestro 20. The four-story Renaissance-style building housed apartments and offices and stood in one of the most elegant neighborhoods in Milan. Across the street, amid tall cedars and poplars, stretched the clipped lawns and winding paths of the Giardini Pubblici, an oasis of foliage and serenity in a smoggy, fast-paced city.

Over the weekend, a warm wind had blown through the city, clearing the ever-present cap of smog and blowing the last dried leaves from the trees. Onorato had found his entryway littered with leaves that morning and hurried to sweep them up before people started coming in and out of the building. His military training had instilled in him a strong sense of order and duty, although it hadn't broken his spirit. Fifty-one years old, he was always neatly dressed and impeccably groomed, his white mustache perfectly trimmed, his remaining hair clipped close. A Sicilian from the town of Casteldaccia, he had come north like so many others looking for work and a new life. Following his retirement from the army in 1980 after fourteen years as a noncommissioned officer, Onorato had decided to settle in Milan, where he worked for several years at various odd jobs. He took the doorman's post on Via Palestro in 1989, traveling back and forth on a small motor scooter from the apartment where he lived with his wife in the northwest section of the city. A gentle man with clear blue eyes and a sweet, shy smile, Onorato kept the entryway immaculate. The six highly polished, red granite steps that rose immediately inside the massive front doorway, the sparkling glass doors at the top of the steps, and the shiny stone floors of the foyer reflected his efforts. At the back of the foyer, Onorato had a small glassed-in cubicle made of wood with a table and chair, but he rarely sat there, preferring to keep busy with his chores. Onorato had never quite felt at ease in Milan, which had offered him work but little else. He was sensitive to the bias many northern Italians have against *meridionali,* or people from the south, and it took little more than a glance to make him bristle. He never talked back and he obeyed his superiors as he had learned to do in the army, but he refused to bow his head.

"I am just as worthy as the next man," Onorato would think, "even if he is rich or from an important family."

Onorato glanced up as he swept and noticed a man across the street. Onorato had seen the man immediately that morning upon opening the two great doors. The man had been standing behind a small green car parked perpendicular to the street with its nose facing the Giardini Pubblici, away from Onorato's building. Usually cars lined the curbs of Via Palestro, one of the few streets in downtown Milan that still had free parking. The cars parked at an angle, facing the curb. It was early, and the car was still alone. The license plate caught Onorato's eye because it was hanging so low it almost touched the ground. Onorato wondered what business the man had at that hour. Clean shaven and well dressed, the man was wearing a light brown overcoat. He kept looking down the street toward Corso Venezia as though expecting someone. Absently stroking his own balding crown, Onorato noticed with some envy that the man had a full head of dark, wavy hair.

Ever since a bomb had gone off up the street in July of 1993, he had kept his eyes open. With a blast that shook the city, a car packed with dynamite had exploded, killing five people and destroying the Padiglione d'Arte Contemporanea, the modern art museum, which collapsed in a rubble of cement, steel girders, and dust. That same evening, another bomb had exploded in Rome, damaging San Giorgio Velabro, a church in the city's historic center. The bombs were later linked to an earlier explosion in Florence on Via dei Georgofili that also killed five people, wounded thirty, and destroyed dozens of pieces of artwork that were stored in the building above the explosion. The bombings were later traced to a Sicilian mafia boss, Salvatore "Toto" Riina, who had been arrested earlier that year for the 1992 murder of Italy's top mafia prosecutor, Giovanni Falcone. Riina had ordered the bombings of some of Italy's most precious cultural monuments in retaliation for his arrest. He was later convicted for both the Falcone murder and the bombings and is currently serving two life sentences. The DIGOS, Italy's political police, which has a specific mandate to move against acts of terrorism, had interviewed all the *portinai,* or doormen, in the Via Palestro neighborhood. Onorato had told them he'd seen a suspicious-looking camper parked near one of the gates to the park that day. From then on, he made little notes on a pad he kept in his cubicle to record anything he saw that seemed unusual.

"We are the eyes and ears of this neighborhood," Onorato explained to one of his army buddies who often stopped by for coffee. "We know who comes and goes and it's part of our job to observe."

Onorato turned and pulled the right-hand door toward him in order to sweep the last few leaves out from behind it. Stepping behind the door, leaving it half-closed, he heard quick footsteps on the stairs and a familiar voice call out to him: *"Buongiorno!"*

Onorato turned to see Maurizio Gucci, who had offices upstairs on the first floor, sprinting up the entry stairs with his usual energy, his camel coat swinging.

"Buongiorno, Dottore," Onorato replied with a smile, lifting a hand in greeting.

Onorato knew Maurizio Gucci was a member of the famous Gucci family of Florence that had founded the luxury goods firm of the same name. In Italy, the Gucci name had always been associated with elegance and style. Italians were proud of their creativity and artisan traditions and Gucci was one of those names, along with Ferragamo and Bulgari, that symbolized quality and craftsmanship. Italy had also produced some of the world's greatest designers, such as Giorgio Armani and Gianni Versace, but Gucci was a name that went back generations, before the designers had even been born. Maurizio Gucci had been the last of the Guccis to run the family firm before selling it two years earlier to his financial partners who that spring had begun to study a plan to take Gucci public. Maurizio, no longer involved in any aspect of his family business, had opened his own offices on Via Palestro in the spring of 1994.

Gucci lived just around the corner in a stately palazzo on Corso Venezia, and walked to work every morning, usually arriving between 8:00 and 8:30. On some days, he let himself in with his own key and was already upstairs even before Onorato swung open the heavy wooden doors.

Onorato often wondered wistfully what it would be like to be in Gucci's shoes. He was a rich, attractive young man with a beautiful girlfriend who was tall, thin, and blond. She had helped Gucci furnish his offices upstairs on the first floor, as the second floor is called in Europe, with exotic Chinese antiques, elegantly upholstered sofas and armchairs, richly colored draperies, and valuable paintings. She frequently came to meet Gucci for lunch, dressed in her Chanel suits, her mane of blond hair perfectly coifed. To Onorato, they seemed a perfect couple with a perfect life.

As Maurizio Gucci reached the top step and started to walk into the foyer, Onorato saw the dark-haired man step into the doorway. In a flash he realized that the man had been waiting for Gucci. He wondered why the man had stopped at the foot of the stairs, where the wide, brown-bristled doormat ended and the gray cloth runner started, held in place at the base of each step with brass step rails. Gucci hadn't noticed the man step in after him and the man did not call out his name.

As Onorato watched, the man opened his coat with one hand, and with the other pulled out a gun. He straightened his arm, raised it toward Maurizio Gucci's back, and started firing. Onorato, no more than a yard away, stood frozen, broom in hand. In shock, he felt powerless to stop the man.

Onorato heard three quick, muffled shots in fast succession.

Motionless, Onorato watched in horror. He saw the first bullet enter Gucci's camel topcoat at the right hip. The second shot hit him just under the left shoulder. Onorato noticed how Gucci's camel coat shivered as each bullet pierced the fabric. "It doesn't look that way when someone gets shot in the movies," he thought.

Gucci, stunned, turned with a puzzled expression on his face. He looked at the gunman, showing no sign of recognition, then looked past him directly at Onorato as though to ask, "What is happening? Why? Why is this happening to me?"

A third bullet grazed his right arm.

As Gucci moaned and slumped to the floor, his attacker fired a final, fatal shot into his right temple. The gunman spun around to leave, only to stop short at the sight of Onorato staring at him in horror.

Onorato saw the man's dark eyebrows rise in surprise, as though he hadn't taken Onorato's presence into consideration.

The gunman's arm was still outstretched and now it pointed directly at him. Onorato looked at the gun, noticing it had a long silencer covering the barrel. He looked at the hand grasping the gun, at the long, well-groomed fingers, the fingernails that looked as though they had been freshly manicured.

For an instant that seemed an eternity, Onorato looked into the gunman's eyes. Then he heard his own voice.

"Noooo," he cried, shrinking back, raising his left hand as though to say, "I have nothing to do with this!"

The gunman fired two more shots directly at Onorato, then turned and ran out the door. Onorato heard a tinkling sound and realized it came from the falling bullet casings dancing on the granite floor.

"Incredible!" he found himself thinking, "I don't feel any pain! I didn't know that it doesn't hurt when you get shot." He wondered if Gucci had felt any pain.

"So this is it," he mused. "Now I am going to die. What a shame to die like this. This is not fair," he thought.

Then Onorato realized he was still standing up. He looked down at his left arm, which was hanging strangely. Blood dripped from his sleeve. Slowly, he lowered himself to sit on the first of the granite steps.

"At least I didn't fall," he thought, preparing mentally to die. He thought of his wife, of his days in the army, of the view of the sea and the mountains from Casteldaccia. Then he realized he was only wounded; he had been shot twice in the arm, he was not going to die. A wave of happiness washed over him. He turned to see the lifeless body of Maurizio Gucci lying at the top of the stairs in a spreading pool of blood. Gucci was stretched out as he had fallen, lying on his right side, his head resting on his right arm. Onorato tried to scream for help, but when he opened his mouth, he couldn't hear the sound of his own voice.

A few minutes later, the wailing of an approaching siren grew louder and louder, then shut off abruptly as a police car braked to a screeching halt in front of Via Palestro 20. Four uniformed carabinieri jumped out, weapons drawn.

"It was a man with a gun," moaned Onorato weakly from his seat on the first step as the men rushed toward him.

2

THE GUCCI

DYNASTY

Bright red blood spatters formed Jackson Pollock–like patterns on the doors and the white walls on either side of the entryway where Maurizio lay. A scattering of shell casings had fallen on the floor. The proprietor of a kiosk across the street in the Giardini Publicci had heard Onorato cry out, and quickly called the carabinieri.

"That is *Dottor* Gucci," said Onorato to the officers, using his right arm to gesture up the steps to Maurizio's motionless body while his left arm hung limply. "Is he dead?"

One of the carabinieri knelt by Maurizio's body and pressed his fingers to Maurizio's neck, nodding when he found no pulse. Maurizio's lawyer, Fabio Franchini, who had arrived a few minutes earlier for an appointment, huddled disconsolately on the cold floor next to Maurizio's body—and stayed there for the next four hours while law enforcement officials and paramedics worked around him. As ambulances and more police cars arrived, a small crowd of curious onlookers formed in front of the building. The paramedics attended quickly to Onorato, whisking him away in one of the ambulances just before the homicide squad of the carabinieri arrived on the scene. Corporal Giancarlo Togliatti, a tall, lanky blond officer with twelve years experience in the homicide division, began to examine Maurizio's body. In the past few years, Togliatti's main job had been investigating murders among warring clans of Albanian immigrants who had moved into Milan. This was his first case among the city's elite—it wasn't every day that a leading businessman was gunned down in cold blood in the center of town.

"Who is the victim?" asked Togliatti as he bent down.

"That's Maurizio Gucci," one of his colleagues told him.

Togliatti looked up, smiling quizzically. "Right, and I'm Valentino," he said sardonically, naming the perpetually suntanned, dark-haired Rome fashion designer. He had always associated the Gucci name with the Florentine leather goods house—what was a Gucci doing with an office in Milan?

"For me, he was a corpse, just like any other," Togliatti later said.

Togliatti gently pulled a cluster of blood-spattered newspaper clippings out of Maurizio's limp hand and removed his watch, a Tiffany, still ticking. As he carefully went through Maurizio's pockets, Milan prosecutor Carlo Nocerino arrived. The scene was near pandemonium; cameramen and journalists jostled paramedics and law enforcement officials from both the carabinieri and *polizia*. Italy has three law enforcement corps—the carabinieri, the *polizia*, and the *guardia di finanzia,* or fiscal police. Concerned that key evidence might be destroyed in the uproar, Nocerino asked which corps had gotten there first. One of the basic unwritten rules among Italy's law enforcement agencies is that the first to arrive at the scene of the crime handles the case. Upon learning that the carabinieri had arrived first, Nocerino quickly dispatched the *polizia,* and ordered the great doors to the foyer closed and the sidewalk around the front doors cordoned off to keep the growing crowd at bay. Then Nocerino walked up the steps to where Togliatti was examining the body of Maurizio Gucci.

Nocerino and the investigators thought the shot to Maurizio's temple made the murder look like a mafia-style execution. The skin and hair around the wound had been burned, indicating close-range firing.

"This is the work of a professional killer," said Nocerino, studying the wound and then the floor where the investigating team had outlined six shell casings with chalk circles.

"It is the classic *colpo di grazia*," agreed Togliatti's colleague, Captain Antonello Bucciol. Yet they were perplexed. Too many bullets had been fired and two eyewitnesses, Onorato and a young woman who had nearly collided with the killer as he ran out the door, had been left alive—hardly the work of a professional bent on administering a traditional coup de grâce.

It took Togliatti the next hour and a half to examine Maurizio, but it would take him the next three years to learn every detail of Maurizio's life.

"Maurizio Gucci was essentially unknown to us," Togliatti said later. "We were going to have to take his life in our hands and open it like a book."

To UNDERSTAND MAURIZIO GUCCI and the family he came from, it's necessary to understand the Tuscan character. Different from the affable Emilians, the austere Lombardians, and the chaotic Romans, Tuscans tend to be individualistic and haughty. They feel they represent the wellspring of culture and art in Italy, and they are especially proud of their role in originating the modern Italian language, thanks in large part to Dante Alighieri. Some call them the "French of Italy"—arrogant, self-sufficient, and closed to outsiders. Italian novelist Curzio Malaparte wrote about them in *Maledetti Toscani,* or *Damned Tuscans.*

In the *Inferno,* Dante describes Filippo Argenti as *"il fiorentino spirito bizzarro."* The bizarre Florentine or Tuscan spirit can also be cutting and sarcastic, ready with the quick comment or joke, as seen in Roberto Benigni, the Oscar-winning director and lead actor of *Life Is Beautiful.*

When a writer from *Town & Country* asked Roberto Gucci, Maurizio's cousin, in 1977 if Gucci could have come from another part of Italy, Roberto looked at him in amazement.

"You might as well ask me if Chianti could come from Lombardy," he roared. "It wouldn't be Chianti any more than Gucci would be Gucci," he bellowed, flinging his arms wide. "How could we not be Florentine if we are what we are?"

The rich history of the centuries-old Florentine merchant class pulsed in the Gucci veins. In 1293, the Ordinances of Justice defined Florence as an independent republic. Until the Medicis took power, the city was governed by *arti,* twenty-one merchant and artisan guilds. The names of these guilds remain today as street names: Via Calzaiuoli (shoemakers), Via Cartolai (stationers), Via Tessitori (weavers), Via Tintori (dyers), and many more. Gregorio Dati, a Renaissance silk merchant, once wrote: "A Florentine who is not a merchant, who has not traveled through the world, seeing the foreign nations and peoples and then returned to Florence with some wealth, enjoys no esteem whatsoever."

To the Florentine merchant, wealth was honorable and carried with it certain obligations, such as financing public buildings, living in a grand palazzo with gorgeous gardens, and sponsoring painters, sculptors, poets, and musicians. This love of beauty and pride in creating beauty has never died despite war, plague, floods, and politics. From Giotto and Michelangelo to the craftsmen in their workshops today, the fruits and flowers of the arts, propagated by merchants, have flourished there.

"Nine out of ten Florentines are merchants, and the tenth is a priest," joked Maurizio's uncle, Aldo Gucci. "Gucci is as Florentine as Johnnie Walker is Scotch, and there's not much that anybody can teach a Florentine about merchandising or craftsmanship," he continued. "We Guccis have been merchants since around 1410. When you say Guccis, you are not thinking of Macy's."

"They were simple people with an incredible humanity," a former employee once said of the Guccis, "but they all had that terrible Tuscan character."

Maurizio's own story starts with his grandfather, Guccio Gucci, whose parents struggled with their failing straw hat–making business in Florence at the end of the nineteenth century. Guccio fled his home and his father's bankruptcy by signing on a freighter and working his way to England. There he found a job at London's famous Savoy Hotel.[*] He must have gaped in amazement at the guests' jewels and fine silks, and at the piles of luggage they brought with them. Trunks, suitcases, hatboxes, and more, all made of leather and embossed with crests and flourishing initials, overtook the lobby of the hotel, a mecca of high society in Victorian England. The guests were rich and famous or wanted to rub shoulders with those who were. Lillie Langtry, the mistress of the Prince of Wales, kept a suite for fifty pounds a year where she entertained her guests. The great actor Sir Henry Irving often came to dine in the restaurant, while Sarah Bernhardt claimed that the Savoy had become a "second home" to her.

Guccio's wages were low and the work hard, but he learned fast and the experience would have a profound effect on his life. It didn't take him long to figure out that the people who came to the hotel brought with them posses-

---

[*]Varying accounts have said he worked as a dishwasher, a bellboy, a waiter, and even a maître d', but the hotel has no records of his employment.

sions that showed their affluence and taste. The key to it all, he realized, lay in the piles of luggage that the bellboys spirited up and down the long carpeted hallways and in and out of the elevators, then called "ascending rooms." The leather was something familiar; he knew it from the workshops of his Florentine youth. After he left the Savoy, according to his sons, Guccio found a job with Wagons Lits, the European sleeping car company, and toured Europe by train, serving and observing the wealthy travelers and their entourages of servants and luggage before returning to Florence four years later with his savings.

Back at home, Guccio fell in love with Aida Calvelli, a dressmaker and daughter of a neighboring tailor. It didn't appear to bother him that she already had a four-year-old son, Ugo, from a love affair with a man who had come down with terminal tuberculosis and was thus unable to marry her. On October 20, 1902, slightly more than a year after Guccio came back to Italy, he married Aida and adopted Ugo as his own. He was twenty-one; she was twenty-four. She was already pregnant with their first daughter, Grimalda, who was born three months later. Aida eventually gave Guccio four more children, of whom one, Enzo, died in childhood. The others were also boys: Aldo in 1905, Vasco in 1907, and Rodolfo in 1912.

Guccio's first job back in Florence was probably in an antiques shop, according to his son Rodolfo. Then Guccio moved to a leather firm, where he learned the basics of the trade before being promoted to manager. When World War I broke out, he was thirty-three years old with a large family: nevertheless, he was called up as a transport driver. When the war ended, Guccio, now working for Franzi, a leather crafts company in Florence, learned how to select raw hides, and studied curing and tanning as well as the art of working with different hides and grades of leather. He quickly became manager of the firm's branch in Rome, to which he went alone. Aida, at home with the children, refused to leave Florence. Guccio came home every weekend and longed to open his own business in Florence catering to customers who understood finely made leather goods. One Sunday in 1921, during a stroll around Florence with Aida, he noticed a small shop for rent on a narrow side street, Via della Vigna Nuova, running between the elegant Via Tornabuoni and Piazza Goldoni on the banks of the river Arno. He and Aida started discussing the possibility of taking over the space. With Guccio's savings, and, according to one account, a loan from an acquaintance, they founded the first Gucci company, Valigeria Guccio Gucci, which later became Azienda Individuale Guccio Gucci, a sole proprietorship, in 1921. Close to Florence's most elegant street, Via Tornabuoni, the neighborhood was strategic for the kind of clientele Guccio hoped to attract. Between the fifteenth and seventeenth centuries, some of the city's richest noble families—Strozzi, Antinori, Sassetti, Bartolini Salimbeni, Cattani, and Spini Feroni—had built fine palazzi along the Via Tornabuoni, where, starting in the 1800s, fancy restaurants and shops began opening up on the ground floors of their houses. The Caffè Giacosa, still there today, had been serving homemade pastries and drinks to its fashionable clientele since it opened at number 83r* in 1815. Suppliers to Italy's royal family, Giacosa first created the Negroni cocktail, named after a patron, Conte Negroni. The Ristorante Doney, founded in 1827 across from where Gucci would later open, catered to Florence's aristocratic families and hosted the ladies' counterpart to the all-male Florence Jockey Club. Next door, a florist shop, Mercatelli, served Florence's aristocratic families. Other establishments still operating today include Rubelli, selling fine Venetian fabrics, the Profumeria Inglese, and Procacci, known for its mouthwatering truffle sandwiches. Wealthy European travelers stayed at the Albergo Londres et Suisse, which in turn wasn't far from the American travel agency Thomas Cook & Sons, located at the corner of Via Del Parione.

At first, Guccio bought high-quality leather products from Tuscan manufacturers as well as from Germany and England to sell to the tourists who flocked to Florence then, as they do today. Guccio selected sturdy, well-made bags and luggage at reasonable prices. If he didn't find things he liked, he commissioned special pieces. He aspired to elegance himself and was always impeccably dressed in fine shirts and crisply pressed suits.

"He was a man of great taste, which we all inherited," recalled his son Aldo. "His imprint was on every item he sold."

Guccio opened a small workshop behind the store where he could make his own leather goods to supplement the imported products and also started an active repair business that quickly became profitable. He hired local craftsmen and built up a reputation for offering service in addition to reliable goods. At the end of the first year, Guccio acquired a larger workshop across Michelangelo's Santa Trinità Bridge on the opposite bank of the Arno along the avenue Lungarno Guicciardini. Guccio ordered his sixty craftsmen to work late into the night if necessary to fill the rising number of orders.

The Oltrarno area south of the Arno had become home to many small workshops, which harnessed the river's water to power machinery that treated and wove wool, silks, and brocades. The wide avenues bordering the river and the smaller streets leading south in this working-class neighborhood rang with sounds of hammering and sawing wood, washing and beating wool, and cutting, stitching, and polishing leather. Antiques dealers, framers, and other craftsmen also settled here. Just across the river, the area around Piazza della Repubblica had become the commercial and financial heart of Florence, dating back to the Middle Ages when it was the headquarters of the powerful trade guilds that regulated the city's thriving craftsmanship.

As Guccio's children grew, they began to work in the family business with the exception of Ugo, who showed little interest. Aldo had the keenest sense of trade, while Vasco, nicknamed *Il Succube,* "The Underdog," took on responsibility for production, although he actually preferred hunting in the Tuscan countryside whenever he could. Grimalda, nicknamed *La Pettegola,* "The Gossip," worked behind the counter in the shop alongside a young sales assistant Guccio had hired. Rodolfo was still too young to work in the shop; when he became older, he turned his nose up at the idea and followed his dream of working in films.

Guccio ruled his children strictly and insisted they address him with the formal *Lei,* rather than the intimate *tu.* He demanded good behavior at meal-times and used his napkin as a whip, flicking it at those who were out of line. When the family spent weekends at their country home outside Florence near San Casciano, on Sundays Guccio hitched up the horse to their wooden two-wheeled cart, loaded in Aida and all the children, and trotted them all off across the fields to morning mass.

"He had a very strong personality and commanded respect and distance," said Roberto Gucci, one of his grandsons. Thrifty, he ordered the side of prosciutto sliced as thinly as possible in order to make it last. He impressed these values on his children; it became family legend that Aldo would top off the bottles of mineral water from the tap. Guccio had his pleasures, too, and one of them was the hearty Tuscan food that Aida served up at the large family table. Perhaps because of the poverty he knew in his youth, Guccio let himself enjoy his later years and both he and Aida grew stout on her savory home cooking.

"I will always remember him with his Havana cigar and the seemingly endless gold watch chain that girded his waist," said Roberto.

Guccio tried not to distinguish between Ugo and his natural children, but the boy didn't seem to want to fall into the pattern set by his father and brothers and sister. His large size and tough manner earned him the nickname *Il Prepotente,* "The Bully," from his brothers. When Ugo didn't show any interest in helping out in the family shop, Guccio found him a job with one of his wealthy customers, Baron Levi, a successful landowner. Baron Levi employed Ugo as assistant manager of one of his farms on the outskirts of Florence. The situation seemed ideal for the brawny young man. Soon Ugo, who was already married, began boasting about how well he was doing. Guccio, still eager to pay off his early debt, asked Ugo for a loan. Ugo, in financial difficulty himself due to an extravagant girlfriend he was secretly courting, was too embarrassed to confess that he didn't have the money and instead promised his father he would give him a loan. In the meantime, Guccio arranged a bank advance with which he paid off his loan. After paying back the bank, he agreed to repay Ugo over time, with interest. What he didn't know was that Ugo, ashamed to admit to his father he wasn't as successful as he claimed, had stolen 70,000 lire (the equivalent of about $3.50, a significant amount of money at the time) from Baron Levi's cash box. He gave his father the 30,000 lire (about $1.50) he had asked for and ran off with the rest for three weeks with his girlfriend, a dancer who performed in the chorus of a small local theater.

Baron Levi reported to Guccio his strong suspicion that Ugo had stolen from him, crushing Guccio's joy at having paid off his partner at long last. He could hardly believe his son would resort to stealing, but a review of the facts left no doubt in his mind. He agreed to repay the baron at the rate of 10,000 lire (about 50 cents) a month.

Ugo distressed his parents in other ways as well. In 1919, a young Benito Mussolini had founded the Fasci di Combattimento, the precursor to his Fascist Party, and by 1922, after Mussolini had already been elected to Parliament, the Partito Nazionale Fascista had attracted 320,000 members across Italy, including bureaucrats, industrialists, and journalists. Ugo joined up—perhaps in rebellion against Guccio—and became a local official. He then used his power to terrorize the baron and others in the neighborhood where he had once worked, arriving at all hours with groups of drunken friends, demanding food and drink.

Meanwhile, Guccio struggled to make his business successful. In 1924, after two years of business, some suppliers who had let Guccio have goods on credit to launch his business were demanding payment. In turn, some of his own clients had not paid what they owed. The young merchant did not have enough cash to pay his bills. One night, in a closed-door meeting with his family and closest staff, a tearful Guccio told the small assembly he was going to be forced to close his shop.

"Unless a miracle happens, I can't stay open another day," Guccio said.

The strong, robust Guccio "looked like a man facing a death sentence," recalled Giovanni Vitali, Grimalda's fiancé. A local surveyor, he knew the family well, having gone to school with Ugo and later Aldo at the Roman Catholic College of Castelletti.

Vitali, who worked in his father's construction business, had put aside some savings for his future with Grimalda. He offered to help Guccio out. Guccio humbly accepted the loan, gratefully thanking his son-in-law-to-be for saving the small enterprise. During the following months, he paid Giovanni back in full. As business improved, Guccio expanded the workshop and encouraged his craftsmen to produce original articles for the shop. He identified skilled artisans and built a qualified team of leatherworkers who were more artists than laborers. They produced fine bags of delicate kidskin and genuine chamois, telescope purses with gussets on the sides, and suitcases inspired by the Gladstone bags Guccio had seen in his Savoy days. Other products included car robe carriers, shoe boxes, and linen carriers—in those days upper-class tourists traveled with their own bed linens.

The business did so well that in 1923 Guccio opened another shop on Via del Parione and during the next few years expanded the shop on Via della Vigna Nuova. The shop changed its location several times in the history of the company, with the last at numbers 47–49, currently occupied by the Valentino and Armani boutiques.

Aldo started working in the family business in 1925, at the age of twenty, delivering packages with horse and cart to customers staying at the local hotels. He also did simple shop tasks, such as sweeping and tidying, eventually helping with sales and rearranging the merchandise displays.

Aldo's knack for mixing work and pleasure was evident from the beginning. In addition to developing salesmanship skills, Aldo adeptly turned his contacts with pretty young female customers into exciting flirtations. An attractive young man with a lean figure, bright blue eyes, chiseled features, and a wide, warm smile, he quickly charmed the young women who stopped in the shop. Guccio appreciated the effect Aldo's captivating manners had on the business and he closed his eyes to his son's amorous escapades until one of his most prestigious clients, the exiled Princess Irene of Greece, came to the shop one day and asked to speak with him privately. Guccio ushered her into his office.

"Your son has been seeing my servant," she reproached him. "This must stop or I shall be forced to send her home. I am responsible for her."

Guccio was reluctant to tell Aldo which young women he could or couldn't escort, but he did not want to offend such an important client. He called his son into the office for an explanation.

Aldo had first met Olwen Price, a bright-eyed, red-haired girl from the English countryside at a reception at the British consulate in Florence. Olwen had also visited the shop during her rounds for her mistress. Daughter of a carpenter and trained as a dressmaker, she had been eager for the chance to go into service overseas as a ladies' maid. She had entranced Aldo with her shy, modest manner, her musical English accent, and simple ways. He persuaded her to meet him privately and quickly discovered that her quiet demeanor hid an adventurous spirit; they soon became lovers, disappearing into the Tuscan countryside for their amorous retreats. Aldo quickly realized that the relationship with Olwen was more than a passing flirtation. When Guccio and the princess confronted him, Aldo surprised them both, announcing that he and Olwen intended to marry.

"From now on, Olwen is no longer your concern," Aldo declared gallantly to the princess. "She is mine and I will take care of her." He didn't tell them that Olwen was already pregnant.

Aldo brought Olwen home, placing her in the care of his older sister, Grimalda, while continuing to meet her for furtive excursions into the countryside. Aldo then followed her home to England to meet her family. They were married on August 22, 1927, in a little church in the English village of Oswestry, near Olwen's hometown of West Felton, near Shrewsbury. He was twenty-two years old; she, nineteen. Their oldest son, Giorgio, whom Aldo always called *il figlio del amore,* his love child, was born in 1928. Two other boys followed: Paolo in 1931 and Roberto in 1932. The marriage wasn't destined to be happy, however. Aldo's and Olwen's sweetheart escapades had thrilled them both, but settling down to family life in Florence was different. First, the couple had to live with Guccio and Aida, forcing Olwen to fit into Italian family life and submit to Guccio's strict, commanding style. They all crammed into the elder Guccis' apartment on Piazza Verzaia, near the old stone San Frediano entrance to the once-walled city. After they moved into their own home on Via Giovanni Prati on the outskirts of Florence, tensions eased for a while. Olwen dedicated herself entirely to the three boys, while Aldo became more and more involved in the family business. She never learned Italian well, was painfully shy, and had a hard time making friends. As he began to expand his horizons through the business, she grew fiercely possessive and resentful.

"Aldo loved life, but she put a damper on anything he wanted to do," recalled his older sister, Grimalda. "She never let him take her out anywhere, always making the excuse of having to look after the children. It wasn't what he married her for at all."

Rodolfo, the youngest son of Guccio and Aida, showed no interest in working in the family business, even after his brothers and sisters were already helping behind the counter at their father's shop on Via della Vigna Nuova. Rodolfo had other dreams. He wanted to act in films.

"I wasn't born to be a shopkeeper," the young Rodolfo, whom his family called "Foffo," protested to his father as the elder Gucci shook his head. "I want to work in the movies."

Guccio couldn't understand where his youngest son had gotten such ideas and he tried to discourage him. One day in 1929, when Rodolfo was seventeen, his father sent him to Rome to deliver a package to an important client. The Italian director Mario Camerini spotted him in the lobby of Rome's Hotel Plaza and invited the handsome young man to do a screen test. Shortly after, a telegram confirming the appointment arrived at the Gucci home in Florence. When Guccio read it, he blew up.

"You are out of your mind!" he thundered at his son. "The film world is full of nutty people. You might get lucky and have your five minutes of fame but what happens when you are suddenly forgotten and never work again?"

Guccio realized that Rodolfo was determined and allowed him to go to Rome to shoot the screen test, which was successful. At the time, the young Rodolfo still wore short pants, as was customary for boys in those days; he had to borrow a pair of long pants from his older brother Aldo for the occasion. Camerini liked Rodolfo and gave him a role in *Rotaie,* one of the masterpieces of early Italian cinema, a dramatic story about two young lovers who decide to commit suicide in a cheap hotel along the railroad tracks. Rodolfo had a sensitive and expressive face, perfect for the stylized cinema of the time. After *Rotaie,* he became best known for his comical roles, in which his contorted expressions and laughable antics reminded viewers of Charlie Chaplin. He used Maurizio D'Ancora as his screen name. None of Rodolfo's later films had quite the same success, although he did have a part in *Finalmente Soli* alongside the young Italian actress Anna Magnani, with whom he is said to have had a love affair.

During the shooting of one of his early films, Rodolfo noticed a bubbly blond actress on the set who played a minor part. Vivacious and unconventionally free-spirited for her time, she was Alessandra Winklehaussen, known professionally as Sandra Ravel. Alessandra's German father was a chemical-plant worker; her mother was from the Ratti family near Lugano on the northern bank of Lake Lugano in the Italian-speaking region of Switzerland. Shortly after she had caught Rodolfo's eye, Alessandra played opposite him in *Together in the Dark,* an early talkie about an adventurous young starlet who enters the wrong hotel room by mistake and slips into bed next to Rodolfo—who in life, as in the movie, had fallen head over heels in love with her. Their filmed encounter between the sheets led to off-screen love. Alessandra and Rodolfo married in 1944 in a romantic ceremony in Venice. Rodolfo had the wedding filmed, complete with footage of the young couple skimming the waters of the lagoon in a gondola and toasting happily at the reception dinner. When their son was born on September 26, 1948, they named him Maurizio in honor of Rodolfo's nom de cinema.

In 1935, when Rodolfo was still developing his film career with no thought of ever joining the family business, Mussolini invaded Ethiopia. While far from Italian shores, this event nonetheless greatly affected the Gucci business. The League of Nations imposed an international trade embargo on Italy. As fifty-two countries refused to sell their products to the nation, Guccio could no longer import the fine leathers and other materials he needed to make his exclusive bags and luggage. Terrified that his small venture would collapse as had his father's straw hat business years earlier, according to some accounts, Guccio geared up the factory to make shoes for the Italian army in order to keep operating.

Guccio also came up with alternatives, as did other Italian entrepreneurs, such as his neighbor, Salvatore Ferragamo, who created some of his most remarkable shoes during the darkest years of the embargo. Ferragamo didn't overlook any possibility, cunningly using cork, raffia, even cellophane from candy wrappers to make shoes. The Guccis sourced as much leather as they could from within Italy and began using *cuoio grasso* from a local tannery in Santa Croce. Veal calves specially reared in the lush Val di Chiana were fed in their stalls to avoid abrasions on their hides. Their skins were then cured on the outside and treated with fishbone grease. The treatment made the skins soft, smooth, and supple; scratches miraculously disappeared with the swipe of a finger. *Cuoio grasso* soon became a Gucci trademark. Guccio also introduced other materials, such as raffia, wicker, and wood, into the products in order to reduce the leather content to a minimum. He made bags out of fabric with leather trim. He ordered a specially woven *canapa,* or hemp, from Naples. Using this fabric, the Guccis developed a line of sturdy, lightweight, and recognizable luggage that quickly became one of their most successful products. Guccio developed the firm's first signature print—a precursor to the famous double-G print—with a series of small connecting diamonds printed in dark brown across the natural tan background. The print looked the same any way one turned the fabric. Guccio had also begun to make other items besides the bags and luggage that were the core of his business. He discovered that smaller leather accessories such as belts and wallets generated a nice income by bringing into his shop people who weren't looking for large items.

In the same period, Aldo traveled around Italy and parts of Europe to test interest in the business. The positive response he met first in Rome, then in France, Switzerland, and England, convinced him that having a shop only in

Florence limited Gucci potential. If so many customers were coming to Gucci, why not take Gucci to them? He tried to persuade his father to open shops in other cities.

Guccio would have none of it. "What about the risk? Think of the enormous investment. Where are we going to get the money? Go to the bank and ask them if they will finance you!"

During their family battles Guccio shot down Aldo's every idea, but behind his back he went to their bankers and told them that he backed Aldo's plan.

Aldo finally got his way. On September 1, 1938, just twelve months before the outbreak of World War II, Gucci opened its doors in Rome on the elegant Via Condotti at number 21, in a historical building called Palazzo Negri. At that time, the only other names on Via Condotti were the exclusive jeweler Bulgari, and a maker of fine shirts, Enrico Cucci, whose clients included Winston Churchill, Charles de Gaulle, and the Italian royal family, the House of Savoy.

Long before the days of *la dolce vita,* Aldo had identified Italy's capital city as one of the most popular playgrounds of the world's elite. While his father shook his head over the bills, Aldo insisted that no expense could be spared to make the Gucci shop a magnet for wealthy and cultivated tourists. The store occupied two floors and had double glass doors and ivory handles carved in the shape of olives stacked one on top of the other.

"The handles were copied from the doors of the shop in Via della Vigna Nuova, and were one of the first symbols of Gucci," recalled Aldo's third son, Roberto.

Massive glass-covered mahogany cases displayed the Gucci products; handbags and accessories downstairs, gift items and luggage upstairs. Rich-looking wine-colored linoleum covered the ground floor, while carpeting of the same color ran up the stairs and along a corridor leading to the first-floor sales area. Aldo moved to Rome with Olwen and the children, renting an apartment on the second and third floors above the shop. Having initially taken the boys to her home in England, Olwen decided to bring them back to Italy when the war broke out. The Allies treated Rome as an open city and didn't bomb it at first. While Aldo managed to keep the shop open and profitable, the boys went to a school run by Irish nuns and Olwen worked with a group of Irish priests, helping Allied prisoners escape. In the final weeks, however, Allied planes began bombing railway yards on the outskirts of the city. Aldo moved Olwen and the boys out into the country, but was forced to return to Rome when city administrators ordered shopkeepers to keep their doors open for business.

During the war, the Gucci family scattered. Ugo, who had participated in the Fascists' march on Rome in 1922, became a Fascist administrator in Tuscany. Rodolfo signed up with the armed forces entertainment unit and moved with the troops, playing the comedy roles of his early silent films and talkies, while Vasco, after a short period of military service, had been allowed to return to the factory in Florence, where he oversaw shoe production for the war effort.

At the end of the war, Olwen was given a special citation for her work. Loyal to her Italian family as well, when she learned that Ugo had been captured and was being held prisoner in Terni by the British army, she used her connections first to plead for better treatment for her brother-in-law, and later for his release. She also went to Venice with Aldo to rescue Rodolfo, who had been stranded with the troops after Italy's capitulation.

It took time for the country to rebuild. The factory along Lungarno Guicciardini had been cut off as departing Germans blew up the Florentine bridges, including Michelangelo's Santa Trinitá. The family began to look for a new site to resume its production of leather goods. In the meantime, Guccio, terrified that Ugo's position within the Fascist Party would prompt the new, democratic Italian government to sequester Ugo's shares in the company as a penalty for his wartime activities, sat down with his adopted son one day and offered him land and a significant sum of money in exchange for his shares. Ugo accepted and went his own way, founding a leather workshop in Bologna where he crafted fine leather bags and accessories for the ladies of that city, in addition to supplying his products to the family business.

Although Rodolfo had thrived on the acting life, the film industry changed dramatically after the war. Early talkies had superceded silent films and the new Italian realist directors—Rossellini, Visconti, and Fellini—weren't looking for the stylized actors of their predecessors, so the young Gucci soon realized that the big parts and good scripts weren't coming his way. With a wife and a young son to support, Rodolfo—at Alessandra's insistence—asked his father if he could come back to the family business. Aldo, an advocate of the family-run business from the beginning, urged his father to welcome Rodolfo back. As the business expanded, he and Guccio needed more help. Guccio initially put Rodolfo to work in the Via del Parione store. Rodolfo proved an instant success with the ladies, who were thrilled to discover such a gracious and handsome salesman in the Gucci shop.

"But aren't you Maurizio D'Ancora? You look just like him!" some of the boldest customers would ask him curiously.

"No, madam, my name is Rodolfo Gucci," he would answer with a gallant bow and a delighted twinkle in his eye.

For a year, Guccio observed his son and was pleased with his work. Dedicated, determined, and attentive to the problems of the business, Rodolfo proved his reliability. In 1951, Guccio invited the young couple to move to Milan to manage the new Gucci store on Via Monte Napoleone. Running between Via Alessandro Manzoni and Corso Matteotti in downtown Milan, Via Monte Napoleone was Milan's principal shopping avenue, lined with fine jewelers, tailors, and leathermakers, among other establishments, putting it on a level with Via Tornabuoni in Florence or Via Condotti in Rome. The new shop also began to cater to Milan's literary and artistic crowd, which gathered just around the corner at the Trattoria Bagutta, a popular meeting place.

Meanwhile, Aldo's gamble on opening in Rome was paying off. American and British troops who were there after the war bought up Gucci's handcrafted leather bags, belts, and wallets, which were just the kind of souvenirs they were looking for. Particularly successful were suitcases called "suiters," covered with the Gucci *canapa* and fitted inside with hangers and used by American and British officers to transport their uniforms. At first, business in Florence lagged behind that of Rome, but later caught up as American tourists flooded to Italy to visit its historical and cultural monuments, as well as to spend their abundant dollars in its elegant shops. Soon Gucci's problem was keeping up production in pace with demand. In 1953, Guccio opened another workshop in the Oltrarno district across the river. Housed in a historic building in Via delle Caldaie, this workshop continued to be an important site for Gucci production well into the 1970s.

Via delle Caldaie, named for the huge vats used in the thirteenth and fourteenth centuries to die wool, ran south from Piazza Santo Spirito. The palazzo Guccio bought had originally been a shop selling felt and wool fabric until a merchant family named Biuzzi built a spacious palace, Casa Grande, on the site in the late 1500s. In 1642, the building was acquired by the cardinal and then archbishop of Florence, Francesco de'Nerli, whom Dante mentions in his *Divine Comedy*. During the next two centuries, the palace figured in various accounts of diplomacy. After 1800, several leading Florentine families owned the property until Guccio Gucci bought it in 1953. Old frescoes covered many of the rooms; the most elaborate crept up the walls and across the ceiling of the large first-floor rooms where Gucci's artisans cut and stitched the smooth *cuoio grasso* into graceful bags. Downstairs, under the arched ceilings of the ground-floor halls, other artisans made luggage.

As demand grew, more young artisans were hired and apprenticed to Gucci's senior leatherworkers, all under the watchful eye of the *capo operaio,* or head artisan. Each team, consisting of a junior apprentice and seasoned expert, was assigned to a workbench, or *banco,* and each artisan was issued a pin bearing the Gucci seal and an identification number—the same number on the time card he punched mornings and evenings. By the time Gucci opened a modern factory on the outskirts of Florence in 1971, the number of workers had more than doubled to 130.

The Tuscan leatherworkers saw Gucci as the ultimate employer, who offered cradle-to-grave security no matter what the ups and downs of the market.

"It was like getting a government job," said Carlo Bacci, who started working in Via delle Caldaie as a young apprentice in 1960. "Once you got in at Gucci you knew you were set for life," he explained in his warm, lilting Tuscan accent. "Other firms would send people home when work was scarce, but at Gucci you had security," Bacci said. "Gucci just kept producing; they knew they could always sell what they had." After working for more than eleven years at Via delle Caldaie, Bacci opened his own leatherworking company, as did other Gucci artisans, and still supplies Gucci today.

"We reported to work every morning between eight and eight-thirty," recalled Dante Ferrari, another longtime Gucci employee. "The coffee break was at ten," he recalled, "if the *capo operaio* saw you fumble for a *panino* under the bench, he would report you! Not only because you were wasting time, but because your hands could get greasy and ruin the leather!"

The leatherworkers specialized in either preparing the hides or assembling the bags. In those days, preparing the hides also meant scraping down the inside of the precious skins, which often arrived with animal tissue still clinging to them. Other artisans cut out the pieces and still others pressed down the edges with a special tool, making the seams thinner and easier to stitch together, an operation called *scarnitura.*

The true artists, however, were the artisans who assembled the bags. Each artisan was responsible for completing an entire bag, from start to finish, a task that sometimes involved putting together one hundred different pieces and took an average of ten hours.

"Each workman was responsible for what he did and his number went into each bag—if there was some defect, they would go back to him. It wasn't like an assembly line where someone did the pockets and someone else did the sleeves," explained Ferrari, who kept a collection of black, cardboard-bound notebooks in which he painstakingly sketched and numbered each handbag style as it was created in order to keep a record, although the Gucci Archive has recuperated duplicates.

"Aside from the sewing machines, all you needed was a table, a good pair of hands, and a good brain," said Ferrari.

Most of the time, the designs for the bags came from the various members of the Gucci family, who also encouraged the artisans to develop new styles themselves, with family supervision and approval.

The bamboo-handle bag, which was simply called by its code number, 0633, probably came into being this way. Although there is no longer a record of exactly when the bag was developed and by whom, fashion historian Aurora Fiorentini, who has helped create a Gucci archive, dates it around 1947. The introduction of bamboo came with the use of new materials under the prewar trade embargo. Some think the first "bamboo bag" was initially developed by Aldo and the *capo operaio* of that time, with a leather handle, possibly based on a bag Aldo brought back from one of his trips to London. The distinctive shape of the bag was inspired by the side of a saddle. Its rigid shape—more in the style of a small case, unlike the softer, less constructed bags Gucci had produced up to then—also distinguished it. The bamboo, shaped by hand over a hot flame, gave Gucci products a distinctive, sporty look. A few years later, in Roberto Rossellini's 1953 *Viaggio in Italia,* a young Ingrid Bergman carries a Gucci bamboo-handle bag and Gucci umbrella.

The Guccis established a friendly, personal relationship with the artisans who worked for them and spent time in the workshop, calling the workers by name, jovially slapping the backs of the old master craftsmen, inquiring about their families.

"We knew each worker by name and we knew about their children, their problems, their joys," said Roberto Gucci. "If they needed help to buy a car or put a down payment on a house—they came to us. After all, we all ate from the same plate—though obviously some of us had bigger spoons than others," he added sheepishly.

Vasco Gucci, who became responsible for the factory, jaunted around Florence on a small motor scooter called the Motom that was popular at the time. The workers in Via delle Caldaie knew when he was coming as the buzz and sputter of his scooter bounced off the buildings closely facing each other in the narrow street.

" '*Uffa! Eccolo arrivato!*' we used to say," recalled Ferrari. "Vasco was like a psychologist, he could really sense if you were interested in what you were doing or not!"

The workers came to have a love/hate relationship with the Gucci family. Proud and highly critical of their own work, they would nonetheless outdo themselves in order to hear a hearty "Bravo!" from Guccio, Aldo, Vasco, or Rodolfo.

In the spring of 1949, Aldo, ever on the lookout for new opportunities, had gone to one of the first industry trade fairs in London. He spotted a stand featuring pigskin hides and was struck by their beautiful ginger color. He commissioned several skins from the tanner, a Mr. Holden from Scotland, asking him if he could have some of the pieces dyed in various colors, including blue and green.

"The tanner said, 'Well, my boy, we have never done this before, but if you want, we'll try,' " Aldo later recalled. "He presented me with six skins in different shades, shaking his head and saying, 'It's up to you; we think they're awful.'"

According to family accounts, Mr. Holden was also the source of the brindle pigskin that became a famous Gucci trademark. As the story goes, the first spotted pigskin was actually a mistake. Something went wrong in the tanning process, marking the pigskins with darker, slightly raised spots.

"Wait a minute, it looks new," said Aldo, who ordered the skins made up into bags. Whether or not his decision was merely thrift, as some suggest, because Aldo was reluctant to throw the skins away, the decision created another signature look for the company that later proved a marvelous defense against counterfeits because it was difficult to reproduce. The pigskin became so crucial to the Gucci business that Aldo acquired the tannery outright in 1971.

The postwar years marked Aldo's rise within the Gucci business and the emergence of the ingenious marketing that made the Gucci name known worldwide. Guccio, growing older, wanted to consolidate the business in Florence. Reluctant to put all they had achieved at risk with Aldo's far-reaching plans, he challenged his son's ideas.

Puffing irritably on his Havana cigar, Guccio would reach theatrically into his left pants pocket—he kept his pocket watch in the right one—and pull out an empty hand. "Do you have the money? If you have the money you can do what you want," he would say.

Nonetheless, Guccio privately acknowledged Aldo's flair for the business. The Rome store flourished. Hollywood stars frolicked in the capital city, as portrayed in *La Dolce Vita.* The stars gave Gucci a new cachet, attracting still other customers. Slowly Guccio let Aldo have his way. While they still argued heatedly over Aldo's ideas about expansion, privately Guccio backed him, again going to the banks to support his son's plans.

Meanwhile, Aldo began to look abroad to New York, London, and Paris.

Why, he reasoned, wait for their customers to come to them? Why not go to them? He didn't seem to worry about where the money for his schemes would come from. Despite Guccio's reservations, Aldo had faith his ideas would pay for themselves.

With his innate sense of marketing, Aldo picked up on his father's dedication to quality and coined the motto "Quality is remembered long after price is forgotten," which he had embossed in gold letters on pigskin plaques and displayed strategically around the stores.

Aldo also promoted a "Gucci concept," a harmony of styles and colors that would unify their products and identify the Gucci name. The world of stables and horses became a rich source of ideas for Gucci products. The double stitching used in saddlemaking, the green and red webbing from girth straps, and hardware shaped like linked stirrups and horse bits became Gucci trademarks. Soon Aldo's marketing genius began spinning the myth that the Guccis had been noble saddlemakers to medieval courts—a fitting image for the elite clientele to which the Guccis were catering. Saddle tack and riding accessories displayed in the stores enriched the saddlemaking legend and some items were even sold. The myth lives on. Even today, members of the Gucci family and former employees still say that the Guccis were saddlers long ago.

"I want the truth to come out," Grimalda told a journalist in 1987. "We were never saddlemakers. The Guccis come from a family in the San Miniato district of Florence," she said. According to a history of Florentine families, the Guccis of San Miniato were active as early as 1224 as lawyers and notaries, although this story is likely to have been embellished later, according to historian Fiorentini. The family crest featured a blue wheel and a rose on a gold banner floating above vertical red, blue, and silver stripes. Roberto spent a fortune in heraldic research and worked the rose and the wheel—said to symbolize poetry and leadership—into the company logo. The original logo featured a bellboy carrying a suitcase in one hand and a soft traveling bag in the other. As Gucci gained success, a knight in armor replaced the humble porter.

By the early 1950s, a Gucci bag or suitcase established its owner as someone with refined style and taste. Princess Elizabeth, soon to become the Queen of England, visited the Gucci shop in Florence, as did Eleanor Roosevelt, Elizabeth Taylor, Grace Kelly, and Jacqueline Bouvier, soon to marry John F. Kennedy. Many of Rodolfo's movie star connections from his acting days became customers, including Bette Davis, Katharine Hepburn, Sophia Loren, and Anna Magnani.

"In the years after World War II, Italy became a center for fine-quality luxury goods—handcrafted leather shoes, handbags, and fine gold jewelry," recalled retail veteran Joan Kaner, currently senior vice president and fashion director at Neiman Marcus.

"Gucci was one of the first status labels to come out of Europe—after so many years of not having things—people really wanted to show off. That's when I first became aware of the Gucci name. People felt with Gucci they were really getting quality for the money."

At the same time, the first Italian apparel designers gained recognition. A young Florentine nobleman, Giovan Battisti Giorgini, who had opened a buying office for American department stores in 1923 and toward the end of the war managed an Allied Forces Gift Shop, organized a fashion show in his own home in February 1951. He timed the event to follow the Paris couture shows and invited leading fashion journalists and buyers from American department stores such as Bergdorf Goodman, B. Altman & Co., and I. Magnin. The journalists raved over the stylish yet wearable designs, and the buyers cabled home for more funds. Giorgini's showings evolved into Italy's first pret-a-porter fashion shows, where names such as Emilio Pucci, Capucci, Galitzine, Valentino, Lancetti, Mila Schön, Krizia, and others debuted under the gleaming chandeliers of the Sala Bianca in Palazzo Pitti.

3

GUCCI GOES

AMERICAN

As American interest in Italian design grew, Aldo resolved to take Gucci to America, and especially to New York. Americans were Gucci's best clients. They loved the quality and style of the handcrafted leather bags and accessories. Aldo pressed Guccio to let him open a shop in New York, and Guccio's hand went into that left-hand pocket.

"Risk your neck if you must, but don't expect me to pay for it," Guccio fumed. "Go to the bank if you must, see if they'll stick their necks out for you! You may be right. After all, I am an old man," he began to relent. "I'm old-fashioned enough to believe that the best vegetables come from your own garden."

Aldo didn't need to hear any more. Guccio, in his way, had given him a green light. He flew to New York, a trip that in those days took nearly twenty hours with stops in Rome, Paris, Shannon, and Boston. Aldo met a lawyer, Frank Dugan, who said he could help him with his plan. He later returned to New York with his brothers Rodolfo and Vasco. When they got into the city, he animatedly walked them up and down Fifth Avenue, gesturing at the elegant shops in excitement.

"How would you like to see the Gucci name in big letters along this chic avenue?" he asked them. They settled on a small shop at 7 East Fifty-eighth Street, just off of Fifth Avenue, with two display windows on Fifty-eighth Street. With Dugan's help, they incorporated the first Gucci company in America, Gucci Shops Inc., with initial capital of $6,000. The new Gucci company was also given the right to use the Gucci trademark in the U.S. market—the only time the trademark was ever granted outside Italy. All of Gucci's subsequent foreign operating companies were extended franchise agreements.

Aldo sent a telegram to Guccio in Florence, informing him they had appointed him honorary president of the newly founded company.

Guccio was furious.

"Come home immediately, you crazy boys!" Guccio cabled back. He accused them of being foolish and irresponsible, reminded them he wasn't dead yet, and threatened to cut off their inheritance if they pursued such a reckless scheme. Aldo brushed off his father's misgivings and threats. He also managed to bring the old Guccio to New York to see the new store shortly before he died. Guccio became as enthusiastic as if the New York opening had been his own idea—he even told his friends it was his idea!

"Oh, *Commendatore!*" his friends would say to him, using the title bestowed on him by a national order connected to Italy's former monarchy. "You are a man of great vision!"

"He had lived to see that Aldo's ideas were not so crazy after all," recalled Grimalda.

Guccio, by then in his seventies, had every reason to be satisfied. His business was plowing full speed ahead. The Gucci name had been received as well in faraway America as in Italy. His three sons were working actively and had produced grandchildren who would one day take on roles in the family company. When each new grandchild was born, as the family saying went, Guccio would say, "Let him smell a piece of leather, for it is the smell of his future."

Guccio encouraged Giorgio, Roberto, and Paolo to work in the shop wrapping and delivering parcels, as his own children had done, firmly believing that the only way to learn the business was from the ground up. At the time, Rodolfo's son Maurizio was still a young child living in Milan and hadn't yet been inducted into the Gucci family school.

Just fifteen days after Aldo inaugurated the New York store in 1953, Guccio dropped dead of a heart attack one November evening as he was preparing to go to the cinema with Aida. He was seventy-two years old. When she came upstairs to see what was taking him so long, she found him lying still on the bathroom floor. The doctor said his heart had just stopped like an old watch. His devoted wife followed him two years later, at age seventy-seven. Once a poor dishwasher, Guccio Gucci had become a millionaire and his business had become famous on two continents. His sons were carrying on the empire he had created and he had been spared the bitter family quarrels that would come to characterize the Gucci dynasty years later. But Guccio himself had set the precedent; he had often played his sons off against each other, believing that competition would stimulate them to perform better.

"He pitted one against the other, challenging them to show what kind of blood ran in their veins," recalled Paolo.

Guccio also caused the first major family rift: he excluded his eldest child and only daughter, Grimalda, from any inheritance in the company solely because she was a woman. Grimalda, who was fifty-two when he died, had served faithfully in his shop for many years and her husband, Giovanni, had helped save the Gucci business from bankruptcy in 1924. The old Guccio handed down an unwritten credo to his sons: no woman could inherit control of the company. Grimalda didn't realize what had happened until her brothers refused to let her have an active role in business decisions. She discovered with dismay that they had inherited equal parts of the Gucci company; she received a farmhouse, some land, and a modest amount of cash.

"It was an archaic concept," admitted her nephew Roberto years later. "I never saw the statute, but my father told me that no woman was permitted to be a partner in Gucci."

After failing to reach an agreement with her brothers, Grimalda called in a lawyer to try and obtain her due. Her efforts were in vain. She said later she misunderstood a key question during the court hearing and inadvertently signed away her rights to the Gucci estate in exchange for a settlement, an experience that left her bitter for years.

"What I really wanted was a part in the development of the company I had seen grow from nothing," she said. Extremely fond of her brothers, she never imagined they would take advantage of her.

"She didn't get a stake in the company, but she did get other assets,"

Roberto said years later, "though there is no doubt that the company subsequently appreciated in value and was worth much more."

For his sons, Guccio's departure was a mixed blessing. Although they missed his firm, guiding hand, for the first time they were free to follow their own objectives and between them they divided up the business into three areas of influence that initially worked well for all of them. Aldo, finally free to pursue his dream of expanding Gucci overseas, traveled constantly. Rodolfo oversaw the Milan store while Vasco ran the factory in Florence. Harmony also reigned because Rodolfo and Vasco let Aldo have his own way, rarely countering him unless they felt he strayed too far from the values and directives Guccio left behind.

Aldo moved Olwen into a spacious villa he built on land next door to Villa Petacci, a grand residence where Mussolini's mistress, Clara Petacci, is said to have lived, along Rome's Via della Camilluccia, an idyllic road bordered with greenery that wound up into one of the hills outside Rome and is today home to some of the city's most exclusive residences. Aldo spent little time there as he traveled between Europe and the United States, opening new frontiers for the Gucci name. Although he and Olwen didn't divorce until much later, their relationship had long since faded, and Aldo picked a dark-haired shop girl he had hired for the Via Condotti store to come to New York as his assistant. Her name was Bruna Palumbo and she resembled the sultry Italian film actress Gina Lollobrigida. She became Aldo's companion and eventually moved into the small apartment he took at 25 West Fifty-fourth Street, across from the Museum of Modern Art. They lived together discreetly at first. Aldo worshipped Bruna, showered her with expensive gifts, and tried to share with her his excitement over the steady expansion of the Gucci business. He pleaded with her to travel with him, but she hesitated, in part due to her discomfort over her status as his mistress. He finally married Bruna in the United States many years later—even though Olwen had never consented to a divorce. After that, Bruna sometimes agreed to accompany Aldo to parties and openings, where he introduced her as "Mrs. Gucci."

Rodolfo, meanwhile, designed Gucci's most expensive handbags and hardware, in addition to running the Milan store.

"Rodolfo had very refined taste," recalled Francesco Gittardi, who worked for Gucci for eighteen years and managed the Milan store under Rodolfo from 1967 to 1973. "He was the one who designed the eighteen-karat gold clasps for the crocodile bags; he loved those things and spent hours on them."

The most romantic of the three brothers, Rodolfo dressed like the actor he once was. He wore plush velvet jackets in unusual colors such as forest green and gold with shining silk pocket scarves, and in summer wore elegant beige linen suits and jaunty straw hats.

At this time Vasco had begun to produce his own designs in the Florence factory, where he also supervised Aldo's son Paolo, who started working in the factory in 1952. Vasco's main passions in his free time were still hunting, his extensive shotgun collection, and his Lamborghini, pastimes that earned him a new nickname, "The Dreamer."

Of Guccio's three sons, Aldo became the driving force behind the business, making most of the important decisions, though he always sought consensus from his brothers.

"Aldo always wanted to do things with the agreement of the entire family," recalled Gittardi. "He may have brought the ideas, but the decisions were always taken by the family board. That said, they usually let him have his way because he always had the right instincts, especially about where to open stores," Gittardi said.

Aldo flew between the United States and Europe, where in 1959 he moved the Rome store to Via Condotti 8, its current location across from the historic Caffè Greco and down just a few paces from the Spanish Steps. In 1960 he secured Gucci's first direct Fifth Avenue exposure with a new store in the St. Regis Hotel on the corner of Fifty-fifth Street. The following year Gucci opened its doors in the Italian spa town of Montecatini, on London's Old Bond Street, and in Palm Beach's Royal Poinciana Plaza. Gucci's first Paris shop, on Rue du Fauburg Saint-Honoré near Place Vendôme, also opened in 1963. A second Paris shop opened on Rue du Faubourg-Saint-Honoré at Rue Royal in 1972.

Aldo pushed himself constantly and hardly took more than three or four days of vacation a year. He made at least a dozen transatlantic trips a year, kept apartments in London and New York, and later bought an oceanfront estate in Palm Beach, the only place he used to say he really relaxed. When a friend asked him if he had hobbies, he just laughed. Even if he were visiting Palm Beach on a Sunday, he would find an excuse to go into the store and look over some papers or check the merchandise. Every two or three weeks he met Rodolfo and Vasco in Florence to discuss business. No longer having a residence in Florence, he stayed at the Hotel de la Ville on Via Tornabuoni, which had opened in the early 1950s to rival the city's older fine hotels, the Excelsior and the Grand.

As his father had before him, Aldo encouraged his sons to join the business. Thanks to Olwen, the boys all spoke fluent English—they even called Aldo "Daddy." Aldo brought his youngest son, Roberto, to New York to help him open the Fifty-eighth Street store, and Roberto stayed for nearly ten years, until 1962, when he returned to Florence to establish new administrative offices and showrooms back at the family headquarters. Roberto also opened the firm's first franchise in Brussels in the late 1960s, a successful venture that would later be used as a model on which to develop Gucci's franchise business in the United States. In Florence, he also established a complaints office to handle any problems customers had with Gucci's goods or service. Aldo relied more and more on Roberto, whom he nicknamed "Sonny."

In 1956, Roberto had married Drusilla Cafferelli, the fair, blue-eyed daughter of a noble Roman family and a refined and pious woman. They had six children: Cosimo (1956), Filippo (1957), Uberto (1960), Maria-Olympia (1963), Domitilla (1964), and Francesco (1967). Of Aldo's sons, Roberto was the most conservative and respectful of his parents, obedient and docile. Paolo later nicknamed him *"Il Prete,"* or "The Priest," because of his formal ways and religious beliefs. Even Aldo at times found Sonny's style a little somber. During the summer months, Roberto and Drusilla and their children lived in Villa Bagazzano, a family home of Drusilla's in the countryside outside Florence. Winters, they moved back to their apartment in the city.

"When we would invite Aldo over to lunch or dinner at our country house," Roberto recalled, "he would look up at all the portraits of the Virgin Mary in our dining room and say to me, 'My God, Roberto! I feel like I'm in a cemetery.' "

Giorgio joined Roberto in New York for a brief stint, bringing with him his first wife, Orietta Mariotti, the mother of his two sons, Alessandro, born in 1953, and Guccio, born in 1955. Orietta cooked up big spaghetti dinners in the Guccis' small rented apartment and fed the entire clan at dinnertime in classic Italian family style. But the hectic pace of life in New York and having to live in his father's shadow grated on Giorgio. He soon returned to Italy, took over the management of the Rome store, and looked after his mother, whom he would ferry to the nearby Porto Santo Stefano for sea holidays.

"Giorgio was very timid," recalled Chantal Skibinska, whom Aldo hired in 1974 as director of European public relations and international fashion coordinator. "He was crushed by the enormous personality of his father."

Aldo, like Guccio, was a tough and domineering father. Once, when Paolo was fourteen or fifteen and did something wrong, Aldo gave away his dog as punishment. Paolo, devastated when he discovered the dog missing, cried for a week. "My father was much tougher on his own sons than on his staff," agreed Roberto.

Giorgio, surprisingly, was the first son to break out of the family mold in adulthood. Despite his shyness, Giorgio had a spirit of his own and he infuriated both his father and his uncle Rodolfo in 1969 when he decided to open his own shop, Gucci Boutique, along with Maria Pia, a former Gucci saleswoman who would become his second wife. Located on Rome's Via Borgognona, parallel to Via Condotti and one street to the south, Giorgio's boutique had a slightly different concept from the other Gucci stores. He catered to a younger clientele, stocking the shop with lower priced accessories and gift items. He and Maria Pia developed their own line of bags and accessories, which were produced in the Gucci factory. Giorgio's rebellion initially amounted to treason, although it paled compared to later family discord.

When asked by a journalist about Giorgio and the second Rome shop, Aldo replied: "He is the black sheep in the family. He has left the cruise liner for a rowboat, but he will be back!" Aldo was right. In 1972, Gucci Boutique was reabsorbed by the family, although Giorgio and Maria Pia continued to manage it.

After helping customers in the Rome store as a young boy, Aldo's youngest son, Paolo, established himself in Florence. Considered by many the most creative of the three, he began working for his uncle Vasco in the factory, where he discovered he had design talent. He put his ideas into production and soon brought out an entire line of Gucci products. Knowing how difficult it was to be around his dynamic and authoritarian father, Paolo initially resisted going to New York, happy to work on his own designs back home in Florence. In 1952 he married a local girl, Yvonne Moschetto, and they had two daughters, Elisabetta in 1952 and Patrizia in 1954.

Paolo lacked the deference and diplomacy of his older brothers and bitterly resented his father's tyrannical attitude. His experiences working in the Rome shop as a boy had humiliated him—only begrudgingly did he offer gracious treatment to customers, who were often VIPs and celebrities. He grew a mustache in defiance of Guccio's rule; his grandfather hated to see hair on men's faces.

Paolo flourished as long as he was given free rein to design and develop new products, and he created the firm's first ready-to-wear items. In his free time, he raised carrier pigeons and housed some two hundred of them in an aviary he built near his home in Florence, later introducing dove and falcon motifs into the scarves he designed. Aldo saw early on, however, that it wasn't going to be easy to make Paolo toe the family line.

"Aldo always used to say that Paolo, who loved horses himself, was a purebred, but that unfortunately he would never allow himself to be ridden," said longtime Gucci employee Gittardi.

Aldo's drive, energy, and ideas seemed limitless. While in New York, if he wasn't jetting off to open a new store or give an interview, he rose between 6:30 and 7:00 A.M. and breakfasted in the Fifty-fourth Street apartment with Bruna, who watched his diet, did his laundry, and generally took care of him. After breakfast, Aldo's first stop in New York (or whatever city he was in) was the Gucci store, where he greeted all the personnel by name.

"Never say, 'May I help you?' to a customer!" he instructed the sales staff. "Please, always 'Good morning, madam!' or 'Good morning, sir!' "

He then checked the merchandise and the displays before taking phone calls in his office from the other continent. Once while visiting a store franchised to carry Gucci products, he ran his finger along a shelf and discovered it full of dust. He canceled the franchise contract instantly.

Aldo's mind worked double time thinking of new products, new store locations, and new merchandising strategies. He paced up and down in his office by day and in his bedroom by night, stopping only to make notes on what he needed to do.

"He was a kind of one-man market research firm," recalled a former employee.

"He always burst in the store with that globe-trotter's walk of his," recalled Chantal Skibinska. "He scaled the stairs of the Rome store two and three steps at a time, staff members fluttering around him."

Aldo inspired loyalty in his employees through his own dedication and conviction that they were all working for something they admired and should be proud of. By treating his staff as extended family, he got their undying commitment and loyalty—a management model common in Italian family-run enterprises.

"He stimulated the people who worked for him; he promised them a lot individually," recalled one former employee. "That made them work very hard." Some ended up disillusioned when they realized that even after a lifetime of hard work, they could never really become part of the family and, in those days, stock option plans weren't part of the program."

Mercurial and intense, Aldo could be alternately a warm, paternal caretaker or a tough, domineering tyrant.

"I was twenty-one years old when I went to work for Aldo," recalled Enrica Pirri of her early days in the Via Condotti store. "For me, he was like a father or an older brother," she said, recalling that she went to him for help when she needed it, including asking for a loan for a down payment on her first apartment, which he granted.

"He was also very hard on me," she said. "When I made a mistake, he would yell at me and make me cry. But he always had time for us; he was somebody you could joke with. He loved to laugh," she recalled.

Playful and mischievous as a child, Aldo charmed troublesome customers to their faces and made fun of them behind their backs, a practice that embarrassed his clerks as they tried to keep straight faces and ultimately set the tone for shabby treatment of Gucci customers that would later make news headlines.

Once, at a formal dinner in London, an Englishwoman asked Aldo innocently why there were so many Guccis and he responded delightedly, "Because in Italy we start making love very early!" relishing the shocked expression on her face.

Aldo loved women and had many lovers. According to company lore, he even set one of his mistresses up in a luxurious apartment on the outskirts of Rome where he installed his own private entrance directly from the hallway into her bedroom where he could pass unnoticed by her servants or her children. He flirted shamelessly and greeted fashion editors he liked with a full kiss on the lips. He knew how to be gallant, never forgetting that women were Gucci's best customers.

"He was a scoundrel," recalled Enrica Pirri with a smile. "He knew perfectly well that every kiss on the hand of a wealthy lady of Palm Beach meant the sale of another handbag!"

Aldo also had a knack for embellishing the truth to suit the message he wanted to give and was probably himself one of the most active architects of the stories about Gucci's noble, saddlemaking past. Domenico De Sole, Gucci's CEO today, who got to know Aldo very well when he was a young lawyer representing first the family and then the company, recalled that Aldo would nonchalantly make statements that flew in the face of logic and all objective proof of the contrary.

"He was the kind of guy who could come in out of the rain and look you in the eye and tell you it was a gorgeous sunny day outside," said De Sole.

If irritated, Aldo paced up and down even faster than usual, arms crossed over his chest, snorting to himself and rubbing his chin obsessively with the fingers of one hand, "Ahem, ahem, AHEM!" When he finally exploded, his face turned reddish purple, the veins on his neck swelled, his eyes bulged, and he banged his fists on the table or desk, breaking whatever he happened to have in his hands at the time. Once he inadvertently smashed his own eyeglasses; when he saw they were broken, he slammed them hard again and again and again on the table.

"You don't know Aldo Gucci!" he would roar. "When I decide something, I get my way!" Former employees have even seen irons and typewriters fly across rooms during Aldo's rages.

Aldo retained some of the thrift he had learned from his father, Guccio. In New York he loved to lunch, either alone or with a staff member, at the employee cafeteria under the St. Regis that served a warm meal for $1.50. He also patronized the Primeburger and Schraft's restaurant, where he ordered a club sandwich and a hot apple pie. Another favorite was the roast beef sandwich at Reuben's across Fifty-eighth Street from the store. An expensive lunch at "21" or La Caravelle was a big event, and sometimes his penny-pinching struck others as contradictory.

"He would skimp on the hors d'oeuvres for a press lunch and then spend a fortune on a transatlantic phone call to discuss the invitations," recalled Logan Bentley Lessona, an American writer based in Italy whom Aldo hired in 1968 to handle press relations—the first person Gucci took on in that capacity.

Always impeccably dressed, Aldo cut an elegant figure in his distinctly Italian handmade suits and shirts. Winters, he wore fedora hats, cashmere coats, blue blazers, and gray flannel pants. Summers, he dressed in neatly tailored linen suits in light colors and white moccasins. Initially, he snubbed Gucci's own loafers in favor of more traditional Italian styles—usually handmade wing tips from London. In those days, moccasins would have been considered too feminine for men. By the mid-1970s, however, Aldo made it a point to complete his attire with a pair of gleaming horse–bit loafers. He often wore a flower in his lapel too. "His suits were always just a little bit too tight, he was just a little bit too polished," recalled Lessona.

Aldo loved to be called *dottore* in Italy or "Dr. Aldo" in the United States, and he took full advantage of an honorary bachelor's degree in economics he received from the San Marco College in Florence. In 1983, Aldo got his American title of "Doctor" in the form of an honorary Doctor of Humane Letters degree from the Graduate School and University Center of the City University of New York.

Aldo continued the drive to open new stores. He identified Beverly Hills's then-sleepy Rodeo Drive as a choice location long before it became a chic shopping avenue, and in October 1968 inaugurated an elegant new store there with a star-studded fashion show and reception. Set back from the sidewalk on North Rodeo Drive, the Beverly Hills shop was designed for the stars. It had an open, plant-filled loggia where bored husbands could watch the California girls go by while waiting for their wives. The massive glass and bronze door opened into an elegant interior featuring an emerald green carpet and lighted by eight Giotto-inspired chandeliers made from Murano glass and Florentine bronze. Rodolfo even hired a film crew to record the opening.

The year before, in a long-standing dream come true, Gucci opened its doors on Florence's Via Tornabuoni. The most elegant and luxurious shop to date, the Via Tornabuoni store had elaborate street doors, pastel decor, deep pile carpeting, gleaming walnut showcases, and discreet mirrors. An elevator, lined with leather and trimmed with the ubiquitous red and green webbing, carried the family and staff between the four floors of selling and office space. The Guccis also had a bank of video cameras installed in Roberto's office, from which he could control every angle of the selling floor. "I could see everywhere," Roberto recalled with a chuckle, "but after three years the unions made me take them out—they said it was an invasion of privacy of the workers."

With the opening of Via Tornabuoni, Gucci also required the sales staff to wear uniforms: white shirt, black jacket, black tie, and black and gray striped pants for the men; three-piece skirt suits for the women in burgundy for winter and beige for summer. The saleswomen wore simple pumps, never Gucci moccasins—it wasn't considered appropriate in those days for the staff to wear the same items as were offered to customers.

The Tornabuoni opening, initially set for December 1966, had been delayed by the famous flood of that November, when the swollen waters of the Arno overflowed its banks and flooded the city, damaging and destroying priceless works of art and historical archives and filling local shops and offices with five and six feet of water. When the alarm spread the morning of November 4, 1966, Grimalda's husband, Giovanni, and Roberto, Paolo, and Vasco were the only family members in Florence.

Together, they carried hundreds of thousands of dollars worth of stock and merchandise to safety from the basement of the shop on Via della Vigna Nuova up to the second floor.

"We weren't due to move into Via Tornabuoni for several weeks yet and all the merchandise was still in Via della Vigna Nuova," Giovanni recalled.

The carpeting under their feet began to bulge and bubble as they carried the last of the goods from the basement up to the second floor. As they finished, they were wading in water up to their waists.

"The shop was a mess, but we had saved ninety percent of the stock," Paolo recalled, "and we didn't have to go to the expense of redecorating because the new premises in Via Tornabuoni were due to open in a few months' time. All in all, we got off lightly."

Fortunately, the factory in Via delle Caldaie was on higher ground and hardly suffered any damage at all. The floodwaters retreated, but the flood of orders continued to flow. The artisans in Via delle Caldaie worked overtime and still couldn't keep up. The Gucci family soon realized they needed to expand and in 1967 the firm acquired a site in the Scandicci suburbs of Florence. Grimalda's husband, Giovanni, was commissioned to build a new factory for the growing Gucci empire. It was to be a modern, 150,000 square-foot factory complete with design, production, and storage facilities. Aldo also envisioned hotel and meeting facilities for the twice-yearly company meetings of employees from around the world, yet these facilities were never built.

In 1966, Rodolfo created another Gucci icon, the Flora scarf, with the help of Italian artist Vittorio Accornero. One day, Princess Grace of Monaco came into the Milan store, where Rodolfo hurried down from his office to greet her and show her around the shop. At the end of the tour, Rodolfo turned to the princess and said he wanted to give her a gift.

She demurred, but when Rodolfo persisted, she said, "Well, if you insist, how about a scarf?"

What Princess Grace didn't know was that Gucci had hardly developed any scarves, except for some small, 70-centimeter (28-inch) square scarves with stirrup or train or Indian motifs on them that Rodolfo didn't feel were appropriate for a princess. Caught off guard and trying to buy some time, Rodolfo asked her exactly what kind of scarf she had in mind.

"Well, I don't know," she replied. "How about one with flowers on it?"

Rodolfo didn't know what to do. His mind raced.

"Princess," he said with a charming smile, "it just so happens we are developing just such a scarf right now. As soon as it is completed, I promise you, you will be the first to have it."

With that, he gave her a bamboo-handle bag and bade her farewell. The instant she walked out of the store, Rodolfo called Vittorio Accornero, whom he had met during his acting days. "Vittorio, can you come to Milan immediately? Something fantastic has happened!"

Accornero arrived in Milan from nearby Cuneo and Rodolfo described Princess Grace's visit.

"Vittorio," Rodolfo said to his friend. "I need you to design a scarf that is an explosion of flowers! I don't want a linear design, I want an explosion. I want it so that every way one turns to look at this scarf, one sees flowers."

Accornero agreed to try, and when he returned with the completed drawing, it was exactly what Rodolfo had envisioned, a magnificent cornucopia of flowers. He asked Fiorio, one of Italy's great silk printers in the Como district just north of Milan, to print it in a large 90-centimeter (36-inch) square. Fiorio had developed a technique, similar to silk-screening, with which he could print more than forty separate colors without the hues bleeding. When the scarf was completed, Rodolfo hand-delivered it to the Princess. Although neither the original design nor the scarf itself have since been located, the Flora propelled the expansion of Gucci's silk division and was subsequently adapted for use on apparel, bags, accessories, and even jewelry. A smaller version, called the "Mini-Flora," became popular as well. The Flora also opened the door to an entire range of lighter-weight apparel a few years later. Accornero began creating two or three new scarves each year for Gucci.

By the mid-1960s, Gucci was known to a savvy elite, who found its products high quality, tastefully elegant, and practical. However, the product that made Gucci a status symbol around the world had been an insignificant sideline up to then: a classic, low-heeled loafer with a metal snaffle bit across the instep. The men's shoe, a classic, low-heeled moccasin, was called Model 175. A classier women's version soon followed.

"Gucci hadn't made it yet," recalled Logan Bentley Lessona. "It was known to the carriage trade, but not to the upper middle class. The shoe made the name take off," Bentley Lessona said.

Thought to have first been created in the early 1950s at the suggestion of a factory worker who had relatives in the shoemaking business, the shoe was put into production and sold in Italy for the equivalent of about fourteen dollars. When Gucci began selling the loafers in the New York store, stiletto heels were all the rage and the shoes were regarded as bizarre and hardly sold at all. But stylish women soon caught on to the chic comfort of the affordable, low-heeled moccasin.

The original Gucci women's moccasin, known within the company as Model 360, was made of soft, supple leather trimmed with the snaffle bit and had two raised seams on top that narrowed toward the toes and then widened. In 1968, the original model was modified slightly and named Model 350, the so-called status shoe that became widely copied. Slightly dressier, it featured a stacked leather heel with a narrow gold chain embedded in it and a matching chain across the front vamp. It came in seven leathers (calf, lizard, ostrich, pigskin, alligator, reversed calf, and patent) and a new range of colors, including an unusual pinky beige and a pale almond green. The *International Herald Tribune* hailed its debut with a long article and a large photo: "Gucci has a new moccasin, which in itself is almost worth a visit to Rome," wrote Hebe Dorsey, the paper's respected fashion critic.

By 1969, Gucci was selling some 84,000 pairs a year in its ten U.S. shops, 24,000 pairs a year in New York alone. At the time, Gucci was one of the few Italian labels with its own store in New York City, along with that of clothing designer Emilio Pucci, whose colorful graphic prints had become famous thanks to Giorgini and the Sala Bianca fashion shows. The jingle among fashionable New Yorkers was "Gucci-Pucci."

Some observers were mystified by the boom of the Gucci moccasin, which continued well into the seventies and early eighties. Paul P. Woolard, then senior vice president of Revlon and an avid wearer of the shoes, was amazed at how Gucci made fashion out of what he considered an established trend. "It's only an Italian penny loafer," he said to the *New York Times* in 1978.

Aldo always felt that the shoe had caught on when the wives of rich Italian industrialists wore it while traveling. Low-heeled (less than an inch), comfortable, and versatile, it looked chic either with skirts or slacks.

Priced at thirty-two dollars, the Gucci loafer was one of the most affordable—and visible—status symbols one could buy. "The status symbol has always been semi-secret, shared by women who really care about clothes and worn like a club insignia," wrote fashion columnist Eugenia Sheppard at the time. A comfortable working shoe that looked fashionable at an affordable price, the loafer quickly became popular with secretaries and librarians. With that success came new problems.

"So many secretaries and shopgirls started coming in and buying the moccasins that the regular clientele was finding itself elbowed aside and not happy about it," recalled Lessona.

Aldo, in another stroke of genius, made a deal with the St. Regis Hotel and took over its cigar store–newsstand space, which he turned into a shoe boutique in the fall of 1968. This gave New York's working women plenty of room to try on shoes and left the main Fifth Avenue store freer to serve its traditional clientele.

The loafer also found its way onto the feet of lawmakers and lobbyists in Washington, D.C., earning the halls of Congress the nickname "Gucci Gulch." In 1985, the Gucci loafer was displayed at the Metropolitan Museum of Art in New York in an exhibit developed by Diana Vreeland. The loafer is still part of the museum's permanent collection.

Men liked the idea of the status symbol, too, so Gucci redesigned the loafer for them. The new Beverly Hills branch of Gucci hadn't even opened its doors when Frank Sinatra sent his secretary over to buy a pair of moccasins to add to his forty-pair Gucci collection. Gucci also created men's belts, jewelry, and driving slippers and even produced a man's purse, called a "document carrying case." Red Skelton had a set of maroon crocodile suitcases, Peter Sellers a crocodile attaché case. Laurence Harvey commissioned a "bar briefcase" complete with insets to hold bottles, glasses, and an ice bucket. Sammy Davis, Jr., bought two white leather sofas like the one in the Beverly Hills store. Other famous male Gucci customers included sportsman Jim Kimberly, Nelson Doubleday, Herbert Hoover III, Charles Revson, Senator Barry Goldwater, and film stars George Hamilton, Tony Curtis, Steve McQueen, James Garner, Gregory Peck, and Yul Brynner.

As Gucci bags and shoes became consolidated status symbols, the company moved into ready-to-wear—starting a decades-long challenge. Paolo designed the first Gucci outfits, mostly leather or leather-trimmed items, in the mid-1960s. Gucci presented one of its first dresses at the 1968 opening of the Gucci Beverly Hills store. The long-sleeved A-line dress was made of a brilliant silk floral print with thirty-one different colors. Three gold chains attached with tiny mother-of-pearl buttons accented the cossack-style neck and front slit, and solid colors from the flower motif banded the collar, sleeves, and hems. Another style featured silver buttons shaped like horseshoes. The following year, Gucci came out with the first scarf dress, made out of four scarves with the signature floral and insect motifs.

In the summer of 1969, Gucci debuted its GG monogrammed fabric, which was an evolution of the old diamond-print *canapa*. In the new version, two Gs were placed facing each other 6-to-9 and arranged in a diamond-shaped pattern. The new monogrammed fabric was used for a full line of luggage, trimmed with the by-then-famous pigskin, including a cosmetic case for women and a toilet case for men—similar to what was being done at the time by Louis Vuitton. Gucci presented the new luggage to an enthusiastic audience at a fashion workshop at the Smithsonian Institution, which had invited Aldo to Washington, D.C., to give him an award. As a gimmick to promote the luggage, Gucci sent male and female models dressed in pants and skirts made from the same printed fabric down the runway carrying the monogrammed bags and suitcases. The show received a storm of applause.

Gucci presented its first full-fledged apparel collection in July 1969, during the Rome Alta Moda fashion week. The new apparel was sporty and practical; Aldo wanted women to wear Gucci every day of the week—not just on special occasions.

"Elegance is like manners," he used to say. "You can't be polite only on Wednesday or Thursday. If you are elegant, you should be every day of the week. If you are not, then it's another matter."

The collection included a sporty blond tweed pants suit with tunic top banded in glove leather, a long leather dinner skirt with a narrow fox hem and fox suspenders, sporty short skirts and shifts, and a suede bra and skirt set that could be clipped together at the waist with clasps.

The *International Herald Tribune*'s fashion columnist Eugenia Sheppard raved about the new clothes, praising in particular a black leather raincoat with raglan sleeves and a wide red and blue canvas belt that coordinated with one of Gucci's most popular handbags. She also highlighted the new enamel jewelry and watches with malachite and tiger-eye faces.

By the early 1970s, Gucci products ranged from the $5 key chain to an 18-karat-gold chain-link belt weighing nearly two pounds and worth several thousand dollars. Over the next decade, the variety of Gucci products would grow at a dizzying pace.

"It was difficult for anyone to walk out of a Gucci store empty-handed because there was something for everyone at every price range," Roberto recalled. "There was every product, except underwear, to dress a person from head to toe for every occasion, from staying at home to fishing, horseback riding, skiing, playing tennis, polo, even deep-sea diving!" Roberto said. "We had more than two thousand different products."

By the 1970s, Gucci had come to symbolize status on three continents. Ten fully owned stores had opened their doors in leading capitals around the world, while the first Gucci franchise was operating in Brussels under Roberto's watchful eye. Aldo had even been called the "first Italian ambassador to the United States" by President John F. Kennedy due to the popularity of Gucci's classic chic styles.

4

YOUTHFUL
REBELLION

Be careful, Maurizio," Rodolfo growled. "I have received information about the girl. I do not like the sound of her at all. I am told she is vulgar and ambitious, a social climber who has nothing in mind but money. Maurizio, she is not the girl for you."

Maurizio struggled to maintain his composure, shifting his weight from one foot to another, wanting to run out of the room. He hated confrontation, and most of all with his domineering father. *"Papà,"* he said. "I can't leave her. I love her."

"Love!" snorted Rodolfo. "This isn't about love, this is about her wanting to get her hands on our money. But she won't! You must forget her! How about taking a nice trip to New York? You know how many women you'll meet there!"

Maurizio fought back tears of rage. "Ever since

Mamma died, you haven't thought of me at all!" he exploded. "You've only cared about the business. You have never bothered to think about what mattered to me, what my feelings were. You just wanted me to be a robot who obeyed your orders. But this is it, Papa! I'm going to have Patrizia, whether you like it or not!"

Rodolfo watched his son, stupefied. Shy, docile, young Maurizio had never talked back to him before. He watched Maurizio spin around, leave the room, and run upstairs with a resolve he had never seen before. Maurizio had decided to pack his suitcase and leave. It was no use arguing with his father but he wasn't going to give up Patrizia. He would cut ties with Rodolfo.

"I will disinherit you!" Rodolfo bellowed after Maurizio. "Do you hear me? You will not get a cent from me and neither will she!"

Patrizia Reggiani had mesmerized Maurizio with her violet eyes and petite figure when they met the night of November 23, 1970. For him, it was love at first sight; for her, it was the beginning of her conquest of one of Milan's most prominent young bachelors—and one of Italy's most glamorous names. He was twenty-two years old, she twenty-one.

Maurizio knew most everybody at the debutante party for his friend Vittoria Orlando. The Orlando family apartment was on Via dei Giardini, a prestigious tree-lined avenue in the heart of the city that was home to some of Milan's wealthiest entrepreneurs. Maurizio knew most of the other guests— sons and daughters of the city's leading families. During the summers, the same group met on the Ligurian beaches of Santa Margherita, about three hours west of Milan by car. There they gathered at the Bagno del Covo, a popular bathhouse with a seaside restaurant and discotheque, where leading pop singers of the time, such as Patty Pravo, Milva, and Giovanni Battisti, performed.

Maurizio didn't drink, didn't smoke, and hadn't yet developed his talent for engaging small talk. Tall and gangly, he hadn't dated seriously, aside from a few teenage crushes. Rodolfo had quickly discouraged any amorous escapades, admonishing Maurizio more than once to associate only with girls from good families.

Maurizio had found the evening rather boring—until Patrizia came into the room wearing a bright red dress that showed off her curves. He couldn't take his eyes off of her. Maurizio, wearing an odd-looking tuxedo without lapels, stood talking absently with the son of a prominent businessman, glass in hand, watching as Patrizia laughed and chatted with her friends. Her violet eyes, dramatically made up with dark liner and heavy mascara, flashed his way from time to time and then slid away as she pretended to be unaware that the young man with dark blond hair hanging limply around his neck had been staring at her since she arrived. She knew exactly who he was. Vittoria had told Patrizia—who lived in the same building—all about Maurizio.

Maurizio finally leaned over and whispered to his friend, "Who is that girl over there in the red dress who looks so much like Elizabeth Taylor?"

The friend smiled. "Her name is Patrizia and she's the daughter of Fernando Reggiani, who operates an important transport company in Milan," the friend replied, following Maurizio's gaze toward the red dress. He paused, then added meaningfully, "She's twenty-one years old and I think she's available."

Maurizio had never heard of Reggiani and he wasn't used to making overtures to girls—they usually approached him—but he summoned up his courage and moved over to the other side of the room where Patrizia was talking with her friends. He found his opening at the drinks table by handing her a tall, thin glass of punch.

"Why have I never seen you before?" Maurizio asked, brushing his fingers against hers as he handed her the cool glass. It was his way of asking her if she had a boyfriend.

"I guess you just never noticed me," she retorted coyly, casting her dark lashes down and then back up as she fixed her violet eyes on his face.

"Has anyone ever told you you look just like Elizabeth Taylor?" he asked her.

She giggled, flattered by the comparison—though she had heard it before—and shot him a long glance.

"I can assure you I am much better," she replied, provocatively pouting her coral-red lips, which were outlined in a darker shade of red.

Maurizio tingled from head to toe. Shocked and enchanted, he gazed at her wordlessly, dazzled and excited. Desperate for something to say, he asked her awkwardly, "Ahhh, wh-wh-what does your father do?" flushing when he realized that he had stuttered slightly.

"He's a truck driver," Patrizia answered with a giggle, then laughed outright at the puzzled expression on Maurizio's face.

"But . . . ah, I thought . . . isn't he a businessman?" Maurizio faltered.

"You are silly." Patrizia laughed, elated. She knew she had captured not only his attention but his fancy.

"At the beginning, I did not like him at all," recalled Patrizia. "I was engaged to somebody else. But when I broke off with my fiancé, Vittoria revealed to me that Maurizio was deeply in love with me—so little by little, everything started. He is the man I loved most despite what he became after all his mistakes," Patrizia said.

Friends of hers at the time said Patrizia never made it a secret that she not only wanted to marry a rich man, but a man with a name. "Patrizia had been seeing a very rich industrialist who was a friend of mine, but he didn't have enough of a name for her mother so Patrizia dropped him," a friend said.

Maurizio and Patrizia began double dating with another couple from the Santa Margherita crowd. Before long Patrizia discovered that Maurizio wasn't as available as she had thought.

Maurizio's mother, Alessandra, had died when he was five years old, and he had grown up under his father's doting, yet strict hand. Her health had started to decline just as she and Rodolfo were beginning to enjoy their new life in Milan, and friends close to the family said she developed a tumor in her uterus following Maurizio's cesarean birth. Gradually the cancer spread through her body, ravaging her beautiful face and figure. After she was hospitalized, Rodolfo brought the young Maurizio to visit her regularly. Alessandra died on August 14, 1954; published reports attributed the cause of death to pneumonia. She was only forty-four. On her deathbed she pleaded with Rodolfo, then forty-two, to promise her that Maurizio would call no other woman *Mamma.*" Profoundly shaken, Rodolfo told his friends sadly that Alessandra had given him the most wonderful years of his life—and she had left him and Maurizio in what should have been still happier years. Even though their relationship hadn't always been smooth, he sanctified her.

Despite Guccio's and Aida's concerns that the young Maurizio needed a mother figure, Rodolfo refused to remarry or seek other steady female companionship. Though from time to time he saw a few women—mostly former acquaintances from his acting days—he limited the relationships, afraid to take time away from Maurizio or make him jealous. Every time the young Maurizio caught him talking with a woman, Rodolfo would say, the little boy tugged nervously at his father's coat jacket. Tullia, a simple, robust, young girl from the Florentine countryside, was already Maurizio's governess and she stayed on after Alessandra's death to help Rodolfo raise his young son. Long after Maurizio had left home, Tullia remained to look after Rodolfo. Although Maurizio and Tullia grew close, she never became a second mother to him—Rodolfo would not have tolerated that.

Maurizio lived with Rodolfo in a luminous tenth-floor apartment on Milan's Corso Monforte, a narrow street lined with imposing eighteenth-century palazzi and few shops. Rodolfo liked the apartment not only because it was an easy walk to the Gucci store, but because it also stood directly opposite the *prefettura,* or police headquarters. In the days of frequent kidnap-pings of prominent and wealthy Italian figures, Rodolfo felt reassured that help was just across the street. The apartment wasn't large, having just enough room for Rodolfo, Maurizio, Tullia, and Franco Solari, Rodolfo's personal driver and assistant. It was tastefully, though not grandly, furnished, as Rodolfo wasn't prone to excess. Each morning, Rodolfo would dress in one of his rich-colored suits, join Maurizio, Tullia, and Franco for breakfast, and walk the few blocks to Gucci's Via Monte Napoleone store. In the evenings he would return for dinner, insisting that Maurizio remain at the table until he had finished. If Maurizio's friends called while they were still at the dinner table, Tullia answered the phone.

"Il signorino," she would say—embarrassing and infuriating Maurizio—"is eating dinner and can't come to the telephone."

After dinner, Maurizio rushed to meet his friends while Rodolfo retreated to the basement of their building, where he had set up a personal film studio. He loved to watch his old silent movies over and over again, reminiscing about the glamorous early days with Alessandra. Rodolfo still traveled frequently for business, which meant Maurizio grew up often feeling lonely and sad.

The death of his mother had traumatized Maurizio. For years afterward, he couldn't bring himself to say the word *Mamma.* When he wanted to ask his father about his mother, he referred to her as *"quella persona,"* or "that person." Rodolfo, working on an old Moviola in his basement studio, began to piece together all the bits of film he could find to show Maurizio what his mother had been like. He assembled scenes from their old silent films, footage of their wedding in Venice, and family scenes showing Maurizio playing in the Florentine countryside with his mother. Bit by bit, he created a feature-length movie about the Gucci family called *Il Cinema nella Mia Vita,* or *Film in My Life.* The movie became Rodolfo's life's work, an all-consuming project that he revised and edited continuously over the years.

One Sunday morning, when Maurizio was nine or ten and attending a private grade school, Rodolfo invited Maurizio's entire class to the first screening of his film at the Ambasciatori movie house located under the Vittorio Emanuele pedestrian shopping arcade and just a short walk from their apartment. For the first time, Maurizio saw his mother as he had never known her, a glamorous young actress, a romantic young bride, and a happy young mother—his mother. After the screening, he and Rodolfo walked the few blocks back home. As soon as they were inside, Maurizio threw himself on the living room couch, sobbing *"Mamma! Mamma! Mamma!"* over and over again until he could cry no more.

As Maurizio grew older, Rodolfo expected him to work in the store after school and on weekends in the Gucci family tradition. Rodolfo apprenticed him to Signore Braghetta, an institution in the Via Monte Napoleone shop, who taught Maurizio how to wrap masterful packages.

"Braghetta's packages were beautiful," recalled Francesco Gittardi, who managed the Milan store at the time. "Even if you only bought a 20,000-lire key chain, you took it home in a package that made it seem like a jewel from Cartier," he said.

Rodolfo's relationship with Maurizio was intense and exclusive, dominated by Rodolfo's possessiveness. Terrified that Maurizio could be kidnapped, Rodolfo ordered Franco to follow Maurizio in the car even when he went for a bicycle ride. On weekends and holidays, father and son would retreat to the estate Rodolfo had bought up, piece by piece, in Saint Moritz. Over the years, Rodolfo had invested his share of Gucci's steadily growing proceeds in buying up property on the hill of Suvretta, one of the most exclusive areas of Saint Moritz, until he had assembled an idyllic estate measuring more than two hundred thousand square feet. Gianni Agnelli, chairman of the Fiat automotive group, Herbert von Karajan, and Shah Karim Aga Khan also had vacation homes there—and Agnelli was said to have made several overtures to purchase the choice property from the Gucci family. Rodolfo named the first chalet he built on Suvretta Chesa Murézzan, or "Maurizio's house" in the local Swiss dialect. Rodolfo personally selected and transported slabs of peach-tinged stones from a nearby valley for the outside walls, where he mounted the family crest high up under the eaves, along with a fleur-de-lis, the symbol of Florence. Chesa Murézzan became Rodolfo and Maurizio's retreat until Rodolfo built the second house, Chesa D'Ancora, a few years later. Located higher up on the hill with a view of the scenic Engadine valley, Chesa D'Ancora had wooden balconies and exposed wooden beams. Chesa Murézzan was then used for servants' quarters while its living room became a giant screening room for Rodolfo's beloved films. Rodolfo kept his eye on a neighboring chalet, a charming wooden house with hand-painted flowers on the shutters in the old style and blue flowers in the front lawn. Built in 1929, L'Oiseau Bleu, as the chalet was called, was the home of the elderly woman who had sold him the Saint Moritz property over the years. Rodolfo had cultivated the old woman over time, stopping in for tea and seemingly endless afternoon chats. He thought L'Oiseau Bleu might be the perfect place to live out his old age.

Rodolfo tried to teach Maurizio the value of money by withholding it, and gave him limited pocket money. When Maurizio was old enough to drive,

Rodolfo bought Maurizio a mustard-yellow Giulia, a popular Alfa Romeo model. A sturdy, high-end car with a powerful motor—for years in Italy it was associated with the national *polizia,* which commissioned it for their squad cars—it wasn't the Ferrari Maurizio yearned for. Rodolfo also kept a strict curfew for Maurizio, who was expected home well before midnight on school nights. Intimidated by his father's autocratic and slightly neurotic personality, Maurizio loathed asking him for anything. He found his truest friend and companion in a man twelve years his senior—Luigi Pirovano, the man whom Rodolfo hired in 1965 to drive him on business trips. Maurizio was just seventeen years old. When he ran out of pocket money, Luigi advanced him the cash he needed; when he racked up parking fines, Luigi paid them; when he wanted to take a girl out on a date, Luigi gave him the car—and fixed it all with Rodolfo.

As Maurizio progressed in his law studies at Milan's Catholic University, Rodolfo worried that his son was too trusting and gullible. One day, Rodolfo sat him down for a father-son talk.

"You must never forget, Maurizio. You are a Gucci. You are different from the rest. There are a lot of women who would like to get their claws into you—and your fortune. Be careful, because there are women who make their careers out of trapping young men like you."

Summers, while Maurizio's peers vacationed at Italian beach resorts, Rodolfo sent Maurizio to New York to work for his uncle Aldo, who was overseeing the expansion of Gucci America. Maurizio himself never gave Rodolfo cause for worry—until the party on Via dei Giardini.

In the beginning, Maurizio couldn't bring himself to tell Rodolfo about Patrizia. He had dinner with his father every night as usual. Rodolfo, sensing Maurizio's impatience, inevitably slowed his pace—dragging out the meal as long as he could while Maurizio fidgeted in agony. The minute Rodolfo finished eating, Maurizio excused himself from the table and rushed off to meet Patrizia, his "pocket-sized Venus," as one friend called her.

"Where are you going?" Rodolfo would call out after him.

"Out with friends," Maurizio would answer vaguely.

Rodolfo would descend to his basement screening room to work on his masterpiece. While he watched the old black-and-white film clips over and over again, Maurizio raced to his *folletto rosso,* or "little red elf," as he had nicknamed Patrizia because of the red dress she had been wearing the night they met. She called him her "Mau." They often ate dinner at Santa Lucia, the homestyle trattoria in the center of town that continued to be Maurizio's favorite restaurant for years. He nibbled halfheartedly at his meal while Patrizia enjoyed the savory, home-cooked pastas and risotti, wondering at his lack of appetite. She discovered only later that Maurizio was eating two dinners—the first at home with his father and the second out with her. Maurizio was swept away by Patrizia, who was only a few months older, but seemed far more worldly and experienced than he. If he noticed that her dark, seductive looks were the result of hours at the hairdressers and in front of the makeup mirror, he didn't care. Even when she was a young girl, Patrizia's style was artificial and overdone. Their friends used to ask themselves what Maurizio saw in her after she removed her false lashes, combed out her teased hair, and stepped down from her high heels—but Maurizio adored everything about her. He asked her to marry him on their second date.

It took Rodolfo some time to recognize the change that had overcome Maurizio. One day he confronted his son with the telephone bill in hand.

"Maurizio!" he barked.

"*Si, Papà?*" Maurizio answered, startled, from the next room.

"Are you the one who has been making all these telephone calls?" Rodolfo asked as Maurizio poked his head into his father's study.

Maurizio turned red and didn't answer.

"Maurizio, answer me. Just look at this telephone bill! It's outrageous!"

"*Papà,*" Maurizio sighed, knowing the moment had come. "I have a girlfriend," he said, walking into the room. "And I love her. I want to marry her."

Patrizia was the daughter of Silvana Barbieri, a red-haired woman from a simple background who grew up helping out in her father's restaurant in Modena, a town in Emilia-Romagna less than two hours south of Milan. Fernando Reggiani, the cofounder of a successful transport business headquartered in Milan, often stopped for lunch or dinner at the family restaurant when he passed through town. Also from Emilia-Romagna, he enjoyed both the hearty regional cooking with which he had grown up and watching the owner's pretty red-haired daughter as she moved about the tables and rang up checks at the cash register. Even though he was in his mid-fifties and married, Reggiani couldn't stay away from Silvana, no more than eighteen at the time. She thought he looked like Clark Gable.

"He courted me assiduously," recalled Silvana, saying they started an affair that lasted years. She claims that Patrizia, born on December 2, 1948, was actually Reggiani's daughter, saying that he couldn't recognize her at the time because of his marriage. In talking about her own childhood, however, Patrizia always referred to Reggiani as her *patrigno,* or stepfather. Silvana married a local man named Martinelli to give her daughter a last name and followed her Clark Gable to Italy's business capital.

"I have been the lover, concubine, and wife of one man, and one man only," insisted Silvana, who moved herself and Patrizia into a small apartment on Via Toselli in a semi-industrial neighborhood near the headquarters of Reggiani's trucking business.

Over the years, Reggiani had made a comfortable fortune with Blort, as his company was called, named for the initials of four founding partners who had pooled their resources before the war to buy their first truck. Although the German army subsequently confiscated Blort's trucks, Reggiani built the business back up after the war, buying his partners out one at a time until he remained the sole proprietor. He became a respected member of Milan's business and religious community and a generous contributor to charities, earning him the title of *commendatore*. Reggiani's wife died of cancer in February 1956, and by the end of that year, Silvana and Patrizia moved into Reggiani's comfortable home on Via dei Giardini. Some years later, Reggiani quietly married Silvana and adopted Patrizia.

Silvana and Patrizia discovered they were not alone in Reggiani's house. In 1945, Reggiani had adopted the son of a relative who couldn't care for the boy. Enzo, then thirteen years old, had a troubled and unruly personality and resented the newcomers.

"Silvana will be your new teacher," Fernando told the boy.

"How is she supposed to teach me anything?" Enzo protested to his father. "She is ignorant, she makes mistakes in grammar."

Enzo didn't get along with Patrizia, either; the two children fought constantly and life in the Reggiani household became unbearable. Silvana, who had been brought up in the old school of strict rules and heavy punishments, tried unsuccessfully to control Enzo. She finally went to Reggiani.

"He isn't bright, Fernando, he is not doing well in school," Silvana told him, and he sent Enzo away to boarding school.

Patrizia, thrilled with her new father and family life, captured Fernando's heart. He coddled her shamelessly; she called him *"Papino"* and adored him. When she turned fifteen, he gave her a white mink coat that she flaunted proudly in front of her classmates at the Collegio delle Fanciulle, an exclusive school for girls on the east side of Milan near the city's music conservatory. For her eighteenth birthday she found a Lancia Fulvia Zagato sports car parked in front of their home wrapped with a giant red ribbon. She teased him, scandalizing him with questions about his faith.

"Papino, if Christ is supposed to be eternal, then why is it necessary to make wooden statues of him?" she would say as he growled a response. *"Papino,* at Eastertime that wooden Christ you bend to kiss used to be a tree!" She'd throw her arms around his neck while Reggiani sputtered and fumed.

"*Papino*, I'll come to church with you on Sunday!"

While Reggiani coddled Patrizia, Silvana groomed her. Silvana had gotten them from Modena to Milan; it was up to Patrizia to take the next step—into the living rooms of the best families in town. Patrizia became the living image of Silvana's ambition. But the cars, furs, and other status symbols only turned up the gossip among Patrizia's schoolmates, who whispered loudly about her mother's simple origins and made fun of Patrizia's outrageous style. Patrizia cried at home with her mother at night.

"What do they have that I don't have?" she asked miserably. Silvana reprimanded her, reminding her that they had left behind another life in the small apartment on Via Toselli.

"You don't accomplish anything by crying," she said. "Life is a battle and you must fight. The only thing that matters is substance. Don't listen to the evil voices. They don't know who you are."

After Patrizia graduated from high school, she enrolled in a school for translators. She was smart and learned easily but having fun was her main interest. Classmates recalled how she would shimmy into class at 8 A.M., slipping yet another of her ostentatious fur coats off her shoulders to reveal she was still wearing a skimpy, rhinestone-studded cocktail dress from the night before.

"She went out every night," said Silvana, shaking her head. "She would come into the living room to say goodbye with her coat clasped tightly across her chest and say, '*Papà*, I'm going out now.' Fernando would look at his watch and say, 'OK, but at twelve-fifteen I am locking the door—if you aren't inside by then, you can sleep on the stairs!' After she would leave he would look at me and say, 'You two think I am an idiot, but I know why she had her coat wrapped across her chest like that. You shouldn't let our daughter go out dressed like that!' It was always my fault!"

Although Patrizia hardly seemed to care about her lessons, she easily became fluent in English and French in addition to Italian, making her *Papino* Reggiani beam at her good grades. At the same time, she became known around Milan for her provocative ways.

"I first met Patrizia at the wedding of a friend of mine," recalled a former acquaintance. "She was wearing a beautiful lavender voile dress, only she wasn't wearing anything underneath it. At the time, it was scandalous!" the friend said. "While Maurizio had received such a strict upbringing from his father, all the boys in our group knew what kind of girl she was. In fact, they used to tell me they knew *very* well, but Maurizio didn't want to hear about it. He completely fell for her."

Rodolfo was taken aback by Maurizio's declaration of love for Patrizia.

"At your age?" thundered Rodolfo. "You are young, you are still in school and you haven't even begun your training to work in the family firm," Rodolfo protested as Maurizio listened silently. Rodolfo wanted to groom Maurizio to take charge of Gucci one day. He could see that none of his brother Aldo's sons was up to the task, something he knew Aldo realized as well.

"And just who is the lucky one?" Rodolfo asked his son apprehensively. Maurizio told him. The name didn't mean anything to Rodolfo, who hoped the whole matter would blow over and Maurizio would lose interest in the girl.

Probably no woman was good enough for Maurizio in Rodolfo's eyes. For some time, Rodolfo had hoped Maurizio would marry a childhood friend, Marina Palma, who later married Stavros Niarchos and whose parents had a house near Rodolfo's in Saint Moritz. Marina and Maurizio had played together as children.

"She was the one person who Rodolfo thought might have been good enough for Maurizio," recalled Liliana Colombo, who worked first for Rodolfo and later became Maurizio's loyal secretary. "Rodolfo dreamed that Maurizio would marry Marina because she came from a good family; he knew her father. He wasn't sure about Patrizia."

About six weeks into Maurizio and Patrizia's relationship, an episode forced tensions out into the open. Patrizia had invited Maurizio to join her for the weekend at Santa Margherita, where her father had a small two-story villa with a flower-filled terrace overlooking the water. Furnished with elegantly carved Venetian pieces, the house was a meeting point for Patrizia and her friends.

"That house was like a port city," recalled Silvana. "Nando would bring home the focaccia and I would make trays full of little sandwiches and within a few hours there would be nothing left!"

But that weekend, Patrizia didn't care how many people had flocked to the house, she only cared about the one who hadn't shown up. Patrizia called Maurizio's home to find out if something had happened, and was surprised when he answered the phone himself.

"I told my father I wanted to come and he wouldn't let me," Maurizio told her sheepishly.

Patrizia was furious and amazed at his diffidence.

"You are a grown man! Do you have to ask permission for everything? We are supposed to be in love, yet it's a crime for you to come swimming with me? Why don't you just come down for the day?"

On Sunday Maurizio finally arrived, having promised his father he would be back that evening, but at dinner Patrizia persuaded him to stay the night. When

Rodolfo realized Maurizio wasn't coming home, he called. Silvana answered the phone only to hear Rodolfo storming on the other end of the line. He asked to speak to Patrizia's father. When Fernando Reggiani came to the phone, Maurizio's father roared, "I am not happy about what is going on between my son and your daughter. She is distracting Maurizio from his studies."

Reggiani tried to calm Rodolfo down, but Maurizio's father cut him off.

"*Basta!* Tell your daughter that she is not permitted to see Maurizio anymore. I know she is only after his money, but she will never have it. Never! Do you understand?"

Fernando Reggiani wasn't a man to take abuse lightly and Rodolfo's attack offended him deeply.

"You are very rude! You should know that you are not the only one in this world to have money," Fernando shot back. "My daughter is free to see whom she pleases. I trust her and her feelings, and if she wants to see Maurizio Gucci or anyone else she is free to do so," he shouted, slamming down the receiver.

Maurizio, overhearing the telephone call, was mortified. He and Patrizia went out dancing that night at the disco down on the beach, but he couldn't enjoy himself. The next morning he left at dawn and drove back to Milan. Maurizio apprehensively opened the solid wooden door to his father's study. Rodolfo, seated behind his massive antique wooden desk, glared at his son and delivered the warning that sent Maurizio marching out of the house.

Less than an hour later, Maurizio set his large suitcase, which bore the trademark green and red Gucci stripe, down on the step in front of Via dei Giardini 3. He rang the bell to Patrizia's home. When she greeted him at the door, her eyes widened at the sight of the heavy suitcase and his sad blue eyes.

"I've lost everything," he cried. "My father has gone crazy. He has disinherited me, he has offended both you and me. I can't even tell you the things he is saying."

Patrizia hugged him silently, stroking the back of his head. Then she straightened her arms and smiled up at him, her arms still encircling his neck.

"We're like Romeo and Juliet, and their families, the Montagues and the Capulets," she said. She squeezed his hand to try and stop the trembling, then kissed him softly.

"What am I going to do now, Patrizia?" he pleaded. "I don't have a cent to my name," he said in a voice that was almost a whine.

Patrizia's gaze grew serious. "Come with me," she said, pulling him into the living room. "My father will be home soon. He likes you. We should talk with him."

Fernando received his daughter and the young Gucci in his study, a simply though elegantly furnished room with bookshelves, an antique wooden desk, two small armchairs, and a sofa. He liked Maurizio, despite his fury over Rodolfo's insult.

"*Commendatore* Reggiani," Maurizio said in a low voice. "I have had a disagreement with my father that has forced me to leave my home and my family business. I am still in school and I don't have a job. I am in love with your daughter and I would like to marry her, although now I have nothing to offer her."

Fernando listened carefully and questioned Maurizio further about the falling-out with Rodolfo. He trusted what the boy was telling him, both about his fight with his father and his feelings for Patrizia. He pitied Maurizio.

"I will give you a job, and I will open my home to you," Fernando finally said, choosing his words carefully, "on the condition that you finish your studies and you and my daughter stay away from each other. I will not tolerate any funny business under my roof, and if there is, all deals are off," Fernando said, looking sternly at the boy. Maurizio nodded silently.

"As for getting married, that remains to be seen, first because I am still smarting from the treatment your father gave me, and second, because I want to be sure you two are convinced. I will take Patrizia away on a long trip with me this summer and when I return, if you are still in love, then we will think about it."

In a move that would become a pattern throughout his adult life, Maurizio had closed down his relationship with Rodolfo—who criticized and circumscribed him—and found a new source of protection and strength in Patrizia and her family. To the Reggianis, Maurizio appeared so well intentioned and vulnerable they were glad to welcome him into their lives and save him from the irate and irrational Rodolfo. The sofa in the study became Maurizio's bed for the next few months while he went to work for Reggiani by day and finished his studies at night.

The news that the two young lovers were living under the same roof traveled like wildfire through Milan's social circles. Patrizia's friends brimmed with questions about what it was like to live with her boyfriend. Patrizia played her role discreetly.

"*Papà* makes sure we hardly even pass each other in the hallway," she complained, delighted at the eagerness of her listeners. "I never see Maurizio anymore. During the day he works with *Papà*'s business and at night he studies for his exams," she pouted.

While Maurizio learned the ropes in the trucking business, Rodolfo brooded bitterly, unable to accept Maurizio's ready departure and willingness to give up all that awaited him just for a woman. Rodolfo's pride kept him from seeking a reconciliation. Missing the evening meals he had shared with Maurizio, Rodolfo stayed in the office later and later each night, instructing the cook to leave him only a cold meal he would eat by himself—usually just fruit and a plate of cheese. When his brothers Aldo and Vasco came to see him, concerned about the rupture between father and son, he cut them short.

"For me, that *bischero*, that fool of a son doesn't exist anymore, do you understand?" he screamed.

"His father never refused me as Patrizia Reggiani, but as the woman who was taking away his beloved son," Patrizia said later. "For the first time, Maurizio was defying his orders and he was furious about it."

In the meanwhile, Reggiani left with Patrizia on a trip around the world. When they returned in September 1971, Patrizia and Maurizio were more in love than ever. Fernando's managers reported that Maurizio had proven himself to be a serious worker with a good head on his shoulders. He didn't hold back, and even did hard physical labor such as unloading containers at the docking bay. He took to heart the problems of the company, carefully coordinating the schedules of the truck drivers. Several days after their return, Reggiani called his daughter into his study.

"*Va bene,*" he said to her. "OK. You two have convinced me that you are serious. I will agree to your marriage with Maurizio. It is a shame that Rodolfo is so stubborn, for by acting this way he will lose a son and I will gain one," Reggiani said.

The wedding date was set for October 28, 1972, and under Silvana's watchful eye wedding plans gathered speed. When Rodolfo realized Maurizio was not going to relinquish Patrizia, he decided to take drastic measures. One morning in late September 1972, he went to see the cardinal of Milan, Giovanni Colombo—but not to seek spiritual solace. After a long wait in the somber, high-ceilinged hall outside the cardinal's office which was located in a building just behind the Duomo, he made his appeal.

"Your Eminence," he begged the cardinal, "I need your help. The marriage between my son and Patrizia Reggiani must be stopped!"

"On what grounds?" Cardinal Colombo asked.

"He is my only son, his mother is dead, and he is all I have," Rodolfo told him, trembling. "This Patrizia Reggiani is not the right woman for him and I am afraid. You are the only one who can stop them now!"

The cardinal heard Rodolfo out.

"I'm sorry," he said finally, standing up to signal the end of the audience. "If they are in love and want to marry, there is nothing I can do to prevent it," he said, ushering Rodolfo to the door.

Rodolfo turned in on himself, brooding about his lost son. At the same time, Maurizio seemed reborn. He had received his law degree from Milan's Catholic University. In the months he lived with the Reggianis, he realized that the world didn't revolve around his father. He seemed more mature, and felt more in control of himself and his future—even if it wasn't to be in his family firm. He was doing well and enjoying his work with Patrizia's father, of whom he had grown fond. The Reggianis grew fond of him too; Maurizio even called Fernando *"Papà Baffo"* for his bristly gray mustache—though never to his face.

"Maurizio even said openly that he enjoyed unloading the trucks!" marveled one of his friends. "Those were the years of the student movements in Italy. In Milan, as in other cities, there were marches and gang wars and tear gas in the downtown streets. Maurizio wasn't involved in the student riots, but Patrizia was Maurizio's rebellion. He had found his independence," the friend said.

Maurizio wasn't completely at peace with himself, however. Several days before his marriage to Patrizia, he went to confession in the Duomo, Milan's magnificent fourteenth-century cathedral. He walked into the lofty, shadowy nave and headed over to one of the confessionals along the side. He liked the feeling of anonymity, of being one among many, sensing murmuring voices, softly echoing footsteps, light filtering down hazily from high stained-glass windows.

"Forgive me, Father, for I have sinned," Maurizio muttered, kneeling on the low padded bench inside the confessional. He lowered his head toward his hands, which he held, fingers knitted together, in front of the faded burgundy curtain.

"I have disobeyed one of the ten commandments," he said. "I have not honored my father's wishes. I am going to marry against his will."

THE FOURTEENTH-CENTURY red brick basilica Santa Maria della Pace stands in a walled, tree-filled courtyard located directly behind the twentieth-century Milan courthouse. As is the custom in Italy, for the wedding Silvana had the pews draped in burgundy velvet and decorated with bunches of wildflowers. *Papino* Reggiani splurged and hired an antique Rolls-Royce to deliver his daughter to the church and six ushers in tails escorted the guests. A brief reception in the halls of the Order of San Sepolcro under the church followed the ceremony, and later the five hundred guests sat down to dinner under the twinkling chandeliers at the Club dei Giardini—the same Milan social club where, with pulsing music and dramatic spotlights, Gucci would stage its modern fashion comeback twenty-three years later.

Maurizio and Patrizia's wedding was one of the big social events of the year—but not one of Maurizio's relatives was there. Patrizia's family, aware that Rodolfo opposed the marriage, had not invited him. Early that morning, Rodolfo had summoned his driver, Luigi, and ordered him to drive them to Florence on a pretense. "It seemed the whole city was celebrating this wedding," Luigi recalled. "The only thing for Rodolfo to do was to leave town."

While the church overflowed with Patrizia's friends and acquaintances, Maurizio's guests included only one of his professors and some of his school friends. His uncle Vasco sent a silver vase.

Patrizia was convinced that Rodolfo would come around. "Don't worry, Mau," she consoled him. "Things will sort themselves out. Just wait until a grandchild or two comes along; your father will make up with you."

Patrizia was right, but she wasn't the type to leave things to chance. She lobbied Aldo, who had always been a strong advocate of the family nature of the business. He had been watching Maurizio and was impressed by his nephew's determination to stand up to his father. He was beginning to realize that none of his own boys had the desire to join him in the United States to work with him, nor the ambition to carry on his work. His son Roberto had settled in Florence with his wife, Drusilla, and their flock of children; Giorgio had established himself in Rome, where he oversaw the two boutiques; and Paolo was working for Vasco in Florence.

In April 1971, Aldo hinted to the *New York Times* that he was looking for a successor because his own sons could not be spared from their functions within the business. He said he might train a young nephew, soon to graduate from college. "Perhaps before he meets some unattractive young girl and settles into family life," he added, "I will give him the challenge of becoming my replacement." It was a strong signal for Maurizio.

Aldo went to speak with Rodolfo.

"Rodolfo, you are more than sixty years old. Maurizio is your only son. He is your true fortune. Look, Patrizia isn't such a bad girl and I am convinced she really does love him." He studied his brother, who had closed himself off with a rigid glare. Aldo realized he was going to have to get tough in his peacemaking effort.

"Foffo!" Aldo said sharply. "Don't be a fool! If you don't bring Maurizio back into the fold, I am telling you, you will only be a bitter and lonely old man."

Two years had gone by since Maurizio had left home. That evening when he came home for dinner to the cozy attic apartment Reggiani had given them on Via Durini in the center of Milan, Patrizia greeted him with a mysterious smile.

"I have good news for you," she said. "Your father wants to see you tomorrow." Maurizio looked surprised and happy.

"You have your uncle Aldo to thank . . . and also me," she said, as she threw her arms around him.

The next day Maurizio walked the few blocks to his father's office over the Gucci store, worrying over what they would say to each other. He didn't have to. His father greeted him warmly at the door as if nothing had happened between them—in typical Gucci style.

"*Ciao,* Maurizio!" Rodolfo said with a smile. "*Come stai?* How are you?"

Neither mentioned their disagreements nor the wedding. Rodolfo asked about Patrizia.

"How would you and Patrizia like to live in New York?" Maurizio's eyes lit up. "Your uncle Aldo would like you to come over and give him a hand."

Maurizio was ecstatic. Less than a month later, the young couple moved to New York. Despite her enthusiasm about arriving in Manhattan, Patrizia was not thrilled with the third-rate hotel Rodolfo had arranged for them to stay in until they could find an apartment.

"Your name is Gucci and we have to live like peasants?" she complained to Maurizio. The next day she moved them into a suite at the St. Regis Hotel on the corner of Fifth Avenue and Fifty-fifth Street, a few paces from the Gucci store. From there, they moved to one of Aldo's rental apartments, where they lived for about a year until Patrizia spotted a luxury apartment in the Olympic Tower, the bronze-tinted glass skyscraper built by Aristotle Onassis. She loved the look of the elegant porter at the door, the floor-to-ceiling picture windows looking out over Fifth Avenue.

"Oh, Mau, I want to live here!" she said, throwing her arms around him as he blushed in the presence of the real estate agent.

"Are you crazy?" he protested. "How am I going to go to my father and say I'd like to buy a penthouse in Manhattan?"

"Well, if you don't have the courage to do it, I will," she retorted.

When Patrizia approached Rodolfo, he was furious. "You want to ruin me!" he accused her.

"If you think about it, it is an excellent investment," Patrizia retorted coolly.

Rodolfo shook his head, but promised to think about it. Two months later, Patrizia had her apartment, which measured some 1,600 square feet over two floors. She covered the walls with taupe faux-suede fabric, furnished the rooms with modern pieces trimmed with smoked glass, and draped leopard and jaguar skins over the couches and on the floors. She drove happily around New York in a chauffeured car with vanity plates that read "Mauizia," and generally enjoyed their New York life. She confessed once in a television interview that she would rather "weep in a Rolls-Royce than be happy on a bicycle." Over the years, other gifts followed: a second apartment in Olympic Tower, hillside terrain in Acapulco on which she wanted to build, Cherry Blossom Farm in Connecticut, and a duplex penthouse in Milan.

Rodolfo's generosity was entirely in line with custom in Italy, where Italian parents generally provide living quarters for their children when they marry. Until marriage, grown children usually live at home with their parents. The gift of housing may range from accommodation within the family home to a co-op apartment or sometimes even an independent house. Wealthy parents, of course, can provide vacation villas and even overseas properties in addition to a principal residence.

Because of Rodolfo's rupture with Maurizio over Patrizia, the young couple had initially moved into an apartment that *Papino* Reggiani had offered them in Milan. Patrizia fretted, feeling they had a right to more. After Rodolfo and Maurizio reconciled, the presentation of the Olympic Tower apartment and the other properties to the young couple represented Rodolfo's efforts to make amends—and, Patrizia felt, to thank her for all she was doing for Maurizio.

"Rodolfo became more and more generous with me," Patrizia recalled. "Every present was his way of thanking me for the happiness I was creating around my husband. In particular, it was his silent appreciation for my diplomatic work with his brother Aldo."

However, Patrizia did not receive title to the New York apartments, the Acapulco hillside, the Connecticut farm, or the penthouse in Milan. An offshore family holding company based in Liechtenstein called Katefid AG—probably established as a tax shelter—held title to all of them. Putting family assets into holding companies was also an effective way to prevent the escape of family wealth. So if a daughter-in-law, for example, left the fold, she might have a very hard time establishing legal claim to any property "given" to her but actually deeded to the holding company.

Patrizia, in love with Maurizio and elated over Rodolfo's generosity, didn't pay much attention to ownership issues back then. She devoted herself to being a good wife and mother. Alessandra, their first daughter, born in 1976, was named for Maurizio's mother—a decision that made Rodolfo profoundly happy. Their second daughter, Allegra, followed in 1981.

"We were like two peas in a pod," Patrizia said. "We were faithful to each other and gave each other serenity. He let me take all the initiative in the house, with our social life, with the girls. He smothered me with attention, loving gazes, gifts . . . He listened to me."

In honor of Allegra's birth, Maurizio made the most ambitious purchase of all—a 64-meter (208-foot), three-masted yacht called the *Creole* that had once been owned by Greek tycoon Stavros Niarchos. Sailors said it was the most beautiful ship in the world, although when Maurizio and Patrizia first saw *Creole,* she was little more than a dilapidated, rotting hull. Maurizio had bought the boat for what was considered a bargain price—less than $1 million—from a Danish drug rehabilitation program that could no longer use it. He shipped the yacht from the Danish shipyard where he had first seen it to Italy's Ligurian port, La Spezia, for initial repairs. He planned to restore the *Creole* to its original beauty.

Commissioned by Alexander Cochran, a rich American carpet manufacturer, from noted English shipbuilder Camper & Nicholson in 1925, the yacht was originally called the *Vira* and was one of the largest schooners built in its time. But the history of the schooner was also linked with tragedy. Cochran died prematurely of cancer and his heirs sold the ship shortly thereafter. It then changed ownership and name several times. After the war, when the vessel was decommissioned by the British navy, it returned to the commercial yacht market. Stavros Niarchos fell in love with it and bought it from a German businessman in 1953, rehabilitating it and renaming it the *Creole.* He replaced the small deckhouse with a spacious cabin in teak and mahogany large enough to contain a master bedroom and a studio—he was loathe to sleep belowdecks, terrified of drowning in his sleep. Whether or not one believes the sailor's adage that it's bad luck to change the name of a boat—and the *Creole*'s name had been changed three times—tragedy came to Niarchos. His first wife, Eugenia, took an overdose of pills and committed suicide on the *Creole* in 1970. A few years later his second wife, Tina, who was Eugenia's younger sister, also killed herself on the yacht. In his grief, Niarchos came to hate the ship and never set foot on it again. He finally sold it to the Danish Navy, which turned it over to the drug rehabilitation institute. Maurizio bought the *Creole* in 1982.

Though thrilled at the prospects of idyllic cruises once the *Creole* had been restored, Patrizia worried that the tragic deaths of Niarchos's wives had cast a negative aura over the boat. An attentive client of astrologers and psychics, Patrizia convinced Maurizio to go aboard with Frida, a psychic, to exorcise the evil spirits she was sure still haunted the sailing vessel. It had been taken out of the water for repairs and was propped up in a hangar in a La Spezia shipyard like an old beached whale. As they stepped aboard, Frida asked everyone, including two crew members who were guiding their tour with flashlights, to stand back. She went into a trance and started walking slowly along the deck, into the central cabin, and down one of the halls, mumbling incomprehensible words. Patrizia and Maurizio and the two crew members followed at a distance. The two workmen exchanged skeptical glances with each other.

"Open the door, open the door," Frida cried out suddenly as Maurizio and Patrizia looked at each other, puzzled. They were standing in the open corridor; there was no door. But the Sicilian crew member turned ashen. Before the reconstruction, there had been a door in that very spot, he said. The group continued to follow Frida, who walked in and out of the cabins, muttering. She stopped suddenly near the kitchen.

"Leave me alone!" she shouted. The Sicilian crew member looked at her in horror and then turned to Maurizio.

"That is where Eugenia's body was found," he whispered. Suddenly a rush of cold air swept through the vessel, chilling the small group.

"What's going on here?" cried out Maurizio, trying to figure out where the current of cold air had come from. The *Creole* was enclosed in the construction hangar, and there were no open doors or windows that could have caused the sudden draft. At that moment Frida snapped out of her trance.

"It's all over," she said. "There are no more evil spirits on the *Creole*. Eugenia's ghost promised me that from now on, she will protect the *Creole* and its crew."

5

FAMILY

RIVALRIES

While Maurizio was a young man pursuing his law studies in Milan, the spectacular growth of the Gucci empire charged ahead. In 1970, Aldo had ushered in the new decade by opening a dramatic new shop on the northeast corner of Fifth Avenue and Fifty-fourth Street. The new Gucci store replaced an I. Miller shoe store in the sixteen-story French Renaissance Aeolian Building at 689 Fifth Avenue. Aldo had called in the Weisberg and Castro architectural firm, known for its remakes of top-notch stores on New York's fashionable shopping streets. The architects created a contemporary look by using plenty of glass, imported travertine marble, and stainless steel treated to resemble bronze.

Casting around for new ways to finance further expansion, Aldo called on the board of directors in 1971 to reexamine an old principle established by their late father, that ownership of the company should never leave the family.

"I think we should float part of the company, which is now worth some thirty million dollars, on the stock market," Aldo said, as his brothers listened silently. "We could sell forty percent, keep sixty percent in the U.S. company. If we start at ten dollars, I bet in a year we will be at twenty," he said enthusiastically.

"The timing is perfect," Aldo continued. "Gucci is a symbol of status and style not only with the Hollywood set, but also with traders and bankers! We must not fall behind; we have to keep pace with our competition. We can use this money to stay on top in our consolidated markets in Europe and the U.S., but also to move into Japan and the Far East."

Rodolfo and Vasco had exchanged long glances across the massive walnut conference table in the offices above the store on Via Tornabuoni where the directors had gathered. Neither was convinced, despite Aldo's persuasive argument. Fundamentally conservative, they didn't see the merit of their brother's ambitious plans. The Gucci business was giving them a comfortable living and they didn't want to put their incomes at risk. With their two-thirds majority, they not only turned Aldo down, but agreed not to sell any of their shares outside the family for at least a hundred years. Typically, Aldo didn't waste any time sulking. His style, as he instructed his sons, was to push ahead.

"Turn the page!" he would bark at the boys. "Go on. Don't look back. Cry if you must, but shoot!"

By "shoot," Aldo meant act and react, which is exactly what he did. He accelerated Gucci's expansion to high speed. New stores followed in Chicago in 1971, then in Philadelphia and San Francisco. In 1973, Aldo opened a third store on Fifth Avenue in New York, next to its shoe boutique at 699 Fifth Avenue. The new store carried fashion apparel, while the corner boutique at 689 Fifth Avenue carried luggage and accessories. Gucci also opened its first U.S. franchises, including Gucci boutiques in the Joseph Magnin specialty stores in San Francisco and Las Vegas. Aldo boasted publicly and privately about Gucci's great strength: it remained an entirely family-owned business.

"We are like an Italian trattoria," he once said. "The whole family is in the kitchen."

Now Aldo could realize his dream of opening the next frontier for Gucci—in the Far East, and in particular, Japan. For several years, Japanese shoppers had flocked to Gucci's stores in Italy and the United States. Initially, even the business-minded Aldo had underestimated the importance of the Japanese consumer to the Gucci business.

"I was serving a Japanese gentleman who had come into the Rome store one day," recalled Enrica Pirri. "When he wasn't looking, Aldo waved me over. *'Vieni qui!'* he said, 'Come here! Don't you have anything better to do?' "

Pirri made a face at her boss and shook her head. The gentleman had been looking at a series of ostrich skin bags in bright candy colors.

"They were really horrible, but they were in style back in the sixties," Pirri recalled. "The man kept looking at the bags and saying, "Ahem, ahem, ahem." I told Dr. Aldo I wanted to finish the sale. I went back to the man and he bought about sixty bags! It was the biggest single sale we had ever done," Pirri said.

Aldo soon changed his tune. "They have excellent taste!" he told the *New York Times* in 1974.

"I tell my staff that the Japanese are the aristocrats of customers," Aldo told a reporter in 1975. "They may not be very good looking, but right now they are the aristocrats." He also instituted a rule that the sales staff could not sell more than one bag to any one customer—he had figured out that Japanese buyers had been coming to Gucci, buying large quantities, and then reselling the bags in Japan for many times what they had paid in Italy. He realized he needed to find a way to take Gucci directly to the Japanese.

Aldo received a proposal from a Japanese entrepreneur, Choichiro Motoyama, for a joint venture to operate a string of shops in Japan. The relationship was to become an important and lasting one, paving the way to Gucci's overwhelming success in the Far East. Motoyama opened the first Gucci shop in the Far East in Tokyo in 1972 under a franchise agreement. The first Hong Kong store opened in 1974, also in partnership with Motoyama. The Gucci empire now numbered fourteen stores and forty-six franchised boutiques around the world.

In just twenty years Aldo had built Gucci from a $6,000 corporation and a small shop in the Savoy Plaza Hotel into a glittering empire spanning the United States, Europe, and Asia. Gucci's biggest presence was in New York, where Gucci now had three boutiques on Fifth Avenue between Fifty-fourth and Fifty-fifth Streets in what the *New York Times* called "a sort of Gucci city."

By the mid-seventies, Aldo's early philosophy that "the customer is always right" evolved into a kind of autocratic rigidity that quickly got attention. Aldo laid down his own policies, whether or not they were in step with what other merchants were doing. He did not accept returns, for example, or give refunds or discounts. At most, a customer could exchange merchandise with the receipt within ten days of purchase—this while most other luxury names, including Tiffany and Cartier, offered full refunds after thirty days.

Anyone wishing to pay by check had to wait while the saleswoman called the bank to confirm that the funds were available. If it was a Saturday, she simply informed the customer she would hold the merchandise in the store and have it delivered on Monday after the bank approved the check. The sales staff also griped about an internal Gucci practice: at the end of the day, employees had to pick marbles, all white except for one, out of a hat. The person who picked the black marble had to have her bag searched before leaving the store.

What infuriated customers most of all was Aldo's insistence on closing the store for lunch every day between 12:30 and 1:30 P.M., a practice he instituted in 1969. The custom was a carryover from Italy, where even today most stores still close between 1:00 and 4:00 P.M.

"The people would line up outside and start knocking on the door to get us to open," recalled Francesco Gittardi, who managed the New York store for several years in the mid-1970s. "I would look at my watch and tell them, 'Five more minutes,' " Gittardi recalled.

Aldo claimed that after experimenting with lunch shifts, he preferred to let all of his employees eat at the same time. By doing so, he said, he could simultaneously promote the family-style management he was so proud of and avoid the risk of slow service because of rotating lunch breaks for the sales staff. He also said he hoped to avoid having customers come in and not find their favorite salesperson.

"We would stagger the lunch hours for some of our employees, but some wouldn't have lunch until late in the afternoon," he explained to the *New York Times*. "So I decided that the customers would understand and now everybody eats lunch at the same time." Instead of hurting business, the practice only seemed to raise Gucci's cachet.

"What is the Gucci mystique?" queried the *New York Times* in December 1974, describing how customers lined up three-deep at counters as Aldo stood, "fingering his blue tie with the famous horse-bit pattern, beaming at the mink coats jostling the blue jeans at the counters." The crowds swelled during the Christmas season, when Aldo himself would hold court in the store, personally signing gift packages.

Customers continued to crowd into Gucci—and leave irate over the service. One of the reasons was Aldo's practice of hiring the sons and daughters of prominent Italian families with little work experience. He inspired them with the intriguing offer of a glamorous job in New York and offered to put them up in one of the apartments he had rented nearby. But as the long hours, low pay, and Aldo's strict supervision took their toll, the inexperienced young people became more abrupt and less courteous with customers. Sometimes they would snicker behind customers' backs, or deride them in Italian—not unlike Aldo's own behavior—thinking the customers couldn't understand them.

My-Gucci-story-is-more-outrageous-than-yours became one of the more popular forms of local one-upmanship among certain New York circles. By 1975, Gucci's service had become such an issue that *New York* magazine dedicated a four-page cover story to Gucci titled "The Rudest Store in New York." "Gucci's staff has mastered the art of the drop-dead put-down and the icy stare, flashing signs that the customer is unworthy," wrote the author, Mimi Sheraton. Despite the rude treatment, she said, "customers came back for more, and paid handsomely for it!"

When Aldo finally agreed to an interview with Sheraton, she was rather apprehensive about meeting the man she knew was called *L'Imperatore* in certain circles. She was ushered into his subdued, taupe-walled office. The Aldo who came to receive her from behind a semicircular desk had come a long way from being the shy, dark-spectacled young man who had given one of his first interviews to a journalist in his spartan office above the Rome store on Via Condotti fifteen years earlier.

Dressed in a shimmering palette of blues—a bright hyacinth blue linen suit, powder blue shirt, and cerulean tie touched with red that accentuated his china blue eyes and flushed pink complexion—Aldo bowled her over with brio.

"I was totally unprepared for the effusively charming, ebullient, vigorously well-preserved 70-year-old who greeted me," Sheraton wrote. "He was far more colorful than his surroundings."

In his most operatic style, complete with changing voice parts, he recounted Gucci's five-hundred-year history, including its supposed saddle-making beginnings. He emphasized Gucci's pride in the quality of its products and the attention to detail.

"Everything must be perfect," he said with a grand sweep of his arm. "Even the bricks in the walls must know they are Guccis!" he said.

Despite his charming and magnetic personality, Sheraton concluded the Gucci stores' reputation for snobbishness came right from the top: "Gucci's rudeness . . . is undoubtedly a reflection of what Dr. Gucci considers to be pride, but which the rest of the world recognizes as arrogance," she ended the story. Far from being offended or angry, Aldo was so thrilled with the article—he thought it was fabulous publicity—that he sent the writer flowers.

Even as he continued opening new stores, Aldo also developed new Gucci product categories. He went back to the family boardroom and urged his brothers to consider selling a Gucci perfume. Again, Rodolfo and Vasco dragged their heels.

"Our business is leather," protested Vasco, who thought Aldo too impulsive and in need of being slowed down. "What do we know about fragrance?"

"Fragrance is the new frontier of the luxury goods market," Aldo insisted. "Most of our clients are women and everybody knows women love perfume. If we make a prestige scent that is expensive, our clients will buy it."

Vasco and Rodolfo grudgingly relented, and in 1972 a new company, Gucci Perfume International Limited, was born. Aldo had a dual motive in launching the fragrance business. He was convinced it was a potentially lucrative diversification that would complement their business in leather goods; he also wanted to use the new perfume company as a vehicle to bring his sons into the business—without giving them too much power. He found scant resistance from his brothers to his proposal to include the next generation of Guccis as a limited benefit for his sons. Vasco was indifferent, as he had no recognized heirs, and Rodolfo was battling Maurizio at the time over his marriage plans and was too angry to give his son a share in the new business.

Another important category for Gucci came about when Aldo met a man named Severin Wunderman in 1968. Wunderman had grown up in the school of hard knocks and as a result his philosophy in life was "He who throws the first punch, wins." The son of Eastern European immigrants, Wunderman was orphaned at fourteen. He grew up between Los Angeles, where his older sister lived, and Europe. At the age of eighteen he started working for a watch wholesaler, Juvenia, now defunct. Wunderman realized that the watch business could earn him a good living.

At the time he met Aldo, Wunderman was working as a U.S. salesman on commission for a French watch company called Alexis Barthelay. On a business trip to New York, where he already met with the likes of Cartier, Van Cleef, and leading jewelers up and down Forty-seventh Street, he decided to visit representatives of Gucci, who were meeting at the Hilton Hotel. Unfamiliar with the new push-button telephone in the lobby, he dialed Aldo's direct line by mistake. To Wunderman's amazement, Aldo himself picked up the phone. The two men began to speak.

"Aldo was waiting for a phone call from someone who was supposed to introduce him to a girl, and he thought I was stalling because I couldn't speak freely," Wunderman recalled.

Not being a man of great patience, Aldo couldn't figure out why his caller wasn't getting to the point, Wunderman recounted. Finally, Aldo exploded in Florentine dialect with the equivalent of "Who the f—— are you?"

Wunderman understood him perfectly because at the time he was dating a woman from Florence.

"I'm not the kind of person to take something like that," Wunderman said, "so I dished it right back to him."

"Who the f—— are you?" Wunderman said.

"Where are you?" barked Aldo.

"Downstairs!" Wunderman barked back.

"Well, why don't you come upstairs so I can beat the sh—— out of you?"

Wunderman marched upstairs, ready to throw the first punch.

"So he grabbed me and I grabbed him and then we both looked at each other and started laughing and that was the beginning of my relationship with Aldo and with Gucci," Wunderman said.

Their relationship would go far beyond a business relationship. They not only became fast friends and sparring partners, Aldo became Wunderman's mentor and Wunderman became one of Aldo's closest confidants.

In 1972, Aldo issued Wunderman a license to manufacture and distribute watches under the Gucci name. Wunderman established his own company, Severin Montres Ltd., in Irvine, California, and over the next twenty-five years built the Gucci watch business into one of the leading players in the business. With his street smarts and unpredictable, colorful personality, he had inched his way into the closed Swiss watchmaking establishment, securing production and distribution operations and the trade show exposition space he needed to become an industry player. Gucci became the first fashion label to become a significant Swiss watch business.

"Every major watch company in the world has had at least one successful model; very few of them have had two. We had eleven!" Wunderman said.

The first Gucci watch under the new license was another classic style called Model 2000, which Wunderman sold in collaboration with American Express in an unprecedented direct-mail campaign. Overnight, sales of the Gucci watches soared from some 5,000 units to 200,000. That watch even made it into *The Guinness Book of Records* for selling more than 1 million units in two years. A women's watch, which came to be known as the ring watch, soon followed. The watch face was set in a gold bracelet and came with changeable colored rings that clipped around it. The business was a bonanza overnight—both for Wunderman and for Gucci, which had secured a lucrative 15 percent royalty, considered high even today.

"If you went to Oshkosh, Wisconsin, and mentioned Gucci," Wunderman said, "people would say, 'Oh yes, they also make shoes!' "

Wunderman, who had translated his from-the-gut intelligence into business acumen, was soon chartering private jets between his London offices and his Swiss production facilities to make the most of his workdays. And though he may have become the bête noir of the conservative Swiss watch-making community, doors opened quickly for him in the best restaurants and hotels around the world, which had learned to offer extra-special service in exchange for Wunderman's generous tips.

Wunderman would hold the Gucci watch license—the first and only watch license Gucci ever issued—for twenty-nine years. By the late 1990s, the Gucci watch business commanded sales of some $200 million a year and generated a royalty to the tune of some $30 million—providing key income to the Gucci company in its times of greatest need. Wunderman, meanwhile, had made his own fortune, establishing sumptuous homes in California, London, Paris, and New York and later buying his very own château in the south of France.

During the 1970s, one event dramatically changed Gucci's ownership structure: Vasco died of lung cancer on May 31, 1974, at the age of sixty-seven. Under Italian inheritance law, his one-third stake in the company passed to his widow, Maria. They had no children. Aldo and Rodolfo proposed to pay her for the shares in order to keep the ownership of the company in the family, and to their relief, she agreed. Aldo and Rodolfo became the sole controlling shareholders of the Gucci empire, with 50 percent each—a share-holding ratio that would profoundly condition Gucci's future. Rodolfo, still stubbornly pursuing his confrontation with Maurizio, refused to consider sharing company ownership with him, but Aldo felt it was time to bring his boys into the Gucci mother company. He split 10 percent of his shares between his three sons, giving 3.3 percent each to Giorgio, Paolo, and Roberto. He acted as a generous and fair father, not concerned that he had given away his power to command. Any one of his sons could now ally with Rodolfo to create a 53.3 percent majority at the family board meetings. At the same time, the two senior brothers created a series of offshore holding companies in which they deposited their Gucci shares. Panama-based Vanguard International Manufacturing became Aldo's; Anglo American was Rodolfo's.

While the watch business took off almost immediately, Gucci's initial effort to start a perfume business on its own stumbled—the costs and the expertise required were beyond the reach of the family. Reluctant to give up, Aldo reconsolidated the venture as Gucci Parfums SpA in 1975, and issued Gucci's first license to Mennen to develop and distribute the first Gucci fragrance. Ownership of the new company was divided equally among Aldo, Rodolfo, and Aldo's three sons, each with 20 percent.

Aldo secretly felt, as his sons did, that Rodolfo's 50 percent stake in Guccio Gucci was disproportionate to his contribution to the family business. He planned to steer more and more of the company profits into Gucci

Parfums by developing a new business under its umbrella. To do so, Aldo retained the right to develop and distribute a new line of bags and accessories for sale in perfumeries as well as in Gucci stores. He also wanted to give a hand to his son Roberto, who had a family of six to maintain, and so named him president of Gucci Parfums. The new line was called the Gucci Accessories Collection, or GAC. Roberto Gucci oversaw the business from Florence, while Aldo supervised its development in New York. The new line consisted of cosmetic cases, tote bags, and similar items made out of a treated canvas printed with the double G monogram and trimmed with Gucci's signature pigskin in brown or dark blue, with coordinating striped webbing. The collection was known either as GAC or as the "canvas" collection. Cheaper to produce than Gucci's handcrafted leather bags and accessories, the GAC was designed to bring the Gucci name to a wider range of consumers. The idea was to sell the Gucci cosmetic cases and totes, among other products, in perfumeries and department stores alongside the Gucci fragrances.

An apparently well-intentioned and well-thought-out move that seemed in step with the times when introduced in 1979, the Gucci Accessories Collection ultimately turned into a destabilizing force in the business and family alike. Its launch represented the moment Gucci lost control over the "quality" factor in the business. Roberto inserted more and more products under the GAC umbrella—including notions such as lighters and pens—and the fragrance subsidiary soon started reaping higher profits than the mother company. At the time, most of the Gucci business was done through directly owned stores or franchises. In agreement with Aldo, a businesswoman named Maria Manetti Farrow, who had run Gucci's franchise shops in Joseph Magnin, began a wholesale distribution operation for GAC directed at a wider range of retailers. Also of Florentine origin, Manetti Farrow had a flair for business and zeal for success and soon became well known in U.S. retail for her management of the GAC wholesale business. Already familiar with both production and retail operations, she took the GAC business from zero to $45 million wholesale in just a few years, buying the canvas bags directly from the mother company in Florence and selling them to department and specialty stores across the United States. She started with eighty points of sale. By the time Gucci wrested the business back from her in 1986, Maria Manetti Farrow was selling some 600,000 pieces a year, of which some 30,000 canvas duffel bags, best-sellers at $180 each, sold in more than 200 cities across the United States. She sold the GAC to more than three hundred accounts for retail sales of more than $100 million. By the end of the decade, Gucci's canvas bags were sold in more than one thousand stores across the country.

"I was reaching the person who didn't travel so much, people who were too intimidated to go into the shop," she explained.

By the end of the 1980s, the GAC would be the product—massively distributed through department stores and cosmetic counters—that professional buyers associated with Gucci's "drugstore image."

The GAC also intensified another phenomenon—counterfeiting. It was much easier to copy the cheaper canvas bags than the painstakingly hand-crafted leather bags; poor-quality fakes soon flooded the market. Wallets with GG initials and bags with red and green trims jammed the shops and markets of Florence and cheap accessories shops in leading U.S. cities. Aldo knew that fakes could destroy his business.

"Why should a woman see an expensive handbag she has just purchased copied all over three months later?" Aldo observed in *New York* magazine.

Gucci fought a long and determined legal battle against counterfeiting. In 1977 alone, Gucci started thirty-four lawsuits in six months, including a suit to halt the manufacture of Gucci toilet paper. The precedent for that had come several years earlier when Gucci brought suit against Federated Department Stores for inscribing loaves of bread with the words "Gucci Gucci Goo." Aldo didn't pursue the manufacturer of a canvas shopping bag inscribed "Goochy," because he thought it was funny. But mock-Gucci shoes from Venezuela, Gucci T-shirts in Miami, and a pseudo Gucci store in Mexico City didn't amuse him.

"Prominent bargain hunters," Roberto Gucci told the *New York Times* in 1978, "including the wife of a former president of Mexico, have tried to have defective goods purchased from the so-called Gucci in Mexico City repaired at the New York store, only to be told they don't have the real thing."

In the first half of 1978 alone, Gucci's legal efforts caused the confiscation of some two thousand handbags and the liquidation of fourteen Italian manufacturers of counterfeits. As the Guccis fought off threats to their name, they overlooked the greatest threat of all festering within their own ranks. Creative and eccentric Paolo, frustrated by his failure to secure a larger role within the company, had begun to butt heads with his uncle Rodolfo, to whom he reported, over the creative direction of the company, as well as its business strategies. Rodolfo, who saw himself as the creative leader of the business, didn't welcome Paolo's suggestions or criticisms. Although Aldo's gift of 3.3 percent in the company placated Paolo for a while, he began using his shareholder status during the family board meetings to put his ideas about design, production, and marketing on the table.

Paolo, by then estranged from his wife and their two daughters, had found a new girlfriend, Jennifer Puddefoot, a plump, blond Englishwoman who wanted to be a singer. Jenny, who had a biting sense of humor, had also left her failed first marriage. The couple eloped to Haiti in 1978, where he became a resident in order to marry her because of the difficult, if not impossible, prospects of obtaining a divorce from Yvonne, whom he had married in the Roman Catholic church. Five years later, Paolo and Jenny had a daughter, Gemma.

After Vasco's death in 1974, Paolo had taken over the supervision of the Scandicci factory outside Florence. From his glassed-in office he could see through to the order department, where large clocks on the walls showed what time it was in Gucci shops around the world. Through the other window he could see the purchasing staff who ordered textiles and precious skins from around the world: ostrich and crocodile skins from Indonesia and North Africa, boar and pigskin from Poland, cashmere from Scotland, and bolts of GG fabric from Toledo, Ohio, where the fabric was routinely sent to Firestone for a special waterproofing process. Across the hall, the design studio was a kaleidoscope of color wheels and textile samples pinned to the walls along with sketches of handbags, buckles, watches, table linens, and pieces of china. The idyllic view from Paolo's window showed cabbage fields, rolling Tuscan countryside dotted with villas and cypress trees, and, in the distance, the dark rise and fall of the Apennine mountains.

Downstairs in the factory, sewing machines whirred and cutting machines thumped, all against the backdrop of buzzing fans used to aspirate the glue fumes. In one corner, artisans expertly passed the flames of gas torches over stiff lengths of bamboo, blackening and softening them into gently curving handles for Gucci's famous bags. Buggies rolled back and forth filled with goods in various stages of production, some to be glued, others for stitching, cutting, or trimming or to have the hardware attached. With the exception of more modern leather cutting and pressing equipment, the artisans used the same techniques they had on Via delle Caldaie and Lungarno Guicciardini before that. After being inspected, each piece was slipped into a white flannel wrapper and prepared for shipping, as is still done today.

To the workers and salespeople who watched him dart back and forth from the store and offices in Via Tornabuoni to the factory in Scandicci, Paolo was an ebullient, likeable, and outlandish figure who became known for his outpouring of ideas and for dashing around in a pair of monogrammed Gucci slacks he had designed. His staff quickly learned that like his father, he could be alternately ecstatic and furious. After a successful presentation, he would turn to his design assistant and say, "They are applauding me, but I know you did it." Yet if the same assistant contradicted him, he would throw a handful of sketches in her face and stalk out of the room.

Paolo's absorbing, apparently serene life amid the rolling Tuscan hills merely masked the turbulence beneath the calm. He thought the company lacked vision and planning and disparaged his uncle Rodolfo for completely lacking organizational skills. His father, on the other hand, was a born leader, but poorly advised.

"My uncle was a good actor, but as a businessman he was rubbish," Paolo once said. "He'd been smart enough to surround himself with good people, but he was no leader. My father, on the other hand, was exactly the reverse: a born leader but with rubbishy advisors."

From Florence, he wrote daily letters of complaint to his uncle Rodolfo in Milan: Gucci should license and distribute cheaper products for the younger, more hip customer; Gucci should open a second string of stores, modeled after Giorgio's successful shop in Rome. Beyond promoting his ideas—speedily rejected—about Gucci's business development, Paolo used his position at family board meetings to ask uncomfortable questions about the company finances. Sales galloped around the world, the factories in Florence produced at full speed, Gucci employed hundreds of people world-wide, yet there never seemed to be any money in the company coffers. The year he and Jennifer married, Gucci Shops Inc. posted a record turnover of $48 million in the United States and no profit. How was it possible? Paolo wondered aloud. Furthermore, he felt the monthly stipend he and his brothers received was hardly enough to live on. Aldo kept his boys on tight salaries to keep them humble and in line. Every once in a while he would give them a bonus to keep them happy. "Let's give the boys something to make them smile," Aldo would say jovially, and slip something extra into their checks at the end of the month.

The lack of visible profits began to cause wider consternation within the family. Rodolfo blamed the poor result on Aldo's hunger for expansion. The launch of Gucci Parfums had been expensive and, owning only 20 percent, Rodolfo saw only a fraction of the profits, 80 percent of which went to Aldo and his sons. In turn, Paolo and his brothers resented Rodolfo's 50 percent stake in the mother company, which they felt had been built up by Aldo. As the written complaints from Paolo piled up on his desk in Milan, Rodolfo lost his patience.

One small episode in the late 1970s that Gucci employees hardly considered unusual reportedly triggered the beginning of major conflict. One day, after arriving at the store in Via Tornabuoni, Paolo had one of Rodolfo's favorite handbags removed from the display window because he, Paolo, had not been consulted about its design. When Rodolfo learned of the change, he demanded to know who had dared to tamper with his window display. When he was told, he exploded. Shortly thereafter, at a press presentation Rodolfo publicly upbraided Paolo, who stalked out. At another meeting in the Florence design office, handbags flew, some sailing through the open window and landing on the lawn below. The episode became part of Gucci lore after the following morning the custodian found the bags outside on the ground upon opening the plant and called the police—thinking there had been a theft.

"This was business as usual," recalled a former employee, referring to the flying bags. "That kind of thing happened all the time."

But Paolo's critical letters and insolent behavior had become too much for Rodolfo. He confronted his nephew angrily on the telephone, summoning him to his office in Milan. When Paolo was shown into Rodolfo's office over the Via Monte Napoleone, Rodolfo wasted little time.

"I have had enough of your insolence!" he shouted. "I am finished with you. If you can't make it in Italy, then you had better go work for your father in New York!"

Paolo counterattacked—demanding to see the company's books. "I am a Gucci director and shareholder," he shot back. "I have a right to know what is going on in this company! What is happening to all the millions of dollars that are pouring in here?"

Paolo called his father and claimed Rodolfo was obstructing his rights within the company, undercutting his role as design director, initiating things without consulting him. Aldo, ever the peacemaker, waved the problem aside and invited Paolo to come work for him in New York.

"You need a break, Paolo," Aldo said benevolently on the other end of the telephone. "America is a wonderful place to live and work—you can take charge of accessories and design here. Jenny will like it too—perhaps she can advance her singing career." Paolo and Jenny were thrilled. Aldo gave Paolo and Jenny an apartment less than five minutes by foot from the Fifth Avenue store and made him vice president of marketing and managing director of Gucci Shops Inc. and Gucci Parfums of America, with an executive salary to go with the position. An ecstatic Paolo brimmed over with new ideas to exploit the seemingly unlimited potential of the U.S. marketplace. It was 1978.

In 1980, Aldo opened a glamorous new store across Fifty-fourth Street at 685 Fifth Avenue in the former Columbia Pictures Building, which he bought in 1977. Workmen hollowed out the first four floors of the sixteen-story building while maintaining elevators and other services for tenants on the floors above. It cost $1.8 million alone to install new steel and concrete girders in the opened space to keep the building supported. By the time it was finished, the store featured a spacious atrium in which the huge tapestry *The Judgment of Paris,* woven in 1583 for the Grand Duke Francesco de' Medici, hung between a pair of glass-walled elevators. The first three floors, again designed by New York architects Weisberg and Castro, were finished in glass, travertine marble, and statuary bronze. The first floor showcased handbags and accessories, the second, men's products, and the third, women's. This store remained with essentially the same decor until it was closed for renovations under Gucci's current management in 1999.

Aldo invested more than $12 million in the venture, including $6 million alone in an art collection that he hung on the fourth floor of the shop, the "Gucci Galleria," designed by Giulio Savio of Rome. For years, marrying art with commerce, he had organized impromptu spaghetti dinners for friends after concerts by the Italian tenor Luciano Pavarotti, also a friend. Gradually these events evolved from informal gatherings to gala benefits, such as the 1978 first night of *Don Pasquale* with Beverly Sills. Gucci contributed to the evening by sponsoring a gala dinner and Gucci fashion show after the performance.

Aldo hired Lina Rossellini, the wife of Renzo Rossellini, the brother of film director Roberto Rossellini, as a VIP hostess in his belief that personal contact was the best advertising for Gucci. Mrs. Rossellini, as she was always referred to, was well connected socially in New York and always welcomed important customers to the Galleria. She graciously ushered them over to soft taupe couches and easy chairs where white-gloved waiters served coffee or champagne on travertine marble tables. There they could admire originals by De Chirico, Modigliani, van Gogh, and Gauguin, among paintings by other artists, and choose limited-edition Gucci-designed jewelry or handbags made of precious skins and featuring 18-karat-gold hardware priced from $3,000 to $12,000.

"You may ask, where are the people to buy these things in time of recession?" Aldo said to *Women's Wear Daily* the eve of the opening. "I have a saying about beautiful women," Aldo continued, answering his own question. "Only 5 percent are truly beautiful. And it's the same with people of great possibility. They are only 5 percent of the population. But 5 percent is enough to make us smile." He predicted that the Gucci U.S. business would hit $55 to $60 million by the fiscal year ending August 1981.

One of Paolo's favorite tasks was personally to hand over to VIP clients Gucci's gold-plated key—another one of Aldo's inventions—that granted them access to the "Galleria." In no time at all, the little gold key—fewer than a thousand were issued—became a must-have in certain New York circles.

Gucci, by then considered the ultimate in class and style, was imprinted on the American mentality as top-of-the-line chic. In 1978, the characters in Neil Simon's *California Suite* all carried Gucci luggage and even mentioned it by name. To set the scene for his 1979 film *Manhattan,* Woody Allen rolled his cameras in front of Gucci's gleaming Fifth Avenue windows. Ronald Reagan wore Gucci moccasins while Nancy carried the bamboo bag for everyday use and picked up Gucci's satin slippers and beaded evening bags for special occasions. Sidney Poitier's joke went around the world: during a trip to Africa, a journalist asked the actor how it felt to set foot on the soil of his ancestors. With a withering glance he retorted, "Fine, through the soles of my Gucci shoes." In 1978, gossip columnist Suzy referred to Peter Duchin in the *Daily News Sunday* as "the Gucci of all society orchestra leaders." In 1981, *Time* magazine described the new Volkswagen as a new subcompact four-seater design that "looks more like a Gucci slipper than a car."

While Paolo enjoyed his New York life, his uncle had not forgotten his nephew's campaign against him. Rodolfo resented Aldo's breezy solution and Paolo's leaving his Italian post with no notice or replacement. Now that Maurizio was back in Rodolfo's good graces, the elder Gucci could no longer accept that Paolo had more standing in the company than his own son. In April 1978, Rodolfo wrote a letter in his own hand to Paolo, firing him from the Italian company for failing to carry out his duties at the factory in Florence. The equivalent of a declaration of war on Aldo, the letter showed that Rodolfo felt he had been provoked beyond toleration.

Paolo received the letter early one morning in New York as he was leaving home to head for the store. Rather than frighten him, it only made him more determined. "If they are going to kill me, I am going to kill them," he told Jenny. He vowed to destroy Rodolfo's position in the company through the power his own father wielded. He reckoned that the growing importance of the Gucci Parfums business with the lucrative Gucci Accessories Collection, of which Rodolfo only had 20 percent, would weaken his uncle's bargaining power.

The problem was that Paolo didn't get on much better with his father. While Maurizio humored Aldo, Paolo clashed with him. Working side by side constantly frustrated them both. Aldo was authoritarian and all-encompassing and had his own very clear ideas about how he wanted things done.

"I wasn't allowed to do anything," Paolo complained. "I had no authority."

When, for a change, Paolo had handbags stuffed with colored tissue paper instead of white, he incurred Aldo's wrath: "Don't you know colors fade? You idiot!" Aldo screamed.

Or when he sent back goods that had been ordered but arrived late, Aldo fumed, "We've been working with these suppliers for years, you can't treat them like that!"

They also disagreed over the advertising budget and the catalog because of Aldo's preference for promoting Gucci by word of mouth. Only Paolo's window displays, which won recognition, seemed to please Aldo—until Paolo hired the hot young window dresser of the moment and Aldo fired him the first day on the job. Even socially, Aldo was the only Gucci who ranked in New York. Dubbed "The Guru of Gucci" by the press, only Aldo appeared in the whirlwind of fashion-related Gucci benefits.

Paolo found his father's tyrannical ways insufferable and wondered what to do. Going back to Florence was out of the question for him. Since he had built up a circle of friends and contacts in New York, he explored the possibility of doing something under his own name. It didn't take long for his family to get wind of his plans.

"Aldo, what is that *bischero* of your son up to?" Rodolfo shouted into the telephone from his office in Scandicci. He had heard from several local suppliers that Paolo had approached them about his own line—the PG collection—and it wasn't just talk. There were styles, prices, delivery dates. And the distribution plan was massive; he even wanted to sell in supermarkets, according to one report.

Aldo hung up the phone, livid. Paolo had completely miscalculated his father's reaction. Instead of siding with him against Rodolfo, Aldo was furious with his own son. Even though Aldo and Rodolfo argued constantly, when it came to protecting the well-being of the company, they were united. They both perceived Paolo as a threat to the Gucci name and all they had achieved. Aldo thumped his fist on his desk, enraged. After all he had done for Paolo, this was his thanks.

He called Paolo to his offices over the Fifth Avenue store. The premises trembled from his shouting.

"*Bischero!* You are fired! You are an idiot to try to compete with us! A fantastic idiot! I cannot protect you anymore."

"Why are you letting them kill me?" Paolo shot back. "I only wanted to make the company better, not destroy it! If you fire me I will found my own company and then we will see who is right!"

He stormed out of the store and called his lawyer, Stuart Speiser. A few days later the papers were filed for the registration of the new trademark: PG.

It wasn't long before his own father's dismissal letter arrived—a registered letter from the board of directors dated September 23, 1980. When Paolo realized that there was no severance provision after twenty-six years with the company, he went to court again, filing papers against the mother company in Italy—which served to convince Rodolfo even more that Paolo was a potent danger. The family convened a board meeting in Florence, to which Paolo was not invited, and authorized some $8 million to fight Paolo's venture. Giorgio, who had tried to stay out of these family battles, was there, as was Roberto, who felt Paolo had gone too far in wanting to have everything his way. He had tried to reason with his brother: "You can't be a part of us and be a competitor at the same time. If you want to play, respect the rules of the game. You can't fight the company and remain inside it. If you want to go your own way, then sell your shares."

Paolo resented the pressure against him. "Everybody else was protecting their own interests within the company, I didn't see why I shouldn't have pursued my own," he said.

Rodolfo made sure Maurizio was present at the meeting too, even though he was not a shareholder. Rodolfo had been diagnosed with prostate cancer and although still highly active in the company, he wanted to bring Maurizio into the fray as quickly as possible.

"You must fight Paolo with everything you have got," Rodolfo confided to Maurizio privately. "He must be defeated, utterly and quickly. He is threatening everything we have and I will not be here forever." By that time, Rodolfo was nearly seventy years old and undergoing intensive radiation therapy to try to halt the cancer.

The Gucci company sprang into action against Paolo, hiring lawyers, instantly putting all the licensees Paolo had contacted on notice that any attempt to distribute products under the Paolo Gucci name would be blocked. Rodolfo personally wrote to all of Gucci's suppliers that anyone who did business with Paolo would be dropped. The battle against counterfeiters was just a skirmish compared to this. Family conflict had escalated into a full-fledged trade war. Over the next decade, the family war would pull back the curtains on the normally private world of a closely held family business, revealing shifting alliances, sudden betrayals, and rapprochements widely characterized in the press as a "*Dallas* on the Arno," but actually more reminiscent of the intrigues of Niccolò Machiavelli's Renaissance Florence.

6

PAOLO

STRIKES BACK

As Gucci marshaled its defenses and drew its battle lines, Paolo's quest to develop his own name became determined and relentless. His assault began in 1981 with the first suit seeking the right to use his own name. By 1987 he had initiated ten cases against his father and the Gucci company. When his father and his uncle stymied all of his efforts to sign up suppliers, he explored the potential of manufacturing his designs in Haiti, where his family discovered he had even made his own Gucci counterfeits.

Meanwhile, Aldo and Rodolfo clashed over the growing importance of Gucci Parfums. Although Rodolfo acknowledged that he had been able to live the life that he had thanks in large measure to Aldo, at the same time he was envious of his older brother's confidence and power and wanted to be everything he was.

He was no match for Aldo's genius, yet he resisted and resented the control Aldo had over the business. Rodolfo was also concerned about the lack of power Maurizio, his sole heir, had in the company.

At the outset of the struggle with Paolo, Rodolfo tried to claim control over aspects of the business that were eluding his grasp. He had figured out Aldo's strategy to shift the lion's share of Gucci's revenues over to the Gucci Parfums subsidiary, in which he only had 20 percent and Maurizio had nothing. Rodolfo pressured Aldo to give him a larger chunk of the perfume business, which Aldo refused to do.

"I can't see any reason now for making my sons part with their shares so that you can have more," Aldo said. Having failed to secure a larger stake in the perfume business, Rodolfo tried to exert his influence in a different way.

He hired a young, Italian-born lawyer, Domenico De Sole, who had established a successful law career in Washington, D.C. De Sole was the first person Rodolfo had ever met—besides Paolo—who stood up to Aldo. Born in Rome, De Sole was the son of an Italian army general from a small town named Cirò in Calabria in southern Italy. As a boy, De Sole had traveled extensively around Italy with his family because of his father's career and he grew up knowing that the world extended far beyond Calabria, a region ravaged by poverty and Mafia activity. After completing a law degree at the University of Rome, De Sole decided to apply to Harvard University Law School for a master's degree at the suggestion of a friend, Bill McGurn, who was studying there.

Harvard accepted De Sole, with a scholarship. Bright, ambitious, and motivated, De Sole quickly identified the United States as a land of opportunity.

"I loved it," De Sole said later. "It was part of my personality. Italians of my generation were all about *'Mamma'* and *'pasta,'* but to me, everything about the United States was new and exciting." He often quoted a study to his friends that showed that most of the wealthy people in America were self-made, while those in Europe were generally born rich. He realized that his ambition and energy was a good fit for the scope of opportunity in the United States. He also liked the idea of being thousands of miles away from his mother, whom he described as strong-willed and controlling.

"In the American mentality, going away to college is a rite of passage," De Sole observed. "I still remember my awful dorm room in Dane Hall the first year. [He later moved to Story Hall.] My mother came to visit me there and looked around and she said, 'Your bedroom at home is still waiting for you.' At that point I realized I didn't want to go back!"

"De Sole is two-hundred-percent American," said his longtime colleague Allan Tuttle, who is Gucci's internal legal counsel today. "He moved from a relatively closed society into a more open society and today he is more American than he is Italian, especially in his enthusiasm for the system."

De Sole studied hard, completed his master's degree in 1970, and worked briefly for Cleary, Gottlieb, Steen & Hamilton in New York before moving to Washington, D.C., with the venerable law firm Covington and Burlings. He had an apartment on N Street in Georgetown across from where Senator John F. Kennedy had lived. He met his wife, Eleanore Leavitt, in June 1974 on a blind date and fell in love with her baby blue eyes, strong character, and WASP value system—feeling that with her he had entered the heart of America.

De Sole was thirty years old, seven years Eleanore's senior. He swept her off her feet.

"He was charming, dashing, and attentive," she said. A career woman with a promising future at IBM, she was also impressed by his hardworking determination—Covington and Burlings accepted only one foreign lawyer within its ranks each year. Soon after they met, he introduced her to his parents, who had come to visit him in Washington, D.C.—and stayed for six weeks. De Sole's mother liked Eleanore immediately and let him know it. By August he had proposed, and by December 1974, they were married in the Saint Albans Episcopal Church on the grounds of the National Cathedral, he in white tie and tails, she in her mother's wedding gown.

De Sole passed the bar and joined Patton, Boggs & Blow, a young, dynamic, growing firm on M Street, today called Patton & Boggs. The firm was well regarded and doing a lot of international work, which interested De Sole. He became determined to make partner—a competitive prospect in the growing firm of three hundred lawyers—and pushed himself incessantly.

"Making partner became my absolute goal," he said. "I worked harder than anybody else, I never asked for any breaks, I was obsessed with it," De Sole said.

After making partner in 1979, De Sole developed himself as a tax lawyer—one of the most difficult areas of the profession for a non-American—and began to draw in lucrative business for the firm by handling major Italian companies who were seeking to expand their U.S. operations.

De Sole met the Gucci family the following year on a trip to Milan, where he was associated with a leading local lawyer, Professor Giuseppe Sena. One day Sena invited him to participate in a Gucci family meeting. As the family members arrived, they arranged themselves in factions around the long conference tables, which were arranged in a rectangle in the center of the room: Aldo, his sons, and their advisors along one side; Rodolfo, Maurizio, and their advisors along the other. De Sole and Sena were seated at the head of the room. At the beginning of the meeting, De Sole paid scant attention. He kept his head down, reading a newspaper under the table. As the meeting heated up—and Sena feared little would be accomplished—he asked De Sole if he would like to run the meeting. De Sole agreed and put the newspaper away.

A no-nonsense, hands-on kind of person, De Sole was not intimidated by the Guccis. In turn, they weren't particularly impressed with him—at first. Though bright and accomplished in his field, he lacked elegance and polish. If in the United States a person could become successful based on merit, Italian business and personal relationships were still highly conditioned by people's family background and social standing. Having the right name, the right address, the right friends, and the right style were all part of the Italian concept of *bella figura,* or having the right form at all times. The Guccis looked De Sole over, taking in his straggly beard, ill-fitting, threadbare American suit and the white socks worn with black business shoes. But when the ebullient Aldo started to speak out of turn, De Sole said crisply, "It is not your turn to speak, Mr. Gucci; please wait your turn." Rodolfo's eyes widened in amazement and admiration. After the meeting broke up, Rodolfo cornered De Sole as they were leaving the building and hired him on the spot—cheap suit and white socks notwithstanding.

"Anyone who can stand up to Aldo like that must come and work for me!" he said excitedly. Together with De Sole, Rodolfo developed a campaign to incorporate Gucci Parfums into Guccio Gucci—a move that would raise and consolidate Rodolfo's control over the lucrative GAC business to 50 percent, from 20 percent.

Aldo, angered by his brother's challenge, summoned Paolo one day to his Palm Beach office to ask for his allegiance at a shareholders meeting in which he hoped to straighten out Rodolfo's position. Rodolfo, who couldn't attend the meeting, asked De Sole to interrupt his holiday on the Florida keys and pop over to represent his interests at the meeting. The three of them sat around a small conference table at the end of Aldo's long, narrow office, which was divided in half by Aldo's desk.

Paolo wasn't in the mood to do his father any favors. His loyalty to the firm and the family had been breached by what he saw as unfair treatment. He told Aldo he could have his vote if he could work under his own name.

"How can you expect me to help you fight Rodolfo when you won't even let me breathe?" Paolo asked his father, who had sprung up from his seat and was pacing agitatedly. "If I can't work within the company, I must be able to work outside it. You fired me, I didn't ask to be fired," he said hotly.

Aldo paced faster. The thought that his son was trying to force his own hand was unacceptable to him. As he stalked back toward his desk, his temper boiled over. He picked up the nearest thing on his large desk, a lead crystal Gucci ashtray that Paolo himself had designed.

"You son of a bitch!" Aldo roared as he threw the ashtray across the room toward his son. The ashtray smashed against the wall behind the conference table, showering Paolo and De Sole with a hailstorm of crystal fragments.

"You are crazy!" Aldo screamed, red-faced, the veins on the sides of his neck bulging. "Why don't you do what I tell you?"

The incident shattered any hopes Paolo had of striking an agreement with his family, and from that moment on, he determined to bring the house of Gucci down. He knew his family was staunchly against him; it was up to him to show them they had made a grave mistake.

But Aldo was unhappy about the conflict. On the business side, it was draining precious resources and energy from the company and generating negative publicity. On the personal side, it pained him to fight his own son. He believed in the strength of the family and wanted more than anything to be reunited with Paolo. Aldo decided to try an armistice. He invited Paolo and Jenny to join him and Bruna in his Palm Beach home between Christmas 1981 and New Year's 1982. Father and son greeted each other warmly, in typical Gucci style, as though nothing had ever come between them. Aldo called Rodolfo, in Milan, wishing him holiday greetings. Then he came right to the point.

"Foffo, I've had a long talk with Paolo. I think he's willing to come back into the fold. We need to put an end to this war." They agreed to make an offer to Paolo, which they did that January. They made sweeping changes to the structure of the Gucci empire: the Guccio Gucci parent company and all of the sister companies, including Gucci Parfums, would be consolidated into one master company, Guccio Gucci SpA, to be quoted on the Milan stock market. Aldo's three sons would receive 11 percent each of the whole business, Aldo would retain 17 percent, and Paolo would be named vice chairman of Guccio Gucci SpA. In addition, a new division would be established under Gucci Parfums to be called Gucci Plus, which would have licensing authority. Paolo would become the director of that business and would be able to bring the licensing agreements he had already signed into the company under the Gucci name. In addition, he would be paid his severance money with interest and an annual salary of $180,000. It seemed to be everything Paolo had wanted. Under the terms of the agreement, both parties would drop all their charges and Paolo would give up his right to design and promote products under his own name.

Paolo remained suspicious. His doubts were confirmed when he was told all his design proposals would have to be approved by the board, of which Rodolfo was president. Nonetheless, Paolo decided to accept. He finally signed the agreement in the middle of February—but the truce wasn't destined to last.

The Gucci board summoned Paolo in March 1982, telling him to bring a detailed list of the product lines he had already contracted as well as his new ideas for the Gucci Plus line. Paolo worked hard to prepare all the materials, but the meeting did not go as he expected. The board voted down all of his proposals, explaining that the whole concept of the cheaper product lines was "contrary to the interests of the company." Paolo, more bitter than ever, felt he had been tricked. De Sole later denied Paolo had been misled, recalling how detrimental his actions had been to the company.

In no time, the board suspended Paolo's right to sign for the company. He was a board member, but without power to operate or execute his own designs. After having received his severance money in February, three months later he was fired again. "I felt like a fool," Paolo said. "All those agreements and assurances given me by my uncle were worthless."

By the time the famous board meeting of July 16, 1982, took place in Florence in the offices in Via Tornabuoni above the Gucci shop, tensions had surged to the boiling point. Paolo no longer had an operative role in the company, but was using his position as a shareholder to create leverage over business decisions. As Aldo, Giorgio, Paolo, Roberto, Rodolfo, Maurizio, and the other company directors took their places around the walnut table, the summer heat was no less oppressive than the atmosphere in the room. Aldo settled into his chair at the head of the long conference table, with his son Roberto to his right and his brother Rodolfo to his left. Paolo sat at the other end of the table with Giorgio on one hand and Maurizio on the other.

Aldo opened the meeting and asked the secretary to read the minutes of the previous meeting, which were approved. Then Paolo asked if he could make a statement, which immediately provoked mutterings and glances.

"Why? What do you have to say?" asked Aldo, irritated.

"I want to say that as a director of this company, I have been denied any opportunity to see or go through any of the company's books or documents," Paolo said. "I want my position clarified before we go any further."

He was interrupted by shouts of disapproval.

"Who are the two mysterious shareholders in Hong Kong who are receiving money from the company?" Paolo blurted out. More shouts.

Paolo noticed that the secretary—Domenico De Sole—wasn't taking the minutes.

"Why aren't you writing down my questions? I demand to have a record of this meeting!" Paolo exclaimed. De Sole glanced around the room, saw that no one else was in agreement, and remained motionless. At that, Paolo pulled a tape recorder out of his briefcase, turned it on, and began reciting his grievances. Then he threw his list of questions down on the table. "And I want these introduced into the minutes," he shouted.

"Turn that thing off," Aldo yelled at him as Giorgio reached across the table and grabbed the tape recorder from Paolo, inadvertently breaking it.

"Are you crazy?" Paolo yelled at him.

Aldo ran around the table toward Paolo. Maurizio jumped up, thinking that Paolo was going to lunge at Giorgio and Aldo, and gripped his cousin in a headlock from behind. Aldo reached Paolo and tried to wrestle the tape recorder away from him. In the scuffle, Paolo's face was badly scratched along one cheek and he began to bleed. When they saw the blood, which was minimal, the group hushed nevertheless. Maurizio and Giorgio loosened their hold on Paolo, who grabbed his briefcase and ran from the room, shouting at the astonished office workers, "Call the police, call the police!"

He grabbed the phone from the switchboard operator and called his doctor and his lawyer, then took the elevator downstairs, where it opened directly into the Gucci shop. Paolo ran through the store on his way out the door, shouting at startled clerks and customers. "Just look! This is what happens at a Gucci board meeting! They tried to kill me!" Then he rushed off to meet his doctor at a local clinic, where he was treated, and ordered that his wounds be photographed. At the time, Paolo was fifty-one years old; Giorgio, fifty-three; Aldo, seventy-seven; Rodolfo, seventy; and Maurizio, thirty-four.

When Paolo came home that night, pale and bandaged, Jenny was shocked. "I couldn't believe it. All of them, grown men, fighting like hooligans!" she said.

"Paolo's face was not badly scratched," said De Sole years later. "It was just a little scratch, but the incident was blown into a fiasco."

Just a few days later in New York, Paolo's lawyer, Stuart Speiser, filed the next round of lawsuits against Gucci. This time, the charges included assault and battery, as well as breach of contract, for being refused his right as a company director to investigate company finances.

He asked for a total of $15 million for the abuses he had suffered: $13 million for breach of contract, calling the so-called peace proposal a trap to neutralize him; and $2 million for assault and battery. To Aldo's dismay, the press gleefully covered the ruckus.

"Move over, *Dallas:* Behind the Glittering Facade, a Family Feud Rocks the House of Gucci," wrote *People* magazine; "Violent Fight in the House of Gucci," added Rome's *Il Messaggero;* "Gucci Brothers Fight," said *Corriere della Sera.* The New York court ultimately refused to hear the case on the grounds that the episode occurred in Italy, but the story riveted the court of public opinion on both sides of the Atlantic. Some of Gucci's most important clients were mystified and disturbed. Jackie Onassis's one-word cable to Aldo: "Why?" has become part of company legend. Prince Rainier of Monaco also called the family to ask if he could help.

The day after the stories broke, buyers from all over the world had already gathered at Gucci headquarters in Scandicci, where the sales presentation of the fall collections were under way. When Aldo learned that not only was Paolo suing him but the news was in all the papers, everybody in the plant that day heard his enraged bellows.

"If he is going to file suit against me, then by God, I'm going to file suit against him!" Aldo thundered into the telephone to whoever had given him the news. Aldo, swallowing his displeasure over Rodolfo's successful bid to increase his control of Gucci Parfums, which was incorporated into Guccio Gucci in 1982, hired De Sole to defend him and the Gucci company against Paolo's assaults. The next day, Aldo gave an interview to *Women's Wear Daily,* minimizing the conflict. "What father has never given an unruly son a slap?" Aldo said, reinforcing his image as the firm's patriarch. Aldo added that the family was close to an agreement with Paolo. But he didn't realize the lengths to which Paolo was willing to go in order to have his way; Paolo had only just rolled out the heavy artillery.

During his years working at Gucci, Paolo had been quietly collecting and analyzing all the financial documents he could get his hands on. He wanted to know about the inner workings of the company and draw his own conclusions about how things were being handled. Discovering that millions of dollars in taxable revenues were being siphoned to offshore companies under a system of false invoicing, he decided to use the evidence as a weapon in his battle for the freedom to use his own name. The first time, Gucci's lawyers succeeded in having the case dismissed and the papers sealed. Undeterred, in October 1982, using his severance money from Gucci to pay his lawyers in part, Paolo filed the damning documents in New York's federal court in support of his claim of wrongful discharge. He hoped the evidence would force

Aldo to change his tune and either invite him back into the family company or give him the green light to launch his own line.

"The papers were only intended to force his hand," Paolo said later.

The Paolo battles divided not only the family but those who were close to them. While some condemned Paolo for turning his father over to the authorities, others felt he had been pushed to the limit.

"Paolo was castrated," said Enrica Pirri, who admitted having a special affection for Aldo's middle son. "If he wasn't the genius of the family, he was the one who gave the most. If he turned in his father, it was because his father had given him the reasons to do it."

"Paolo wasn't bamboozled," countered De Sole. "He was making deals behind the family's back and they had to make sure he wasn't giving the company away. He was not dealing in good faith."

The papers Paolo filed showed explicitly how Gucci was masking profits. Panamanian companies based in Hong Kong were posing as creative design suppliers to Gucci Shops Inc. A damning letter to Gucci from Gucci's chief accountant in New York, Edward Stern, pulled away the window dressing covering up the scheme: "In order to substantiate the services for which such invoices were rendered, and to document the underlying need for the company, it will be necessary to send a variety of fashion designs and sketches to Gucci Shops for approval or rejection. *This is only to build up some sort of record* [italics added]," Stern wrote.

In 1983, as Rodolfo's health took a turn for the worse, the IRS and the U.S. attorney's office started looking into Aldo Gucci's personal and professional tax liabilities. Edward Stern died well before the case was closed, but investigators found enough evidence to turn the matter over to a grand jury.

Of all the lawsuits Paolo brought against his family company, only one of them ever made it to trial. It wasn't until 1988 that New York District Court Judge William C. Conner ruled on the case. Judge Conner found an even-handed solution to the family feud that had dragged on for nearly a decade: he prohibited Paolo Gucci from using his name as a trademark or trade name because of the confusion it would cause among consumers over the Gucci trademark. On the other hand, he allowed Paolo Gucci to use his own name to identify himself as a designer of products sold under a separate trademark that did not include the Gucci name.

"Since the time of Cain and Abel, family disputes have been marked by the irrational and impulsive decision of those involved, the fierce battles which ensue, and the senseless destruction they cause," Conner wrote in his opinion.

"This case is but a skirmish in one of the most publicized family disputes of our time," he continued, noting that the Gucci family at that time had "legal issues being litigated before judges and arbitration panels around the world at enormous cost to members of the family and the businesses they control."

Conner's decision authorized Paolo to produce and distribute goods under the name Designs by Paolo Gucci. Ever creative, Paolo took out a paid advertisement in *Women's Wear Daily* on November 30, 1988, in which he published a poem dedicated "To the Retail Community," announcing his debut as an independent designer.

On Wednesday August tenth
nineteen hundred and eighty-eight
in an open letter "Gucci America"
announced its present status and future fate.

They have claimed victory
in a lawsuit mandate
stating clearly, Paolo Gucci, family member,
former shareholder, had been given the gait [sic].

I am pleased with the outcome
to use my rightful name
to create fashion and home accessories
is my goal and my aim.

The Federal Court in New York
affirmed this decision
leaving me a free man
to continue my vision.

My association of trademark and name Gucci
ends after twenty-five years
as an independent designer I'll continue
to work hard, thank you my patrons
for your praise and kind cheers.

In agreement with "Gucci America" regarding
sacrosanctity of trademark and name,
hopefully my continued efforts will now
draw individualized acclaim.

*The Paolo Gucci name now found
on a label will certainly combine
outstanding quality, continued
perfection and excellence in design.*

*Aside from the trade, this non-conventional
response letter directed to the refined,
informed consumer,
is my public introduction to say hello,
welcome and do it with some humor.*

*With great pleasure and pride
in my traditional view
I present "Designs by Paolo Gucci"
everything more than that "other"
company could ever strive to do.*

*In closing, it is funny how things
may happen, life can be such a game,
I know in my heart one day "Gucci
America," you will buy my name.*

Paolo's prophecy that Gucci America would buy out his name came true just eight years later. After the court ruling, Paolo had revved into overdrive with preparations to launch his own business, even renting premium retail space on New York's Madison Avenue, where he paid rent for some three years, but never managed to open the store. Professionally, his business venture stalled, then failed; personally, his marriage with Jenny disintegrated. Paolo took up with another Englishwoman called Penny Armstrong, a fresh-faced, redheaded young stable girl he had hired to look after the purebred stallions on his eighty-acre Sussex estate, Rusper. Paolo and Penny had a little girl, Alyssa. Paolo moved Penny into the manor house and moved Jenny out, dumping her belongings into boxes he left to stand out on the grounds in the rain. Jenny, protesting indignantly, sent her sister to recover the boxes while she camped out with their by then ten-year-old daughter, Gemma, in an unfinished $3 million luxury apartment they had bought in 1990 in New York's Metropolitan Tower. The apartment offered breathtaking views of Central Park—and exposed wiring and pipes that Jenny tried to cover with yards of borrowed gold lamé fabric. After she served Paolo with divorce papers in 1991, he stopped paying the bills. In March 1993, she had Paolo jailed briefly for failing to pay some $350,000 in alimony and child support. That November, authorities raided Paolo's New York estate, Millfield Stables in Yorktown Heights, to discover more than a hundred emaciated and unkempt prize Arabian horses Paolo had neglected in order to prove to Jenny he didn't have the funds she claimed. Some fifteen of the horses hadn't even been entirely paid for. Paolo filed for Chapter 11 bankruptcy protection.

"What you have to understand about the Guccis," Jenny told a journalist in 1994, "is that they are all completely mad, incredibly manipulative, and not very clever. They have to be in control, but as soon as they get what they want, they crush it! They are destroyers, it's as simple as that!"

Paolo, plagued with debts and liver problems, retreated into the dark rooms of Rusper, where, according to Penny Armstrong, he no longer had the money to pay the electric and telephone bills. Authorities sequestered starving and uncared-for horses, some of which had to be put down, at Rusper as well.

"I spent my last thirty pence to buy milk and I don't know what is going to happen tomorrow," Penny told an Italian newspaper in 1995.

Paolo's lawyer, Enzo Stancato, ruefully remarked later that when he had first started working for Paolo, he thought he had struck gold. "Just a year before I was the most exciting guy in the world, I was working for Gucci! And all of a sudden I was practically supporting this guy—I gave him clothes, ties, shirts, and suits. When he came to New York, he had nothing, I dressed him up. He came to me and said, 'I'm sick, I have a liver problem. I need a transplant. That is the only way I will be able to survive.' "

The transplant didn't come in time and Paolo died of chronic hepatitis on October 10, 1995, in a London hospital. He was sixty-four. His funeral was held in Florence and he was buried in the small cemetery of Porto Santo Stefano along the Tuscan coast, next to his mother, Olwen, who had died just two months before. In November 1996, the bankruptcy court approved the sale of all rights in the Paolo Gucci name to Guccio Gucci SpA for $3.7 million, a price the company willingly paid to end the Paolo battles once and for all. There were several competing bidders, none of them well-known names, including Stancato and former licensees to whom Paolo had promised the right to use the name. One of them challenged the sale all the way up to the Supreme Court, but ultimately lost.

Paolo's death and the company's purchase of his commercial name and trademark did not, however, put an end to the internecine agitations within Gucci. The conflict simply shifted to another part of the family. Paolo's initial estrangement and ultimate exit from the family's business operations had coincided with the rise of his young cousin Maurizio, who would soon enter the family battlefield.

7

WINS

AND LOSSES

On the evening of November 22, 1982, an audience of more than thirteen hundred invited guests, murmuring in excited anticipation, gathered at the Cinema Manzoni in Milan. Rodolfo had instructed Maurizio and Patrizia to invite friends for a showing of what would be the last version of his film *Il Cinema nella Mia Vita,* or *Film in My Life.*

Formal printed invitations went out announcing the screening with the melancholy phrase: "Never lose touch with the importance of the soul and one's sentiments. Life can be a vast, arid field where the seed one sows often grows away from all that is good."

After working in New York with Aldo for seven years, Maurizio, Patrizia, and their young daughters moved back to Milan in early 1982. Rodolfo's health was deteriorating, his illness a well-kept secret. The Verona-based doctor who administered cobalt therapy to treat his prostate tumor died suddenly, sending Rodolfo on a desperate search for a new cure. He called Maurizio back to Milan to head up a new phase in Gucci's growth.

Rodolfo made a grand gesture to Maurizio and Patrizia by turning the showing of his film autobiography into a social occasion. He wanted to close the door on their conflicts and show friends and acquaintances in Milan that the family warmly welcomed the young couple back.

Patrizia greeted the guests graciously, radiant in an Yves Saint Laurent dress and Cartier "Truth's Eye" brooch. Things were working out just as she had envisioned. Maurizio's reconciliation with Rodolfo put her husband in a prime position to bring fresh leadership to the family firm, which she felt had lost its glamour on Aldo's and Rodolfo's watch. For Patrizia, the premier at Cinema Manzoni marked the beginning of a new age, which she called "the era of Maurizio."

As the lights dimmed and the velvet curtains swept open with a whisper, the documentary opened with a scene of young Maurizio running and tumbling in the snow at Saint Moritz with Rodolfo, just months after losing his mother.

"The following is a pathetic love story, a story that I wish would never end . . . the story of a man who wants to tell his son about his family, and help him see the world in the right perspective," the narrator explained as the screen filled with the black-and-white images of Guccio and Aida and their children, of the family dinner table, of the original workshop in Florence. Then came stylized film clips of Rodolfo and his wife acting under their stage names, Maurizio D'Ancora and Sandra Ravel. Contemporary footage then chronicled the growth of the Gucci name: the opening of Via Tornabuoni; Rodolfo in the Milan store on Via Monte Napoleone, complimenting the manager, Gittardi, on a good sale; Aldo in his jaunty fedora entering the revolving doors of Gucci's Fifth Avenue store; the dancing frenzy of Gucci-clad disco dancers in the seventies; Maurizio and Patrizia directing workmen in the renovation of their new Olympic Tower apartment; and the baptisms of Alessandra and Allegra. The movie ended with an idyllic scene of Rodolfo with Alessandra as a toddler on the immaculately clipped lawn at Chesa Murézzan in Saint Moritz playing with the manual crank of his old movie camera. Rodolfo's narration ended with a touching message: "If there is anything left that I can teach you, it is to help you understand the deep relationship that exists between happiness and love and that life isn't lived in decades, or even seasons, but in beautiful sunny mornings like this, watching your daughters grow up . . . true wisdom lies in what we can do with the real riches of this world—beyond the ones we can trade or manage—the riches of life, youth, friendship, love. These are the riches we must treasure and shelter always."

The movie was an exact expression of Rodolfo's character—romantic, grandiose, overdone. His masterpiece, his testament of love for his late wife, and for their son, the film symbolized his reconciliation with that son. But it also contained a message for Maurizio: Rodolfo had seen his son's ambition, his zeal, and the way he managed his money. Through the frames of the film he wanted to remind Maurizio not to lose sight of what he, Rodolfo, in his final years, felt were the true values of life.

"Every human creature," he used to say, "has three essential things that must always be in harmony among themselves: a heart, a brain, and a wallet. If these three elements don't work together, problems will come."

The guests were moved and impressed as the lights came back up.

"When is the next screening?" one of them asked Rodolfo.

"We'll see, we'll see," he answered with a sad smile. Only those closest to him knew that cancer was consuming his body, that he had tried clinic after clinic searching for a cure to keep him alive. He tired more easily, his expression grew more melancholy. He still reported regularly to his offices in Via Monte Napoleone, but he began spending more and more time in his beloved Saint Moritz—where he had finally bought the charming L'Oiseau Bleu from his elderly neighbor—content to let Maurizio take more of a role in the business.

Maurizio returned to Milan from New York filled with enthusiasm for his new mandate. Uncle Aldo had taught him a lot and their relationship was affectionate and mutually respectful, although Aldo, as with his own sons, always made sure to keep Maurizio in his place.

"Vieni qui, avvocatino," he would say to Maurizio when he wanted to talk to him. "Come here, little lawyer," waving him over with a hand as though he were a child, making fun of his nephew's law degree even though Maurizio at that point was the only one in the family who had completed advanced studies. Unlike Aldo's sons, who bristled at their father's domineering personality, Maurizio kept his head down and humored Aldo. He knew that if he wanted to learn from Aldo, he had to survive in Aldo's tough school. He also knew there would be rewards.

"It wasn't a question of living with my uncle, but surviving," Maurizio once said. "If he does one hundred percent, you have to do one hundred and fifty percent to show you can do as well as he does."

So he bided his time, knowing that to get what he wanted, he couldn't always take the shortest route.

Still reserved and hesitant, Maurizio had absorbed much of Aldo's teachings, bringing out his own charisma, charm, and ability to infect others with his enthusiasm. Aldo, more than Rodolfo, was Maurizio's mentor.

"The difference between my father and my uncle was that my uncle was a marketing man, a developer," recalled Maurizio. "He . . . had a completely different influence on everyone. He was very human, sensitive, creative. He was the one who was building everything up in the company and I saw how he was able to establish rapport with the people he worked with, as well as the customers. What fascinated me most was how different he was from my father, who was an actor in everything he did. My uncle wasn't playing a part, it was the real thing with him," Maurizio said.

As Aldo grew more outrageous and extroverted, Rodolfo grew more reflective and introverted, rarely confronting his brother directly. Over and over again, he furiously called Maurizio to drive to Florence with him to challenge yet another instance of Aldo's abuse of power. With Rodolfo's trusted driver, Luigi Pirovano, at the wheel of a sleek silver Mercedes, they pulled out onto the A-1 Autostrada leading south from Milan.

"This time he has gone too far! I am going to give him a piece of my mind," Rodolfo sputtered as Maurizio consoled him and Luigi listened silently, guiding the speeding car down the autostrada—first along the plains to Bologna and then around the twisting switchbacks over the Apennine mountains to Florence. By the time, three hours later, that Luigi swung the car through the gates and past the guardhouse of the Scandicci factory, Rodolfo's anger had calmed; his resolve faded.

"Ciao, carissimo!" he invariably greeted Aldo with an affectionate hug.

"Foffino! What are you doing here?" Aldo would say with a surprised smile, as Rodolfo shrugged, made some excuse about a new bag he was developing, and invited Aldo to lunch.

Aldo, at seventy-seven, had hardly slowed his pace, though he was more interested in his parties and charity balls than in running the company day to day. He did abolish the noon closing policy in New York in 1980 and promoted the Gucci name to the masses with the Gucci Accessories Collection, but he began to seek his own rewards after a lifetime devoted to Gucci. He spent more time with Bruna and their daughter Patricia at his waterfront mansion in Palm Beach, gardened, socialized, and still strove to convert his merchant status to an artistic calling.

"We are not businessmen, we are poets!" Aldo intoned at his marquetry desk during an interview in his office on Via Condotti. "I want to be like the Holy Father. The Pope always speaks in the plural."

Where starkly framed certificates once hung on bare white walls, now seventeenth- and eighteenth-century oil paintings glowed against velour the color of burnt umber under a vaulted ceiling painted with frescoes. The Gucci heraldic seal hung nearby with the key to the city of San Francisco that Mayor Joseph Alioto gave to Aldo in 1971.

While Aldo pontificated, someone needed to plan for the future of the business, and Maurizio, propelled by Rodolfo and Patrizia, became the heir apparent. By the time Maurizio returned to Milan in 1982, a wave of change had reshaped the Italian fashion industry, up to then centered on Rome's Alta Moda couture presentations and Giorgini's ready-to-wear shows in Florence's Sala Bianca. The fashion spotlight shifted to Milan as newly recognized fashion designers such as Tai and Rosita Missoni, Krizia's Mariuccia Mandelli, Giorgio Armani, Gianni Versace, and Gianfranco Ferré emerged in Italy's financial and industrial capital. Valentino, who had started his couture business in 1959 in Rome, snubbed Milan for Paris, where he presented first his couture and later pret-a-porter collections.

Milan fashion organizers wrested the semiannual presentations of women's ready-to-wear collections away from Florence, marking the end of the Sala Bianca–style shows and establishing Milan as the new center for women's fashion. Since the postwar disappearance of the master tailor, young new designers had emerged to fill a creative gap. Initially, they created innovative styles for the brand-name collections of medium-sized Italian clothing manufacturers in Northern Italy: Armani, Versace, and Gianfranco Ferré all worked for small apparel producers. Growing demand for trend-setting designs showed them they could capitalize on their own names. As their budding businesses flourished, the young designers established ateliers along Milan's most fashionable streets—Armani on Via Borgonuovo, Versace on Via Gesù, Ferrè on Via della Spiga, and Krizia on Via Daniele Manin, to name a few. Inspired, they worked long hours alongside faithful teams of design assistants to perfect their new styles, crowding late at night into the few surviving family-style trattorias in downtown Milan—Bice on Via Borgospesso, Torre di Pisa in the Bohemian Brera district, Santa Lucia near the Duomo— all of which are still popular among the fashion and business set.

Armani and Versace emerged as the sparring leaders of Milan fashion. Versace championed hot, flashy, provocative styles; Armani created cool, reserved, elegant looks. Versace bought impressive palazzos in Milan and on nearby Lake Como and filled them with precious art in the gaudy, baroque style he promoted. Armani, known as "The King of Beige," preferred his quiet retreats in the Lombardy countryside outside Milan and on the island of Pantelleria off Sicily that he furnished in his understated, minimalist style.

Italian fashion buzzed with new energy. New money pumped up the designer names with the help of cutting-edge photographers, top models, and glossy advertising campaigns. Family-operated accessories houses such as Fendi and Trussardi bought into the new way of doing business—they updated their images and stole market share from Gucci, which began to seem old hat. In those days, Prada, where founder Mario Prada's granddaughter, Miuccia, took over in 1978, was still considered a sleepy luggage company.

Maurizio understood that to remain competitive, Gucci had to find a new direction. Gucci still symbolized class and style, but the glamour it had personified in the sixties and seventies had faded. Maurizio's mission in Milan became to realize Aldo's long-held dream of making the Gucci name as famous for ready-to-wear as it was in accessories. Patrizia, an avid consumer of designer clothing, had been pushing Maurizio for some time to hire a big-name designer for Gucci apparel.

"For Gucci, ready-to-wear was the big challenge," recalled Alberta Ballerini, who had started working on the first Gucci apparel alongside Paolo in the 1970s and is still with the company today as ready-to-wear product manager. Paolo's sportswear collections had met with success, but they remained a minimal part of the overall business.

One day in the late 1970s, Ballerini recalled, Paolo gathered his staff around him in the design studio in the Scandicci factory.

"My cousin Maurizio has come up with a crazy idea," he said. "He wants to hire an outside designer."

"Well, maybe it isn't such a crazy idea," volunteered Ballerini.

"He keeps talking about this guy called Armani," continued Paolo. "Who is he?" When no one seemed to know, Paolo concluded, "We don't need him."

Paolo continued to design the collections for several seasons and did bring in a young Cuban designer named Manolo Verde for one season, but as relations soured with his family, he left Florence for New York in 1978 and was ousted from any operational role in the company by 1982. Gucci found itself without a designer for ready-to-wear at a moment when the other Italian fashion names surged in popularity. For a few seasons, the family tried to manage on its own, working with Ballerini and the internal staff, but they soon realized they needed help.

Maurizio again floated the idea that Gucci needed a known designer to revive its image. He knew Armani's work and thought he could do the kind of casually elegant sportswear that was right for Gucci. By that time, however, Armani had dedicated himself to his own business, which was growing rapidly. Gucci openly started looking for someone.

In leading Gucci into the new territory of ready-to-wear, Maurizio had to tread a fine line: he needed to relaunch the Gucci name in a changing fashion market, but he didn't want a designer who would overshadow the Gucci brand or alienate the traditional customer. He wanted Gucci to be recognized as a trendsetter without losing its identity as a luxury house.

In June 1982, Gucci hired Luciano Soprani, a designer from Italy's central Emilia-Romagna region who had distinguished himself with a limited color palette and expertise with wide-weave, gauzy fabrics, to design its ready-to-wear. Maurizio prepared the company for its first fashion presentation in Milan that fall. He wanted to establish Gucci's presence in the Milan fashion network—away from Florence, which he viewed as provincial.

Gucci presented the first Soprani collection, which featured an Africa theme, in Milan in late October 1982. Unmoving mannequins posed in tableaux decorated with 2,500 red dahlias imported from the Netherlands. It was an instant commercial success.

"I'll never forget that first presentation," recalled Alberta Ballerini, the longtime Gucci employee who helped develop and coordinate the apparel collections. "The showroom stayed open all night and all these exhausted buyers kept coming in with swollen feet and we were all working around the clock. Everybody bought so much, too much; we sold an incredible amount. That was the beginning of a glory period," she said.

The Italian press praised Gucci's new direction as keeping pace with the times: "In the moment of crisis, Gucci shed its Florentine roots and turned its sights on Milan as a laboratory for new ideas and new entrepreneurial strategies," wrote Silvia Giacomini in *La Repubblica*. "They decided to enter the star system of Milan fashion, taking advantage of all the resources the city offered."

"Gucci is drastically updating its image," wrote Hebe Dorsey for the *International Herald Tribune* after viewing the collection. With Aldo uncharacteristically home in Rome with the flu, Maurizio explained the company's new direction to the respected fashion journalist.

"We want Gucci to set trends instead of following them," Maurizio explained. "We are not fashion designers and we don't want to create fashion but we want to be part of it because fashion today is the vehicle to reach people faster," he said.

But Dorsey didn't rave about the Soprani influence and had trouble picking a theme out of the plethora of looks Gucci presented.

"The new image is a sharp departure from the classic—and classy—leather-skirt-with-colorful-silk-blouse image. The new style had several facets, including a Colonial look—a fashion takeoff from Agatha Christie's 'Death on the Nile,' " Dorsey wrote. She noted that the new coordinated Gucci luggage in white and beige, without the GG monogram, was the most noteworthy part of the tableaux.

Maurizio hired Nando Miglio, who ran a leading fashion communications and advertising agency at the time, to produce a campaign—a sharp departure from Aldo's strategy of personal contacts. When Aldo saw the images by noted fashion photographer Irving Penn, he blew up.

"It's clear he doesn't understand the least bit about what Gucci really is," said Aldo, fuming and firing off a stinging letter to Penn. But Aldo was too late. The campaign, featuring a top model of the period, Rosemary McGrotha, posing against Penn's signature white background, had already been committed to a wide range of fashion and lifestyle magazines. Maurizio refused to cancel it. The next four campaigns, one of which featured Carol Alt, were shot by Penn's student, a young Bob Krieger, in the same vein. The new images promoted clean, fun, sporty fashion—just the kind of look Aldo said he wanted back in the seventies. They had little to do with the sexy power look of Gucci promotions today.

During the following years, Maurizio also oversaw a much less glamorous but equally important change within Gucci: a review of the company's thousands of products and styles in order to pare down the numbers.

"The company had decided it needed to have some internal control of all the products that were being developed and produced for the company," recalled Rita Cimino, a longtime Gucci employee who oversaw the handbag collections and is still with the firm. Up until that point, the business had evolved around each family member, with no oversight or coordination among the various camps. Rodolfo had his group of staff and suppliers that did what he wanted, Giorgio together with Aldo had theirs, and Roberto, head of the Gucci Accessory Collection, had his own direction. The result became such a diverse mix of products that the only thing they had in common was the Gucci name—far from the concept of stylistic harmony Aldo had pioneered. "I worked side by side with Maurizio to catalog all the products and try to bring some order to it all. Maurizio had very clear ideas about what he thought Gucci luxury products should be," Cimino added.

It didn't take long for Maurizio's imprint to be noticed. In December 1982, *Capital,* a leading Milan business monthly, published a cover story about Maurizio, identifying him as the young scion of the fashion dynasty.

Patrizia was thrilled with the article—it underlined what she already felt. She wanted Maurizio to become a leading figure in the Milan fashion industry.

"I knew he was weak, but I was not weak," said Patrizia. "I pushed him so hard he became president of Gucci. I was social, he didn't like to socialize;

I was always out, he was always in the house. I was the representative of Maurizio Gucci, and that was enough. He was like a child, a thing called Gucci that had to be washed and dressed."

"The era of Maurizio has begun," Patrizia repeated to him and anybody else who would listen. She propelled him forward, acting as his behind-the-scenes advisor. Even before Maurizio became known in Milan circles, Patrizia played the role of the celebrity wife, cruising around town in her chauffeur-driven car dressed in her Valentino and Chanel suits. The society pages nick-named her the "Joan Collins of Monte Napoleone." Maurizio and Patrizia moved into a luminous penthouse apartment that Rodolfo had bought for them on Galleria Passarella in downtown Milan above the San Babila shopping square. A terrace garden ran entirely around the outside of the penthouse, which she decorated with warm wooden paneling and a ceiling painted to look like a Tiepolo heaven, and furnished with antiques, bronze statues, and Art Deco vases.

"Patrizia really helped Maurizio," recalled Nando Miglio. "While he was shy, reserved, and awkward at public functions, she knew how to sparkle," Miglio said. "Patrizia pushed the accelerator. She wanted Maurizio to become somebody. 'You have to show everyone you are the best,' she would tell him.'"

Patrizia persuaded Maurizio to let her design a line of gold jewelry for Gucci called Orocrocodillo. The line featured chunky, stand-alone pieces imprinted with a crocodile-skin pattern and encrusted with precious stones. Patrizia hoped that Orocrocodillo would become for Gucci what the three gold bands of the rolling ring were for Cartier—a signature product that iden-tified the brand. Sold in the Gucci stores, Orocrocodillo was impossibly expensive—some pieces cost as much as twenty-nine million lire (more than $15,000 depending on the exchange rate) each—yet looked like flashy cos-tume jewelry. Gucci's salespeople just shook their heads, slid the jewelry away in the display cases, and wondered who would ever buy it.

At the end of April 1983, Gucci inaugurated its new boutique on Via Monte Napoleone across the street from the existing store, which continued to sell luggage and accessories. The new store, in the corner spot occupied today by Les Copains, sold the expanded apparel collection by Luciano Soprani. The company persuaded city traffic authorities to close Milan's most exclusive shopping street to traffic for the inauguration of the boutique. Tables and chairs and cascades of gardenias filled the sidewalks. The adjacent cross street, Via Baguttino—also closed to traffic—became an impromptu restaurant where white-gloved waiters bore silver trays of oysters and caviar among the guests as the champagne flowed. That day, it was Maurizio who greeted the guests and circulated among the crowd. Rodolfo had been quietly taken to Madonnina, one of the best private clinics in Milan, several weeks earlier.

Rodolfo left the clinic briefly, accompanied by his nurses, to see the new store shortly before it opened. He walked shakily across the spacious selling floor propped up by Tullia on one side and Luigi on the other, admiring the decor and greeting his employees by name.

"His clothes were hanging off him, he was so thin," recalled Liliana Colombo, then assistant to Rodolfo's secretary, Roberta Cassol.

Maurizio had given strict instructions that no one should be allowed to visit Rodolfo at the clinic—except for him, his U.S. lawyer, Domenico De Sole; and his close advisor Gian Vittorio Pilone. Pilone, a native of Venice, had established a lucrative accounting business in Milan working for many of the city's old industrial families. Maurizio trusted him and grew reluctant to make a decision or organize a meeting without Pilone at his side.

While Maurizio tried to hide from the world the fact that his father was dying, Rodolfo remained mystified at his isolation. Of his Italian employees, only Roberta Cassol and Francesco Gittardi came to see him in the clinic, where Maurizio and Patrizia had delivered two enormous white potted azalea bushes to Rodolfo's room.

Rodolfo carried himself elegantly to the end, wearing his silk dressing gowns and scarves around the clinic even during his final days. A flurry of lawyers and accountants came and went as he settled his affairs, yet Rodolfo remained unsettled. He asked repeatedly for his brother Aldo, who had returned to the United States after the Monte Napoleone opening just a week earlier without stopping in to see him. On Saturday, May 7, Rodolfo slipped into a coma. Maurizio and Patrizia rushed to his bedside, but he no longer recognized them. Aldo arrived the next day to find Rodolfo calling his name.

"Aldo! Aldo! Aldo! *Dove sei?*" Rodolfo called out. "Where are you?"

"I'm here, Foffino! I'm here," cried Aldo, leaning over his younger brother, bringing his face close to Rodolfo's unseeing eyes. "Tell me, tell me, what can I do for you, little brother, how can I make you feel better?"

Rodolfo couldn't answer him. The cancer had run its course. Rodolfo died on May 14, 1983, at the age of seventy-one. The Romanesque basilica of San Babila overflowed with mourners as Rodolfo's coffin was carried in by four of Rodolfo's faithful employees, including Luigi and Franco. At the end of the ceremony, Rodolfo's coffin was taken to Florence for burial in the family tomb. An era had ended—and a new one had begun.

8

MAURIZIO
TAKES CHARGE

For Maurizio, aged thirty-five, his father's death was at once a shock and a liberation. Maurizio had been the sole object of his father's obsessive, possessive, authoritarian love and Rodolfo had kept him under strict control. Up to the end, their relationship was stiff and formal. Maurizio reluctantly confronted his father or asked him for things—he still went to Luigi Pirovano, Rodolfo's driver, or Roberta Cassol, Rodolfo's secretary, when he needed pocket money.

"I always used to say, Rodolfo gave him the castle, but he didn't give him the money to maintain it," said Cassol. "Maurizio was always asking me for spending money because he was afraid to ask his father."

Even as a grown man, Maurizio jumped to his feet when his father walked into the room. His only rebellion against Rodolfo had been to marry Patrizia, whom in the end Rodolfo grudgingly accepted. Although he never grew close to his daughter-in-law, they made their peace. Rodolfo could see that she loved Maurizio and that they were happy together and bringing up Alessandra and Allegra in a loving home.

Rodolfo left Maurizio a multimillion-dollar inheritance: the Saint Moritz estate, luxury apartments in Milan and New York, some $20 million in Swiss bank accounts, and 50 percent of the Gucci empire, which was generating profits hand over fist. Among all the riches of his estate, which at the time was valued at more than 350 billion lire (about $230 million at the time), Rodolfo also left Maurizio a simple, yet symbolic gift, a crocodile-skin wallet with a Gucci insignia from the thirties. Rodolfo's grandfather, Guccio, had given him the thin black wallet. An antique English shilling was set into the clasp—a souvenir from Guccio's Savoy days. Now it was Maurizio's turn to hold the purse strings.

Holding the purse strings meant making decisions—for the first time in his life, Maurizio was free to make his own choices. However, he lacked experience—Rodolfo had managed everything for him up to then. Furthermore, in Maurizio's lifetime, the decisions would become more difficult. The lessons Aldo taught him in New York had served his uncle well—but in a different era. Maurizio's world was far more complex. The luxury goods business was more competitive and the Gucci family battles were more cutthroat.

"Rodolfo's biggest mistake was not to trust Maurizio earlier on," said Maurizio's advisor, Gian Vittorio Pilone, during an interview in his Milan office shortly before his death in May 1999. "He held the purse strings so tightly and never gave Maurizio a chance to stand on his own two feet."

"There were times when Maurizio became overwhelmed at the enormity of the decisions facing him," added Liliana Colombo, who became his faithful secretary. "Rodolfo had always taken care of everything for him."

Before he died, Rodolfo worried that despite his efforts to bring Maurizio up with a sense of values and the meaning of money, he hadn't succeeded. Lacking the genius business flair of his brother Aldo, he had nevertheless amassed a fortune with the estate in Saint Moritz and an unmarked Swiss bank account. Rodolfo boasted that he had only made deposits to the account and never a withdrawal, but he wasn't sure that Maurizio had the same fiber. He saw how Maurizio could spend millions at the drop of a hat, how focused he was on the trappings—rather than the substance—of success. Rodolfo also worried Maurizio would be devoured by the bitter family battles.

"Maurizio was a sweet, sensitive young man," recalled Pilone. "His father was afraid that his very character left him open to attack."

Many of Rodolfo's advisors recalled that he took them aside in the months before he died and asked them to look out for Maurizio after he was gone—a request that couldn't have done much to build Maurizio up in their eyes.

One day when Rodolfo was still active in the business, but already traveling frequently to Verona for his cancer treatments, he spoke with Allan Tuttle, a colleague of De Sole's at Patton, Boggs & Blow in Washington, D.C. Tuttle, a litigator, had defended Rodolfo, Aldo, and the Gucci company in court against Paolo and knew the family well. He had just arrived on holiday in Venice, which was less than an hour away from Verona. Rodolfo met him there and invited Tuttle to lunch on a cold and rainy day. Tuttle, who had just arrived from hot, sunny Washington, D.C., found himself unprepared. "Rodolfo literally gave me the coat off his back, because I didn't have one," he recalled.

The two men lunched at a local restaurant and then went for a long walk along the winding Venetian canals. Rodolfo described his wedding to Sandra Ravel there years earlier, recalling how the canals were lined with well-wishers tossing flowers on their gondola.

"He knew he was dying, although he didn't tell me so," Tuttle said. "He gave me a little speech about Maurizio and how he was worried about him. He wanted me and Domenico De Sole to look out for him."

When he had finished, Rodolfo stepped into a water taxi, waved an elegant hand, and was gone.

"He was the actor to the end," Tuttle said. "It was very well staged and very moving."

De Sole later got the same speech from Rodolfo. "Rodolfo was scared," De Sole said. "He could see that Maurizio had no sense of limits."

Despite his early mistrust of Patrizia, Rodolfo even confided in his daughter-in-law. "Once he gets money and power, he will change," Patrizia said Rodolfo told her. "You will find you are married to another man." She didn't believe him at the time.

In the early months after Rodolfo died, Aldo watched Maurizio carefully. He knew that the death of his younger brother could shake up the status quo that they had managed to maintain despite the wars with Paolo. They had divided the company between them according to some simple principles; first, the company must remain in family hands and only the family could decide about how fast to grow, where, and with what products. Second, they had carved up the business into two clearly defined areas—Aldo controlled Gucci America and the retail network while Rodolfo controlled Guccio

Gucci and production in Italy. That division of power had been successful; when Rodolfo died, Gucci was generating sales hand over fist. The company controlled twenty directly owned stores in leading capitals around the world, forty-five franchise shops between Japan and the United States, a lucrative duty-free business, and the successful GAC wholesale business. The battles against Paolo had calmed down and Aldo found time to enjoy his status as family patriarch.

"I was the engine and the rest of the family was the train," he would later recount with satisfaction. "The engine without the train is worthless and the train without the engine—well, it doesn't move!"

Aldo hoped that despite Rodolfo's death, the Gucci business would continue as it had. He underestimated three things. One, Maurizio's ambition to take Gucci far beyond the family policies that had made the company successful up to then. Two, his son Paolo's determination to win the right to do business under his own name. Three, the attitude of the U.S. Internal Revenue Service about tax evasion. Gucci's old status quo reigned for a scant year.

Before Rodolfo died, there had been no question but what Maurizio would inherit his 50 percent stake in the business upon his death. Rodolfo used to say openly to staff, friends, and family that Maurizio would inherit everything when he died, "but not a minute before." He had seen in Aldo's experience with Paolo the consequences of giving over power too soon. He decided Aldo's gesture in passing ownership to his sons was premature and destabilizing and vowed not to make the same mistake.

Rodolfo's will wasn't found immediately after his death, but Maurizio, as his only child, was still the legal heir under Italian inheritance law. Several years after Rodolfo died, when Maurizio found himself embroiled in legal problems over the inheritance, a squad of investigators from the Guardia di Finanza, the fiscal police, found the will in the company safe, which they had opened with a blowtorch after being unable to find the key. Rodolfo had penned his wishes in his own flourishing longhand, leaving everything, as expected, to his *"unico, adorato figlio,"* his sole, adored son. Rodolfo also made provisions for his loyal household staff—in particular for Tullia, Franco, and Luigi.

At the first family board meeting after Rodolfo's death, Maurizio, Aldo, Giorgio, and Roberto awkwardly sized each other up. Despite Maurizio's little speech about wanting to work together for Gucci's future, the others didn't take him seriously.

"Avvocatino!" Aldo said. "Don't try to fly too high. Take some time to learn."

To them it was no surprise that Maurizio had inherited 50 percent, but their mouths dropped open in amazement when he produced the signed share certificates showing that his father had actually signed his shares over to him before he died—saving him some 13 billion lire ($8.5 million) in inheritance taxes. They suspected the signatures had been forged.

Maurizio, frustrated by his inability to gain his relatives' support at the meeting, soon after went to see Aldo privately in Rome. He hoped to secure Aldo's blessing for his plans to modernize Gucci. One of Aldo's Rome assistants overheard them as Aldo, shaking his head patronizingly, ushered Maurizio out.

"Hai fatto il furbo, Maurizio, ma quei soldi non te li godrai mai," she heard Aldo telling him. "You were very clever, Maurizio, but you will never enjoy that money," he said.

Maurizio, undaunted by his relatives' resistance, developed a new vision for Gucci as a global luxury goods firm with professional, international management; streamlined design, production, and distribution processes; and sophisticated marketing techniques. His model was the French family firm Hermès, which had evolved without sacrificing either its family character or its high-end products. Maurizio wanted Gucci to climb back into the league with Hermès and Louis Vuitton; he feared it was more on a par with Pierre Cardin, the Italian-born French designer who made fashion history by authoring Christian Dior's best-selling Bar suit before he made licensing his name almost an art form, selling his scrawling signature across everything from cosmetics and chocolate to home appliances.

Maurizio's concept for Gucci was good; his problem was how to achieve it. The company had been balkanized around the family members and each one defended his right to do what he perceived as best for Gucci. Even though Maurizio was Gucci's largest single shareholder with 50 percent, his hands were tied. Facing Maurizio across the boardroom table were Aldo, with 40 percent of Guccio Gucci SpA, and Giorgio, Roberto, and Paolo, with 3.3 percent each. In Gucci America, Aldo had 16.7 percent, while his sons had 11.1 percent each. Maurizio could not do much without their consensus and they had little patience for his ideas. Gucci survived on its past glories and still generated ample profits to support their lifestyles—they saw little need to change things.

Maurizio pressed forward with his plans anyway, to the extent he could. He relied on Roberta Cassol to help him update Gucci's staff. Uncomfortable with confrontation, as his father had been, Maurizio asked Cassol to fire many long-term employees he felt were no longer viable in the changing luxury goods industry.

"Just as in the past he would tell me things he didn't have the courage to say to his father, now he was saying to me, 'Roberta, the time has come to get rid of so-and-so,' " Cassol said. "He had a fragile, insecure personality."

At the same time, Aldo's own position at Gucci America grew precarious. In September 1983, on the basis of the court documents filed by Paolo, the Internal Revenue Service started examining the financial affairs of Aldo Gucci and Gucci Shops. By May 14, 1984, the Justice Department authorized the U.S. attorney's office to open a grand jury investigation into the matter. Aldo—very smart in his business affairs—hadn't understood the American attitude toward paying taxes, even though he had become a U.S. citizen in 1976. In Italy, the average citizen, skeptical and mistrustful of government, feels that paying taxes is tantamount to throwing money at corrupt politicians for little in return. The American saying—only two things in life are certain: death and taxes—wouldn't make any sense to an Italian and especially wouldn't have in the 1980s. Today the Italian government is trying to curb rampant tax evasion, but in those years, the more money one managed to avoid paying in taxes, the smarter one was considered. It was almost something to boast about. De Sole, who was more American in his thinking than Italian, had specialized in tax law. He tried to drive home the seriousness of the situation to Aldo.

"I made a big presentation to the whole family at the Hotel Gallia in Milan," De Sole said. " 'This is a major problem,' I told them.

" 'Don't be ridiculous!' they said to me. 'Aldo is a great man and has done great things for the community; they won't touch him.'

" 'You don't understand,' I told them. 'This is America, not Europe. We are talking about massive fraud—Aldo Gucci is going to go to jail!' "

No one took De Sole seriously and the "Guru of Gucci" brushed the whole matter aside. "You are always so pessimistic," he said condescendingly to De Sole, who had continued to work for the company after Rodolfo's death.

"Aldo was being his old domineering self and wouldn't discuss it," recalled Pilone.

In the meantime, De Sole had discovered that in addition to illegally transferring millions of dollars out of Gucci America into his own offshore companies, Aldo had personally cashed a stack of checks worth hundreds of thousands of dollars that had been made out to the company.

"Aldo was living like a king, but there was massive fraud at every level!" De Sole said. "It was going to wreck him personally and it was going to wreck the company."

De Sole begged Aldo to see reason. He flew Aldo and Bruna to

Washington, D.C., where De Sole and his wife, Eleanore—at the time living in Bethesda, Maryland, with their two young daughters—invited them home to dinner.

"I told Aldo, I don't have anything against you, please understand," De Sole said. At one point during the dinner, Bruna, in tears, took De Sole aside to try to understand.

"I told her, 'I'm sorry, but he's going to go to jail,' " De Sole said. "Aldo denied reality. He viewed Gucci as his own personal toy. He had no understanding of the difference between personal and corporate—his attitude was that he had built the company and he deserved to get something back from all he had done."

In the beginning, De Sole said he even had trouble convincing Maurizio of the consequences Aldo would have to face. "You don't understand," De Sole said to Maurizio. "If Aldo goes to jail, he is not going to be there anymore to run the company. Something must be done!"

Maurizio finally agreed. Aldo's vulnerability on the tax issues favored Maurizio's far-reaching goal to create a new Gucci. With the help of Pilone and De Sole, he developed a plan to take over the board of directors. The only way to get power was to create an alliance with one of his cousins. But which one? Giorgio was too reserved, traditional, and loyal to Aldo. He wouldn't want to rock the boat. Roberto was even more conservative and worried about ensuring a future for his six children. Both of them were too comfortable with Gucci as it was. The only possibility was Paolo, the black sheep, who had stopped speaking to Maurizio two years earlier, after the boardroom incident. But Maurizio also knew that Paolo was pragmatic and in financial difficulty—he had already managed to spend the settlement he had received from Gucci. Maurizio decided to make him an offer. He picked up the phone and dialed Paolo's number in New York.

"Paolo, this is Maurizio. I think we should talk. I have an idea that could resolve your problems and mine too," Maurizio said to him. They agreed to meet in Geneva the morning of June 18, 1984.

Paolo and Maurizio arrived at almost the same time at the Hotel Richemond. As they sat in the sun at a table on the terrace, overlooking Lake Geneva, Maurizio told Paolo his plan to create a new company, Gucci Licensing, to be based in Amsterdam for tax purposes, which would control all licensing under the Gucci name. Maurizio would control the new company with 51 percent, Paolo would have the remaining 49 percent and the title of president. In exchange, Maurizio wanted Paolo to cast his 3.3 percent vote on the board of Guccio Gucci with Maurizio's 50 percent. Maurizio would buy out Paolo's shares at a later date for $20 million. And finally, Paolo and Maurizio would drop all the suits pending against each other. At the end of their meeting, the two cousins shook hands and agreed they would ask their lawyers to start preparing the necessary documents.

They signed their pact a month later, in the Lugano offices of Crédit Suisse, where Paolo deposited his share certificates and Maurizio made a good faith payment of $2 million. Maurizio would gain control of the shares when the new company, Gucci Licensing, was founded, and when he paid Paolo an additional $20 million, for a total of $22 million. In the meantime, he had Paolo's vote and effective control of the Gucci company.

The board of Gucci America met in New York every year at the beginning of September. Only a few items were on the agenda: to approve the results for the first six months of 1984, a plan for new store openings, and a few new personnel appointments.

In the old days, when Rodolfo, Vasco, and Aldo were running the business, board meetings were enjoyable family reunions when the three brothers would get together and rubber-stamp what Aldo wanted to do, recalled his son Roberto. "There was such trust that they would just vote through what he wanted without contesting anything, then they would go out and have a good time," he said.

The weekend before the Gucci America board meeting, Domenico De Sole flew secretly to Sardinia, where Maurizio and Pilone were following the runoff races to select the Italian challenger for the America's Cup sailing competition. They stayed at the Hotel Cervo in Porto Cervo, which the Aga Khan had developed along with nearby Porto Rotondo. Many consider these exclusive vacation resorts among the finest in Italy. The pre-planned village of Porto Cervo extends out from a central piazza complete with cafes, restaurants, and designer boutiques, all painted the same soft pink and overlooking the bay where Italy's wealthy vacationers moor their luxury yachts and powerboats. The sun-drenched terraces and pruned gardens of luxurious private villas peek out from the rugged mountainside rising from the water. Porto Cervo's and Porto Rotondo's artificial style, symbolic of Italy's nouveau riche, clash with Sardinia's spartan natural beauty.

By day, Maurizio, Pilone, and De Sole plowed through foaming waters behind the sleek racing boats in Pilone's Magnum 36 high-speed motorboat; by night they dined on the candlelit terraces of Porto Cervo and reviewed their plan, which was remarkably simple. De Sole, who was secretary of Gucci America's board of directors, would fly to New York and attend the board meeting as Maurizio's representative. He had already met with Paolo's representative, who had committed to vote with De Sole. De Sole would propose to dissolve the existing board and nominate Maurizio as the new chairman of Gucci's U.S. operation. With control of the majority of the votes, there could be no effective opposition from the other board members. In minutes, Aldo would have lost control of Gucci.

A few weeks later in New York, the plan worked even more smoothly than they had dreamed. The meeting took place in Gucci's boardroom on the thirteenth floor of the Fifth Avenue store building. Before the start of the meeting, De Sole deposited his proxy to vote on Maurizio's behalf. A few minutes later, Paolo's representative did the same. Aldo, downstairs in his office on the twelfth floor, had decided not to attend the meeting, expecting it to be routine as usual. He sent Gucci's chief executive officer, Robert Berry, in his place.

De Sole asked for the floor as the dark eyes of a grinning, cigar-puffing Guccio Gucci stared down from a large-as-life oil portrait of the company's founder that hung on the wall behind the conference table.

"I would like to request that a motion to dissolve the board be placed on the agenda," De Sole said matter-of-factly.

Berry's eyes widened as his jaw dropped open.

Moments later, Paolo's representative seconded the motion.

"I . . . I . . . I would like to request a temporary suspension of the meeting," Berry stammered before he dashed out the door and rushed down to Aldo's office to tell him what was happening.

Aldo, chatting animatedly on the telephone with someone in Palm Beach, hung up the phone when Berry interrupted him.

"Dr. Gucci! Dr. Gucci! You must come upstairs immediately," panted Berry. "There is a revolution going on!"

Aldo listened silently to what Berry had to say.

"If that is the way things are, then there is no use going upstairs. There is nothing we can do," Aldo said tersely. He had misjudged the young Maurizio, who he feared was making a grave mistake.

Berry returned and tried in vain to suspend the meeting on the grounds that Aldo's lawyer, Milton Gould of a prestigious New York law firm, couldn't attend because it was a Jewish holiday. De Sole and Paolo's representative voted to dissolve the board and appoint Maurizio Gucci chairman of Gucci Shops Inc.

Aldo left the building, his face drawn. His own nephew, the very man he had once thought could be his successor, had toppled him in a coup d'état. Now Maurizio was the enemy.

Aldo met soon after with Giorgio and Roberto, but they sadly realized there was nothing to be done; Maurizio, allied with Paolo, effectively controlled the company. The same scenario would take place at the next meeting of the Guccio Gucci board in Florence.

The Guccis reached an agreement beforehand, which they signed in New York on October 31, 1984, and ratified by a shareholders meeting in Florence on November 29. Maurizio obtained four seats on the seven-member board and was nominated chairman of Guccio Gucci. Aldo was nominated honorary president, while Giorgio and Roberto were nominated vice presidents. Giorgio would continue to manage the Rome store, just as Roberto would continue as company administrator in Florence.

Maurizio, ecstatic, had gotten exactly what he wanted. Aldo retained an important title, but had essentially been neutralized; the cousins had been allowed to maintain their roles in the company, but Maurizio had control. Moreover, he had managed to transform Paolo's shares into a stabilizing factor. The press, gleefully covering the family feud, held him up as a hero; the *New York Times* dubbed Maurizio as the "Family Peacemaker," painting him as the image of tranquillity amid the steamy battles that had filled gossip columns.

Maurizio called a meeting of upper-level employees in Florence, inviting the group of some thirty people into the oval-shaped conference room that the staff had nicknamed the "Sala Dynasty," a tongue-in-cheek reference to the popular television series. The workers gathered around the massive wooden conference table, surrounded by dark, wood-paneled walls and four marble busts that represented the four continents. Maurizio explained his vision of the new Gucci to the group of office and factory workers.

"Gucci is like a fine racing car," he began hesitantly, looking at the old familiar faces clustered around him. "Like a Ferrari," he said, using a reference he thought they could relate to. "But we are driving it like a Cinquecento," he said, referring to the small, postwar utilitarian model produced by Fiat.

"As of today, Gucci has a new driver. And with the right engine, the right parts, the right mechanics, we are going to win the race!" he said with a broad smile, warming up to the subject. At the end of his speech, he asked the silent faces if there were any questions. Amid the nervous shifting of feet and clearing of throats, Maurizio's glance fell on Nicola Risicato, a man who had started as a clerk in the Milan shop, and worked his way up to manage the Via Tornabuoni store. Risicato, by then well into middle age, had watched Maurizio grow up.

"Nicola, not even you? Don't you have anything to say to me?" Maurizio asked with a smile, looking fondly at the elder man and hoping for approval.

"No, I don't give away compliments," Risicato said dryly, echoing the misgivings of many of his colleagues. They had grown comfortable with the spontaneous, backslapping style of Aldo and Rodolfo, and didn't quite know what to make of Maurizio's talk of Ferraris.

That December, the *Wall Street Journal* published an extensive exposé on Aldo Gucci's alleged financial transgressions, reporting that he was under investigation by a federal grand jury for allegedly siphoning off some $4.5 million from company coffers between September 1978 and the end of 1981. The article noted that Aldo had declared annual earnings of less than $100,000, "a small sum for a man of his status."

The Italian press picked up the news too. Gucci had reached a pinnacle in the United States—but perhaps now was heading for its downfall. "For the first time, the Gucci name wasn't being mentioned in connection with style and class, but with a serious crime," wrote the Italian weekly *Panorama* in January 1985.

Maurizio trusted De Sole implicitly and had asked him to become the new president of Gucci's U.S. business with a specific mandate: clean up the company's tumultuous fiscal affairs, prepare its response to the tax fraud allegations, and hire professional management. Before De Sole's arrival, the previous president of Gucci Shops Inc. had been a woman named Marie Savarin. Savarin was an accountant and had been a loyal assistant of Aldo's for years; she was probably the only woman Aldo had ever really trusted—even to the point of giving her authority to sign his signature.

De Sole agreed to do what Maurizio asked him, on the condition that he could keep his home and law firm position in Washington, D.C., and execute his new corporate duties part-time. De Sole began traveling to New York once a week. He hired a man named Art Leshin as Gucci's new chief financial officer to help him sort out the company's accounts.

"When we got in there, we freaked out!" De Sole recalled. "It was a disaster, total chaos. There were no inventories, no accounting procedures. It took us months to make head or tail of what was going on. Aldo ran the business with intuition—and his marketing genius was so great, he had gotten away with it!"

De Sole's once-a-week trips to New York became Monday through Friday, and his wife, Eleanore, dutifully packed him off with a suitcase of clean clothes at the beginning of each week and welcomed him home each weekend—along with his bagful of dirty laundry. De Sole eventually moved his family to New York.

In 1986, under his cleanup program, De Sole reincorporated Gucci's

U.S. business under a new name: Gucci America. In January 1988, Gucci America paid the IRS $21 million in back taxes and fines covering misappropriations by the family between 1972 and 1982. In exchange, De Sole extracted a promise from fiscal authorities to clear the company from any further liability in that period. The company was forced to go into debt in order to make the IRS payment. But De Sole both expanded and streamlined Gucci's operations. He bought back six of Gucci's independent franchisees, bringing the number of Gucci-owned stores in the United States to twenty, and took back wholesale distribution of the GAC from Maria Manetti Farrow in what became a nasty lawsuit—but instantly increased direct revenues. He also nixed a cigarette license that had been signed by the family with the R. J. Reynolds Tobacco Corporation, arguing that the association of Gucci with a cigarette would kill the brand in the United States. The license was later issued by Yves Saint Laurent. By 1989, Gucci America reported annual sales of some $145 million and profits of about $20 million, despite the continued family battles.

While De Sole tackled problems at Gucci America, Maurizio authorized the company's participation in an Italian consortium which was sponsoring a boat to race in the 1987 America's Cup sailing competition. The race had captured the interest of Italians in 1983 when the Italian boat *Azzurra* competed in the elite competition, creating enormous returns for its sponsors, Italy's largest automobile manufacturer, Fiat, and Cinzano, distiller of aperitifs. The historic race attracted the attention of elite viewers in the United States and Europe—just the kind of public to which Gucci catered. Maurizio's idea was to use the race to promote the strength of the "Made in Italy" label and he rounded up other corporate sponsors including the then–chemicals giant Montedison and pastamaker Buitoni. Maurizio was named image director of the new consortium and took his role seriously, promoting Italy not only as a country with traditions in art and craftsmanship but also as a growing source of advanced technology. The consortium bought a boat, *Victory,* which had performed well in the previous America's Cup, as a prototype on which to model its own boat, *Italia,* of which three models were subsequently made. It also hired a leading skipper, Flavio Scala from Verona, and a top-notch crew.

To the consternation of Aldo, Giorgio, and Roberto, who thought the sponsorship was an enormous waste of time and money, Maurizio threw himself—and much of the Gucci staff—into designing uniforms for the crew. Every item was technically tested to make sure it could withstand the wear and tear of work on a racing boat, as well as being aesthetically beautiful. The crew's racing gear was even designed to flash the rippling colors of the Italian flag as the men bent to wind and unwind the winches.

"I was the one who got handed the project," recalled Alberta Ballerini ruefully. "And I had a small staff that had become passionate about this race. We designed and produced everything for the crew, from T-shirts to jackets, pants, and bags. They were the best-dressed sailors I had ever seen!"

The tricolor look that Gucci created for *Italia*'s crew was so striking that *Italia* quickly became known as "the Gucci boat." Prada's competition in the America's Cup 2000 in Auckland with *Luna Rossa* is not unlike what Maurizio had hoped to do with the *Italia* consortium.

In October 1984, the competition to select the Italian boat that would compete in the America's Cup was held in Sardinia, off the Emerald Coast. Gucci established a base at Porto Cervo, where a few months earlier Maurizio, De Sole, and Pilone had planned their coup.

After several days of grueling competitions, *Italia* won the runoff, to everyone's surprise, beating out the favored *Azzurra*.

Unfortunately, not only did *Italia* not win the America's Cup, it became most famous for the day one of its prototypes sank in port after being transferred to Perth, Australia, where the America's Cup challenge was to be held. On launch day, the crane lifting the boat toppled over, sinking the boat under its weight. The boat was recovered damaged, and there wasn't time to reconstruct it before the race.

The Caffè Italia restaurant that Maurizio operated in Perth during the races was much more successful, quickly becoming the central meeting place and watering hole for all of the race participants. Table linens, silverware, crystal, and china were all imported from Italy for the occasion, as were the chefs, waiters, and all provisions, including mineral water, wine, and pasta.

When Maurizio wasn't off following the America's Cup endeavor, he found his new responsibility for Gucci all-consuming. He worked twelve- and fifteen-hour days, traveling constantly, tireless in his quest to realize his dream for Gucci. Lunch and dinner became opportunities to organize business appointments. He even traveled on weekends to supervise store openings and renovations, sacrificing his personal life, the sports he loved, his family.

As Rodolfo predicted, Maurizio changed. He relied on De Sole and Pilone for advice, becoming increasingly annoyed by Patrizia's efforts to guide him. As a younger man, Maurizio had looked to Patrizia to support him, giving him the strength to stand up to his own father. As he gained power, she had somehow taken over his father's role—telling him what to do, how and when to do it, and criticizing his decisions and advisors. Though he had finally won control of his family company, he felt oppressed.

"Patrizia really beat him up," recalled De Sole. "She set him up against his uncle, his cousins, or anybody else she didn't feel was treating him properly. At Gucci events she would say things like, 'I didn't get offered champagne first, that means they don't respect you!'"

"She became a real nuisance," agreed Pilone. "She was an ambitious woman and she wanted a role in the company. I told her to stay out, 'no wives allowed,' and she hated me for it."

Meanwhile, Rodolfo's warning rang in Patrizia's head. She finally admitted that her father-in-law had been right about Maurizio. Her husband, obsessed with his dream for Gucci, excluded all else—including his own family. He rejected her opinions and advice, and the distance between them started to grow.

"He wanted Patrizia to tell him *'bravo'* all the time; instead she reprimanded him constantly," said Roberta Cassol. "She became unpleasant."

De Sole and Pilone replaced Patrizia as his trusted advisors and she deeply resented them. Driven by her own ambition, she envisioned herself as the strong woman behind the weak man—but then suddenly found herself on the sidelines.

"Maurizio became unstable . . . arrogant and unpleasant," Patrizia recalled. "He stopped coming home for lunch, weekends he went off with his 'geniuses.' He gained weight and dressed badly . . . he surrounded himself with unsubstantial people. Pilone was the first. Bit by bit he changed my Maurizio. I realized it when Maurizio stopped telling me things, his tone grew detached. We spoke less. We grew cold and impassive with each other," she said.

Maurizio began to call his *folletto rosso* the *strega piri-piri* after a witch in a popular children's cartoon.

On Wednesday, May 22, 1985, Maurizio opened the wardrobe in their Milan penthouse and packed a small suitcase. He told Patrizia he was going to Florence for a few days, said goodbye to her, and kissed the girls, Alessandra, nine, and little Allegra, four. They spoke the next day by phone; nothing seemed to be out of the ordinary.

The next afternoon, a doctor who was a close friend and confidant of Maurizio stopped by to tell Patrizia that Maurizio wasn't coming back for the weekend—if ever. Patrizia was stunned. The doctor offered some consoling words—and the bottle of Valium he had tucked in his little black bag. She promptly sent the doctor and his bag packing. Patrizia knew that she and Maurizio had grown apart, but she never imagined that he would leave her and his children. A few days later, Patrizia's good friend Susy invited her over for lunch to deliver another message from Maurizio.

"Patrizia, Maurizio isn't coming back home," Susy said. "He wants you to prepare a couple of bags with his clothing and he will send a driver to pick it up. His decision is final."

"Tell me where I can find him," snapped Patrizia, "the least he can do is tell me to my face."

In July, Maurizio called and arranged to see the children on weekends. In September, he came home and asked Patrizia to accompany him to a polo match Gucci had sponsored and to present the winner's cup. During the week he was home, they finally had a chance to talk about their relationship. He invited her for dinner at Santa Lucia, the cozy trattoria where he had courted her.

"I need my freedom! Freedom! Freedom!" he explained. "Don't you understand? First I had my father, who told me what to do, now I have you. I have never been free in all my life! I didn't enjoy my youth and now I want to do what I want to do."

Patrizia sat speechless as her pizza grew cold. Maurizio explained that he wasn't leaving her for another woman, but because he felt "castrated" by her relentless criticism and bossiness.

"What is this freedom you want?" she finally replied. "To go rafting in the Grand Canyon, to buy a red Ferrari? You can do those things if you want to anyway! Your family is your freedom!"

Patrizia couldn't understand why Maurizio wanted freedom to come home at three o'clock in the morning when he was the kind of man who usually fell asleep at 11 P.M. in front of the television. She suspected he had been seduced by his own growing importance in the luxury goods business and by the respect given him by his new lieutenants in the office.

"My intelligence disturbed him," she said later, "he wanted to be number one and thought he had found the people who were going to make him number one!"

"Do what you must do," Patrizia finally told him coldly. "But don't forget you have obligations to me and to the children." Cold and impassive on the outside, inside, Patrizia felt her world falling apart.

They agreed not to tell the children immediately and Maurizio left. Initially he rented a residence on Milan's tree-lined Foro Bonaparte; later he took a small apartment in Piazza Belgioioso, although with all his travels, he rarely slept there. He never went back to Galleria Passarella to empty his wardrobe—he simply had new shirts and suits custom made, new shoes ordered.

After Maurizio left home, Patrizia turned to an unlikely companion for solace—a Neapolitan woman named Pina Auriemma who had become her friend. She and Maurizio had met Pina many years before at a health spa in Ischia, an island off the coast of Naples known for its thermal springs and mud baths. In Pina, who came from an industrial family that operated in the food sector, Patrizia found a lively and entertaining companion. They spent several summers together in Capri, where Pina had helped find Patrizia a house. Pina's sarcastic Neapolitan banter and skill with tarot cards entertained Patrizia for hours—helping to soothe the pain of Maurizio's departure.

"When we were in Capri, she came to visit me every day," Patrizia recalled. "We talked for hours and she was funny, she made me laugh."

The two women became fast friends and Pina often visited Patrizia in Milan or accompanied her on trips. Patrizia persuaded Maurizio to let Pina open a Gucci franchise in Naples that she operated for several years before turning it over to an associate. Pina was by Patrizia's bedside when Allegra was born in 1981. After Maurizio left home, Patrizia turned to Pina for consolation. When Patrizia became distraught enough to contemplate suicide, Pina talked her out of it.

"She stayed by me in the moment of my deepest depression," said Patrizia later. "She saved my life."

Although Patrizia thrived on the competitive social milieu she had found in Milan, she rarely felt at ease in it and had made few friends in whom she felt she could truly confide. When she really wanted to talk, she turned to Pina. When they weren't together, they talked for hours by telephone.

"I trusted her, I didn't have to watch my words with her, I told her everything," Patrizia recalled. "I knew she wasn't a gossip."

In the early years after Maurizio left home, Patrizia and Maurizio kept up the appearance of their marriage socially and sometimes went to public functions together. She dressed up to look her best whenever he came over to see the girls, but after he left she locked the door to her room, threw herself on the bed, and cried for hours. Even though every month Maurizio deposited some 60 million lire (about $35,000) in a Milan bank account for Patrizia— she began to feel that all she had achieved was slipping through her fingers. She turned to the Cartier diaries she bought each year that were bound in tan calfskin with a miniature photograph of herself set into the cover. She began to record every contact she had with her "Mau," as she still referred to him, in what would become an obsession.

The breakup of his marriage was only one of Maurizio's problems. Aldo and his sons had not taken Maurizio's coup lying down. They turned over a detailed dossier, complete with names of key witnesses, to the authorities in June 1985, indicating that Maurizio had forged his father's signature on his share certificates in order to avoid paying inheritance taxes. Aldo's strategy was to stop Maurizio's advance on Gucci by showing that he hadn't legitimately obtained his 50 percent stake in the company.

The key name in the file was Roberta Cassol, the woman who had worked for Gucci for more than twenty years, starting as a salesgirl and working her way up to become Rodolfo's assistant. Cassol handled all of Rodolfo's business and personal affairs, and when she had finished her tasks in the office, she spent long evenings with Rodolfo in his basement film studio, typing and retyping the narration to his film. As his health deteriorated, Cassol also traveled frequently with him to Saint Moritz to help him handle correspondence and other arrangements even when he was out of the office.

In the early months after Rodolfo's death, Cassol worked side by side with Maurizio as she had with his father. As he laid out his plans for modernizing the business, Cassol asked Maurizio for a promotion to commercial director. However, their relationship soured. He associated Cassol with his father and the past; he wanted to bring new people with fresh ideas into the company and wanted young, motivated professionals to replace Gucci's old guard and carry forward his dream. Maurizio turned down Cassol's request.

"We need fresh air," he said to her, and asked her to leave. They argued and left each other on bad terms.

"In life one must always learn to count to ten," Cassol said years later, admitting that she hadn't handled their breakup in the best way. At the time she felt angry that after years of devotion to his father, there was no room for her in Maurizio's new vision.

"He couldn't stand to have anyone around him who reminded him of his past," Cassol concluded.

That August, the chief of the Florence police, Fernando Sergio, summoned Cassol to his office. She took the train down from Milan, a three-hour trip. When she arrived in his office, he had a forty-page dossier on his desk that had been carefully prepared by Aldo, Giorgio, and Roberto. They accused Maurizio of having falsified his father's signature to avoid paying inheritance taxes of some 13 billion lire (or about $8.6 million).

"Can you confirm what is written here?" he asked her.

"I can confirm it," she said nervously.

"Tell me how things went."

Cassol took a deep breath.

"On May 16, two days after Rodolfo Gucci died, his son, Dr. Maurizio Gucci, and his advisor, Dr. Gian Vittorio Pilone, asked me to imitate Rodolfo Gucci's signature on five share certificates that had been put in his name. We were in the Gucci offices in Milan on Via Monte Napoleone. I didn't think I was able to forge the signature, so I suggested that my assistant, Liliana Colombo, do it. Late morning, in Pilone's house on Corso Matteotti, Colombo executed the signatures. But they didn't come out well and so the certificates were destroyed and new ones were printed, and two days later, twenty-four hours after Rodolfo's funeral, again in the home of Gian Vittorio Pilone, she forged the signatures again on share certificates of Guccio Gucci SpA, Gucci Parfums, and several green certificates she didn't know the identity of."

The dossier identified another key witness who had also been summoned by Sergio that day. Giorgio Cantini, a member of Gucci's administrative staff in Florence, held the keys to the company safe, which was located in Gucci's Florence offices. An old black Wertheim made in Austria in 1911, the safe contained all of Gucci's most important documents.

Cantini told the police chief that the documents had been in the safe from March 14, 1982, until May 16, 1983, when he had delivered them to Maurizio after Rodolfo's death. When Sergio informed him that the share certificates had been signed by Rodolfo on November 5, 1982, Cantini, incredulous, reacted immediately.

"Impossibile, signore!" he said. He was the only person, besides Rodolfo himself, who possessed a key to the safe and he had not opened that black box for anyone. It seemed strange to think that the ailing Rodolfo could have traveled to Florence off-hours, opened the safe with his key, and taken and later replaced the share certificates, all without Cantini knowing about it.

Sergio realized the case was too hot for his jurisdiction and turned it over to his colleagues in Milan, where the alleged forgery had taken place. On September 8, 1985, a Milan court sequestered Maurizio's 50 percent stake in the company pending an investigation into the alleged forgery. Maurizio—who felt that Cassol had aligned with his relatives in a personal vendetta—issued an indignant statement on Guccio Gucci presidential stationery with the company seal at the top. In the meantime, Aldo, Roberto, and Giorgio—not content with the criminal action they had initiated—also filed civil suits against Maurizio. Working with his lawyers, Maurizio managed to have the sequester removed on September 24, but for him, the big fight had only just begun.

The year before, after seizing control of the board of directors, Maurizio felt he had been magnanimous with Aldo, giving him the honorary title and letting him stay in his presidential twelfth-floor office in Gucci's New York building. When Maurizio realized that Aldo had put the dossier on Sergio's desk, he showed Aldo no mercy. He told De Sole what had happened. Overnight, Domenico De Sole called in workers who boxed up Aldo's belongings and moved the Guru of Gucci out of his presidential office. When the New York staff reported for work the next morning, Domenico De Sole sat behind Aldo's curved wooden desk.

"They started the war again," De Sole said. "I told Aldo that he had to be rational and make fair decisions—if he started litigation I would fight him back. He kept telling me that he liked what I was doing, he saw that I was putting things in order. But I think he was being set up by his children, even though he himself used to say all the time he thought they were stupid. He attacked us in court and so I threw him out," De Sole said matter-of-factly. With Maurizio's approval, he banned Aldo from entering the building and issued a press release saying that Gucci management "has decided to terminate Aldo Gucci's role in the company." The statement added that Aldo Gucci had been directed "to take no further actions to represent the company" due to confusion over who represented the business. Then Gucci America filed suit against Aldo and Roberto for allegedly siphoning more than $1 million of company funds for their personal benefit.

When Bruna Palumbo heard what had happened, she called Maria Manetti Farrow, the former GAC distributor, who had become a friend.

"Something terrible has happened," Bruna told Maria, asking her in a trembling voice to light a candle for the Madonna. After thirty-two years, Aldo had been kicked out the door of his own company by his nephew.

During the 1980s, Gucci became better known for its family wars than for its trademark products. The twists and turns of the family fights filled pages of gossip columns as the press had a field day with the stories. The larger and more sensational the headlines, it seemed, the more customers filed into Gucci stores.

"This is a new episode of a new, authentically Italian 'Dynasty' where the players are all real people, not actors," wrote *La Repubblica*, referring to the American television series that had captured a vast audience in Europe. A few days later, *La Repubblica* wrote, "*G* isn't for Gucci, but for *guerra*," which means "war" in Italian. And according to London's *Daily Express*, "Gucci is a multimillion-dollar company where more chaos reigns than in a Roman pizzeria."

"It is the kind of fighting where you go in as pigs and come out sausage," another paper wrote, quoting an English comedian. Even the Florence-based

La Nazione, Gucci's hometown newspaper, cracked irreverently in a full-page spread on the Gucci dynasty: "Wealth can give you everything—except transfusions of blue blood."

By this time Aldo, finally facing up to the seriousness of his legal and fiscal problems in the United States, decided it was time to clean house. In December 1985, Aldo called Giorgio and Roberto to meet with him in Rome. He came straight to the point, telling them he had decided to cede his Gucci shares to them, for two reasons. First, he feared that the impending IRS investigation was going to result in heavy fines on his assets; he wanted to lighten his portfolio, but keep the assets in the family. Second, he was eighty years old and wanted to protect his boys from steep inheritance taxes—especially after what had happened with Maurizio. "Why give money away to the tax authorities?" he reasoned.

On December 18, 1985, Aldo divided his remaining 40 percent in Guccio Gucci SpA between Giorgio and Roberto in a secret pact. He had already divided an initial 10 percent among his three sons in 1974 at the time of Vasco's death. The transaction gave Roberto and Giorgio 23.3 percent each in the Italian mother company and cut Paolo out, leaving him only with his original 3.3 percent. All the sons also had 11.1 percent in the U.S. company, Gucci Shops Inc. Aldo was left with no shares in the Italian company and 16.7 percent in Gucci Shops Inc. Aldo and his boys also had various stakes in Gucci's foreign operating companies in France, the U.K., Japan, and Hong Kong. Maurizio controlled 50 percent of Guccio Gucci and Gucci Shops Inc. and the same stakes Rodolfo had held in the foreign units. Paolo may have suspected he wasn't being treated on par with his brothers, for he had already announced to the family at large: "If Daddy dies leaving me nothing . . . I will put a team of lawyers to work for fifty years on the case if I have to!"

To avoid further confrontation with Paolo, Roberto and Giorgio agreed to vote only with their 3.3 percent stakes at Guccio Gucci board meetings.

In the meantime, Maurizio's agreement with Paolo fell apart in November 1985 at a final meeting they had set to conclude the pact sealed with a handshake that sunny day in Geneva. Messengers for Paolo and Maurizio rushed back and forth between the two camps along the corridors of the Lugano offices of Crédit Suisse, where Paolo's shares were held in escrow. According to legal documents subsequently filed by Paolo, Maurizio hadn't respected the terms of their pact. Maurizio had allegedly frozen him out of the new company, Gucci Licensing Service, which was supposed to be founded with Paolo's participation. The hours passed, with little progress toward concluding the agreement that would have sealed Maurizio's control of Gucci at 53.3

percent. Finally, late that night, well past normal business hours and with the bank officials exasperated, Paolo put an end to what he felt had been a charade. He tore up the draft of the contract on which they had been working, rallied his team of advisors, and stalked out, taking his share certificates with him. A few days later, Paolo filed new charges against Maurizio, declaring that his cousin had seized control of Gucci in violation of their agreement, and asking that Maurizio's nomination as chairman of Gucci be declared null and void.

Maurizio, beginning to understand the dynamics of the family feuds, had anticipated the breakup with Paolo and had another deal with Giorgio up his sleeve. At a board meeting on December 18, 1985, he proposed a new scenario for the company to nominate an executive committee with four members, comprised of himself, Giorgio, and a trusted manager of each. Giorgio would be confirmed as vice president, while the executive committee would ensure a collegial management of the company. Even Aldo agreed to the proposal.

Maurizio left for the Christmas holidays feeling he had reached a solution that could hold—at least for a while. In the meantime, relations with Patrizia had improved slightly as they made an effort to keep up appearances for the two girls. Maurizio had been home often in September and they agreed to spend the Christmas holiday together in Saint Moritz. Patrizia knew how much Maurizio loved his mountain retreat and hoped it would be the site of their reconciliation. She threw herself into festive decorations. When she had finished, Chesa Murézzan glowed with red and silver garlands, candles, moss, and mistletoe. She and Alessandra decorated the Christmas tree erected near the fireplace with blown glass bulbs etched in gold and dozens of real miniature candles. Maurizio had promised to go to midnight mass with her, something she had always loved doing, and her spirits leaped at the thought that everything could return to the way it had been between them. She bought Maurizio a set of cuff links and studs inlaid with diamonds and sapphires and couldn't wait to see the expression on his face when he saw them.

The evening of December 24, Maurizio went to bed at ten o'clock without saying a word—leaving Patrizia to attend the midnight mass alone. The next morning, as was their custom, the family invited the staff to receive their presents, before opening their own gifts privately. Maurizio gave Patrizia a key chain from the yacht *Italia* and an antique watch. She didn't know whether she was more disappointed or furious. She hated antique watches and thought he knew it; the key chain was an insult! That evening, they had been invited to a party together, but Maurizio didn't want to go. Patrizia decided to attend alone and learned there from one of their friends that Maurizio planned to leave the next day. She confronted him angrily with an outpouring of criticism and he reacted, grabbing her around the neck and lifting her petite frame off the ground as the two girls cowered in the doorway, watching them.

"Così cresci!!" he yelled. "This way you'll grow tall!!"

"Keep going!" she wheezed through clenched teeth despite his neckhold. "I could use a few extra inches!"

Their Christmas holiday, for which she had been so hopeful, was over. So was their marriage—Patrizia marked December 27, 1985, in her diary as the day it truly ended.

"Only a real jerk would dump his wife at Christmas," Patrizia said ruefully years later. The next morning, she awoke to find Maurizio packing his bags. He told her he had to go to Geneva. Before he left, he took Alessandra aside and said, "Daddy doesn't love Mommy anymore and so he is leaving. And Daddy has a nice new house where you can come and stay with him, one night with him and one with Mommy."

Alessandra dissolved into tears and Patrizia was shocked at how abrupt Maurizio had been with the girl, especially after their pact not to tell the children yet about their estrangement. That day marked the beginning of their battles over the children, battles that would profoundly affect them all. Maurizio accused Patrizia of trying to keep his daughters from him; she protested that his visits upset them so much she preferred to limit their time with their father. "Patrizia kept the children from him because she wanted to force him to come back home to her," added a former family governess.

If Patrizia used the children against him, Maurizio used his properties against her. He decided to ban her from the Saint Moritz estate and the *Creole*—only he neglected to tell her. One day, Patrizia brought the girls to Saint Moritz—only to find the locks changed. When she called the servants, they wouldn't let her in, saying they had instructions from Mr. Gucci not to allow her on the property. Patrizia called the police. When they determined that she and Maurizio were estranged, but not divorced, the police forced the locks and helped let her and the girls in.

In the meantime, arbitration had started in Geneva to resolve the dispute between Paolo and Maurizio, though no solution had been reached before the next family board meeting in Florence in early February 1986. Aldo knew that Maurizio's agreement with Paolo had fallen through. Now that his nephew was in a weaker position, he thought it might be the right moment to bring him around. Despite all that had happened between them, Aldo greeted Maurizio with a big smile and a hug, in the Gucci tradition of proceeding as though nothing had happened.

"Son! Give up your dreams of being the big boss," Aldo said. "How can you do everything alone, *Avvocatino*? Let's work together." He proposed Maurizio enter into a new agreement including both Giorgio and Roberto, with himself as arbitrator.

Maurizio forced a smile; Aldo's overtures weren't to be taken seriously. He knew Aldo's autonomy was limited. U.S. authorities had nearly revoked his passport over the tax case. On January 19, shortly before boarding a plane to Italy, Aldo had pleaded guilty in an emotional hearing in New York federal court to defrauding the United States government of $7 million in back taxes. Aldo admitted he had taken some $11 million out of the company through various devices, diverting the funds to himself and members of his family. Dressed in a double-breasted blue pin-striped suit, Aldo tearfully told Federal Judge Vincent Broderick that his acts didn't represent his "love for America," of which he had become a citizen and permanent resident in 1976. Aldo turned over a $1 million check to the IRS and agreed to pay the additional $6 million before sentencing. He faced up to fifteen years in prison for the offenses and a $30,000 fine. Domenico De Sole had advised Maurizio it was almost certain that Aldo would have to go to jail.

The family board meeting wound up without any major drama. Maurizio confirmed his accord with Giorgio, promising important jobs within the company to his sons. As Aldo left, he gave Maurizio a pointed message: "I admitted my responsibility [with regard to the U.S. tax issue] to save the company and the family. But don't think that in those years my little brother Rodolfo had his hands in his pockets," Aldo said, implying that Rodolfo also benefited from the arrangement. "I got myself in a mess to help everybody. I have a big heart."

Now that peace reigned in the family—at least temporarily—it was time to deal with Paolo again. After his pact with Maurizio had fallen apart, Paolo had gone back to his pet "PG" project. This time he went into production and brought out a prototype collection of bags, belts, and other accessories that he launched with a big party in Rome that March at a private social club. In the middle of the festivities, judicial police burst in and sequestered the collection as the guests jumped for caviar tarts and a last glass of champagne. A furious Paolo knew who had sent the unwelcome visitors—Maurizio.

"*Maledetto!* You will pay for this!" Paolo, dressed in tails and holding a glass of champagne, yelled out to no one in particular. Paolo was desperate. His legal bills amounted to hundreds of thousands of dollars. He hadn't earned a salary in years. His Gucci stock wasn't yielding anything despite the company's healthy profits because Maurizio had voted through a proposal not to distribute dividends, but to deposit them as reserves to help finance his grand plan. Paolo, forced to give up his home and offices in New York, had returned to Italy. And now Maurizio had ruined his party. He threatened to go to the authorities, but Maurizio paid him no heed.

While Paolo plotted his punishment for Maurizio, he won his revenge against his father, who was sentenced in New York on September 11, 1986. Paolo made sure the press turned out in force, cameras flashing, for the event by calling all the reporters he could think of the day before. In a tearful plea for clemency before the court, Aldo said in halting English, "I am still very sorry, deeply sorry for what has happened, for what I have done, and I apply for your indulgency. It won't happen again, I assure you."

In a breaking voice, he told the court he forgave Paolo, and "anybody who wanted me here today. Some members of my family have done their duty and others have the satisfaction of revenge. God will be their judge."

His attorney, Milton Gould, tried to save the eighty-one-year-old Aldo from going to jail, arguing that sending him to prison "would probably be a death sentence." But Judge Broderick had already made up his mind. He sentenced Aldo to a year and a day in prison for evading more than $7 million in U.S. income taxes.

"Mr. Gucci, I am persuaded that you will never commit another crime," Broderick said, noting that Aldo had already suffered "considerable punishment" from the publicity surrounding the case and from the consequences for his business. "I recognize that you are from another culture where our voluntary system of assessment of taxes does not pertain," Broderick said, but he explained he felt compelled to send a strong signal to other would-be tax evaders. Aldo received the jail sentence on one count of conspiracy to evade personal and corporate income taxes, as well as three years each on two counts of tax evasion, to which Aldo had pleaded guilty in January. The judge suspended the sentence on the two tax counts, instead ordering Gucci to serve five years of probation, including a year of community service.

Broderick allowed Aldo to remain free until October 15, when he was admitted to a federal detention center in Florida at the former Eglin Air Force Base in the Florida panhandle. The judge had said it wasn't his intention to strain a man of eighty-one years. To the displeasure of its warden, a Mr. Cooksey, Eglin was nicknamed "The Country Club Clink" for having facilities that made it sound more like a Club Med resort than a prison. The facilities included courts for basketball, racquetball, tennis, and even bocce, an old Italian game similar to bowling played with wooden balls on a narrow dirt court. There was a softball field equipped with night-lighting, a soccer field, a running track, and even a volleyball court on the beach. The recreation building featured pool and Ping-Pong tables, television, and a bridge club; there were even two horseshoe pits, and inmates could subscribe to newspapers and magazines. For a while Aldo was even allowed a telephone in his room, although his wardens later suspended the privilege because he spent all his time talking on the phone.

Even from jail, Aldo made his presence felt back in Florence, where his letters and telephone calls became part of company lore.

"*Dottor* Aldo?" said Claudio Degl'Innocenti in disbelief the first time he picked up the ringing telephone on his desk in the Scandicci plant to hear Aldo's jovial Tuscan accent on the other end of the line. "Aren't you supposed to be in jail?"

"He used to call all the time," recalled Degl'Innocenti. "He had a crush on a girl who used to work with me and he would always call to talk to her."

Aldo also kept in touch with the home front through letters that showed he was making the best of life in jail and thinking actively about springing back into action as soon as he was released.

In December 1986, he responded to a letter from Enrica Pirri, the former saleswoman he had hired in Rome more than twenty-five years earlier. "My dear Enrica . . . I am glad to be here because I am finding it incredibly restful, both mentally and physically," he wrote, his flourishing script dashing across the page. Aldo added that his family was urging him to resume "his post" at Gucci that he had been "forced to abdicate."

"The image of Gucci has been undone in the hands of those who can't seem to maintain the pace," he continued. "*Sto benissimo*, I am doing great and it will be a surprise for all, *i buoni e i cattivi*—the good and the evil—when . . . I will return among you," Aldo concluded.

After five and a half months at Eglin, Aldo was transferred to a Salvation Army halfway house in West Palm Beach where he was required to perform community service in a local hospital during the day. Paolo claimed he felt no remorse at the news of his father's jail sentence, though his wife, Jenny, later revealed that privately he was mortified.

Despite Maurizio's conflicts with Aldo, the fate of his uncle saddened him. He didn't think Aldo deserved what had happened to him. "If they had killed him, he would have suffered less," Maurizio said. To keep Aldo far from his company, in one place, after a life lived dashing around the world, was punishment enough.

Aldo's circumstances only made Paolo more determined to get his revenge against Maurizio, who he felt had cheated him. On his desk in Rome, where he had set up operations, he spread out an array of documents describing all the offshore companies in the Gucci empire, including photocopies of bank accounts and a detailed description of how Maurizio had bought the *Creole* by using funds diverted through the Panama-based Anglo American Manufacturing Research, Rodolfo's creation. Paolo sent copies of the dossier to everyone he could think of: the *Procuratore Generale,* or the chief prosecutor of the Republic of Italy; Italy's fiscal police, Guardia di Finanza; the tax inspection office, the Ministries of Justice and Finance, and four of the country's then-leading political parties. For good measure he sent his material to the *Consob,* the Italian stock market watchdog agency equivalent to the SEC. In October, Florence prosecutor Ubaldo Nannucci summoned Paolo, who told him everything he knew. The repercussions for Maurizio were immediate.

While Maurizio was in Australia following the *Italia,* investigators burst in the door of his Milan apartment in Galleria Passarella. Patrizia, who was at the Paris Ritz on a shopping spree, heard the news from a friend who was staying with the two girls, who were then aged five and ten. The girls were about to leave for school when five investigators burst in with a warrant to search the house. They even followed Allegra to her school, the Sisters of Mercy, later that morning, shocking the mother superior and demanding to see some drawings she had taken in her satchel. The investigators also searched Maurizio's offices on Via Monte Napoleone.

Meanwhile the papers that Aldo and his sons had filed against Maurizio over the summer were also making their way through the Italian judicial system. On December 17, 1986, Milan prosecutor Felice Paolo Isnardi issued a request to once again sequester Maurizio's 50 percent stake in Gucci. Maurizio knew it was going to be more difficult than he had ever imagined to realize his dream of turning Gucci into a topflight competitor in the luxury goods market. He had to move quickly, before Isnardi's request was granted.

9

CHANGING
PARTNERS

Dottor Maurizio! Venga subito!" cried
Maurizio's loyal driver, Luigi Pirovano.
Luigi had burst into the offices of
Giovanni Panzarini, one of Milan's leading civil
lawyers, where he had finally found Maurizio after
searching for him around downtown Milan for more
than an hour. Maurizio, chatting with his consultant,
Gian Vittorio Pilone, and Panzarini around an antique
wooden conference table, looked up in surprise at
Luigi's alarmed voice and saw the worried look on the
face of the dark-haired, mustached driver. Seeing his
calm, steady-going Luigi so upset, Maurizio knew
something was very wrong.

"Luigi?" Maurizio said, rising from his chair in
concern. *"Cosa c'è . . . ?"*

"Dottore! There is no time!" Luigi said. "The *finanza* is waiting for you in Via Monte Napoleone! You
must leave or they will arrest you. Come with me, NOW!"

When Luigi had gone to wait for Maurizio at his Monte Napoleone office after lunch, the *portinaio* downstairs had blocked him at the entrance and nervously pulled him aside before he could take the elevator up to the fourth floor.

"Signor Luigi!" the doorman had whispered. *"Lassù c'è la finanza! Vogliono il Dottor Maurizio!"* he said, describing the group of uniformed financial police that had gone up to Maurizio's office just minutes before. The Guardia di Finanza, Italy's fiscal police, is an armed police corps that specializes in financial crimes—primarily those against the state, such as tax evasion or disrespect of other financial norms. Just the sight of their gray uniforms and hats with yellow flame symbol is enough to make most Italians tremble and try to slip out of sight. Italians view *finanza* officers with far more trepidation than the regular blue-uniformed *polizia* or the carabinieri, who wear a characteristic red stripe down each pant leg and are the target for derisive Italian jokes.

Luigi knew exactly why the *finanza* had come. Maurizio had told him all about Paolo's accusations, the early-morning raid in the Galleria Passarella apartment the year before, and the December attempt to sequester his Gucci shares. Through his lawyers, Maurizio knew that prosecutors were preparing a warrant for his arrest as a result of the campaigns against him by his uncle Aldo, Paolo, and his cousins. When he could, Maurizio spent time out of the country, and when in Milan, he varied his daily patterns. Often during the past few months, Maurizio had asked Luigi to drive him out to little-known trattorias in the Brianza countryside north of Milan, where the two of them shared lonely dinners of steaming spaghetti and steak *filetti* before checking into small local hotels for the night because Maurizio was afraid of returning to the residence in Milan where he had been living since he left home. He knew that Italian law enforcement officials habitually arrested their suspects at dawn, when they were sure to find them at home in bed, asleep. Sometimes, not finding a room for the night, they even slept in the car. Nervous and lonely, Maurizio confided in Luigi, who spent night after night away from his own family in order to keep Maurizio company. Sometimes, late at night when he couldn't sleep, Maurizio even called Patrizia to share his worries with her. Now the moment Maurizio feared had arrived.

The minute Luigi heard that the *finanza* was waiting for Maurizio in his office, he had turned on his heel and rushed down the street toward Bagutta, the homey trattoria nearby that was still filled with the colorful oil paintings and sketches by its patrons of years gone by. No longer a hangout for the literary and artistic set, Bagutta now catered to the business elite of Milan's so-called golden triangle—the chic shopping streets that surrounded it. Bagutta had served Gucci managers and their patrons *cotolette alla milanese* and other local specialties for nearly forty years. Luigi knew Maurizio had lunched there with Pilone. However, when he slipped through the bristled strands of rope hanging in the doorway to keep out flies, the smiling, black-suited maître d' told him Maurizio and Pilone had already left. Luigi guessed they might have gone to Panzarini's office several blocks away.

Upon hearing Luigi's words, Maurizio turned and raised his eyebrows at Pilone and Panzarini, then bolted out the door after his driver. Still in good shape from the tennis playing, horseback riding, and skiing he loved but had little time for, he bounded down the back stairs of the office building after Luigi two steps at a time, heart pounding. They jumped into the car Luigi had pulled around to the back in case anyone came looking for Maurizio. Luigi drove the few blocks to Foro Bonaparte, where Maurizio kept his cars and motorcycles in a garage under the residence. Luigi handed him the keys to the biggest bike, a powerful red Kawasaki GPZ, and a helmet.

"Put this on—no one will recognize you—drive like hell and don't stop until you cross the Swiss border. I will follow you later with your things," Luigi said. Once he was in Switzerland, Maurizio was safe—Swiss officials would not extradite Maurizio for financial crimes.

"Keep your helmet on at the Swiss border, DON'T let them see who you are," Luigi instructed him. "Pretend to be relaxed; if they ask, just say you are going to your residence in Saint Moritz. Don't act suspicious, but be swift!"

His heart racing faster than the red Kawasaki he straddled, Maurizio reached the Swiss border at Lugano in less than an hour. He slowed the bike's thundering motor as he approached the guard station, keeping his helmet on as Luigi had advised. After the border guards waved him through with no more than a glance at his passport, he opened up the motor again as he nosed the Kawasaki back onto the highway that would take him north to Saint Moritz—although it was the longer route, the shortest itinerary would have taken him back across the wandering Swiss frontier into Italy, and he couldn't risk being stopped. Little more than two hours later Maurizio pulled the bike into the drive at his Saint Moritz estate, shaking.

After Maurizio fled Milan on the red Kawasaki, Luigi had gone back to the Via Monte Napoleone office, where the *finanza* officials were still waiting in vain for the Gucci chairman. Luigi pretended he too was looking for Maurizio and asked them what they wanted.

Luigi had been right. The officials in Maurizio's office had an arrest warrant issued by Milan magistrate Ubaldo Nannucci charging Maurizio Gucci with the illegal export of capital in buying the *Creole*. Italy's financial markets had not yet been liberalized and it was still illegal to move significant sums of money overseas. Despite the fact that Maurizio was a Swiss resident and the *Creole* flew the British flag, Paolo had achieved his objective. Maurizio was out of Italy—far from the daily operations of his company—and his hands were tied.

The next day, Wednesday, June 24, 1987, the papers blazed the shocking news: "Gucci in a storm over a dream yacht: arrest warrants issued," cried Italian daily *La Repubblica.* "Maurizio Gucci flees arrest."

Likewise, Rome's *Il Messaggero* screamed, "Handcuffs for the 'Gucci Dynasty,' " and Milan's *Corriere della Sera* trumpeted, "The *Creole* betrayed Maurizio Gucci."

Gian Vittorio Pilone and his brother-in-law were also charged in the case, but Pilone was the least fortunate of the three—police arrested him and held him in Florence's Sollicciano jail, near Gucci's Scandicci headquarters, for three days of questioning. Like Maurizio, Pilone's brother-in-law also fled in time, avoiding arrest. As Maurizio watched helplessly from his Swiss exile, two months later a Milan court took control of his 50 percent stake in Gucci and appointed a university professor, Maria Martellini, as company chairman in his place.

For the next twelve months, Maurizio lived in Swiss exile, moving between his Saint Moritz estate and Lugano's best hotel—the lakefront Splendide Royal—which he made his new operational base when he wasn't traveling. Lugano, an attractive Swiss town on Lake Lugano, lies in a pocket of Switzerland that extends deeply into Italy between Lago Maggiore and Lago di Como. Its proximity to Milan made it a beacon for city residents who often traveled to Lugano for its lower priced gas and groceries, efficient postal service, and discreet banking system. For Maurizio, the city offered a comfortable and convenient exile—he could summon his managers up from Italy for reports about Martellini's reign and easily drive up to Saint Moritz for weekends. Maurizio pleaded with Patrizia to bring the girls to Lugano so he could see them, but she inevitably came up with a last-minute reason to cancel. During Maurizio's first Christmas in exile, Patrizia promised that the girls could come, and he spent the morning of December 24 scouring the toy shops of Lugano for gifts for Alessandra and Allegra, whom Patrizia had agreed to send up with Luigi that afternoon. But when Luigi rang the doorbell in Galleria Passarella a few hours later, the maid answered, saying the girls weren't permitted to go with him.

"What could I do?" Luigi said later. "I couldn't bear to go back to Maurizio empty-handed, but the girls weren't allowed to come out with me." On the drive back to Lugano, Luigi stopped to call Maurizio with the news.

"When I returned to him that evening, he cried," said Luigi sadly. That was the beginning of what Luigi called Maurizio's *"periodo sbagliato,"* a time when everything seemed to go wrong.

The one ray of sunshine in Maurizio's life came from a tall American blonde from Tampa, Florida, a former model named Sheree McLaughlin. Maurizio had met her back in 1984 during one of the America's Cup runoff races in Sardinia. Lanky and athletic, with china blue eyes, streaked blond Farrah Fawcett haircut, and ready smile, Sheree responded to Maurizio's good looks and exuberant charm. Patrizia, who participated in some of the *Italia* team dinners and events, had immediately noticed Maurizio's interest in the girl. She let him know exactly what she thought about it. After Maurizio left home, he began to see Sheree regularly as they both traveled back and forth between Italy and New York. Sheree was one of the few people in Maurizio's life who truly cared about him—more than his money or his last name. If he was tied up in meetings when Sheree was in town, he would thrust some bills into Luigi's hand and instruct his driver to take Sheree shopping at Milan's designer boutiques. As Luigi navigated Maurizio's black Mercedes deftly amid the city center traffic, he tried hard to communicate with her—though neither spoke the other's language.

"Luigi, why does Maurizio want to buy me all these things?" Sheree would ask him plaintively. "I don't need fancy dresses. All I need is a pair of blue jeans and to spend time with him," she would say. After Maurizio fled Milan, Sheree met him in Lugano, or slipped up to Saint Moritz for a weekend when Maurizio was sure Patrizia wasn't using the estate. Sheree loved Maurizio and wanted to build a new life with him—but Maurizio wasn't ready. Absorbed with his personal and professional problems, he didn't feel he could make a commitment to her.

When Sheree was away, during the long days and evenings that Maurizio was alone, he threw himself into a thorough study of Gucci's past, writing the monograph that would become his blueprint for relaunching the Gucci name.

Maurizio may have been held at arm's length by the arrest warrant, but he hadn't been immobilized. He also kept busy furnishing the Gucci Room at Mosimann's, an exclusive London dining club operated by the acclaimed Swiss chef Anton Mosimann. Maurizio did the room in grand style, with his favorite Empire antiques, green Gucci print fabric on the walls, and one-of-a-kind period chandeliers and light fixtures. The effort cost a small fortune—sending Gucci's custodial chairman Maria Martellini into fits when she saw the bills, which of course were sent directly to Gucci headquarters.

A tall, bearded man named Enrico Cucchiani became Maurizio's chief representative in Milan, ferrying documents, messages, and instructions back and forth between Gucci's Via Monte Napoleone offices and Lugano's Hotel Splendide Royal. Maurizio had hired Cucchiani just a few months earlier from the McKinsey & Company, Inc., consulting firm to become the new managing director of Gucci.

Earlier that spring, before his exile, Maurizio had confided in Cucchiani about the seriousness of the attacks he knew Aldo and his sons were preparing against him.

"My family is hopeless!" Maurizio had said to Cucchiani one day, pacing back and forth in front of his desk in his Via Monte Napoleone office. "I have tried to work with them, but every time I take one step forward, one of them goes off and does something that has nothing to do with anything else we are trying to do. And now they are waging war against me!" he said, pushing his tortoiseshell glasses back up on his nose with his middle finger in a characteristic gesture. Maurizio turned to look at Cucchiani. A soft-spoken man with long limbs and slender hands and gray beard, Cucchiani crossed one leg over the other as he sat in one of the two Biedermeier chairs facing Maurizio's desk. He stroked his beard with the thumb and forefinger of one hand, listening to his boss.

"We have to find a way to buy them out!" said Maurizio.

Cucchiani had called an investment banker he knew who worked for Morgan Stanley in London, a man named Andrea Morante. Cucchiani asked him if he would like to meet Maurizio Gucci, but stressed that any encounter must be kept highly confidential given the high level of conflict within the Gucci family. Morante, a clever, analytical man who had parlayed his Italian roots and financial skills into a successful investment banking career, was immediately intrigued. Gucci was more than just another dynamic, medium-sized Italian company with a succession problem; there were many companies with succession problems. Gucci stood for glamour, luxury, and untapped earnings potential—an investment banker's dream. Morante agreed to meet Maurizio in Milan the following week.

When he arrived, Maurizio greeted Morante at the door of his Milan office and cordially invited him in, needing only a few seconds to size up some important details about his visitor. He was an attractive man of medium weight and height, with intelligent blue eyes and graying hair he kept clipped close around his head. Morante had put on his best suit for the occasion and an Hermès tie.

"I am very pleased to meet you, Mr. Morante," Maurizio said with a twinkle in his eye, "even if you are wearing the wrong tie!" Morante shot the young Gucci executive a probing look, then broke into an easy laugh. He liked Maurizio immediately. The glint in Maurizio's eye and his gentle reprimand had put Morante immediately at ease. Over the next few months he would come to admire Maurizio's talent for starting important business meetings with a joke that made everybody feel more relaxed. Morante sat back and glanced around the room, taking in the honey-colored Biedermeier furniture, the graceful green leather couch studded with red leather buttons, and the black-and-white glamour shots of Maurizio's parents from their film days. Morante's eyes lingered on Maurizio's beautiful desk, and the antique crystal liquor decanters and silver drinking glasses arrayed on a gleaming console against the wall. To Maurizio's left, light streamed into the room from two windows that looked out on a small balcony running the length of the outside wall. Maurizio carried the conversation from the beginning.

"You see, Mr. Morante," he said, "Gucci is like a restaurant with five different cooks from five different nations—the menu is five pages long and if you don't like pizza you can have spring rolls. The customer is confused, the kitchen is a mess!" he exclaimed, raising his arms dramatically. The formal patina he often put on for strangers wore off as he warmed to Morante.

From behind his aviator glasses, Maurizio's blue eyes studied the investment banker's reaction. Morante nodded, listened, and said little as he tried to figure out what Maurizio was after, and where he—Morante—fit in. Morante had joined Morgan Stanley in 1985 with responsibility for the Italian market and had immediately started work on a major deal—an attempt by Italian tire manufacturer Pirelli to buy U.S. tire giant Firestone. The takeover subsequently failed and Firestone was later acquired by Bridgestone. An international family background and conceptual mind gave him an unusual approach to the investment banking business, where he wasn't afraid to develop creative solutions to the problems of succession and growth plaguing many leading Italian companies. Morante's father, a naval officer from Naples, had met his mother when his ship put into port in Shanghai, where she had been born to Milanese parents. The family had lived all over Italy and abroad in Washington, D.C., and Iran. Morante had studied economics in Italy and completed an MBA at the University of Kansas in Lawrence before moving to London to start his career.

"We have one more chance to recover the Gucci customer, and that is to provide him with product, service, consistency, and image," Maurizio was saying. "If we can do it correctly, the money will flow in significant quantities. We have a Ferrari . . . but we are driving it like a Cinquecento!" he said, using his pet metaphor. "I can't enter a Formula One race unless I have the right car, the right driver, top mechanics, and plenty of spare parts. Do you see my point?"

Morante didn't. When Maurizio ushered him to the door more than an hour later, he still hadn't revealed the real purpose of the meeting. Later that day, Morante called Cucchiani to ask him what he should think.

"Don't worry, Andrea; that is typical of Maurizio," Cucchiani said. "The meeting went very well. He liked you. We should set another meeting, as soon as possible."

The following week, Maurizio, Cucchiani, and Morante met for breakfast at the Hotel Duca, where Morante customarily stayed during his visits to Milan. The hotel stood in a lineup of other large business hotels set back off Via Vittor Pisani, a wide avenue that led to the city's central train station.

This time, as waiters moved quietly around the tables and the high-ceilinged room filled with the sounds of murmured conversations and clinking glasses and china, Maurizio came quickly to the point. He had liked Morante immediately and decided to trust him. But instead of displaying his usual breezy optimism, he seemed nervous and pressed.

"My relatives are undermining everything I want to do," Maurizio had said earnestly to Morante, leaning forward in his chair. "Florence has become a swamp where all initiatives flounder. Now they are starting a campaign against me. I must either buy them out or sell my own holdings. Things cannot go on like this."

Morante realized that somewhere in the story there was a mandate for him to buy or to sell. Cucchiani looked over at Morante with a meaningful "You see? I told you so!" glance.

"*Dottor* Gucci, do you think your cousins might be willing to sell their Gucci shares?" Morante asked in his resonant, musical voice.

"Not to me," Maurizio said, laughing and sitting back in his chair and resting his hands on its arms. "For them it would be like agreeing to marry off their beautiful daughter to a monster!" What Maurizio didn't say, but Morante quickly figured out, was that Maurizio didn't have the money to buy out his relatives even if they would sell to him. "But under certain circumstances"—Maurizio's voice grew serious—"their shares might be purchased."

"Tell me this, *Dottor* Gucci," Morante persisted. "If they decide not to sell, would you be willing to sell to them?"

Maurizio's expression darkened as though a shadow had passed across his face. "Absolutely not! Besides, they don't have the money to buy me out. Before selling to them I would prefer to sell to a third party who I thought had the company's long-term interests at heart."

Morante quickly grasped the solution—to find a third party who would buy out Maurizio's relatives and become a partner to Maurizio in redefining the Gucci name.

Morante also realized that Maurizio—for all his apparent wealth—had a cash-flow problem. He questioned him on what assets he might be willing to sell in order to raise some liquidity—and thus be in a stronger negotiating position with his potential new financial partners.

What he learned surprised him: Maurizio, along with Domenico De Sole and a small group of investors, had quietly purchased control of the venerable U.S. carriage trade department store B. Altman & Company, which had been founded in the late 1860s and by the late 1980s operated seven stores. The investor group installed two former accountants to operate the business: Anthony R. Conti, formerly head of the retail accounting practice of Deloitte Haskins & Sells as CEO, and another former Deloitte partner, Philip C. Semprevivo, as executive vice president. The Gucci name hadn't appeared in connection with the transaction, and few were aware of Maurizio's ownership of B. Altman. With Morgan Stanley's assistance, Maurizio and his partners sold the store for some $27 million in 1987 to an Australian retail and real estate group called the Hooker Corp. Ltd. controlled by a businessman named L. J. Hooker. While the proceeds from the sale represented a welcome influx to Maurizio's bank account, sadly that sale marked the beginning of the demise of what had been an American retail institution. Within three years, B. Altman was out of business.

Morante went back to his London office and at the weekly Monday morning meeting of Morgan Stanley's investment banking division he described his initial meetings with Maurizio Gucci to the group of some twenty colleagues gathered around the conference table. They responded with laughter and raised eyebrows. The Gucci brand name was compelling, but it was also associated with family disputes, lawsuits, and tax schemes.

"Just make sure we get some loafers out of this one!" one of his colleagues cracked.

"The Gucci name instantly attracted everybody's attention," recalled Morante. "Usually the level of interest in those meetings was measured by how much money people thought we could make on a deal, but in the case of Gucci, it was the association with the name that struck everybody."

Though the bankers were intrigued, most of them were highly skeptical that there was any chance of doing a deal in Gucci's tangle of family conflicts.

One young man in the room, however, took Morante's presentation seriously. John Studzinski—"Studs" for short—was then responsible for the bank's think tank activity. Today he directs Morgan Stanley's entire investment banking operation. Studzinski knew that a then-little-known investment bank called Investcorp had made a fortune in 1984 by rehabilitating the historic American jeweler Tiffany & Company and then selling its shares on the New York Stock Exchange. He knew that Investcorp had wealthy clients in the oil-rich countries of the Middle East with a developed taste for investing in luxury brands.

"They are the only ones crazy enough to consider a deal like this," Studs thought to himself, "but I bet they could do it." After the meeting broke up, he took Morante aside and told him about his idea.

"There was a very low probability of success," Studzinski said later. "We saw Gucci as a declined brand with a shareholder situation that was all over the map. I regarded this deal as six-no-trump bridge—but we needed to get all the kings and queens in the right place," he said.

"It required a lot of patience and determination, but we knew Investcorp had the financing, was keenly interested in luxury goods, and had the patience to deal with an intricate shareholder situation," Studzinski said. He put in a call to Investcorp's London representative, a young man from Ohio, Paul Dimitruk.

A slim, tightly built man with dark hair and dark eyes that could be veiled, piercing, or warm, Dimitruk had a reserved demeanor, a strong dose of ambition, and a black belt in karate. The son of a fireman, he had been born and raised in Cleveland before going to law school in New York. Investcorp's founder and chairman, an Iraqi businessman named Nemir Kirdar, had plucked Dimitruk from the company's law firm, Gibson, Dunn & Crutcher, to launch Investcorp's London operations. Kirdar liked Dimitruk's experience working on cross-border deals between American and European industrial companies. Eager to expand his horizons and to live in Europe, Dimitruk had moved to London in 1982 as managing partner of the law firm's London office. He joined Investcorp in early 1985, shortly after the Tiffany acquisition. Dimitruk's job initially was to help develop Tiffany's international business and work on other post-acquisition management issues.

When Dimitruk's secretary told him John Studzinski was on the phone, he took the call immediately. Despite his young age, "Studs" was already widely admired in the investment banking world for his high-level contacts, expertise in the luxury goods industry, and unusual ability as an American to ingratiate himself in the clubby European business world.

"Paul, would you folks be prepared to consider Gucci?" Studzinski said into the telephone, sketching out the scenario. "If you agreed with Maurizio Gucci's vision, would you be willing to help him?"

Like Morante before him, Dimitruk perked up at the mention of the Gucci name. "We are extremely interested in meeting Maurizio and listening to his story," he said.

Once Studzinski got the green light from Dimitruk, Morante called Maurizio from London; Maurizio hardly let Morante finish his greeting.

"Do you have the deal?" he blurted out.

"Wait, wait a minute, one step at a time," Morante protested.

"We need to move fast, there is no time to waste," insisted Maurizio, who was still in Milan at that time. He didn't tell Andrea that he feared serious legal complications because of his relatives' accusations.

"I have someone who is interested in meeting you and hearing your story," Morante said. "Can you come to London?"

In 1987, Investcorp was hardly known in the financial world outside of private equity circles. Founded in 1982 by Kirdar, Investcorp had established itself as a bridge for clients in the Arabian Gulf to invest in Europe and North America.

Kirdar was a charismatic man with a sense of mission. He had a high forehead, a hawklike nose, and all-knowing green eyes that bore into yours when he looked at you. His family, from the northeastern city of Kirkuk, was pro-Western and loyal to the ruling Hashemite family at a time when the anti-Western movements of Nasserism, Pan-Arab nationalism, and Ba'thism electrified the Arab world. The 1958 assassination of the royal family and the bloody coup that later brought Saddam Hussein to power forced Kirdar to flee the country.

After completing a bachelor's degree at the College of the Pacific in California and working briefly at a bank in Arizona, Kirdar returned to Baghdad, where things seemed to have settled down. He developed a trading company that represented Western firms, but one April day in 1969 Kirdar was suddenly arrested and inexplicably held hostage for twelve days—a show of power by the regime. The experience was enough to convince him to leave Iraq again—only this time he was thirty-two and had a young family to support. Kirdar got a job in New York City with Allied Bank International, a consortium through which eighteen U.S. banks channeled their international business. During the day he worked in the basement of the bank's East Fifty-fifth Street town house; nights he studied for his MBA at Fordham University. After completing his degree and a brief stint at the National Bank of North America, Nemir was offered a job at Chase Manhattan, then the Cadillac of

American banks. It was the right place for an ambitious young man seeking a career in international banking.

During his years with Chase, Kirdar had developed a long-term business plan for the Arabian Gulf area, which had grown rich because of the 1970s oil crisis. First in Abu Dhabi and later in Bahrain, he secured important business for Chase and organized the team that would later join with him in forming Investcorp: Michael Merritt, Elias Hallak, Oliver Richardson, Robert Glaser, Philip Buscombe, and Savio Tung. Cem Cesmig, a country manager at Bankers Trust, became a good friend and also joined the group.

Kirdar's idea was to offer wealthy individuals and institutions in the Gulf region attractive investments for the fortunes they had made on oil. Kirdar wanted to connect them to sound real estate and corporate opportunities in the West, and in the process build an Anglo-Arab counterpart to Goldman Sachs or J. P. Morgan—top-notch investment banks known for their deal-making ability. In 1982, he launched his dream in Room 200 of the Bahrain Holiday Inn, with one secretary and a typewriter. By the following year, Investcorp graduated from Room 200 to its own corporate headquarters, Investcorp House, in Manama, and subsequently expanded to London and New York.

The company's mission was to buy up promising but struggling companies, improve them with financial resources and advice, and resell them at a profit. Investcorp's clients could pick and choose their positions in each investment—they were not obliged, as in an investment fund, to automatically take stakes across the board in all of Investcorp's holdings. No dividends were paid out to clients until the end of the cycle, when Investcorp sold the company, either through a private sale or a stock exchange listing.

Investcorp's initial purchases—it bought Manulife Plaza in Los Angeles and took a 10 percent stake in A&W Root Beer, among others—served to develop experience and credibility. But the acquisition of Tiffany & Company in October 1984 from Avon Products, Inc., for $135 million put Investcorp squarely on the deal-making map. After installing former Avon president William R. Chaney as CEO to spearhead Tiffany's successful turn-around, Investcorp took Tiffany public three years later—securing an eye-popping return of 174 percent per year and a reputation for having rehabilitated an American legend.

"We felt you couldn't sell jewelry as though it were cosmetics," said Elias Hallak, Investcorp's chief financial officer years later. "We said first we had to bring back Tiffany's glorious past."

As Morante described Investcorp's background on the telephone to

Maurizio, the mention of Tiffany made Maurizio warm to the idea of joining forces with the Arabian banking institution. "He understood that a partner that had restored Tiffany was a partner that was interested in brand names, that cared about quality, and had the financial sophistication to take the company public," Morante recalled.

Maurizio told him he could come to London at any time. But over the summer, gale-force winds had churned up a sea of troubles for Maurizio— the court sequester of his Gucci shares, the arrest warrant for the *Creole*, and the installation of court-appointed custodians for Gucci. If all that wasn't enough, Maurizio's personal assets had also been sequestered by a civil court investigating his inheritance from Rodolfo. As Maurizio drove the charging Kawasaki over the Italian border into Switzerland that June day, he wondered what he was going to tell the people at Investcorp—whom he hadn't even yet met. Once he had settled into his Saint Moritz home, Chesa Murèzzan, he had summoned up his optimism and called Morante.

"Tell them it is a move by my cousins to sabotage me, tell them that I will work everything out. Tell them that six months from now it will be all over."

Morante found Maurizio's reassurances persuasive and decided to believe him. Even if things didn't work out as well as Maurizio had predicted, Morante advised Investcorp, Maurizio's financial and judicial troubles would make it easier for the investment bank to buy him out.

At the time of Maurizio's escape in June 1987, a total of eighteen cases were pending in various courts around the world regarding the Gucci family, including two new ones instigated after Paolo also fired off dossiers against Giorgio and Roberto, alleging they had established their own network of offshore companies in Panama to siphon profits out of the Gucci business without paying taxes. In Maurizio's absence, Giorgio abandoned their alliance and reunited with his brother Roberto. The two brothers carried the next Gucci board meeting in July; together they controlled 46.6 percent of the company. A mistake had been made in depositing Maurizio's shares, which were represented by a court-appointed custodian, and Roberto and Giorgio prevented him from voting. The two brothers nominated a new board with Giorgio as chairman and reorganized the company themselves even though they didn't have a legal quorum. Milan lawyer Mario Casella, the court-appointed custodian of Maurizio's sequestered 50 percent, shook his head. "Here we have to save Gucci from the Guccis!," Casella muttered under his breath to Roberto Poli, a court-nominated accountant.

When on July 17 the court nominees formed another board of directors with Maria Martellini as chairman, the Gucci company found itself in a bizarre situation: it had two presidents and two boards of directors—one representing the family and one representing the court-ordered custodians. Aldo Gucci, eighty-two years old and recently released from prison, jumped back into action. He flew to Florence from the United States, took a room at his habitual favorite, the Hotel de la Ville, and helped arrange a compromise between the family and the court representatives: court appointee Maria Martellini was confirmed as chairman, while Giorgio Gucci was named honorary president without administrative powers and Roberto's son Cosimo became vice president.

For the first time in the history of the family company, the person in the driver's seat was not a Gucci. While Martellini struggled to keep the company on an even keel and cleanse it of the family fiefdoms, she installed a bureaucratic, unimaginative custodianship that employees recall as one of the dark periods in Gucci's history—with the exception of a lucrative license to manufacture Gucci eyewear with Italian producer Safilo SpA that is still in effect today.

"The company hit a standstill," one long-term employee recalled. "You practically had to get authorization to buy a roll of toilet paper. It became a company legend that one day to order some letterhead, the company required seven signatures," she said. "There was no creativity, no progress, it was just survival."

With Maurizio out of the picture in Italy, Aldo took the war against him to Gucci America, where Maurizio still controlled his 50 percent stake. The board was at a standoff—Aldo and his sons on one side, Maurizio on the other. Determined to regain control of his company after his bruising ouster by Maurizio three years before, Aldo was in no mood to step softly. He filed a lawsuit against Gucci America calling for De Sole to be expelled and the company to be liquidated. But, once again, Maurizio would surprise him.

In September 1987, Maurizio flew to London, where he had booked a room at his favorite hotel, Dukes, on St. James's Place. Near St. James's Park and the Green Park tube station, Dukes offered posh, intimate lodgings—and one of the best martinis in town. The next morning, accompanied by Morante and Studzinski, Maurizio arrived at Investcorp's London office, a charming four-story former mews on Brook Street in Mayfair. The men were ushered up to one of the second-floor sitting rooms, furnished with comfortable sofas and chairs and small coffee tables—a refined and intimate setting for doing business. Here Paul Dimitruk, Cem Cesmig, and Rick Swanson greeted them.

"I will never forget the first meeting we had with Maurizio," said Rick Swanson, a blond, boy-faced former accountant from Ernst & Young, who had recently joined Investcorp. "It was like waiting for a movie star!"

By then, Maurizio had fashioned his own engaging style from a mixture of Rodolfo's drama and Aldo's verve. He swept in the door ahead of his new banking acquaintances with his swinging cashmere camel-color coat, his longish blond hair, dark aviator sunglasses, and his blue-eyed Gucci smile. The waiting Investcorp executives were transfixed and intrigued.

"Here comes an Italian with this famous name whom we had never met before. He walks in, he looks like a movie star, his name is on the door of his company," Swanson said. "But he's being sued by his relatives, his shares have been sequestered, and he doesn't even have control! The tremendous infighting between him and his relatives is all over the papers, and the question to us is—'Would you mind coming in and helping to buy out his cousins?' "

Maurizio launched into the story of grandfather Guccio, the Savoy days, and the small shop in Florence. In his nearly perfect English, he recounted Aldo's triumphs with Gucci in the United States, Rodolfo's design and management role in Milan, and his own experiences as a young man working with Aldo in New York. Then he described the current problems: the cheapening of the brand, the family battles, the tax problems, the great divide between Gucci America and the Italian operation. He expressed his frustrations with trying to move things forward.

"There is a saying in Italy: The first generation is the one that creates the idea, the second develops it, the third must face the big growth questions,' " Maurizio explained. "Here, my view is diametrically opposed to that of my cousins. How can you tie a company that has 240 billion lire [about $185 million at the time] in sales to a closed family mentality? I believe in tradition, but as a base on which to build, not as an archaeological collection to show to tourists," he said heatedly.

"The family war has paralyzed this company for years, at least in terms of its development potential. I often ask myself, how many competing labels have been born and reached success just because Gucci was standing still? Now it is time to turn the page!"

The small group of investment bankers was hanging on his every word.

"There are too many cooks in the kitchen," Maurizio said, his blue eyes intense. "My cousins are all convinced they are God's gift to the fashion world—but Giorgio is totally hopeless, all he cares about is awarding the Gucci Trophy Cup at the equestrian competition at Piazza di Siena. Roberto thinks he is an Englishman; his shirt collars are so stiff he can hardly move. Paolo is a complete liability whose most significant achievement in life was to put his father in jail!

"These are my relatives; I call them the 'Pizza brothers,' " he said, painting his cousins as inept provincials. "Gucci is like a Ferrari that we are driving like a Cinquecento," he continued, dropping in his favorite metaphor with a flourish of a hand.

"Gucci is underexploited and mismanaged. With the right partners, we can bring it back to what it used to be. Once it was a privilege to own a Gucci bag, and it can be again. We need one vision, one direction, and"—he paused for effect—"the money will flow as you have never seen it."

Maurizio had enchanted the group of investment bankers, even though common sense might have suggested they put their money elsewhere. He had also snared them with the potential of the Gucci brand.

"It was crazy! Really dicey stuff," recalled Swanson. "There were no con-solidated financial statements—at least not at the level we were used to—no definitive central management team, no guarantees. But when he started to spin his story of his vision for Gucci, he charmed other people with his dreams."

Maurizio's evident passion for the Gucci name and sense of urgency about bringing it back captivated and inspired Dimitruk as well. Although Dimitruk and Maurizio came from entirely different backgrounds, they were about the same age, had the same driving ambition. Their relationship would prove key over the coming months.

"There was an incredible chemistry with Maurizio," recalled Dimitruk. "He portrayed himself as the shepherd of the brand, which he had a very, very strong conviction about restoring. He was also ready to say, 'I don't know it all.'"

After Maurizio left, Dimitruk picked up the phone and called Kirdar, who was spending his holidays at his favorite retreat in the South of France.

"Nemir, this is Paul. I have just met with Maurizio Gucci; do you know the brand Gucci?"

There was silence on the other end of the phone.

Kirdar was smiling. He said, "I am looking at my feet. I think I am wear-ing Gucci loafers." Gucci's black crocodile loafers with a gold horse bit had always been—and still are—an integral part of Kirdar's wardrobe.

Kirdar immediately gave Dimitruk the green light to pursue an agreement with Maurizio. He knew Gucci could be Investcorp's entry ticket into Europe's closed, chummy business community.

"We had to prove ourselves on both sides of the Atlantic," said Kirdar years later, "we needed to build our pedigree in Europe."

"It was much harder to do deals in Europe than in the United States," recalled Investcorp CFO Elias Hallak, saying the business environment at the time was small and clubby. "It was strategically important for us to do a big deal in Europe." An investment in Gucci would have made people sit up and take notice on both sides of the Atlantic.

The next step was to introduce Maurizio to Nemir Kirdar, who would make the final decision before they could go forward. Kirdar liked to initiate his business relationships with a fine meal—either in one of Investcorp's own comfortable dining rooms or at a gourmet restaurant. He preferred to size up new associates in a relaxed social setting rather than a stiff business meeting. Kirdar invited Maurizio to Harry's Bar—a refined private club known for its gourmet Italian cuisine and fine service.

Surrounded by the understated luxury of Harry's Bar's dining room—hardwood floors, round tables, comfortable chintz-covered chairs, and soft lighting—the two men studied each other. Kirdar and Maurizio liked each other instantly. Kirdar found a well-intentioned, inspired young man of thirty-nine intent on his dream to relaunch his family company. Maurizio found a gracious, reassuring man of fifty willing to take a risk on his plan.

"It was a total honeymoon," recalled Morante. "They were completely in love with each other."

Kirdar made the Gucci case a top priority project for Investcorp, assigning Dimitruk and Swanson full-time to help Maurizio. They code-named the Gucci project—which had to be kept top secret—"Saddle," and got to work reviewing the company accounts.

Dimitruk and Swanson worked out a succinct agreement with Maurizio that set out principles and key points of their collaboration: relaunch the brand, install professional management, and establish a unified shareholder base for the company—which meant in business jargon to buy out the other family members. Ultimately, they agreed, Gucci would seek a stock market listing once the relaunch was complete. Those few pages, dubbed the "Saddle Agreement," formed the basis of what would become a remarkable business relationship.

"We shared Maurizio's conviction about the value of the name. That it was special and deserved to be restored," Dimitruk recalled. "I had Nemir's complete support." Investcorp committed itself to buy up 50 percent of Gucci from Maurizio's relatives.

"There was only one path—buying out the cousins," said Paul Dimitruk. "Maurizio never saw a moment's hesitation or fear from us. We were just going to persist. We communicated all the time."

Maurizio was elated. He sensed he was finding his way out of the "Pizza brothers" quagmire. From Maurizio's headquarters in exile at the Splendide, in a suite overlooking Lake Lugano, Maurizio and Morante plotted the best way to approach Maurizio's relatives. Morgan Stanley would front the acquisition. Investcorp wanted to remain anonymous until it was clear it could acquire the entire 50 percent.

Maurizio said that Paolo, whom he viewed as unscrupulous, shrewd, and self-interested, should be approached first. Paolo was the key to the puzzle because, although he had only 3.3 percent, he was the least loyal to the family. Paolo knew that even his small handful of shares would break the 50 percent deadlock between Maurizio and the others. He was well aware his sellout would wound his brothers and his father—a sweet revenge for their refusal to grant him importance within the company. Paolo was also poised to launch his business in the United States under the PG label, and needed the money. He didn't want to know if Maurizio was behind the transaction—or he didn't care. Morante arranged a meeting with one of Paolo's lawyers, Carlo Sganzini, at an office in Lugano, across the lake from the Splendide. Maurizio claimed he watched them through binoculars from his hotel window. "I never believed him, but it was all part of the folklore," Morante said.

At one point, the negotiations with Paolo hit a snag over a clause the lawyers had inserted to make sure Paolo couldn't compete with the Gucci business. "There was a big desire to close the book on the Paolo problems," Morante recalled. "Our demands touched Paolo's most sensitive nerve."

Furious at the effort to limit his freedom to use his own name, Paolo grabbed the contract, threw it up in the air, and stalked out as the pages floated down around Morgan Stanley's bankers and lawyers. Morante reported back to Maurizio, who was happily expecting the deal to be closed.

When Morante said that a problem had come up, he watched as Maurizio's friendly enthusiasm transformed into violent fury; his mouth set into a thin line and the cheerful blue eyes turned to ice. "Tell that Paul Dimitruk if he doesn't do this deal I am going to sue him for the rest of his life," Maurizio seethed as Morante stepped back in surprise.

"He had every right to be upset by the failure of the deal, but he had no right to say what he did. He became nasty," Morante said later. "I realized I had seen the other side of him—he had the litigious genes in his body too."

Morante patched up the problem with Paolo and cleared the first hurdle for the Gucci bid in October 1987, when Morgan Stanley bought out Paolo for $40 million. Paolo's lawyer also received a $55,000 watch from Bregeut, the luxury watchmaker Investcorp had bought earlier that year. As they walked out after signing the transfer papers, the lawyer turned to Swanson, saying, "You know, we talk so much about representations and warranties, but I want you to think about this transaction as though you were buying a car off a used car lot—'buyer beware.' "

Swanson was shocked. " 'Buyer beware'? What was that supposed to mean?" he said later. "We had just spent millions of dollars and he had the gall to say 'buyer beware'?"

Paolo's decision to sell marked a critical turning point in Gucci's history. Although he had the smallest shareholding of the family—11.1 percent in Gucci America, 3.3 percent in Guccio Gucci SpA, and various stakes in Gucci's French, U.K., Japanese, and Hong Kong companies—Paolo became the linchpin that definitively ruptured the sanctity of family control. His decision effectively stabbed his father and his brothers in the back by handing majority control to Maurizio and his new financial partners. There was little choice for them but to follow in his footsteps or remain minority shareholders in their own company. Though Paolo had fought Maurizio alongside Aldo, Roberto, and Giorgio, his own rupture with his father and brothers ran deeper, and he turned his back on them in the end—as he felt they had with him.

Maurizio now had a secure majority of Gucci, thanks to his alliance with Morgan Stanley and Investcorp. It was time to end the war with Aldo over Gucci America. Aldo and his sons had brought suit in July 1997, attacking De Sole's management and calling for the company to be liquidated.

"You have taken a real thoroughbred racehorse and reduced it to a carriage horse!" Aldo wrote to De Sole at the time.

Now that Maurizio controlled the board, there were no longer grounds to say that the company was deadlocked and should be dissolved. Paolo, in the meantime, had withdrawn his support of the charges against Gucci America.

"It was a very dramatic hearing," recalled Allan Tuttle, the lawyer with Patton, Boggs & Blow who then represented Maurizio. When Tuttle and his team presented the ownership change before Justice Miriam Altman in New York's Supreme Court, Aldo's lawyers jumped up in protest, requesting time and more information in an effort to stop the judge from throwing out the suit. Justice Altman, who by this time had seen one Gucci case too many, cut them short. "I know every piece in the Gucci line and I know that two-thirds of the price of every wallet goes to lawyers' fees. It's quite clear what happened," she said as she pounded the gavel. "You've been stabbed in the back!"

Maurizio's elation over the buyout of Paolo's shares and his new relationship with Investcorp buoyed his optimism in the face of a steadily rising tide of legal problems in Italy. On December 14, 1987, a Milan magistrate called for Maurizio's indictment for allegedly forging Rodolfo's signatures on his Gucci share certificates. The indictment was returned in April 1988. According to the charge, Maurizio had not only forged the signatures, he owed the government a total of 31 billion lire (or about $24 million) in unpaid taxes and fines. On January 25, 1988, Maurizio was indicted for illegal export of capital for buying the *Creole* and again on February 26, for the $2 million he had paid to Paolo under the agreement they had reached that sunny afternoon in Geneva. In July, however, the tide began to turn in Maurizio's favor. Maurizio's lawyers struck an agreement with Milan magistrates, who revoked his arrest warrant. He was required to come back and face the charges against him, but he would not have to go to jail. In October, Maurizio appeared in a Milan court to defend himself from the accusations that he had falsified Rodolfo's signature. Maurizio stood up and produced his father's will. On November 7, the Milan court convicted Maurizio of tax fraud in connection with his falsification of signatures on his father's will, gave him a one-year suspended sentence, and told him he had to pay 31 billion lire (about $24 million) in back taxes and fines. His lawyers immediately appealed and worked out a financing agreement under which the court also restored Maurizio's voting rights over his shares. On November 28, a Florence court acquitted Maurizio of the foreign exchange violations after a reform of financial regulations made the export of capital no longer an offense. Maurizio was finding his way out of the net.

In the meantime, Morante made the rounds of the other Gucci cousins. By that time, Paolo's brothers, Roberto and Giorgio, each controlled 23.3 percent of Guccio Gucci SpA after Aldo had transferred his shares to them back in 1985. They also owned 11.1 percent each in Gucci America and, as Paolo had, varying minority stakes in each of the overseas operating companies. Aldo had retained just 16.7 percent of Gucci America, in addition to his holdings in the overseas units. Morante met Roberto Gucci in the frescoed offices of Gucci's intimidating Florentine lawyer, Graziano Bianchi, a dark, cultured, Machiavellian personality with above-average intelligence. Morante explained that he was an investment banker with Morgan Stanley in London and had important business to discuss with them, after which Bianchi personally frisked him to make sure he wasn't wearing a hidden recording device. Morante sat down in one of the antique high-backed wooden chairs in front of Bianchi's imposing wooden desk and Roberto remained standing. Morante got right to the point.

"I am here to tell you that there has been a change in the shareholding structure of the Gucci company," Morante said. The two men stared at Morante, dumbfounded. "Morgan Stanley has bought out Paolo Gucci's shares."

"Hehhhh, hehh," said Bianchi, uttering a short, cynical laugh that sounded more like a cough, giving the impression he suspected all along something like this would happen.

Roberto, still standing, froze.

Morante let the information sink in.

"*Ecco!* Roberto!" Bianchi's rough voice broke the silence. He waved an elegant hand toward Morante as though presenting him. "Our new shareholder!"

Morante had more to say.

"My visit here today is not just to inform you of what has already taken place, but to say that we have no intention of stopping here. We are acting on behalf of an international financial investor who at this point wishes to remain anonymous. We are committed to going forward." He paused, studying the reaction on the faces of the two men. Bianchi had a gleam in his eye, and Morante could tell that his calculating mind was working fast. Roberto sat down on another wooden chair as though all the air had gone out of him, pain playing across his face. Pain from his brother's betrayal, from the possibility that Maurizio would emerge victorious, from the implications for his future and that of his family.

Morante stopped next in Prato, where he made the same presentation to Annibale Viscomi, Giorgio Gucci's accountant. Subsequently he met with Giorgio's son Alessandro, who acted as his father's agent. Morante entered into negotiations with the two brothers—separately.

Morgan Stanley closed with Giorgio at the beginning of March 1988, and with Roberto at the end of March. Roberto held back a 2.2 percent stake in a final, desperate play to strike a deal with Maurizio—together they could have controlled the company. Maurizio said no—he had already aligned himself with Investcorp.

It quickly became clear to the outside world that something big was afoot at Gucci. Journalists called daily, and their papers speculated about shifts in Gucci's ownership structure. In April 1988, Morgan Stanley confirmed it had bought 47.8 percent of Gucci for an international investment group, but nobody knew who the mystery buyer was.

By June 1988, Investcorp decided to identify itself and confirmed it had acquired Morgan Stanley's "almost 50 percent stake" in Gucci, and had reached an agreement with Roberto Gucci for his 2.2 percent stake. However, Roberto didn't capitulate until March of the following year after failing to convince Maurizio to make a deal with him. Those events have left Roberto bitter and hurt to this day. "It was like losing my own mother," said Roberto years later.

Now Investcorp had to acquire Aldo's 17 percent stake in Gucci America to complete its 50 percent holding in Gucci. Paul Dimitruk called Morante. "It's time to make the final push with Aldo," he said.

In January 1989, Morante flew the Concorde to New York, where he met Aldo in his apartment, not far from Gucci's Fifth Avenue store. Banned from Gucci's executive offices, Aldo used his apartment for business appointments. When Morante arrived in late afternoon, Aldo opened the door himself and graciously ushered Morante into an elegantly furnished drawing room. Over the years, the walls had become a mosaic of photographs of Aldo smilingly greeting presidents and celebrities, as well as plaques, certificates, and symbolic city keys testifying to Aldo's accomplishments in the United States. More memorabilia were elegantly displayed on end tables and coffee tables around the room. Aldo offered Morante a coffee and slipped out to prepare it himself, while Morante studied the souvenirs that told Aldo's story.

"It struck me how well integrated Aldo felt in the United States, where he had met incredible success, yet had never adapted to its fiscal system," Morante recalled. "He welcomed the celebrity and glamour the country offered him, but hadn't accepted the rules of the game—and had paid dearly for it."

Aldo—who knew exactly why Morante had come—had dressed impeccably for their meeting and took care to impress the investment banker with his charisma and style. He sat down amicably with Morante, telling him his story—the store openings, the products, the charities, the awards—glancing at him furtively from time to time out of the corners of his blue eyes from behind thick glasses in a way that reminded Morante of a cat. He dominated the conversation and Morante couldn't help but think that Aldo truly had what Italians call *fascino*—and was keen to show it. Morante realized where Maurizio had gotten his storytelling skill, his vibrancy, his anecdotes. He listened as the hour grew late.

When Aldo finished, he looked Morante in the eye. "Now we can talk about why you've come," he said.

Aldo knew he had no choice but to sell—his sons, to whom he had generously ceded his shares long before his death—had already walked out of Gucci's door; the only thing he could do was follow. With only 17 percent of Gucci America, Aldo no longer had any authority over the company's affairs. Suddenly Aldo's gracious tone grew angry.

"The only thing I want to ensure is that my *bischero* of a nephew doesn't have anything to do with this!" Aldo intoned. "If he wins out, it is the end of everything I have created! I still care for Maurizio—despite all that has happened between us—but I am warning you, he is not equipped to wear the Gucci mantle. He will *not* be able to carry the company forward!"

Morante reassured Aldo that he was working for an international investment institution and dangled a proposal to keep Aldo involved in the business for several years under a glorified consulting contract.

"He knew he had lost the match and had little to negotiate, but the sense that he could maintain his honor and in some way a role in the business was a matter of life or death," Morante said later. "I had the overwhelming feeling that if he sold out entirely, he would die. It was as though he were tearing out a piece of himself. And in that moment, he hated his children for what they had done to him. After all he had given to them, he was left with nothing."

In April 1989, Investcorp sent Rick Swanson to Geneva to close the deal with Aldo. That transaction ended a process that had lasted more than eighteen months, one of the longest, most complicated, and most secretive series of acquisitions in investment banking history.

"Miraculously, nobody found us out until the very end," recalled Swanson. "For more than a year and a half, we had lawyers, bankers, trademark experts—everybody you could think of working for us. Normally, in Italy if you sneeze the whole world knows!" At one point, Investcorp was close to closing on another block of shares with one of the cousins while in the next room a crew from *60 Minutes* interviewed Maurizio and speculated on who could be buying Gucci—all to the tune of the theme song from *Dynasty*.

Investcorp's acquisition of 50 percent of Gucci marked another turning point in the history of the family-owned company. It was the first time since Guccio Gucci started his small business that an outsider owned such a significant block of shares in the family firm. Most important of all, Investcorp was not an individual but a sophisticated, unsentimental financial institution intent on realizing successful returns for its investors—although it would prove far more patient and understanding than many other institutions might have been.

The final meeting with Aldo took place at lawyers' offices in Geneva. The men at Investcorp couldn't believe they had finally come to the end of their long journey. They nervously envisioned a worst-case scenario—what if they wired the money to Aldo's accounts but then Aldo and his lawyers grabbed the share certificates and ran, leaving the bankers empty-handed?

Investcorp's team lined up on one side of the conference table, Aldo and his lawyers on the other. The share certificates lay in front of Aldo. The entire group waited for the bank to call saying the funds had gone through.

"It was so strange, everything had been negotiated and everything had been signed and there was really nothing more to say and we were all just sitting there in silence waiting for the phone to ring," recalled Swanson.

When the phone finally rang, everybody jumped. Swanson picked up the receiver. "When I got off the phone to say OK, the money had gone through, Aldo moved forward in his seat to stand up and our lawyers lunged across the table for the shares. We were so nervous!"

Aldo blinked, startled, with the shares in his hands. Then he got up, walked over to Paul Dimitruk, and gallantly handed him the shares.

"These Guccis, they really were all actors, they never showed their sweat," recalled Swanson. The tension was broken by the pop of a champagne cork and a short speech by Dimitruk about Aldo's heritage and what he had built. Then Aldo made his own speech, faltering as he failed to contain his tears. "It was all very sad," said Swanson.

Everything Aldo had worked for had ended. At age eighty-four, he had followed his sons out of Gucci's door, selling his last remaining piece of the empire he had built to a financial institution.

"When we finished, we just stood there and nobody knew what to say, and there was an awkward silence," Swanson said. Then Aldo put on his cashmere coat and fedora hat and his advisors put their coats on and everybody shook hands and then they went out the door into the cold Geneva night. About thirty seconds later, Aldo came back through the door—the ultimate humiliation—his taxi hadn't shown up.

Two days later Aldo sent Swanson his travel and hotel bills for attending the closing. "That was so Gucci." Swanson laughed.

10

AMERICANS

One warm morning in June 1989, Maurizio welcomed Dawn Mello, the president of Bergdorf Goodman, into a suite that he had reserved expressly for their appointment at New York's Hotel Pierre.

"Miss Mello! I am so glad to see you!" said Maurizio emphatically, as he invited her into the room and gestured for her to sit on the overstuffed couch while he settled into a wing chair to her left. Light from the window streamed in behind him. He had been calling her for weeks, but she hadn't returned his phone calls until just more than a week earlier. Maurizio wanted Mello to help him make his dream for Gucci come true, and said, "My relatives have destroyed this brand and I am going to bring it back." Mello listened carefully, impressed with his fluent, only slightly accented English.

Dawn Mello had become a star on the U.S. retail scene for her revival of the venerable—yet sleepy—Bergdorf Goodman. Maurizio knew it would be difficult to woo her away, but he was determined.

LOCATED ON THE WEST SIDE OF FIFTH AVENUE between Fifty-seventh and Fifty-eighth Streets, Bergdorf Goodman was founded in 1901 by two merchants, Edwin Goodman and Herman Bergdorf. Over the years, the store earned a reputation as one of the most elegant and expensive women's stores in the world, but by the mid-seventies that reputation had started to slip. Goodman's son Andrew had sold the store in 1972 to a three-way partnership, Carter-Hawley-Hale. In an effort to reverse the slide, in 1975 the new owners hired Ira Niemark, a tall, soft-spoken, seasoned retail executive from B. Altman who had started his career at the age of seventeen as a doorman at Bonwit Teller. Niemark brought Dawn Mello with him.

"Bergdorf Goodman was a store that had aged along with its owners," Mello recalled. "The average customer was about sixty years old and very conservative. The image of the store was so dusty that neither the French nor the American designers would sell to us!"

Mello knew from her experience as fashion director at B. Altman that such designer names as Fendi, Missoni, Krizia, and Basile from Italy were starting to gain a following. A young Gianni Versace was turning heads with his designs for Callaghan, the brand name created by an apparel manufacturer named Zamasport in northern Italy.

"We began to buy the Italian collections," Mello recalled, and they also redid Bergdorf Goodman's decor, creating a luxurious yet homey feeling. An antique crystal chandelier from the former Sherry Netherland Hotel now hung in the entrance hall over a new Italian intarsia marble floor and fresh flowers were placed daily in crystal vases throughout the store. By 1981, Bergdorf's carried all the top designer names from Italy and France, including Yves Saint Laurent and Chanel. Even Bergdorf Goodman's pale purple shopping bags became status symbols and were carried by society matrons, rock stars, and princesses alike. When in the early nineties the Yves Saint Laurent name began to lose its shine, Bergdorf's boldly dropped the designer, a move symbolic of how far the store had come. "There is only one New York City Ballet, one Metropolitan Opera, one New York Stock Exchange, one Madison Square Garden, one Museum of Modern Art, and one Bergdorf Goodman," wrote *Town & Country* in 1985.

Maurizio wanted Mello to do for Gucci what she had done for Bergdorf's. Years earlier, Aldo had identified her as a woman with the right balance of smarts and style for the Gucci business and had tried to hire her several times, but she had always turned him down.

Maurizio had first started calling Mello at the end of May 1989. He had just recovered full control of his Gucci stake and thanks to his new alliance with Investcorp, he had been unanimously reelected chairman of Gucci on May 27, 1989. When Mello didn't return his phone calls, he got a mutual acquaintance, Walter Loeb, the Wall Street retail analyst, to call her.

"Maurizio Gucci is anxious to talk to you," Loeb said, "why aren't you responding to him?"

"I'm really not interested," Mello replied. "I love my store. I don't want to leave. What can I possibly do for him?" She had been promoted to president in November 1983, with all the benefits of the position, including the perfect office complete with a picture window looking up Fifth Avenue toward Central Park. Mello had reached the pinnacle of the American luxury retail world, and after thirty-four years in the business, she wasn't about to give it all up for an Italian businessman—even if his name was Gucci.

"Do it as a favor for me, go speak to him for me," Loeb had implored her. Mello agreed.

Mello could see the Hotel Pierre from her office above Bergdorf's. Before going to her appointment with Maurizio that morning she lingered at the window for a few minutes, looking down at the domed canopy over the Pierre's front door. Then she turned briskly, went downstairs, and emerged from Bergdorf's revolving doors into a blast of unseasonable heat. The sun beat down as she paused impatiently on the corner of Fifty-eighth Street and Fifth, waiting for the light to change. She flicked some imaginary flecks of lint from her suit and looked irritably at her watch. "This is a waste of my time," she thought crossly. She had so much to do back at the office and had hoped to get some correspondence done before her afternoon product meeting. She wished she hadn't agreed to the appointment with Gucci. The light changed and she started across the street, her mouth set firmly.

Mello came from Lynn, Massachusets, a small industrial town north of Boston. She had been crazy about clothes from early childhood, cutting out new clothes for her paper dolls and playing dress-up in her mother's outfits. She studied illustration at the Modern School of Fashion and Design in Boston, which no longer exists, and at night took drawing and painting courses at the Boston Museum of Fine Arts. But after hurting her hand in a car accident, she realized she couldn't maintain the skill she had worked so hard to develop. Before she turned twenty, she set out for New York City where she started modeling. But despite the success her attractive face and willowy, nearly six-foot-tall figure brought her, she found the work tiresome. She wanted more. She lied about her age and landed a job with a division of Lane Bryant to open a chain of their Over 5'7" Shops, to retail clothing for tall women around the country. After completing a training program in Boston, she started out.

"It was a big adventure," Mello said. "I had never been outside of Boston except for that brief experience in New York. I had a small salary and a very small expense account, but I knew I was on the right track."

Mello next moved into the training department at B. Altman, where she waited for a job to open up. In those years, B. Altman was a grand old store that took up an entire block at Thirty-fourth Street and Fifth Avenue. A carriage trade store then considered the Harrods of Manhattan, B. Altman had fine products and a loyal following. Mello's moment came in 1955 when Betty Dorso, the glamorous and talented former editor of *Glamour* magazine, came on as fashion director. A former cover girl, Dorso hired Mello as her assistant.

"I learned about style from her," Mello said. "She was into Chanel and wore cardigans and silk shirts and pleated skirts—very modern for her time. I would walk behind her, dressed in the cheaper version of what she had on, affecting the same pelvic tilt."

Mello first saw European fashion when Dorso brought back dresses from the couture shows in Paris that the store then had copied by manufacturers on Seventh Avenue. In those days, couturiers such as Balenciaga, Yves Saint Laurent, Balmain, and Nina Ricci showed custom designs during the Paris couture shows, but the ready-to-wear designer hadn't yet emerged. "There was a huge gap between the couturier and the apparel manufacturer," Mello recalled.

At this time, a few designers had started working in New York. Claire McCardell, Pauline Trigère, Ceil Chapman, and others had staked out new territory. A very young Geoffrey Beene designed for Traina-Norell, while Bill Blass worked for Maurice Rentner, but in those days the manufacturer was still more important than the designer.

In 1960, the May Department Stores Company recruited Mello as fashion director. During the next eleven years, she worked her way up to become general merchandise manager and vice president.

"That's where I learned the basics, that you have to put your pants on one leg at a time," Mello said. Then she fell in love with the president of the company, a man named Lee Abraham, and married him.

"I had to leave, or go to work for my husband," she recalled ruefully. She went back to B. Altman in 1971 when Ira Neimark hired her as fashion director. Neimark had also worked for the May Company and was familiar with her work. They were a close and successful team; he was a talented merchant, and she had a sense of creativity and style, which he encouraged. "They were an unbeatable pair," recalled Joan Kaner, senior vice president and fashion director of Neiman Marcus.

As a woman in a man's world, she had learned to be tough without sacrificing style or manners. Shy yet determined, Mello often struck people as elegant but aloof. Those who managed to delve beneath the surface, however—especially the talented young people she encouraged and promoted—found in her a warm and supportive friend.

Mello stood out in the retail world not only because she was a woman in a high-level position, but because of her creative, fashion-oriented approach to the business. "I was lucky to have worked with people who encouraged me to develop my fashion sense," Mello said. "While the average buyer was worrying how to get which products to her stores at what price, I was able to work on a more creative level."

She developed an eye for quality and stylish products and a nose for coming fashion trends. A whiz at spotting budding new businesses and design talent, she brought many new names into the stores where she worked. In order to keep pace with the razor-sharp competition among New York's top retailers, she drove hard bargains and sought exclusive contracts wherever possible. By the time Mello reached Bergdorf's, she had become a commanding presence in the international fashion world, not just with designers and fellow retailers, but also with writers and editors at the top fashion magazines.

"GUCCI HAS TO RECONQUER the image it had in its youth," Maurizio was saying to Mello as she sat on the couch, listening. "Over the last few years, Gucci has lost its prestige. I want to bring back the glamour it had in the sixties and seventies; I want to regain the confidence of the consumer; I want to re-create the excitement."

Mello remembered well what Gucci had been in its glory days. As a young woman working for Lane Bryant, she had saved up an entire week's salary to buy her first Gucci bag: a brown pig suede hobo bag that at the time cost sixty dollars.

She also remembered the period when people lined up outside the store on Fifth Avenue waiting for it to reopen after lunch. In Maurizio's warm, enthusiastic, and inspired company, her reservations began to melt away. As he spoke, she forgot about her phone calls, the memos waiting to be written, the afternoon meeting, her corner office overlooking Central Park. First entranced, then excited about what Maurizio was saying, she understood in a flash what he wanted to do. The Gucci name had been cheapened. The canvas handbags with their interlocking Gs were everywhere. By the late 1980s, Gucci sneakers had even become status symbols for drug dealers; rappers sang about Gucci in a popular rap tune. Maurizio wanted to wipe the slate clean and bring back Gucci's glory days, when it was the symbol of luxury, quality, and style.

"I need someone who knows what Gucci was like at its peak, I need someone who can believe it can be that again, someone who understands what the business is about. I need you!" Maurizio said, looking Mello earnestly in the eyes.

When Mello finally walked out of the Pierre back into the early June heat two and a half hours later, her head was spinning. She had missed her meeting and, remarkably, didn't care!

"I had the feeling my life had been changed," she said. Maurizio had asked her to help create the new Gucci.

It didn't take long for Maurizio's courtship of Mello to hit the New York City rumor mill and Domenico De Sole started receiving questions from his staff and phone calls from the New York retail fashion community asking him if the stories were true. Not only had Maurizio not told De Sole about Mello, he denied the rumors when De Sole called to ask him. De Sole dutifully reported back to his callers that the rumors were false—only to discover shortly thereafter that the rumors were true and Maurizio had kept him in the dark.

De Sole, upset at how Maurizio had treated him, offered to leave—he could always go back to his law practice in Washington, D.C. Maurizio refused to accept De Sole's resignation and asked him to continue his work at Gucci America.

"The important thing in understanding my relationship with Maurizio is that Maurizio was beginning to enjoy his power," De Sole recalled. "He had been pushed around all his life—first by his father, then by his wife and then by his relatives who had forced him into exile. Suddenly he was back, he was the CEO of Gucci. Investcorp and Dawn Mello and others were showering him with respect—he thought he was invincible. I made him uncomfortable. I had been the hero of the war [with Aldo]. I was a lawyer. I treated him with respect, but I wasn't in awe of him or intimidated by him. I was the only one who wasn't bowing down to him. When he said, 'Let's cut wholesale,' I said,

'Are you sure you want to do this? It represents a lot of business. Do we have the money to do it?' He never understood the concept of money."

De Sole kept his post at Gucci America and Dawn Mello moved to Italy in October 1989 as the new creative director of Gucci with a salary that was double what she was making at the time and a benefits package that included luxury apartments in New York and Milan, Concorde flights back and forth, and a personal car and driver for a total cost of more than $1 million. Mello's news made a splash on the New York fashion scene.

"The fact that Gucci had taken the initiative to hire an American woman of her stature—that made heads turn," said Gail Pisano, senior vice president and general merchandising manager of Saks Fifth Avenue.

"She had a vision, a merchandising background, a passion for fashion, and she understood the New York customer. Because of her, top merchants such as Burt Tansky, Rose Marie Bravo, and Phillip Miller started paying attention. It became clear something was brewing," Pisano said.

Some thought Mello was crazy for leaving her prime spot in New York to join the crazy, unpredictable Gucci family.

"She can never turn things around," one unnamed New York retail executive told *Time* magazine. "The name is too far gone."

Mello's move to Gucci marked the beginning of a wave in the late 1980s and early 1990s, as leading European fashion houses increasingly sought out American and English design talent. A young English design duo, Alan Cleaver and Keith Varty, was already turning out trendy, lighthearted styles at Byblos, the popular label owned by Italy's Genny SpA group in Ancona on the Adriatic coast. Over the next decade, American designer Rebecca Moses was hired for the Genny signature label, while several years later British designer Richard Tyler would replace Cleaver and Varty at Byblos. The Gerani family of Cattolica, also on the Adriatic, contracted American designers Marc Jacobs and Anna Sui for their labels, while Ferragamo turned to Stephen Slowik to rev up its apparel line. Behind the scenes, Prada, Versace, Armani, and others recruited graduates from top U.S. and British design schools for their design teams, and budding talent from Belgian design schools was beginning to be recognized as well.

At Gucci, Mello became the magnet that attracted other young talent. She hired Richard Lambertson, a young, New York-based designer from Geoffrey Beene with a background in buying and accessories who had also worked on product development for Barney's. David Bamber, who is today creative services director at Gucci, recalled he was happily working for Calvin Klein when Mello called him.

"I hadn't thought of moving," Bamber said. "But at my first meeting with Dawn she went through the whole process of what she was trying to do at Gucci. I was very impressed with her and thought to myself, this has to be something serious." A few months later, he had moved to Milan to join the growing design team.

Mello's own arrival at Gucci was rocky, however. Maurizio—typically—hadn't told most of the Gucci employees that Mello was coming. In particular, he hadn't told Brenda Azario, who supervised the design staff for the apparel. When Maurizio fled to Switzerland, Azario took on the coordination of all of Gucci's collections, approaching her new responsibility with courage and determination. When Mello arrived in the morning, Azario left that afternoon, in tears.

"It wasn't so much that Dawn Mello was American or that she didn't speak the language," said Rita Cimino, "it was the way Maurizio presented her, or rather didn't present her. And if that wasn't enough, Maurizio had already encouraged her to visit some of our suppliers, who immediately called us and asked us what was going on. It wasn't pleasant."

Maurizio finally called all the workers in Florence together to present Dawn Mello to them. By that time, they were full of misgivings. Amid rumblings and grumblings and calls to keep quiet, one of them stood up: "I just want to know why we have to listen to you now," the workman complained. "First it was the 'schoolteacher,' " as the Florentine workers had nicknamed the court-appointed chairman Martellini, "and now an American signora from New York." Before he could finish, he was shushed by his colleagues and told to sit down.

Maurizio, enthusiastic about his coup in bringing Mello to Gucci, and anxious that she not lose heart, took very good care of her. He furnished a beautiful apartment for her in Milan's chic Brera neighborhood that overlooked Giorgio Armani's garden and took her to lunch regularly in the city's top restaurants.

Maurizio personally accompanied Mello on visits to many of Gucci's longtime manufacturers and taught her about the leathers, the tanning, the way the bags were stitched together. She learned from him about Gucci's traditions and roots. "Maurizio was always touching the hides and having me touch them and talking about *mano,* or hand—the feel of the leather," Mello said.

Having blazed her trail through the tough world of New York retailing, Mello tried not to let the reactions of Gucci's staff discourage her. She had her mandate from Maurizio and confidence that his dream for Gucci was viable. She simply rolled up her sleeves and got to work.

"The first thing I had to do was understand the company," she recalled.

"The family had taken away a lot of the historical value and promoted a lot of low-level people into important jobs." Morale was a disaster, she said. "It took a long time to convince the workers in Florence about what we wanted to do. Once we did, though, they were great."

Maurizio was pleased with his new team. In addition to Dawn Mello, he had brought over Pilar Crespi, former public relations director for Italian label Krizia in New York, as his new communications director. Carlo Buora, who had been at the sportswear company Benetton, became Gucci's new executive vice president for finance and administration. In 1990, Maurizio hired Andrea Morante—who had become his new star—as Gucci's managing director. After leaving Morgan Stanley in 1989, Morante had moved to Investcorp at the invitation of Kirdar, who had been impressed with Morante's campaign to buy out Maurizio's relatives and hired him to oversee the new investment. He had another reason for bringing Morante over to Investcorp. Kirdar had already seen that the relationship between Paul Dimitruk and Maurizio Gucci had gone beyond an impartial business relationship, and he felt that Dimitruk was smitten with Gucci, throwing into question his allegiance to Investcorp. When a photo of Paul Dimitruk appeared in the *Financial Times* in 1989 alongside the news that the Investcorp executive had been nominated vice chairman of Gucci, Kirdar took the Investcorp executive off the Gucci account—despite the protests of both Dimitruk and Maurizio—and put Morante in his place. Dimitruk, who disagreed with Kirdar's decision, resigned in September 1990.

"Nemir wanted someone who knew the Gucci story intimately, but was less 'in love,'" recalled Morante. "I was ready for a change and very glad to come over."

Investcorp had made Morante an offer too good to refuse: a position on the senior management committee and a mandate to work side by side with Maurizio. "It was an exception because Investcorp never allowed its management to get involved in the business," Morante said. He went to Milan to help Maurizio hire his new team and restructure the commercial and administrative aspects of the business. He also opened talks to reacquire Gucci's franchise in Japan and started streamlining commercial and logistical systems. A strong working relationship grew between the two men, and inevitably, Morante too became impassioned by Maurizio's dream. It didn't take long for Nemir Kirdar to question his loyalty to Investcorp.

"It became clear that I too had fallen 'in love' with Gucci, not with Investcorp, and Nemir was convinced that I was too much on Maurizio Gucci's side," recalled Morante.

At the next annual management committee meeting in Bahrain in January

1990, Kirdar called Morante into his office. He offered him an exciting new position within Investcorp—to move to New York and work on the acquisition of Saks Fifth Avenue. The catch? Kirdar wanted Morante to start the new job the next day.

Morante raised his eyes to look out of the picture window behind Kirdar's desk, which framed both the ocean and the desert in one stunningly beautiful scene. "I was torn," Morante said. "I had all these people who were looking to me as a reference point: Dawn Mello, Carlo Buora, and all the others we had spoken to or whom we had asked to join Maurizio's team." He explained the situation and asked Kirdar to give him sixty days to tie things up.

Kirdar, his green eyes severe, looked at Morante. "You don't understand, Andrea, I am giving you twenty-four hours. This is the only way you can prove to me where your loyalty lies," Kirdar said. "You have to show me that you are an Investcorp soldier."

"I can't do it in twenty-four hours," Morante said flatly.

Kirdar looked at him silently, got up from behind his desk, and came toward Morante, opening his arms and wrapping them around him in a passionless bear hug.

"It was his way of saying goodbye," Morante said.

When Morante called Maurizio in Milan to give him the news, Maurizio hired him on the spot. He glowed with enthusiasm about his new team, which he called "*i miei moschiettieri*," or "my musketeers."

11

A Day

in Court

The morning of December 6, 1989, Maurizio, two lawyers at his side, walked up the concrete steps leading into the cavernous, echoing halls of the Milan courthouse. The three men took their places in the front row before Judge Luigi Maria Guicciardi of Milan's Court of Appeals. To Maurizio's right sat Vittorio D'Aiello, one of the city's top criminal lawyers and almost a fixture in the Milan Tribunale with his mop of white hair and the sweeping black robes of his profession. To his left sat Giovanni Panzarini, Maurizio's civil lawyer, eyes half closed in concentration. Maurizio sat silently in his gray double-breasted suit, hands crossed tensely in front of him. The men stiffened slightly and stood as a buzzer sounded, announcing Guicciardi's arrival. After taking his place at the judge's bench, Guicciardi announced his decision: "In the name of the Italian people, the Court of Appeals of Milan . . ."

Maurizio nervously pushed his glasses up more firmly on his nose and clenched his teeth—the next words Judge Guicciardi would pronounce would either wipe the slate clean of all his judicial troubles, or leave him with an indelible mark on his reputation and a hefty tax bill. Although he had emerged relatively unscathed after his conviction little more than a year before for falsifying his father's signature—with a suspended sentence and no criminal record—the sentence of the Court of Appeals was his last chance to clear his name of the charges. Maurizio held his breath and watched the tassels on the judge's robe.

"... in reform of the sentence issued by the lower court, absolves Maurizio Gucci of all the charges against him."

The words shot through Maurizio's mind like rays of sun after a thunderstorm. He had won! Not only had he survived all the legal attacks from his relatives, now two and a half years after he had been forced to flee Milan on his red Kawasaki, he had cleared his name. Maurizio threw his arms around D'Aiello and wept. Maurizio's Investcorp partners were pleased and comforted by the decision—and didn't really want to know the details. Miraculously, it seemed, Maurizio's promises that he would overcome the accusations against him had proved true. Several Investcorp executives recalled that Maurizio had seemed extremely confident about the outcome even several weeks earlier.

Others were stunned by the verdict. The case against Maurizio had seemed airtight. Two eyewitnesses had testified against Maurizio. Roberta Cassol, Rodolfo's former secretary, had described in detail how the signatures had been forged by her then-assistant, Liliana Colombo. Giorgio Cantini, a custodian in Gucci's Scandicci offices, had testified that the share certificates had been locked in his safe on November 5, 1982—the day Rodolfo had supposedly signed them over to Maurizio. Cantini said the shares had stayed in the safe until after Rodolfo's death in May 1983, when he handed them over to Maurizio. Furthermore, during the course of both the trial and the appeal, four separate court-ordered handwriting analyses had determined that the signatures did not remotely resemble Rodolfo's script—but were similar to Colombo's. Finally, the prosecutor had even analyzed the date of the fiscal stamps affixed to the share certificates at the moment of the alleged transfer—the stamps had been issued by the government printing office three days after Rodolfo's death! Despite all the evidence against Maurizio, he had won, his lawyers arguing valiantly that Maurizio's warring Florentine family had plotted against him. They cast doubt on the handwriting analyses; they debunked Cassol's testimony, saying she sought revenge after Maurizio had fired her;

and they raised the possibility that Rodolfo had another key to the company safe in Cantini's care. They even suggested that the government printing office had inadvertently released the stamps, which were commonly preprinted, before the stated date. Had their reasoning been enough to convince the judge? In his verdict, Guicciardi said it was impossible to prove beyond doubt that the signatures had been falsified. Maurizio was absolved for lack of sufficient evidence.

"It was the worst decision I had ever seen in my entire life," said a government lawyer, Domenico Salvemini, who fought the decision fiercely, taking it all the way to Italy's highest court, La Corte di Cassazione, where he was turned down. "I have my ideas about what happened, but it isn't correct for me to say," said Salvemini, whose friends recall he became so bitter over the decision he nearly abandoned his career. With time, he became more philosophical. "Sometimes you get ruled against—that's life," Salvemini said years later.

Maurizio—ecstatic about his victory—resumed his duties at Gucci with a renewed spirit while Mello and her assistant, Richard Lambertson, began to learn the ups and downs of Italian manufacturing. Maurizio liked Lambertson and took him under his wing, too, introducing him to the Florentine factory workers and showing him about the leathers.

"He took me into the factory in Florence and said, 'Richard is OK,' so we'd go back and forth together. Once we spent an entire week just doing the luggage collection," Lambertson recalled. "Maurizio was fanatical. Everything had to be perfect, down to the last detail. We cleaned up all the hardware and even developed a GG initial that went on the screws for the handbags."

Mello and Lambertson visited Gucci's manufacturers around Florence, who began to confide in them and teach them their business. Many of Gucci's products were unevenly priced, they learned. The silk scarves, for example, cost more than the elaborately stitched handbags! They later discovered one of the reasons for the erratic pricing was a system of payoffs to Gucci employees who brought profitable business to regional suppliers—and expected a kickback for it.

Mello, mystified in many ways by the new world she had found herself in, started receiving anonymous phone calls at night. *"Signora, sono stanco di pagare il signor Palulla,"* an anxious voice said night after night. "I am tired of paying Mr. Palulla."

"I knew nothing about all this, but it wasn't long before I figured out the decisions that needed to be made," Mello said. She went to Maurizio and told him what she had learned. He agreed to make changes, though he didn't always move as quickly as he should have.

Mello soon realized that Gucci to the Florentine manufacturers was something like the queen bee to her swarm—they coddled her, served her, acquiesced to her often-unreasonable requests—and benefited from her. It was widely known in the artisan community that from time to time the suppliers of Gucci bags would slip a handbag or two out the back door and pocket the sale, one of the invisible perks of the trade.

"Gucci is an icon to Florentines," Mello said. "It is a brand they covet, not just another client. The power that goes along with the possession of that icon is not easily understood."

To help catalog what had been lost, Mello wanted to create an archive, something sequential and organized beyond the few old random photographs and samples she had found. She had already collected a few items culled from London flea markets, a rich source for retro fashion; young English girls were scouring the flea markets for men's Gucci loafers to wear themselves.

"These girls were buying the men's loafers for themselves," Mello recalled. She and Lambertson picked up the cue and redid the women's loafer, making it sportier and more hip. "We changed the women's last to the men's last, made the vamp higher, and we did it in suede in sixteen different colors," Mello said.

One day, Mello and Lambertson drove up into the hills around Florence looking for a jewelry manufacturer who had worked for Gucci in the 1960s. When Mello and Lambertson pulled up in front of the place they had been told about, they discovered a wrinkled old man stoking a coal-burning stove in a small silver jewelry workshop. His eyes lit up as they explained their mission. He went over to a little safe and began to take out drawers full of Gucci jewelry he had made over the years.

"We sat on the floor in awe and went through drawer after drawer," said Mello. "It was wonderful. He could easily have sold everything for five times over what it cost him, but he knew someday someone would want to restore the brand—he had saved it all for that day," said Mello, who hired the little old man to start manufacturing for Gucci once again. "That was when we began to realize what we had," she said.

Then they turned to the bamboo-handle bag, the famed Model 0063. Enlarging it slightly to make it more practical, they also added a detachable leather shoulder strap and produced it in calfskin leather (for $895) and crocodile (for $8,000). For fall, they shrank it, manufacturing "baby" bamboo bags in satin, kidskin, and suede in a rainbow of colors from bubble gum pink, canary yellow, and purple to red, navy, and basic black.

Mello was also the first person at Gucci to take the Prada phenomenon seriously. Prada had begun to gather momentum in the mid-eighties when it began to attract a small following of Milan fashion insiders. In 1978, Miuccia Prada had invented an innovative nylon bag made from parachute material that had proved a simple, yet revolutionary concept at a time when most handbags were stiff, boxy, and made of leather. In 1986, a young woman who worked in Gucci's design office under the supervision of Giorgio and his wife, Maria Pia (who had assumed a larger role in product development after Paolo's departure), brought a sampling of the nylon Prada handbags to a design meeting in Scandicci.

"Prada was beginning to become a name among Milan's fashion elite," recalled Claudio Degl'Innocenti, whom Maurizio had recently hired to develop a new range of gift items and coordinate production. The soft nylon bags were scornfully disregarded as the insignificant products of a Milan merchant—they had nothing to do with the refined, highly constructed leather bags Gucci produced.

"The bags were not even taken into consideration," recalled Degl'Innocenti. "The whole concept of a soft bag didn't come to Gucci until several years later, and even then, with a lot of internal conflict—we had to retrain people who were used to making the hard leather bags."

Mello knew that she had to balance the revival of Gucci's traditions with the latest fashion trends, so she responded to women's need for a soft handbag that could be easily packed in a suitcase by reviving the hobo bag she remembered so fondly from her youth—a supple, roomy pouch that had not been sold since 1975. But, like a girl all dressed up with no place to go, Gucci's new look remained invisible to most of the fashion set, which was far more captivated by the exciting shows and whirlwind parties put on by designers such as Giorgio Armani, Valentino, and Gianni Versace.

"We couldn't get anyone to come and see us," recalled Mello. "It was a real problem." After the international press ignored her first presentation for Gucci at Florence's Villa Cora hotel in the spring of 1990, Mello had an idea. She asked her secretary to call up all the influential fashion editors in New York and ask for their shoe sizes; she mailed Gucci's new loafers to everyone she could think of. "That was how we got them," said Mello, with a satisfied smile.

By January of 1990, Maurizio had sent around a letter to some 665 U.S. retail clients announcing he was closing down the canvas Gucci Accessories

Collection and discontinuing the Gucci wholesale business to department stores—effective immediately. A wail of protest went up from top executives of leading department stores, but Maurizio refused to compromise. Domenico De Sole tried to dissuade him, knowing full well the canvas products represented the backbone of Gucci's business in the United States—with total revenues of nearly $100 million. De Sole appealed to Investcorp, telling them what Maurizio had done and warning them of the consequences. He thought it would be better to pare the business back more slowly.

Maurizio not only held fast, he also slashed the duty-free business worldwide. Between the GAC, the wholesale business, and the duty-free, the cuts represented some $110 million in total revenue.

"We can't clean our dirty linens in public," he insisted to the team at Investcorp. "We have to fix up our own house and then go back to the market from a position of strength. Then we will be able to command the terms," he said.

Maurizio knew he had to bury Gucci's "drugstore" image before he could bring the glamour back. From now on, Gucci's business would be limited exclusively to its then sixty-four wholly controlled stores—which Maurizio set about refurbishing with the help of his interior designer buddy, Toto Russo.

Maurizio wanted Gucci's customers to walk into his stores and feel as though they were in a plush, tastefully decorated living room. He left no detail to chance. With Toto, he developed new cabinets and fixtures in polished tanganica and walnut to display Gucci's new accessories and clothing. Cabinets were enclosed with fine, emerald-cut beveled glass. Round polished mahogany tables displayed rainbows of silk scarves and ties. Custom-made alabaster lamps hung from the ceiling with gold linked chains, creating warm, residential-like lighting. Original oil paintings graced the walls. Toto developed two chairs for the selling floor that he copied from original Russian antiques and reproduced in large quantities for the stores: the Czar chair, which went in the menswear selling area was modeled after a neoclassical piece, while the daintier walnut Nicoletta, dating from the 1800s, was for the women's area. The bills for these lavish furnishings mounted, but Maurizio waved them aside. He wanted the stores to be perfect.

"In order to sell style, we must have style!" he insisted.

When Mello saw that Russo's project—beautiful as it was—lacked the merchandising techniques she felt were important to sell the goods, she brought in American architect Naomi Leff to try to streamline some of the fixtures—creating an immediate clash between the Neapolitan interior designer and the American architect.

Maurizio had little time or inclination to mediate—he pressed forward with his plans. Thanks to the long days of cataloging Gucci's product offerings back in the eighties, Maurizio and his staff pared down the product line to some 7,000 items from 22,000, sliced the number of handbag styles from 350 to 100, and reduced the number of stores from more than 1,000 to 180.

In June 1990, Maurizio's new team presented its first fall collection. Gucci, as was its custom, rented space at the old Centro Meeting conference center in Florence for the entire month and invited Gucci's eight-hundred-some buyers from around the world to buy the collection.

Mello and Lambertson had set out the new bamboo bags, the hobo bags, and the loafers, all arranged in a rainbow of colors. When Maurizio arrived to preview the collection he walked slowly through it, looking at each item, speechless. Then he wept. His were tears of joy.

When all the staff and buyers had finally gathered in the showroom, he held up one of the new bamboo handbags for all to see. "This is what my father worked for," Maurizio said. "This is what Gucci used to be!"

Convinced that in order to achieve its new status Gucci needed to have a strong presence in Milan, Maurizio had started to look for an appropriate site for a new Gucci headquarters in Italy's fashion and financial capital. By the late 1980s, Milan already vied with Paris as an acclaimed fashion center. Paris was still the city of couture, while Milan had emerged as the center for modern, elegant ready-to-wear. Armani and Versace had become the kingpins of fashion in Milan, but there were also exciting new designers, such as Dolce & Gabbana. With journalists and buyers flocking to Milan twice a year for the seasonal designer fashion shows, Maurizio felt Gucci needed to be part of the action. Maurizio also felt far more at home in Milan than Florence, where some thought he even felt uncomfortable.

Again, with Toto's help, Maurizio rented a beautiful five-story building on Piazza San Fedele, a small square paved with smooth white stones located between the Duomo and La Scala, the opera house, that backed up onto the stately columns of Palazzo Marino, Milan's imposing city hall. The renovations proceeded at lightning speed and everything was ready in record time, less than five months from start to finish, including remodeling and furnishings—unheard of even for Milan.

The executive offices on the top floor all opened onto a spacious terrace circling the building, where table and chairs were set under a lattice arbor so on sunny days Gucci's top management could lunch outside. Maurizio's executive suite was one of Toto's crowning achievements. Walnut wainscoting, parquet floors, and forest green fabric on the walls gave a warm, elegant feel to Maurizio's office, which opened through double doors into a small conference room furnished with a square table and four chairs. Maurizio spent most of his time in this conference room, rather than at his Charles X desk, and preferred to receive visitors there, where they could spread out their materials and talk. He had brought the famous busts representing the four continents up from the old "Sala Dynasty" in Florence and set one in each corner of the conference room. Here he also hung a black-and-white photograph of his father, Rodolfo, and his grandfather Guccio. He had upgraded the old flip charts from Via Monte Napoleone into a modern, automated system with pages that advanced electronically set into discreet cupboards along one wall, where he also placed a television and stereo set. A pair of sliding doors opened from Maurizio's personal conference room into a large, formal boardroom. Entirely finished in walnut paneling, the room contained a long, oval conference table and twelve leather-covered chairs.

On the wall of his office, diagonally to the right of his desk and over the green leather studded couch from Via Monte Napoleone, Maurizio hung a painting of Venice that had belonged to his father. On the side table next to the couch went the black-and-white photograph of Rodolfo. The photo of his mother stood on his own desk, where he also kept a gimmicky gift from Allegra—a funny, battery-operated Coca-Cola can dressed like a person wearing eyeglasses that shook with laughter when somebody came into the room. Opposite the couch stood an antique console, on which he placed the smiling photographs of Alessandra and Allegra and a miniature trunk filled with crystal liquor bottles. Liliana's desk stood in the green carpeted entranceway in front of Maurizio's office, while Dawn Mello had asked for a small office on the other side of the floor with a view of the spires of Milan's cathedral—if she had to trade in her view of Central Park, at least she wanted to see the Duomo. She especially loved the double French doors that opened onto the terrace.

Administrative offices filled the fourth floor of the San Fedele building, and the design studio and offices took up the third floor. The press office was on the second floor, while Dawn had ordered a small showroom on the first floor for Gucci's seasonal presentations.

By September 1991, the new offices in Piazza San Fedele were ready and Maurizio organized a staff cocktail and dinner party on the rooftop terrace to inaugurate the new building. He welcomed them all with an enthusiastic speech and established a task force for each product area and business activity to study Gucci's relaunch.

Maurizio also believed that the company needed a more sophisticated approach to human resource issues and training to eliminate the factional fief-domlike management of the past and imbue all its employees with a common vision of Gucci. He developed the concept of a "Gucci school" to train employees in the Gucci history, the Gucci strategy, and a Gucci outlook in addition to offering professional and technical expertise.

To this end, Maurizio bought a sixteenth-century villa called Villa Bellosguardo that had belonged to the opera star Enrico Caruso, slated $10 million to refurbish it, and dreamed of establishing the Gucci school there. In Maurizio's mind, the villa would also serve as a cultural, conference, and exhibition center. Located in the Florentine hills at Lastra a Signa, Villa Bellosguardo overlooked the rolling hills and fields of the surrounding Tuscan countryside. A long drive bordered with sculptures of divine figures led to the front entrance of the villa, which was flanked by a gracious double staircase. Out back, steps led from a long, rectangular patio bordered by stone columns down to a Renaissance garden. On initial visits to Bellosguardo, however, Maurizio learned from the watchman that the villa was haunted, and decided to bring Frida—the psychic who had exorcised the *Creole*—down to banish any negative influences that might have lingered.

Maurizio couldn't exorcise the ghosts of his family's past battles as easily as those in the Villa Bellosguardo, however, and Gucci communications director Pilar Crespi recalled that they spent hours talking about how to deal with the past. While Maurizio encouraged a return to the principles of quality and style that had piloted Gucci to success, he shunned the family disputes that had dragged the name through the mud. Crespi found herself at a loss when journalists would call for information about the battle with Paolo, or background about the family wars.

"I kept getting these phone calls and going to him and saying, 'Maurizio, how are we going to deal with the past?'" Crespi said. "He was very angry with Paolo, in particular," she recalled. "He really didn't want to talk about him or the others. He would say, 'Gucci is a new Gucci, don't discuss the past! Paolo is the past—I am the new Gucci!'"

Maurizio had taken up the Gucci mantle, but he didn't know how to wash it of its stains. "I sat with him for hours. He never understood that the past would come back to haunt him," Crespi said.

In the fall of 1990, with the help of the McCann Erickson advertising agency, Mello showed how much she had learned from Maurizio's initial teachings and her visits to the local manufacturers. She created a $9 million advertising campaign featured in top fashion and lifestyle magazines such as

Vogue and *Vanity Fair,* built around the concept "The Hand of Gucci." The portfolio featured the suede loafers, rich-looking leather bags, and sporty new suede backpacks in an effort to show both Gucci's traditions and its come-back.

Though the first campaign was successful, Mello quickly realized that it was going to be difficult to sustain Gucci's new image without giving more importance to apparel. Even though Gucci had always done the bulk of its business in handbags and accessories, Mello knew that clothing was key to establish a concept on which to build Gucci's new identity.

"It was hard to create an image with a handbag and a pair of shoes," Mello said. "I convinced Maurizio that Gucci needed to have ready-to-wear for the image. We were always trying to pull Maurizio forward on the fashion side," she said.

Although Maurizio had pushed the fashion accelerator and hired Luciano Soprani back in the early eighties, during his Swiss exile he had revised his thinking to focus on Gucci's artisanal leather-working roots. By the early nineties, he did not believe pursuing a fashion strategy was right for Gucci.

"Maurizio's philosophy at the time was that he didn't believe in design-ers," said Lambertson, who was trying to build a full-fledged design team for Gucci. "He didn't believe in fashion shows and he didn't believe in promot-ing any one name to the detriment of Gucci's. He thought the accessories should speak for the company."

Up until then, all of Gucci's apparel had been done in-house, a costly, labor-intensive undertaking. Gucci didn't have the capacity to produce, mer-chandise, and distribute apparel competitively and it quickly became appar-ent that the company's best bet was to give a production contract to an apparel manufacturer. After a few seasons, Gucci struck agreements with two top-notch Italian clothing producers: Ermenegildo Zegna for the menswear and Zamasport for women's wear.

Lambertson also spent a lot of time looking for the right people to join their team—and then trying to convince them to move to Italy and work for Gucci. "We mostly spent the first six months just hiring people," he recalled. "It was hard to get anyone to work for Gucci at that point. And Maurizio didn't want to hire too many Americans—he was worried about keeping Gucci Italian."

When Mello and Lamberston arrived at Gucci, there was already a small group of young designers working there. "These kids were all from London and living in Scandicci," Lambertson recalled, "but nobody really paid any attention to them. They were isolated in their own world. The company didn't really believe in designers," he recalled. "Dawn and I kept stressing to Maurizio that we really needed a ready-to-wear designer."

As Mello and Lambertson built their team, a young, unknown New York designer named Tom Ford and his journalist boyfriend, Richard Buckley, were mulling over a move to Europe.

Ford was from a middle-class family in Austin, Texas, where he grew up until his family moved to Santa Fe, New Mexico—the home of his father's mother, Ruth—when he was a teenager. Both of his parents were real estate brokers. His mother was an attractive Tippi Hedren look-alike, who wore tailored clothes, simple heels, and her blond hair in a chignon. His father was a supportive, liberal-thinking man, who as Ford grew older also became a true friend.

"Growing up in Texas was really oppressive for me," Ford said. "If you're not white and Protestant and do certain things, it can be pretty rough, especially if you're a boy and don't want to play football and chew tobacco and get drunk all the time." Ford found Santa Fe much more sophisticated and stimulating and especially loved spending the summers at his grandmother Ruth's house, where he also lived for a year and a half. To Ford, Grandmother Ruth was an Auntie Mame character who dressed flamboyantly in big hats, big hair, big fake eyelashes, and big jewelry: bracelets, squash blossom buckles, concha belts, and papier-mâché earrings. As a boy, Ford loved to watch her get dressed for the cocktail parties she was always running off to.

"She was the kind of person who used to say, 'Ooooh, you like that honey? Well, go ahead and get ten of them,' " Ford said with a sweeping wave of his hand. "She was all about excess and openness and her life was much more glamorous than my parents' life—she just wanted to have fun! I'll always remember her smell. She wore Estée Lauder's Youth Dew—she was always trying to seem younger."

Ford believes those early memories had a fundamental impact on his design sensibility. "Most people are influenced throughout their lives by those very first images of beauty. Those images stick with you and they are the images of your taste. The aesthetics of the era you grew up in come with you."

Ford's parents encouraged him to explore his creative talent from an early age through drawing and painting and other such activities—without placing limits on his imagination.

"It didn't matter to them what I wanted to do, so long as I was happy," Ford said. From a young age, Ford had very specific ideas about what he liked and didn't like.

"From the time I was three I wouldn't wear THAT jacket and I didn't want THOSE shoes and THAT chair wasn't good enough," Ford recalled. As he grew older, when his parents went out to dinner or a movie he would recruit his younger sister into helping him rearrange the furniture, heaving and pulling sofas and chairs into new positions.

"It was never right, it was never good enough, it was always wrong," Ford said. "I really gave my family a complex. Even to this day they all say they get nervous when they see me. Even though I've learned not to say anything, they can feel me looking them up and down, clocking everything."

From the age of thirteen and after, Ford's personal uniform consisted of Gucci loafers, blue blazers, and button-down oxford shirts. He attended an exclusive Santa Fe prep school and dated girls—some of whom he fell in love with. But he had his eyes on New York City, where he went after graduating and enrolled at New York University. One night, a classmate invited him to a party; it didn't take Ford long to realize it was an all-guy party. In the middle of it, Andy Warhol showed up, and in no time the group traipsed off to Studio 54. A sweet, fresh-faced boy from the West with a movie star smile and an air of snob appeal, Ford was welcomed into the crowd. Before the night was over, Warhol was chatting earnestly with Ford and drugs appeared out of nowhere. Ford, whose lifestyle up to then had resembled that of the clean-cut boy in a toothpaste ad, blinked at the fast, hip life quickly unfolding around him. "It was a bit of a shock," Ford admitted later.

"He couldn't have been too shocked," retorted his classmate, the illustrator Ian Falconer, "because by the end of the night we were necking in a cab!" Before long, Ford became a regular at Studio 54. He partied all night, slept all day, and quit going to classes—much more interested in what he was picking up in his new club life.

"I had had friends back in Santa Fe that I had been obsessed with, but I didn't realize until I got to New York that I had been in love with them," Ford said. "I kind of knew it somewhere inside myself, but it was all pushed so far back."

By 1980, at the end of his freshman year, he dropped out of NYU altogether and started acting in television commercials. His good looks, speaking ability, and easy presence in front of the camera made him a success. He moved to Los Angeles. At one point he had twelve commercials on the air at the same time. Then one day the unthinkable happened. A hairdresser doing his hair for a Prell shampoo commercial did a double take at Ford's scalp, where the hairline was receding ever so slightly.

"Ooh, honey!" the male hairdresser said in a high, nasal voice. "You're losin' your hair." Ford's composure shattered.

"He was a bitchy queen and I was only nineteen or twenty and I just got paranoid," Ford recalls. For the rest of the shoot he kept his chin jutting downwards and with his fingers obsessively brushed his bangs ever lower over his forehead.

"The director kept stopping the camera and shouting, 'Would you please fix his hair!' " Ford recalled. The incident stayed with him. As he worked, insecurity about his hair mounting, Ford also found himself thinking, "I can write a better commercial," or "I would direct it this way" or "That looks better over there . . ." He realized that he wanted to be on the control side.

Ford enrolled at Parsons School of Design in New York, where he studied architecture, a field he had been interested in since the early days of rearranging his family living room. Partway through the program he moved to Paris, where Parsons also has a campus. But when he had nearly completed his studies, he realized that architecture was far too serious for his taste. An internship at French fashion house Chloè confirmed his sensation—the world of fashion was a lot more fun. Toward the end of his junior year he traveled to Russia for a two-week holiday; one night he came down with a bad bout of food poisoning and dragged himself back to his drafty hotel room.

"I was miserable and stayed in my room alone that night and I just started thinking," Ford said. "I knew I didn't want to do what I was doing, and all of a sudden, *FASHION DESIGNER* came into my head! It just came to me like a computer printout." He thought he knew what one needed to be a successful fashion designer—smarts, articulate speech, the ability to stand up in front of a camera, good ideas about what people should wear.

Ford's model had been Calvin Klein. Even before Armani was a big name in the United States, Ford remembered buying Calvin Klein sheets for his bed when he was in high school during the mid- to-late seventies.

"Calvin Klein was young, stylish, rich, and attractive," said Ford, remembering himself as a teenager poring over a magazine featuring slick black-and-white shots of Klein in his New York penthouse apartment.

"He licensed his name, he sold jeans, he sold ready-to-wear—he was the first fashion designer as movie star." Ford dreamed of becoming like Calvin Klein, whom he had actually met during his Studio 54 days and had followed around like an adoring puppy.

Back in Paris, the Parsons administration told Ford he would have to start his curriculum over from scratch if he wanted to major in fashion design—something Ford wasn't willing to do. He graduated in architecture in 1986, went back to New York, drew up a fashion portfolio, and started looking for a job; he just didn't mention what department he had graduated from and didn't let himself get discouraged by rejection.

"I guess I'm very naive or confident or both," Ford said. "When I want something I'm going to get it. I had decided I was going to be a fashion designer and one of those people was going to hire me!" He made a wish list and started calling designers every day.

"I told him on the phone I didn't have any positions open," recalled the New York–based designer Cathy Hardwick. "But he was so polite. 'Can I just show you my book?' One day I gave in. 'How soon can you come over?' I asked him. 'In one minute,' he said. He was down in the lobby!" Impressed by his work, Hardwick hired him.

"I didn't know how to do anything," Ford recalled. During his first few weeks with Cathy Hardwick, she asked him to make a circle skirt. He nodded, went downstairs, hopped on the uptown subway, and got out at Bloomingdale's, where he made a beeline for the dress department. There, he flipped all the circle skirts he could find inside-out to see how they were made. "Then I went back, drew the skirt, gave it to the pattern maker, and made a circle skirt!" Ford said.

Ford was working for Cathy Hardwick when he met Richard Buckley, then a writer and editor at fashion publishing house Fairchild Publications and today the Paris-based editor-in-chief for *Vogue Hommes International*. Ford was twenty-five and had movie-star looks—piercing dark eyes, a strong chin, and dark brown, shoulder-length hair. He still wore blue jeans and oxford button-down shirts. Buckley, thirty-seven, had sapphire-blue eyes, a stiff shock of salt-and-pepper hair he wore in a bristly crew cut, and a biting sense of humor that masked his shyness. He dressed in the fashion editor's eternal uniform: trim black pants, black boots with elastic insets at the ankles, a crisp white shirt without a tie, and a black jacket. Buckley had recently moved back to New York to head up Fairchild's then-new *Scene* magazine, now defunct, after working in Fairchild's Paris bureau as European editor of its menswear daily *DNR*. He had spotted Ford at a David Cameron fashion show. When he saw the young, dark-haired Ford, his heart had jumped for the first time in a long time. He hung around after the show with the excuse he had to interview some retailers—and looked around for Ford, who had vanished. Ford had noticed Buckley at the fashion show too.

"At one point I turned around and saw this guy just staring at me," Ford recalled. With his ice-blue eyes, spiky hair, and intent expression, Buckley looked possessed. "He scared me!" Ford said.

To Buckley's amazement, he came face-to-face with Ford himself ten days later, on the roof of the Fairchild building on West Thirty-fourth Street, where he was supervising a fashion shoot for *Scene*. Given the grueling pace of his job—he was fashion editor of the daily trade paper *Women's Wear Daily* as well as editor of *Scene*—he had resorted to the rooftop for a last-minute shoot. Cathy Hardwick had sent Ford over to pick up some clothes, which Buckley hadn't yet finished photographing. Just as Buckley was confiding in the art director about having seen Ford at the fashion show, Ford himself walked out on the rooftop to see about the clothes.

Buckley's eyes widened and he gulped. "That's him!" he whispered to the art director, "the guy I was telling you about . . ."

Buckley tried to greet Ford nonchalantly and asked if he could wait for the clothes, explaining that he hadn't finished shooting them yet. Ford agreed. As they took the elevator back downstairs together later, Buckley—usually witty and polished—found himself blathering shamelessly.

"He must have thought I was a complete idiot," Buckley recalled. Ford didn't.

"It sounds so silly, but I thought he was nice," Ford said later. "And in our business, it's rare to find people who are real and have a good heart."

On their first date, at Albuquerque Eats over on the East Side one November evening in 1986, Buckley and Ford quickly found themselves in deep conversation—which left Buckley impressed with Ford's focus and sense of mission. As they sipped drinks and munched shrimp quesadillas at their table amid the rollicking young crowd, Ford told Buckley exactly what he wanted to be doing ten years from then.

"I want to create clean sportswear with a European flair, more sophisticated and modern than Calvin Klein but with a sales volume like Ralph Lauren's," Ford said as Buckley listened with a mixture of pity and amazement.

"Ralph Lauren is the only designer that has really created an entire world," Ford explained earnestly to Buckley. "You know exactly what his kind of people look like, what their houses look like, what kind of cars they drive—and he is making all these products for them. I want to do that in my own way!"

Buckley leaned back against the padded leather seat of their booth and observed his handsome new friend. "He's so young and he already wants to be a millionaire," he thought to himself. "Just wait until he gets out there and gets beaten up in the rough-and-tumble world of New York fashion," Buckley thought, half feeling sorry for Ford and half hoping the young designer could prove himself despite the odds.

Something had clicked between the two men: one was focused, ambitious, and unknown; the other had become quite a man-about-town through his work for Fairchild—he went on to edit the gossipy "Eye" column—but hadn't lost his friendly, down-to-earth personality.

"Richard was nice, smart, and funny," said Ford. "He just had the whole package." Buckley and Ford moved in together that New Year's Eve. It would become the partnership of their lives.

Buckley had just moved into a 700-square-foot apartment on St. Mark's Place in the East Village; Ford was living in an apartment at Madison and Twenty-eighth that backed up onto a single-room-occupancy hotel. "The building was perfectly nice and so was the apartment, but at night the windows looked into these rooms where you could see people shooting up; it was very scary," recalled Ford.

"We agreed he would move in with me," Buckley said.

Two years later, a smooth-haired fox terrier also moved into the St. Mark's Place apartment, a birthday present from Buckley to Ford. "From the beginning, Tom wanted a dog," Buckley recalled. "I fought it for a long time, but I finally gave in." John, as they named the terrier, became their loyal companion and a shameless model whom they gussied up in wigs and outrageous drag outfits for Polaroid photos they sent to close friends. Despite his initial opposition, Buckley grew so attached to John it often seemed as though the friendly terrier was his own.

Meanwhile, in the spring of 1987, Ford, frustrated with his career, had quit Cathy Hardwick. He dreamed of landing a design job with Calvin Klein, the champion of the kind of clean sportswear Ford wanted to design. After nine separate interviews, two of which were with Calvin himself, Calvin Klein told Ford he wanted to hire him to work in the women's design studio. Ford was ecstatic—until he received the financial offer, which was far below his expectations. Ford asked for more money and Calvin said he had to discuss the request with his business partner, Barry Schwartz. After putting in several follow-up calls, Ford didn't hear anything back from Calvin Klein. When shortly thereafter designer Marc Jacobs asked him to come work with him at Perry Ellis, Ford accepted. Some time later, he came home from work one day to find a message from Calvin Klein's secretary on the answering machine.

"Mr. Klein is still very interested in you and he wants to make sure you haven't taken another job, and before you take another job would you call him first?" the message said. Ford called back to say thanks, he had already taken the job with Perry Ellis.

Buckley's career took a jump the following year when he left Fairchild in March 1989 to join Tina Brown's *Vanity Fair,* but his elation with the new job was quickly dampened. In April, Buckley was diagnosed with cancer. After what he had thought was acute tonsillitis failed to clear up after months of antibiotics, throat cultures, and a sunny trip to Puerto Rico, Buckley finally

Guccio Gucci, right, circa 1904 with his parents, Gabrielle and Elena.
Courtesy of Gucci

Artisans working in Via delle Caldaie. Courtesy of Gucci

Rodolfo Gucci as a young film
actor. Martinis/Croma

Sandra Ravel (Alessandra Winklehaussen), left, in *Those Three French Girls*
with actresses Fifi Dorsay and Yola D'Avril, 1931. Farabolafoto

Vasco (*left*) and Rodolfo Gucci (*right*) with a visitor in front of the handbag display in Gucci's Rome store. Martinis/Croma

Vasco, Aldo, and Rodolfo Gucci board the airplane for New York.
Martinis/Croma

Vasco and Aldo Gucci in New York. Martinis/Croma

Rodolfo Gucci helping a customer in the Milan store,
Via Monte Napoleone. Farabolafoto

Maurizio Gucci as a young boy skiing
with friends at Saint Moritz. Martinis

Sophia Loren leaving Gucci's Rome
store, Via Condotti. Farabolafoto

Jackie Onassis, circa 1979 in New York carrying the "Jackie" bag. The G-G version alone sold a record six thousand pieces when relaunched in 1999.
Farabolafoto

Paolo Gucci.
Edelstein/Grazia Neri

Maurizio and Patrizia
Gucci during the happy
days of their marriage.
Pizzi/Giacomino Foto

Maurizio, Allegra, Alessandra,
and Patrizia Gucci. Armando
Rotoletti/Grazia Neri

Maurizio Gucci in his Milan office with a photo of Rodolfo and Guccio, 1990. Art Streiber

The bamboo-handle bag. Courtesy of Gucci

Tom Ford and Dawn Mello in their favorite Milan restaurant, Alle Langhe. Davide Maestri

Maurizio Gucci and Paola Franchi in the living room of their apartment on Corso Venezia, 1994. Massimo Sestini/Grazia Neri

Maurizio Gucci's body being carried out of the foyer of Via Palestro, March 27, 1995. Farabolafoto

Allegra Gucci, Patrizia Reggiani, and Alessandra Gucci at Maurizio Gucci's funeral. Farabolafoto

Patrizia at home after Maurizio's death. Palmiro Mucci

Gucci creative director
Tom Ford. Courtesy of Gucci

Gucci CEO Domenico De Sole. Courtesy of Gucci

Model Amber Valetta in Gucci's March 1995 fashion show, which helped make Gucci hot again. Courtesy of Gucci

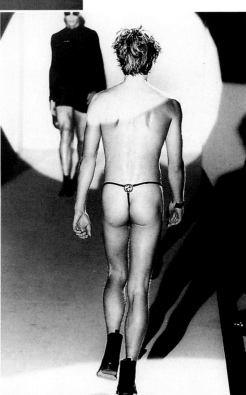

The Gucci G-string introduced in the January 1997 menswear collection.
Giovanni Giannoni

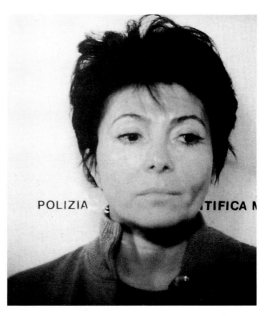

Patrizia Reggiani Martinelli
at the time of her arrest.
Farabolafoto

Pina Auriemma, "*La Maga Nera*," and her lawyers. Farabolafoto

The accused triggerman, Benedetto Ceraulo, and the accused driver of the getaway car, Orazio Cicala, on trial for the murder of Maurizio Gucci. Farabolafoto

(*From left*) Alessandra and Allegra Gucci, Silvana Reggiani, and Patrizia Reggiani Martinelli with one of her lawyers, Gaetano Pecorella, at her trial. Farabolafoto

Alessandra Gucci in a 1998 cover story entitled "No One Can Judge Us," in Italy's *Sette,* a weekly newsmagazine.
Photograph by Armando Rotoletti

Allegra Gucci in Corso Venezia sitting in front of a portrait of her mother.
Rotoletti/Grazia Neri

The Gucci dynasty: (*from left*) Giorgio, Maurizio, Roberto, Aldo, Alessandro, Paolo, Elisabetta, Patrizia, Guccio, and Rodolfo (*in front*).

checked into St. Luke's–Roosevelt Hospital for a biopsy, thinking he was going in for a minor procedure. When he came out of anesthesia, the surgeon at St. Luke's told him he had cancer, that he had to undergo more surgery the following week, and that his chances of surviving were 35 percent.

Buckley swallowed painfully, shook his head, and said, "No! No! No! I want to go home! I want my dog, and my own bed!" Ford went to the hospital and took Buckley home, then he got on the phone. From Buckley's Rolodex he pulled several names of leading New Yorkers who he knew were active in raising funds for the cancer research institute, Memorial Sloan-Kettering. Within twenty minutes, Buckley had an appointment two days later with a top surgeon and radiologist. Buckley then went through more surgery and months of painful radiation treatments. Ford called Buckley's family every day to update them on his condition.

When Buckley's doctors told him that it appeared that he had won his battle with cancer—but that he should lead a less stressful life—Buckley and Ford turned their sights on Europe. Ford felt that a designer working in New York could be a success in the United States, but that a successful designer in Europe could achieve global recognition. Buckley thought he could get a good writing job that would involve less pressure than what he had been doing. In early summer 1990, they financed a European trip out of their own pockets, and started doing rounds of interviews. Ford had already called his friend Richard Lambertson on a previous trip to Milan, and had dinner with Lambertson and Dawn Mello. There Lambertson urged Mello to consider Ford for Gucci's women's ready-to-wear, but she shook her head. Her policy was "no friends." In the meantime, thanks to his fashion contacts, Buckley had lined up a whirlwind round of appointments for Ford with just about every leading design house in Milan. After a sumptuous lunch with Donatella Versace, and meetings with Gabriella Forte at Giorgio Armani and Carla Fendi (who had met with Ford in New York and been impressed with his talent), there was still no job offer for Ford. They lunched again with Dawn Mello, who this time agreed to give Ford a trial project. After their lunch, Ford and Buckley went to the most exclusive florist in Milan and sent her a massive bouquet of the kind only Italians send, drowned in sprays of baby's breath. "We were horrified when we saw all that baby's breath and made them pull it all out!" Buckley recalled.

"Dawn at that point had seen every wannabe in Milan," Buckley said. "All the young designers out there wanted to reinvent the skirt. Tom already knew that you can't reinvent the skirt. The key is what skirt you do at what time," Buckley said. Mello loved the project Ford did for her so much she agreed to bend her own rules and hire him.

"I just sensed he could do anything," Mello said later.

Ford moved to Milan in September 1990, and Buckley joined him in October as the new European editor of *Mirabella* magazine.

For the first few days they lived in classy, though cramped quarters in a chic residence in Via Santo Spirito, located in Milan's golden shopping triangle. The room, which was about the size of a closet, was nonetheless fully equipped with a cooking corner and luxurious trappings such as Frette sheets and Alessi pots and pans. Between Buckley, Ford, and eight enormous suitcases, they could hardly turn around. After a few days they found a pleasant apartment on Via Orti in southeast Milan with a large, wisteria-covered terrace, where John joined them. They furnished their new home with a mix of old pieces they had shipped over from New York and new pieces they had fun collecting in Europe, including a Biedermeier chest, two Charles X armchairs, and patterned upholstery.

Ford and Buckley's life in Milan soon settled into a routine. They made friends with the other young assistants on the Gucci design team, which soon became a tight-knit group. Together, they all learned the ups and downs of living in Milan—the food, the fashion parties, the ski weekends in the Alps, the long hours, the dreary weather.

"Everybody felt a little displaced," recalled David Bamber, the knitwear designer. "Milan was so different from New York."

Ford and Buckley had brought a multisystem VCR and later invested in a satellite dish. When they weren't out to dinner with friends and colleagues, they stayed home and watched old movies in English. Blockbuster Video hadn't yet opened in Milan, but Buckley brought back a stack of home videos every time he came back from New York—where he traveled often for cancer treatments. They watched their favorite movies over and over. Later, Ford would use that habit purposefully to zero in on a mood he wanted to capture for a collection.

Ford and Buckley's apartment became a meeting ground for their new friends in Milan, all of whom were somehow connected to the fashion and design community. The small group would gather on the terrace at Via Orti for home-cooked meals Buckley prepared, and Ford often invited his design team over for evening work sessions.

"We were supposed to be doing a cross between Calvin Klein and Timberland," recalled David Bamber, who also traveled to Scotland to develop a cashmere program for Gucci, commissioning classic cashmere sweaters in a rainbow of colors.

The Americans proved vital to Gucci's future. Dawn Mello went far beyond resurrecting long-lost Gucci designs and artifacts for high-style accessories. She captured the attention of the all-important fashion press, promoted the company's move into mainstream apparel, and recruited the innovative young designers who convinced the doubters that designer clothing indeed belonged in Gucci's constellation. Among the designers, Tom Ford, of course, was the star whose stiletto heels, sleek suits, and fashion handbags would resuscitate Gucci's fame and fortune. Beyond their talent, Mello and Ford offered Gucci something else crucial to Gucci's success—the staying power to ride out the storms ahead.

12

DIVORCE

The sun shone brightly the morning of January 22, 1990, taking the chill out of the air as mourners, wrapped in furs and winter coats, crowded into the church of Santa Chiara off of Rome's Via della Camilluccia to pay their last respects to Aldo Gucci. His death shocked many of his friends and acquaintances. Dynamic and agile up to the end, Aldo appeared much younger than his eighty-four years. Few realized how old he was or that he had been undergoing treatments for prostate cancer. Not even a year had passed since that April afternoon in Geneva when he had been forced to sell his Gucci shares.

Aldo had moved to divorce Olwen in December of 1984, many years after their marriage had ceased to thrive. Although they no longer lived together, he visited her when in Rome, moving in and out of the villa he had built off the Via della Camilluccia as freely and comfortably as though in his own home. His request for a divorce shocked Olwen, who was frail after suffering an attack of thrombosis in 1978. Olwen stood her legal ground, though she had never obstructed him from doing what he wanted. Aldo had pursued his lifestyle where and with whom he pleased—even marrying Bruna in the United States.

Aldo had spent the Christmas holidays quietly in Rome with Bruna and their daughter, Patricia, but he had come down with a virulent, worsening flu. That Thursday night he quietly slipped into a coma; Friday his heart stopped beating.

At the church, Giorgio, Roberto, Paolo, and their families took their places in the front pews near Aldo's casket. Maurizio had flown down from Milan with Andrea Morante. As they entered the church, Morante stayed along the back wall, not wanting to intrude on such a personal, family moment, while Maurizio walked forward to stand alone at one side of the church.

On the opposite side of the church, off to one side, stood Bruna and Patricia, not sure of their proper place in the ceremony until Giorgio welcomed them and brought them over to stand with his family in one of the pews. Roberto accompanied his elderly and frail mother, Olwen, and stood by her protectively. Shortly thereafter, she was admitted to a Rome clinic for her poor health. Even in death, the irrepressible Aldo stirred up controversy: he had left his American estate, worth an estimated $30 million, to Bruna and Patricia, a move that was contested by Olwen and two of their three sons, Paolo and Roberto, although the families later reached an amicable solution.

As Maurizio stood by himself in the chilly church, he looked down at his clasped hands in front of him and let the rise and fall of the priest's voice float through his mind. He pictured Aldo scaling the stairs of his Via Condotti office two at a time, barking orders to his salesclerks right and left, or holding court in the New York store, signing Christmas packages. His mind's ear heard Aldo's voice repeating his old adage about the dynamics of the family—"My family is the train, I am the engine. Without the train, the engine is nothing. Without the engine, well, the train doesn't move." Maurizio smiled. As the mourners around him shifted their feet and dabbed at their eyes with soggy tissues, Maurizio unclasped his hands, then clenched and unclenched his fists as though for warmth.

"Now I must be both the engine and the train," he said to himself. "And I must bring Gucci back under one roof." He repeated his personal mantra over and over again: "There is only one Gucci, there is only one Gucci."

Investcorp had served him well, helping him put an end to the family power struggles, but it was time to do what he had dreamed of for so long—bring the two halves of the company together. He knew that Aldo, despite their differences, would have wanted that. Only he, Maurizio, could bring continuity to Gucci—he was the link between the past and the future. In December, Maurizio had told Nemir Kirdar he wanted to buy back the outstanding 50 percent of Gucci from Investcorp, and Kirdar had agreed. Maurizio wanted to carry out the restructuring himself—he wanted to achieve his dream for Gucci without an outside partner.

After the service, Maurizio lingered to greet his relatives and many of the longtime Gucci employees who had attended the funeral. Giorgio, Roberto, and Paolo received him coolly. They would never forgive Maurizio for the way he had taken over Gucci and for humiliating their father. Maurizio had become an easy scapegoat for the deep sense of loss they felt. Seeing him at Aldo's funeral, dressed in his characteristic gray double-breasted suit and accompanied by Andrea Morante—the man who had bought them all out—didn't make them feel any better. On the drive back to Florence for Aldo's burial, Maurizio reiterated his promise to himself that he would do everything in his power to get all of Gucci back.

Maurizio had successfully negotiated an agreement to buy Investcorp's 50 percent stake in Gucci for $350 million. That same January, at Investcorp's annual management committee meeting in Bahrain, Nemir Kirdar stood up before his colleagues and announced not only that Investcorp had agreed to sell Maurizio its stake, but that it would do everything to help him arrange the financing to do so.

"There is no more important project on our table than helping Maurizio get financing to buy us out," Kirdar said, looking around the room at his team. "We have played our part, we have assembled the shares, now Maurizio Gucci's name is on the door, we must let him take the company and go his own way."

Bob Glaser, one of Investcorp's senior executives, protested to Kirdar that it was highly unusual for a seller to help arrange financing for the buyer. He also pointed out that Maurizio didn't have the tools to explain the Gucci business to the banking community in a way they could understand. Glaser—who hadn't been involved in the acquisition of the initial 50 percent—went through Investcorp's files on Gucci, looking for information.

"I was shocked that we didn't have even the basic level of financial and background information on Gucci that we were used to having before making an initial investment," Glaser recalled. He put Rick Swanson, who had been working closely with Maurizio, on the job; his mission was to research and write a detailed document that would describe the Gucci business and its potential.

"Swanson was doing the work that should have been done by Maurizio—for free!" Glaser pointed out.

Swanson quickly discovered that the task was easier said than done. He struggled to portray Gucci's worldwide companies in Italy, the United States, England, and Japan as a unified whole—when in fact each functioned independently.

"I had to take this disparate group of companies with no global management team and a vision that was only starting to be formed and pull it together into a cohesive business and financial plan that the bankers could understand. It was something that didn't really exist," Swanson said.

Gucci had evolved constantly under Maurizio's restructuring program and Swanson struggled to incorporate all the changes. Maurizio had slashed the canvas business, revamped the product, and closed stores that weren't up to his new standards. He bought the Villa Bellosguardo and talked about selling off some New York real estate to recoup some fresh cash. Through it all, Investcorp gave him a free hand.

"The horse was out of the barn!" Swanson said. "We owned fifty percent but we could not control what he was doing." Swanson flew to Milan and sat down with Maurizio at the flip chart in the conference room, and together they drew boxes and sketched in the management structure. Maurizio had a modern corporate management framework all figured out, including positions in strategy and planning, finance and accounting, licensing and distribution, production, technology, human relations, image, and communications.

"Then we had to price it out," said Swanson. "Maurizio had never bothered to put a figure on what it was going to cost to add all these new positions," Swanson said. The figure, including the elegant new Piazza San Fedele headquarters, came to more than $30 million—an enormous increase, especially in view of the sharp cuts Maurizio had made in products and distribution. Maurizio's plan left Swanson aghast.

"Maurizio, in this region, Gucci did $110 million last year," Swanson said, pointing to his charts.

"Okay," Maurizio replied, leaning back in his chair and squinting his eyes in mock concentration. "One hundred twenty-five, one hundred fifty, one hundred eighty-five."

Swanson looked at him blankly.

"What do you mean?"

"Those are the projections, no?" Maurizio answered, looking matter-of-factly at Swanson.

"Ahh, are you doing those on a percent basis?" Swanson countered, ever the accountant, trying to follow Maurizio's logic.

"Oh, no, no, no, percents are irrelevant," Maurizio said, waving his hand and clucking his tongue. "One hundred twenty-five, one hundred fif—no, let's make that one hundred sixty . . ."

Swanson packed up his documents and flew to London, where he poured out his frustrations to Eli Hallak, Investcorp's chief financial officer, and Bob Glaser, a tough, feet-on-the-ground, red-bearded banker whom Kirdar had also asked to negotiate the terms of the sale to Maurizio.

"Bob," Kirdar had said, "you're the only guy I can trust not to get seduced by Maurizio!" Glaser was one of the close-knit team that Kirdar had recruited from Chase's Middle East operation. He was a clever clear-thinking, straight-talking man who knew how to get things done.

Swanson tried to explain his dilemma to the two Investcorp executives. "I am trying to write this book for Maurizio and make this as easy and risk-free and digestible for the bankers as possible," he complained. "And while I am doing it, not only does the ball keep moving, but Maurizio is pulling sales projections out of thin air!"

Glaser and Hallak looked at each other and shook their heads. Neither of them had been impressed by Maurizio's business acumen and both doubted he could pull off the repositioning by himself.

Glaser feared Maurizio had launched into the repositioning too fast—cutting sales and increasing costs.

"Investcorp had never signed off on the financial implications of Maurizio's plan for Gucci," Glaser recalled. "It was all very conceptual—Maurizio presented his plan and Kirdar had said it sounded good to him."

Swanson finally finished his report—a massive document of some three hundred pages, including company history, family trees, detailed fact sheets, schedules of assets, stores, and licenses. The "Green Book," as Swanson and his colleagues nicknamed the detailed information memorandum, included projections—a temporary decline in sales and operating performance from pruning products and stores. Then the curve came back up as sales were scheduled to improve.

Investcorp helped Maurizio sell his proposal to the banks, identifying the institutions, sending out the memorandums, and introducing Maurizio to the bankers themselves.

Not one of the major international or Italian banks would finance

Maurizio's business plan. One after the other, more than twenty-five financial institutions turned Maurizio down.

"It didn't work," Swanson said later. "The company wasn't doing well, the numbers were heading south. We spun wonderful stories and all the bankers loved Maurizio and it was a wonderful vision, but when you dug below the surface and looked at the numbers, the bankers could see that it fell apart—even though Maurizio could always find some wonderful anecdotes. To hear him tell it, the business was not only performing, but exceeding expectations! Maurizio was like Scarlett O'Hara in *Gone With the Wind*— tomorrow was always another day," Swanson said. "He truly felt that if he couldn't get the financing today, he would get it tomorrow; if he could just survive another day, he would win."

In the meantime, Glaser had spent months trying to negotiate a sales agreement with Maurizio—going through three separate full-fledged contract negotiations, which employed squads of lawyers and pounds of documents. Glaser began to get the feeling that Maurizio was cleverly stringing him along—perhaps an effort to keep him busy and engaged while he searched for the financing.

By the summer of 1990, it became clear even to Maurizio that there wasn't going to be any financing. He and Investcorp changed course once again and agreed to go forward together as fifty-fifty partners under the principles they had laid down three years earlier in the Saddle Agreement. To do so, Maurizio told Investcorp he wanted to streamline all of Gucci's operating companies around the world into a single holding company—a giant modernization step in the corporate structure of the Gucci business. Kirdar agreed, and assigned Bob Glaser the task. Glaser agreed to do it on one condition: that the two partners establish a working set of rules about how they were going to govern the company and the interests of each shareholder. After seeing Maurizio's actions in the years since Investcorp made its investment in Gucci, Glaser wanted to make sure the investment bank had a meaningful say in the running of the business.

The process of fleshing out a precise, legal operating structure for the relationship between Maurizio Gucci and Investcorp put a major strain on their relationship. "Trust is one thing, but we had to spell out how we were going to protect our investment if one day we did not see eye to eye. That's what started the conflict," Kirdar said. "It became a legal nightmare. Maurizio had always been attacked, there was never anyone in his life whom he could really trust and now, all of a sudden, the comfort that he had taken in Investcorp turns into another nightmare of people who he is afraid want to take advantage of him."

At times, the discussions between lawyers on both sides became so confrontational that Maurizio would call a time-out and ask to see Kirdar. He would go to London, shaken by all the obstacles that had been thrown up, and they would sit in the easy chairs in front of the fireplace and talk.

"Tell me, Maurizio, what is the problem?" Kirdar would say, his green eyes smiling benevolently at his visitor.

"Nemir, they are being too harsh," Maurizio would say, shaking his head.

"It is not our intent to be harsh," Kirdar would assure him. "If that is too harsh, let's change it. I am not trying to attack you or trick you; my lawyers are not either. They are just doing their job." And Maurizio would leave, reassured, until the next conflict. By the time the whole process was over, however, Maurizio hated and mistrusted Bob Glaser, whom he nicknamed "the devil with the red beard" or, alternatively, "Mr. What-if?"

"I had to play the hard guy," admitted Glaser later. "It's a role I played reasonably well and Maurizio didn't like it at all. I was the first person at Investcorp to tell him that he couldn't have something he wanted. My experience with Maurizio was that first he would try to charm you. Then he would try to intimidate you. If he could neither charm you nor intimidate you, he would just back down."

Allan Tuttle—true to his promise to Rodolfo—had continued to represent Maurizio personally and was on the front lines for his client in the dealings with Investcorp. Tuttle was a punctilious, tenacious advocate for Maurizio—so much so that Glaser, exasperated, finally forced Maurizio to take him off the account.

"I knew Tuttle was doing a damn good job for Maurizio, but I also realized that I was never going to get the deal signed as long as he was around. I'd had it! I told Maurizio I wasn't going to another meeting if Tuttle was in the room and that he had better find another lawyer!"

Afraid of scuttling the entire deal, Maurizio reluctantly agreed, and hired another lawyer. As a result, Investcorp won several key points in their agreement—which ultimately amounted to some two hundred pages—that would profoundly affect the future of the company. Among other provisions, the agreement forbade Maurizio to put up all or part of his 50 percent stake in Gucci as collateral for financing—although Investcorp was free to do so if it wanted.

"We were a financial institution; borrowing and lending was part of our business," Glaser said. "But we couldn't risk the possibility that Maurizio could borrow, default, and leave us with a new partner. Nemir Kirdar insisted on this."

Asked at the last minute to review the agreement for compliance with New York law, Tuttle was astonished, in particular at the limitations it placed on Maurizio's use of his shares. "Maurizio, they have tied you up tighter than a drum!" said Tuttle, who tried to make some last-minute changes that would have given Maurizio a little more flexibility.

"He was a rich man, but he didn't have any money," Tuttle said later.

Glaser went even further. After the grueling process of hammering out the new business partnership between Investcorp and Maurizio Gucci, he stood up at an Investcorp meeting in London and denounced Maurizio as either an incompetent CEO, possibly a crook, or both. A murmur traveled around the room of Investcorp executives, most of whom had been charmed by Maurizio—it was as though Glaser had said the emperor had no clothes. Nemir's piercing green eyes narrowed in anger.

"You have no right to say those things about Maurizio!" he shouted. "We are trying to help him!"

"I'm sorry if you don't agree with me," said Glaser. "It's just my opinion. I can't prove anything, but there is no reason for the company to be generating the losses that it is! I think it's suspicious and I want to hire an independent auditing firm to go through the books from start to finish!"

Bob Glaser, who by then was ready to return to the United States after finishing the tasks at Gucci that Kirdar had assigned him, then recommended that Kirdar replace him on the Gucci account, recognizing how damaging his stand had been to the relationship. Kirdar agreed and asked a thoughtful, soft-spoken banker he had recently hired named William Flanz to take over the case. Flanz came to Milan a few times that fall and started taking note of what was going on at Gucci.

In the meantime, Andrea Morante had carved out a role for himself at Gucci's Milan headquarters as chief operating officer, although he had never been given an official title. He helped Maurizio hire his new team, reviewed pricing worldwide, and acquired sole control of Gucci's business in Japan from its long-standing partner, Choichiro Motoyama. An investment banker at heart, Morante started working on a project he hoped would resolve everybody's problems. He crafted an agreement with Henry Racamier, the expelled chairman of Louis Vuitton. Racamier had formed his own group, Orcofi, as a vehicle for acquisitions in the luxury goods business he hoped would one day rival those owned by Moët Hennessy Louis Vuitton (LVMH). Morante felt Racamier would make a strong partner for Maurizio and could help develop Gucci's business in the Far East, where Racamier had had significant business success with Louis Vuitton. Morante structured a deal that would finally give Maurizio control of Gucci with 51 percent, bring in Racamier with 40 percent and a say on the board, leave Investcorp with a symbolic presence of 7 or 8 percent, and award the rest to management—namely, to Morante himself.

"This deal would have helped Maurizio get control, given Investcorp an elegant exit, and would have been one of the crowning achievements of my career," Morante said.

Maurizio was thrilled. The two of them spent hours analyzing and discussing the opportunity, which would have been one of the first strategic alliances between an Italian company and a French one in the luxury goods business. Up to then, the French luxury industry had viewed the Italian firms primarily as suppliers or second-rate competitors.

In the fall of 1990, while Morante was developing the proposal, Maurizio invited him along with his friend Toto Russo for a sailing weekened on the *Creole* for the Nioularge, an annual regatta of historic sailboats in Saint-Tropez. The regatta was a high-level, not-to-be-missed sea party for Europe's rich industrialists. Conveniently located for boat owners who wintered their mega-yachts in Antibes and other warm-water Mediterranean ports, the Nioularge effectively ended the summer regatta season. All the leading French and Italian industrialists participated, including Raul Gardini with *Il Moro di Venezia,* which had raced in the America's Cup. Gianni Agnelli, the dashing chairman of Italy's Fiat SpA automobile group, invariably showed up to follow the race in whatever boat he had at the time, but rarely competed in the regatta itself. Maurizio's invitation to Morante was significant, symbolic, and meant to impress; only his most intimate and trusted friends received an invitation to sail on the *Creole.* Morante was deeply pleased that Maurizio had brought him into his inner circle.

"The idea of this weekend was to have a good time and at the same time to reflect together, in a pleasant setting, about all that was going on," recalled Morante.

Maurizio chartered a small jet to fly them from Milan to Nice on the Friday afternoon, where they boarded a helicopter to Saint-Tropez, even as dark storm clouds mounted on the horizon. The helicopter swayed and hiccuped in the winds and clouds that quickly enveloped the small port town, shaking up its passengers during the trip. Relieved to land in the small heliport in the center of Saint-Tropez, the three men walked over to the dock where the *Creole*'s mahogany tender awaited them and the three-masted silhouette of the *Creole* rose in the distance. The *Creole,* too large at more than two hundred feet long to enter the port, was anchored just outside the small bay of Saint-Tropez.

The three men bantered lightheartedly about the weather, the boat, the weekend ahead. Maurizio recounted his misadventures in rehabilitating the *Creole,* from the day he fired the architect Patrizia had hired, to the day during the summer of 1986 when the creaking schooner was docked in the La Spezia shipyard for repairs. As Paolo circulated his accusations that the *Creole* had been illegally acquired, Maurizio had grown nervous that the authorities might try to sequester his dream yacht. One morning he had ordered the captain to weigh anchor, hoist the sails, and flee the harbor with carpenters still aboard on the pretense of a trial run. The *Creole* stopped in Malta to let off the perplexed workmen, then set sail for the Spanish port Palma de Mallorca, which would become its new home. Maurizio described for Morante his no-cost-barred efforts to restore the ship to its former glory and equip it with all the modern technology available. Toto Russo had helped Maurizio infuse the schooner's rooms with his luxurious, old-world style—all at spectacular prices. To redo just one of the staterooms he had spent $970,000. The *Creole* truly had become one of the most beautiful yachts in the world—at a cost that would prove far dearer than Maurizio ever imagined.

The men sped over the water toward the yacht in the tender, falling silent as the imposing dark mass of the magnificent schooner loomed overhead.

They stepped on board, greeted the skipper, a smiling Englishman named John Bardon, and, in a ship's ritual, saluted the flag. Then Maurizio gave Morante a quick tour. Maurizio had turned Stavros Niarchos's former deck-top cabin into a sumptuous living room with oil paintings, a marble table, and a state-of-the-art sound system. Just belowdecks in the stern stood four double cabins, each paneled in a different kind of precious wood—teak, mahogany, cedar, and briarwood—and decorated with Oriental paintings; and each with its own bathroom well stocked with fine towels and toiletries, all exclusively prepared for the *Creole.* Opposite Maurizio's master suite on the starboard side of the boat was the ship's dining room, arranged with a comfortable, finely upholstered bench along one side of two folding wooden tables that could be extended to seat twelve, or folded to form two smaller coffee tables. A bar and service station, a laundry, and crew's quarters were on the same deck in the forward half of the ship, while the kitchen and the motor room nestled deep in the belly of the vessel.

Maurizio issued Morante and Russo each an onboard uniform, which he had specially commissioned for guests, consisting of white sweatshirt and slacks with the *Creole*'s emblem, a pair of intertwined mythological seahorses with unicorn heads. Then Maurizio darted off to find Bardon and catch up on the sailing gossip. Morante dutifully changed into the uniform Maurizio had provided and went off in search of Toto, whom he found in the living room, where the sound of Maurizio's voice, chatting and laughing happily downstairs with Bardon, floated up the stairs.

Russo showed Morante around the room, pointing out the seamlessly fitted boiserie, the graceful brass light fixtures shaped like jumping fish that he had had custom-made based on an antique, and a rose-colored marble table with a cast-bronze base in the form of intertwined seahorses—also a well-done copy. Then, drinks in hand, the two men flopped down opposite each other on two leather couches—one cream colored, one gray—two of Maurizio's most prized pieces, and made from real sharkskin. Russo indicated the soft blue-gray sheen on the walls behind their heads and raised his dark eyebrows. "The skin of stingrays imported from Japan!" he said dramatically. Maurizio's idea, he explained, had been to create a refined maritime decor without resorting to kitschy shell and boat motifs.

"Impressive, very impressive," Morante murmured, gazing at the painting on the wall across from him, a sunset scene of the mouth of the Nile, bathed in shimmering light.

Russo could tell that Morante, though admiring, was preoccupied. The two men had clashed recently as Morante began contesting Russo's astronomical bills for remodeling the Gucci stores. Russo, who had thrived on Maurizio's money-is-no-object attitude, sized up the executive, whose growing influence over Maurizio concerned him.

"Andrea, tell me, how are things really going at Gucci?" Russo asked him probingly.

"Not too well, Toto," Morante replied earnestly, setting down his glass.

"Tell me," Toto said.

"Well, it's a difficult time, the market is down, Maurizio's ideas are great, he has the right view for Gucci, but he really needs someone to help him manage it. He needs to delegate that, otherwise things are only going to get worse," Morante said, pressing his lips together under his bristly salt-and-pepper mustache, his forehead creasing into a deep frown.

"That's what I was afraid of, Andrea," Russo said.

"The thing that troubles me is that he doesn't seem to realize what is happening," said Morante. "I mean, he sees all the figures, he knows everything, but somehow, he's oblivious to it all."

"You know, Andrea, we are his only friends, everyone else is out to get something from him," said Russo. "We owe it to him to tell him. We should talk to him—you should tell him—he trusts you."

"I don't know, Toto," said Morante, shaking his head. "He might take it the wrong way. You know how he feels about Gucci, it's as though he has to prove to everyone he can do it himself."

Despite his misgivings, Morante promised Russo he would talk with Maurizio about his concerns. They agreed to wait until Sunday night, so as not to spoil the weekend. Morante hoped the relaxed and beautiful setting would make Maurizio more open to what he had to say.

At that moment, Maurizio bounded up the stairs and into the room, grinning with pleasure, to call them to dinner downstairs in the ship's dining room. The cook had prepared his specialty, one of Maurizio's favorite dishes, *spaghetti al riccio di mare,* or spaghetti with sea urchin, followed by a delicately grilled fish. Maurizio had stocked the ship's coolers with cases of a crisp white Montrachet—wine experts called it the best white burgundy— that he had taken a particular liking to. After dinner they all lounged in the living room, drinking more Montrachet and listening to music. Maurizio played a popular hit of that time, *"Mi Manchi"* (*"*Missing You*"),* over and over again, listening to the sultry voice of Italian pop singer Anna Oxa and thinking about Sheree, with whom he had broken up not long before.

After seeing each other for several years, Sheree had asked Maurizio his intentions—what did he have in mind for her and their relationship? She would have liked to build something more solid with him, perhaps even start a family together. He had to admit to himself—and to Sheree—that he wasn't the man for her. He already had a family—fragmented as it was—and hoped to reunite with his daughters one day. He was also so completely immersed in Gucci's relaunch that he had little time left over for his personal life. He let Sheree go—though he missed her warm, loving, easygoing companionship.

By morning the clouds had cleared and the *Creole*'s passengers awoke to a sunny sky and a brisk breeze that promised an exciting regatta. The men donned *Creole* windbreakers and climbed to the roof of the instrument room, from where they could observe every maneuver without getting in the sailors' way. Crew members scurried about preparing the lines and sails for the race and, as they hoisted the heavy anchor, the *Creole* surged forward smoothly the instant the sails caught wind. Bardon, trilling orders in the old style with a whistle, had the crew test conditions with a few sweeping turns.

Suddenly the men looked up as a sleek blue 97-foot sloop approached. A deeply tanned man with a shock of snow-white hair stood at the wheel. The boat was *Extra Beat* and the man was none other than Gianni Agnelli, then chairman of the Fiat SpA automobile manufacturer, dubbed Italy's unofficial king for his power and stature. An elegant, cultivated man, married to the beautiful Principessa Marcella Caracciolo, Agnelli commanded national respect and pride awarded to few—if any—of the nation's political leaders. The Italian press referred to Agnelli as *L'Avvocato,* or "The Lawyer."

Agnelli directed one of his crew to ask permission to come aboard; it wasn't the first time he had asked. Once, when the boat was in port for repairs, Maurizio had seen Agnelli coming and ducked down into one of the cabins, asking a worker who was on board to say Mr. Gucci was out and decline the request.

Maurizio once again relayed a negative response back to Agnelli through one of his sailors, saying that renovations on the *Creole* weren't complete and that the boat wasn't ready for visitors. At that, Agnelli executed a sharp maneuver and brought *Extra Beat* antagonistically close to *Creole*'s side, alarming the schooner's skipper and crew and attracting a swarm of paparazzi that darted in and out of the churning wakes for shots of the confrontation.

"Agnelli had wanted for some time to pay his respects to this magnificent boat," said Morante, "but Maurizio was always afraid Agnelli wanted to buy it from him, just as he had been afraid Agnelli wanted to buy his Saint Moritz estate."

On Sunday, the *Creole*'s passengers skipped the traditional awards ceremony and that evening motored into town, watching as the clustered medley of yellow, orange, and pink buildings, bathed in twilight, grew closer. Maurizio and his guests had exchanged their *Creole* uniforms for pressed khakis and button-down oxford shirts with colorful cashmere sweaters thrown loosely around their shoulders. They walked past the ranks of sidewalk artists and their easels and through the picturesque streets of Saint-Tropez to Maurizio's favorite restaurant, known for its fish dishes, nestled deep in the old town. They took a table and a waitress served them water and a bottle of wine. Maurizio poured three glasses, joking about the Agnelli episode, and ordered fish for all of them. Russo, sitting to Maurizio's left, glared across the table at Morante and mouthed for him to broach the subject of Gucci, but Morante ignored him and kept on chatting with Maurizio. During the first course, Russo kicked Morante under the table, signaling him to get down to business. Morante finally gave a nod to Russo and cleared his throat.

"Maurizio, there's something Toto and I want to talk to you about," Morante said, glancing over at Russo for support.

Maurizio noted the serious tone in Morante's voice.

"Yes, Andrea, what is it?" replied Maurizio, looking over at Russo as though for clarification, although Russo remained silent.

"You aren't going to like what I have to say to you, but I feel as a true friend of yours, I have to tell you. Please try to take this in the spirit of our friendship," Morante said. "You have so many qualities, Maurizio," Morante started out in his smooth, resonant voice. "You are smart and charming and nobody can get people excited about the changes at Gucci the way you can. You have a whole set of attributes, but . . . let's be realistic, not everyone is a natural manager. We have been through a lot together, but I feel I have to tell you, I don't think you know how to manage this company. I think you should let someone else—"

Maurizio slammed his fist down on the table so hard he knocked over their wineglasses and set the silverware dancing a tinkling tango.

"NO!" said Maurizio loudly as he brought his fist down. "NO! NO! NO!" he repeated in a crescendo, each word accompanied by another pounding of his fist on the table as glasses jumped and the other diners in the restaurant looked over at the three men, all of whom had become red in the face.

"You don't understand me or what I am trying to do with this company!" Maurizio said forcefully, glaring at Morante. "I don't agree with you at all."

Morante, troubled, looked at Russo, who hadn't backed him up at all. The jovial, fraternal atmosphere they had enjoyed on the ride over had been shattered.

"Look, Maurizio, it is just my opinion," said Morante, raising his hands as though in self-defense. "You don't have to agree with me."

Maurizio had surprised himself, as well as Morante and Russo, with the intensity of his reaction. He loathed confrontation, preferring to smooth things over amicably. Ever the diplomat, he tried to downplay his reaction.

"Dai, Andrea," said Maurizio, "let's not ruin a beautiful weekend with such talk." Russo contributed an off-color Neapolitan joke, and by the end of the meal the atmosphere appeared much as it had when they had arrived— though only on the surface.

"Something had turned off inside him," said Morante later. "He had decided he couldn't trust me anymore and so all the rest was window dressing. Maurizio had heard both his father and his uncle say over and over again that he wasn't capable of managing the company. He carried this fear of his father and uncle around with him and I had thrown it in his face. He wanted to hear people say, 'You are a genius.' There were people a lot more agile than me who told him what he wanted to hear, and they survived. With Maurizio, you were either for him or against him."

As he had with his father and Patrizia, Maurizio closed down his relationship with Morante. Back in Milan, a chill settled between them. Everybody noticed.

"At the beginning, Maurizio and Andrea Morante were inseparable," recalled Pilar Crespi, who worked with both. "Maurizio loved Morante. And then it fell apart. He felt betrayed. Morante had suggested to him that perhaps he was overextended and he didn't like that. He liked yes-people."

To make matters worse, the negotiation with Racamier, which Morante had worked on intensively for six months, collapsed at the last minute. Everything had been ready when Morante left for the Christmas holidays, convinced it was just a matter of signing the papers. The deal fell apart in the plush, hushed offices of Rothschild's in Paris.

Maurizio Gucci and his lawyers were ushered in, along with a team of Investcorp executives. But when all parties gathered around the table, the price Racamier put forward was far below what Investcorp expected.

"His offer was so low that we were insulted and walked out," recalled Rick Swanson, who was still working with Investcorp at the time. Racamier had underestimated Investcorp's pride and business standards. Later, Swanson learned from an advisor that Racamier was actually prepared to put another $100 million on the table, but he had so offended the Investcorp executives that they left before he could raise his offer.

"That's when things really started to fall apart," Morante recalled.

When Investcorp reviewed the Gucci business at its annual management committee meeting in January 1991, the numbers painted a dismal picture: sales had plummeted nearly 20 percent, profits had disappeared, and the near-term outlook was even worse. The company had lost tens of millions of dollars. "It was like an airplane flying into a downdraft," said Investcorp executive Bill Flanz, who by then was spending more and more time at Gucci.

"In the span of just a few years, the company went from making about $60 million to losing about $60 million," said Rick Swanson later. "Maurizio had cut more than $100 million in sales and added another $30 million to the expense base. He was like a kid in the candy shop who had to have everything at once. He had no sense of priority—it was, 'I'm here and I'm in control and I can do it,' " Swanson said.

Maurizio begged his partners at Investcorp to give him time. "Demand will come!" "Sales will pick up!" "It is only a matter of time!" Maurizio had trouble getting Gucci's revamped new products into the stores quickly enough. The speed with which Maurizio had cut out the cheap canvas bags hadn't allowed time for the new products Dawn Mello and her design team turned out to get into the stores.

"There was nothing in the stores," recalled Carlo Magello, the managing director of Gucci U.K. from 1989 to 1999. "For a period of about three months the stores were empty—people had the impression we were closing!"

"No one faulted Maurizio for trading the product up, but he could have phased out the canvas gradually," commented U.S. retailer Burt Tansky, who was president of Saks Fifth Avenue at the time and is currently chairman and CEO of Bergdorf Goodman, part of the Neiman Marcus retailing group.

"We used to plead with them—there is no reason to pull a product that is so successful without something to replace it," Tansky said. "That was all the customer knew."

As Investcorp reviewed Gucci's plummeting sales, fighter planes started flying over Iraq. Tension had been building in the Middle East since August 2, 1990, when Iraqi troops invaded Kuwait. On August 8, Iraq formally annexed Kuwait, charging the country with overproducing oil and depressing prices. When Saddam Hussein failed to respond to a U.N. ultimatum to remove his troops by January 15, 1991, U.N. forces led by U.S. General Norman Schwarzkopf started a massive bombing campaign against Iraq, followed by a ground attack. Although a cease-fire was adopted February 28, the Gulf War devastated the luxury goods market.

"It hammered the industry," recalled Paul Dimitruk, who had resigned from Investcorp in September 1990, but remained in close contact with the industry as a member of the board of directors of Duty Free Shops (DFS), the largest retailer of luxury brands in the world through its network of tax-free stores. "The Gulf War created a fear in the world that in hindsight was extreme, but at the time was very real," Dimitruk said. "There was a feeling that something dreadful was going to happen. People did not want to fly at all, much less over the Middle East. Two groups fueled the luxury trade, the Americans and the Japanese. That trade just collapsed," recalled Dimitruk. To make things worse, the Japanese stock market crashed around the same time, prompted by a collapse in the real estate market.

"The Tokyo stock exchange plunged from thirty-nine thousand to fourteen thousand," Dimitruk said. "It was the single greatest destruction of real wealth in world history barring a war."

After the failure of the Racamier deal and the outbreak of the Gulf War, Morante realized there weren't going to be any white knights to rescue Maurizio. He had to dig into the guts of the company and see if it was going to be able to survive.

"I put together figures to try and scare Maurizio into action, but nothing happened," said Morante, who had calculated that Gucci stood to lose as much as 16 billion lire (about $13 million) in 1991. "Sales weren't coming back, profits were not there, costs were skyrocketing, and all the company's cash had been eaten up. Maurizio had no concept how cash flow in a company worked. His style was management by intuition. And today if you try to manage by intuition, you can get away with it if things are good, but you can't get away with it when things are bad." What might have worked for Aldo—who also had a business fiber Maurizio lacked—wasn't going to work for Maurizio.

By the time Morante tried to get Maurizio to focus on the most urgent problems, Maurizio had lost faith in him, so all of Morante's warnings were in vain. Maurizio had found a new star, a consultant named Fabio Simonato, and brought him in as director of human relations. Morante resigned in July, though he stayed a bit longer at Maurizio's request.

Since 1987, Morante had helped Maurizio break through Gucci's stalled family shareholder situation, brought him a new financial partner, helped him bring in a new management team, and drafted a new shareholder proposal that would have delivered control to Maurizio and given Investcorp an elegant exit. "Unfortunately, the dream didn't end the way I had hoped, although not for lack of trying," Morante wrote in his resignation letter. "Now I have to go my own way." Morante joined a small boutique merchant bank in Milan and later moved back to London for Crédit Suisse First Boston (CSFB), where he currently has responsibility for the Italian market. Though he came back in stride with the deal making he knew best, the memories of his days with Maurizio continued to flood back. Like Dimitruk before him—and so many others before them—his experience at Gucci had affected him profoundly.

13

A MOUNTAIN

OF DEBTS

Neither Morante nor anyone else realized
that as Gucci's financial problems grew,
so had Maurizio's own personal debts,
which mounted to the tens of millions of dollars. He
had told nobody about his outstanding loans until
he finally confided in his lawyer, Fabio Franchini, in
November of 1990. He had quickly run through the
cash his father had left him in the Swiss bank
account and had mortgaged his future on the bet
that Gucci's turnaround would generate rich profits.
He had taken out personal loans to finance the refit-
ting of the *Creole,* the furnishing of a grand apartment
on Corso Venezia in Milan, and ever-mounting legal
fees to fight his relatives. Franchini had been initially
hired by Maria Martellini to help straighten out
Gucci's legal affairs during her custodianship—and
was invited to stay on by Maurizio when he resumed

the chairmanship. Franchini had never forgotten one of Martellini's first comments about Maurizio. "Maurizio Gucci," she had said, "is sitting on a mountain of wealth." Instead, Franchini realized in dismay, Maurizio was sitting on a mountain of debts.

"I was flabbergasted," Franchini said later. Maurizio admitted to Franchini that his personal debts amounted to some $40 million. The bulk of the money was owed to two banks: Citibank in New York and Banca della Svizzera Italiana in Lugano. Maurizio explained to Franchini that the banks wanted to be paid back, but he didn't know where to get the money. With the Gucci business in the red, he had no income from his 50 percent stake. His only other assets were his real estate holdings in Saint Moritz, Milan, and New York, most of which were already mortgaged. Maurizio had never responded to his bankers' letters or returned their phone calls. Franchini started a seemingly endless round of appointments with new banks and entrepreneurs in another fruitless search for funding to help Maurizio.

In the meantime, pressure mounted on Investcorp as Gucci's poor performance weighed heavily on Kirdar and his team, especially as they had just spent more than $1.6 billion to buy Saks Fifth Avenue in 1990 amid market criticism that Investcorp had grossly overpaid for the high-end retailer. By 1991, Gucci had lost nearly 38 billion lire, or some $30 million.

"A major complication was that the same investors that had gotten into Gucci were also in Chaumet and Breguet, which weren't exactly home runs. People were unhappy," said a former Investcorp executive. Kirdar sent Bill Flanz to Milan full time to exert more control over Maurizio.

An unassuming, soft-spoken man in his late forties, Bill Flanz had worked on the acquisition of Saks Fifth Avenue. He knew how to listen to people, nodding his balding head understandingly as he blinked his pale blue eyes behind thin tortoiseshell glasses. Even under pressure, he radiated a sense of calmness and peace of mind, qualities that had gotten him through some tight situations. In Tehran, he had negotiated with the Khomeini government in his smooth, measured voice over the nationalization of a bank after the fall of the Shah. In Beirut he had had several close calls during the civil war, where one of his subordinates was killed in the violence. The oldest son of a Czech-born political science professor, Flanz grew up in a working-class neighborhood in Yonkers.

After receiving his bachelor's degree from New York University, where he studied tuition-free thanks to his father's position there, he completed his MBA at the University of Michigan. From there he entered a training program at Chase Manhattan Bank, where he spent the next nineteen years of his career before cofounding Prudential Asia, a private equity business, and then joining Investcorp.

Flanz's placid demeanor hid a sense of adventure and love for the outdoors—on weekends, depending on where he was, he traded his gray banker suits for black leather motorcycle gear and cruised the countryside on a big BMW, or donned hiking gear and disappeared into the woods, or clamped on ski equipment and whirled off in a helicopter in search of untracked pistes. Seen as a bridge builder within Investcorp, Flanz, in Kirdar's view, had the right kind of nonthreatening approach and personality to reconstruct the breach and work closely with Maurizio.

Flanz and another Investcorp executive, Philip Buscombe, flew from London to Milan and met with Maurizio in the spacious new conference room in the Piazza San Fedele offices. They set up an executive committee as a vehicle to get more involved in some of the business decisions Gucci faced, identifying eleven points that needed to be addressed.

"It was our way of trying to create a management spirit without offending Maurizio," recalled Swanson, who was also involved. "A lot of work was done, but ultimately Maurizio was the guy who had to implement it and it just didn't happen."

"Maurizio would say 'Fine, OK,' and then he would go on and do what he wanted to," said Gucci's former administrative and financial director, Mario Massetti. "It wasn't that he denied there were problems, he was just always convinced that somehow he was going to come through it."

Maurizio recognized that the costs of turning his dream into reality were higher than anyone had realized at the outset, and he initially welcomed Flanz, inviting him to set up an office in Gucci's new headquarters.

Flanz, in keeping with his style, came into Gucci with an open mind and took his time evaluating the problems. But once he took a stance, no one could easily dissuade him from it.

"I liked Maurizio, but I became more critical of his decisions and the way he was doing things, the relationship began to feel the strain," Flanz said. "I came to the conclusion that Maurizio was unrealistic as a businessman, ineffective as a manager, and only marginally effective as a leader. I decided that he wasn't going to be able to make a success of the business—ever—and certainly not in the amount of time that the creditors were going to give us."

In February 1992, despite the streamlining of Gucci America, Citibank raised a red flag for the company, calling in payment of its $25 million credit facility, which had been used to the limit. The company's net worth was approximately a negative $17.3 million and sales had plunged to $70.3 million. Under a new goods pricing structure imposed by Maurizio, Gucci America found itself unable to pay its sister company for merchandise and meet payrolls and other operating expenses. That new pricing policy, which included much higher prices for the new, high-quality goods being turned out by Dawn Mello and her new design team, would later became a red-hot subject of contention between Maurizio, De Sole, and Investcorp.

"How were we going to sell thousand-dollar handbags in Kansas City?" protested De Sole.

Citibank assigned a man named Arnold J. Ziegel to the case. Ziegel notified Domenico De Sole that the bank had taken two strong positions on Gucci's financial situation: first, that the bank didn't want Gucci America to repay Guccio Gucci for any merchandise until the loan had been cleared, and second, Citibank would hinge its faith in the company on the continuation of De Sole as CEO. Although De Sole protested the latter stance, reluctant to appear to be milking the troubled situation for his own job security, Ziegel's ultimatum would further deepen the growing schism between the two companies and the two men that ran them—Domenico De Sole and Maurizio Gucci.

At the same time, Ziegel also pressured Maurizio to pay down his delinquent personal loans with Citibank. The loans had been secured by the two apartments in Olympic Tower on Fifth Avenue—the one Maurizio and Patrizia had furnished in the early 1970s, and another Maurizio had bought later but never refurbished. Both had depreciated as New York City real estate values plummeted and by then were worth less than what Maurizio owed.

At the time, Investcorp knew nothing about Maurizio's personal loans, but the financial situation at Gucci was deteriorating so fast that the Investcorp team prepared a slide show to drive home to Maurizio in simple terms the dramatic situation facing the company. Called to London, Maurizio sat silently at the oval marble conference table in the darkened room at Investcorp's elegant Brook Street offices surrounded by Investcorp's Gucci team as the slides clicked by.

"It must have felt like an inquisition," Swanson said. "There were at least ten suits around the table and there it was, in front of everyone's eyes, just how bad things were."

"We finally got to the big conclusion slide, which read 'Conclusion: Increase sales and decrease expenses,'" Swanson said.

At that, Maurizio's eyes widened and he jumped up and turned toward

Kirdar with a big laugh. "Increase sales, decrease expenses! Hey! I could have said that, the question is, 'How?' "

"Maurizio, you're the chief executive," shot back Kirdar, in no mood for laughs. "That's your challenge!"

Maurizio promised he would come back to London with a business plan. He returned to Milan, where a new leather-bound plaque stood alongside Aldo's adage about quality being remembered long after price is forgotten. The new plaque read "Are you part of the problem or part of the solution?"

The agreed-upon date came and went with no plan. Kirdar flew to Milan to speak with Maurizio.

"Maurizio," said Kirdar. "This is not good at all. Let us get you a chief operating officer. You are the visionary, but the company needs an in-house manager."

Maurizio shook his head. "Trust me, Nemir," he said. "Trust me. I'll do it right!"

"I do trust you, Maurizio!" said Kirdar. "But things are not going well. I understand your problem, you have to understand mine. I have to rescue this sinking ship. The company is losing money. I am not your rich partner; I have a responsibility to my investors."

In the meantime, Flanz discovered that Gucci had warehouses full of old stock that Maurizio had removed from stores under his repositioning plan. Flanz found stacks of old canvas bags, bolts of fabric, and piles of leather, all left to rot.

"Maurizio had no concept that unsold inventory declined in value," said Flanz later. "He felt as long as he could put a rug over the old goods and hide them someplace, they didn't exist anymore for him. They might exist on a balance sheet somewhere, but they didn't exist in his mind."

Claudio Degl'Innocenti, the burly production manager at Scandicci, was already familiar with Maurizio's position on inventory. As part of the overall restyling of Gucci products, Maurizio had changed the color of the gold fixtures on bags and accessories from yellow gold to green gold.

One day, during a product meeting in Florence, Maurizio called Degl'Innocenti up from the factory. A big bear of a man with a full head of wild, curly brown hair and a beard, he nodded in greeting as he entered the design studio where Maurizio was working with Dawn Mello and the other designers.

"Buongiorno." He stood to one side as they finished talking, dressed in his usual attire of cotton button-down shirt, jeans, and heavy work boots.

"Okay, Claudio, from now on, instead of using 00 gold, we are going to use 05 gold," Maurizio said, referring to standard codes for the different tinted metals.

"That's fine, *Dottore*," Degl'Innocenti said in his gruff voice, "but what about all the merchandise in the warehouse?"

"Claudio, what do I care about the merchandise in the warehouse?" Maurizio answered.

Degl'Innocenti nodded silently, left the room, and went back to his office, where he made some phone calls and calculations. After less than an hour, he walked back upstairs to Maurizio's office.

"*Dottore,* there are some items that we can repaint with green gold, but many of the clasps can't be treated. We are talking about merchandise worth at least 350 million lire [at that time nearly $300,000]," Degl'Innocenti said.

Maurizio looked at the workman. "Who is the chairman of Gucci, you or me?" Maurizio asked Degl'Innocenti. "The old products are obsolete! Throw them away, do what you like, as far as I am concerned they don't exist anymore!"

Degl'Innocenti shrugged and left the room.

"I didn't throw anything away," Degl'Innocenti admitted later. "In fact, we were eventually able to sell the merchandise. The crazy thing was that we got such contradictory messages. On the one hand, big money would be thrown away; and on the other, we were instructed to save on pencils and erasers, our telephone calls were monitored, and at one point we even had to start turning out all the lights by five P.M."

Flanz pressed Maurizio to find a buyer for the old goods and offered to help. Finally, one day Maurizio proudly announced he had found the solution to the inventory problem. He had signed a contract to sell the entire lot in China. Maurizio reassured Flanz that he had taken care of everything.

"He was just as pleased as he could be, and he was strutting around the office telling everyone on the board that they could relax because he was taking care of the problem personally," Flanz said. Gucci shipped out huge containers of the old merchandise—which disappeared into warehouses somewhere in Hong Kong. Not only was the company never paid for the merchandise, it paid some $800,000 in advance to an intermediary for arranging the contract. Flanz and his colleagues at Investcorp steamed with frustration and rage over the entire stock episode, which initially cost the company an estimated $20 million in merchandise.

"The whole China transaction evaporated," said Flanz. "It was just another one of Maurizio's rainbows."

Months later, Massetti flew out to Hong Kong, found the merchandise, and finally sold it.

As time slipped away and Gucci showed no signs of improvement, Gucci board meetings grew confrontational. Although the days of flying handbags and tape recorders were long gone, Flanz and the other Investcorp directors now openly challenged Maurizio's decisions.

"You are throwing this company down the drain!" said Investcorp's Elias Hallak, who had replaced Andrea Morante on the board in 1990. "We are not happy with the fifty-fifty relationship. Nobody wants to oust you, we want you to stay at the helm of the company, but we want to bring in an experienced CEO; we have to have control."

In retaliation, Maurizio and his directors conducted the board meetings in Italian, which further infuriated Investcorp's directors.

"I didn't speak Italian at all, but if I picked up a few words, I could make out the whole scenario, and I didn't like what was going on," said Hallak.

Antonio, the white-gloved butler who worked in Gucci's executive suite, faithfully served frothy cappuccinos and strong espressos from polished silver trays as the men glared at each other.

"San Fedele still served one of the best cappuccinos in Milan," said one board member, Sencar Toker, recalling that the coffee service was the least of the abundant excesses being racked up in the name of repositioning. "The entire situation was not unlike the *Titanic* sinking and having champagne and caviar," he said.

As temperatures rose at one meeting, Maurizio dashed off a note in his bold, energetic script and slipped it to Franchini, who was a member of the board and sat next to him.

David Against Goliath
There are Four of THEM.
They count for_____
Forza!!
They have to expose themselves.

"It was very tense," recalled Toker, who had been called in by Investcorp for his deep understanding of the Italian—and European—business climate. "The bottom line is that Investcorp hung on much longer than any normal investor would have under the circumstances. Primarily because it wasn't clear what the alternative was. Second, Nemir liked Maurizio and didn't want to hurt him. And third, everyone was hoping for some kind of miracle—that it might turn around. They would have felt lucky to sell the whole wretched thing for $200 or $300 million at that point—it was leaking like a sieve!"

Flanz said Investcorp spent about a year trying to convince Maurizio to take a nonexecutive chairmanship or another face-saving solution that would have gotten him out of the management.

"Would you want someone else to run your company?" Maurizio would retort as he directed Franchini to continue his rounds of fund-raising appointments in an effort to raise enough money to buy back his company.

"He was insulted," admitted Hallak.

"I talked to him one-on-one," recalled Flanz, "we talked to him in small groups, we tried to convince him to hire a CEO and move out of the day-to-day management. He finally said, 'I'll buy you out!' and promised that if he didn't buy our shares by a certain date, he would step down. When he failed to buy us out, he reneged on that promise. We wasted a lot of time trying to help him work out a way to do it. All we succeeded in doing was postponing the day of reckoning."

Gucci survived 1992 thanks to the annual $30 million royalty check from Severin Wunderman's watch business that allowed the company to pay basic expenses and salaries, though there was little left over for production.

"I kept the company alive," said Wunderman later. "I was the tail that wagged the dog."

In the meantime, the Italian mother company was further choked because Gucci America, under pressure from Citibank, had stopped payments for merchandise. Gucci urgently needed a capital increase, but Maurizio didn't have the money to put up his share and therefore couldn't allow Investcorp to inject money and thus dilute his control.

"Maurizio wanted Investcorp to put in money as loans, but we didn't want to," recalled Hallak. "It wasn't financially sound for the company and we had no confidence in Maurizio's ability to run Gucci profitably—there was no guarantee we would get that money back."

Desperate for money, Maurizio turned to De Sole, who had remained loyal to him. In various transactions, De Sole had already lent him $4.2 million of his own money from the proceeds of the B. Altman sale—the nest egg De Sole had stashed away for his daughters' education and his and Eleanore's retirement. When a desperate Maurizio came back asking for more, De Sole told him he had nothing left. Maurizio pleaded with De Sole to give him cash off Gucci America's balance sheet.

"I can't do that, Maurizio! I could get in trouble!" De Sole said. Maurizio begged him. Finally, De Sole grudgingly agreed to lend him some $800,000 on the condition that Maurizio return the loan before De Sole closed out the next balance sheet. When that deadline came and went with no money from Maurizio, De Sole had to pay back the company himself.

In continued desperation, in early 1993 Maurizio secretly restarted production of the cheap canvas collection in Florence and signed deals with parallel importers in the Far East.

"When Gucci America stopped paying us for their merchandise, we had a huge liquidity problem—we couldn't even pay our suppliers—and so Maurizio had us start producing the old Gucci Plus collection again," said Claudio Degl'Innocenti. "We made tens of thousands of those bags, all based on the old styles.

"Maurizio told us we had to get through this tough moment, and then he was going to buy the whole business back. We made five or six billion lire [around $3 million] a month on this stuff, which was based on all the old styles. It was a so-called 'in-house parallel' business, which a lot of companies were doing at the time. It helped us hang on for a few more months," Degl'Innocenti said.

"It was amazing how much Maurizio was prepared to violate his principles in order to scrounge up some cash," said Flanz. "He went back to doing exactly what he had stopped doing in 1990—just pumping out the cheap plastic-coated canvas stuff with the double G logo. Pretty soon the warehouses were overflowing with these things too."

Then Carlo Magello, managing director of Gucci U.K., generated the all-time largest sale in the history of the company. One day Magello, a tall, resourceful, yet easygoing man with a stylish sweep of white hair over his forehead, had rushed down to the Gucci store on 27 Old Bond Street from his upstairs office to greet an elegantly dressed, soft-spoken gentleman who wanted to buy some crocodile Gucci bags and briefcases.

"These were precious pieces we had had in the store for decades, it seemed," Magello said. The customer wanted a matching set, which Magello didn't have on hand, but he scurried around and made several phone calls and managed to pull a set together. The elegant customer was so pleased that shortly thereafter Magello received—to his astonishment—an order for twenty-seven matching sets in every imaginable color, from Ferrari red to forest green, for a total value of about 1.6 million pounds, or about $2.4 million. The soft-spoken client whom Magello had so graciously served was a representative of the Sultan of Brunei, who wanted the matching luggage sets as gifts for all of his relatives.

"When I passed the order to Italy, they came back to me and said, 'Carlo, we don't have the money to buy the crocodile skins!' so I went back to the customer and got a ten percent deposit," Magello said later. Instead of paying for the skins, the money paid employee salaries. So Magello scrambled again and ordered the Florence workers to search the warehouses until they turned up enough of the precious skins to produce the first two or three sets of luggage in exchange for a partial payment. With that, more skins were bought, the order was filled, and salaries were paid.

In February 1993, Dawn Mello went to New York for minor surgery. Maurizio, in the United States on business, came to visit her as she recuperated in Lenox Hill Hospital.

"He sat on my bed and held my hand and said, 'Don't worry, Dawn, everything is going to be fine,' " Mello recalled. "He was so gentle and reassuring, he really made me feel better."

Yet when she came back to Milan three weeks later, Maurizio had grown cold toward her. "He wouldn't speak to me," Mello said later. "A curtain had come down. He thought I had turned against him." She struggled to understand what had gone wrong and tried to speak with him, but Maurizio avoided her. In a matter of days, they passed each other in the halls of San Fedele without speaking as the Gucci staff marveled at the change in their relationship. Although each relationship had been different, like Rodolfo, Patrizia, and Morante before her, now Mello too had been taken off Maurizio's list.

"Maurizio was like a sun that pulled people to him like planets with the force of his personality, but if they got too close he would burn them up and throw them away," said Mario Massetti. "We learned that the trick to surviving with Maurizio was not to get too close to him."

Maurizio—swayed by his new star, Fabio Simonato—had started blaming Mello for many of Gucci's troubles, especially the negative press, fearing she had leaked news of the difficulties to journalists. Maurizio also felt she had disregarded his orders, taking her own design direction without respecting the Gucci traditions he had tried to instill. He also accused her of being too expensive—though he had been the first to wine and dine her, rent private jets for her business trips, and furnish and refurnish her apartment and office until she was satisfied.

"First Maurizio blamed me," said De Sole, "but he couldn't blame me for the product, so he decided that Dawn was the cause of all his problems."

Maurizio soon felt that the entire design team, led by Dawn Mello, worked against him and his vision for Gucci. An offending red jacket from one of the men's collections, which Maurizio felt had nothing to do with his image of Gucci, became the symbol of all that was going wrong.

"No real man would ever wear that jacket!" he scoffed, and threw it out of the presentation.

He stopped paying the design team in Italy and sent a three-line fax to De Sole in New York, ordering him to fire Tom Ford and the other designers who were paid by Gucci America. The directive inched out of the fax machine in the middle of the office—rather than out of De Sole's private fax—for all the astonished staff of Gucci America to see.

"I called Investcorp immediately to let them know what was going on," De Sole said. "Then I sent a fax back saying we couldn't fire the designers at that time. It was lunacy! They were all working on the next collection. I could tell Maurizio was really falling apart," De Sole said.

In that same period, Tom Ford, worried that the battle between Maurizio and Investcorp could tarnish his reputation and compromise his chances of getting another job, considered an attractive new job offer from Valentino.

Although dated, Valentino was still one of fashion's most revered names with a fully rounded business that encompassed women's couture and ready-to-wear collections that showed in Paris, menswear, collections for younger clients, and a complete range of accessories and fragrances. Ford had been design director at Gucci for a year and had gradually taken on more and more work as members of the design staff resigned due to the growing hardships at Gucci. At that point, he was single-handedly designing all of Gucci's eleven product lines—including clothing, footwear, bags and accessories, luggage, and gifts—with the help of the few remaining design assistants. Ford worked around the clock, hardly taking time out to sleep. He was tired, but he liked the control.

Ford mulled his future on the flight back to Milan after visiting Valentino's offices in Rome. He thought about Dawn Mello, who had given him a chance and allowed him to prove himself by taking on more and more responsibility. They had grown so close in the past few months as the working environment at Gucci became hostile and unpredictable that they started finishing each other's sentences. Back in the city, Ford went directly to Piazza San Fedele, took the elevator up to the fifth floor, and knocked on the door of Mello's office.

She had been expecting him and looked up from her desk, biting the inside of her lip, her brown eyes worriedly scanning his face. Ford sat down, resting one hand on the smooth black surface of her desk, and looked down at his boots. Then he raised his brown eyes to meet Mello's and shook his head.

"I'm not going," he said emphatically. "I can't leave you in this mess. We have a collection to put out. Let's get back to work."

With the fall shows only a few weeks away, Ford and the other design assistants worked overtime to prepare the collection even as Gucci's administrative directors cut back on supplies and overtime salaries. Mello asked the design staff to come in the back door so as not to stoke tensions.

"Maurizio didn't seem to understand that Tom was designing everything by himself, the company was going to market in March and we couldn't buy fabric, we couldn't do a show!" Mello recalled. She called Magello in London, who by that time had been paid by the Sultan of Brunei. Magello sent her the money to buy the fabrics and pay the Italian design staff.

The company stretched out payments to suppliers from 180 to 240 days; some hadn't been paid for six months. Production and delivery of Gucci handbags and other products slowed to a trickle. One morning, disgruntled suppliers rallied at the gates of Gucci's Scandicci factory, waiting for management to arrive.

The gatekeeper called Mario Massetti at home to warn him of the angry crowd and told him not to come. Massetti came anyway.

"The suppliers jumped all over me," Massetti recalled. "It was very rough, but I had to come. I had relationships with all of them—I was the one they looked to for answers," Massetti said. "I tried to reassure them that they would be paid." The company that had once radiated the security and stability of a government ministry was coming apart at the seams. Massetti pleaded with the banks to extend more credit, borrowing money at figures well beyond the value of expected orders. He worked out a payment plan with the suppliers. Flanz thought of him as the boy with his finger in the Gucci dike—he just kept his head down and did what had to be done as best he could.

Maurizio's bid for time seemed successful until early 1993, when Citibank and Banca della Svizzera Italiana lowered the boom on him—they asked Swiss authorities to sequester Maurizio Gucci's assets for nonpayment of his personal loans. A third bank, Crédit Suisse, also emerged holding unpaid mortgages on Maurizio's Saint Moritz properties. They filed their request with a local judicial official in the Swiss canton of Coira, where Maurizio had his legal residence. The official, a man named Gian Zanotta, responded by sequestering all of Maurizio Gucci's assets—the houses in Saint Moritz and his 50 percent stake in the company, which was held by a Swiss fiduciary company, Fidinam. He set a repayment deadline for early May and, in the event of nonpayment, a date on which all of Maurizio Gucci's assets would be auctioned off to repay the banks, which were owed some $40 million.

When Investcorp learned about the auction, Flanz, Swanson, and Toker came to Milan to make Maurizio a final offer—a $40 million loan to pay off the banks and $10 million for five percent of Gucci. They proposed Maurizio stay on as chairman with 45 percent—and turn the reins over to a professional chief executive officer. At the end of their presentation, Maurizio thanked the men, told them he would think about their offer, and walked out of the room.

"Quite honestly, I feel Maurizio was not totally out of line in not accepting Investcorp's offer," said Sencar Toker later. "If he had given away control of his fifty percent, what was the rest of his stake going to be worth? It takes only a small dose of intellectual honesty to agree with his reasoning."

Maurizio went to Franchini's offices and relayed the latest offer to the lawyer. "I will not be a guest in my own house!" he said angrily to Franchini, who was the only person aside from Luigi with whom he openly discussed his situation. "What are we going to do?" he asked Franchini, pacing in the lawyer's office like a caged animal.

Maurizio had never been under so much pressure in his life. Pale and drawn, he hardly resembled the charming, enthusiastic man who had inspired so many people with his dream. He had become moody, gloomy, and paranoid—even avoiding his own employees in the halls of San Fedele. Luigi worriedly chaperoned his boss wherever he needed to go, pained with what he saw happening to Maurizio, but helpless to change his course.

"He seemed to get thinner and thinner before my eyes, day by day," Luigi said. "Whenever he went upstairs, I was afraid he was going to throw himself out of a window."

Frequently he slipped away from his office, turned off his cellular phone, and walked the few paces over to the Galleria Vittorio Emanuele shopping arcade to meet his *maga,* or psychic, Antonietta Cuomo, at one of his favorite *caffès*. Sipping a cappuccino or an *aperitivo,* anonymous amid the crowds of tourists and students, he shared his worries with Antonietta. She was a simple, motherly woman who ordinarily worked as a hairdresser. In addition, she saw special clients who appreciated her extrasensory talents.

"*Giù la mascara,* Maurizio," she would say to him at the start of each meeting. "Take off your mask."

"I was the only person he really opened up to," she said years later.

"We were desperate, we were beyond desperate," recalled Franchini. He had already been to every leading bank in Italy and Switzerland. He had contacted industrialists, including television magnate and former Italian prime minister Silvio Berlusconi and the then-little-known Patrizio Bertelli, the husband of Miuccia Prada and the architect behind the explosive growth of the Prada fashion label over the past few years. In 1992, "Bertelli didn't have twenty billion lire in the bank," Franchini recalled. No one could—or would—help Maurizio Gucci.

On Friday, May 7, at 7 P.M., the sweet, pungent scent of Valentino perfume wafted through the high-ceilinged hallway of Fabio Franchini's Milan office as his secretary ushered in a dark-haired, full-figured woman wearing a tight miniskirt, fishnet stockings, and dramatic makeup. Her stiletto heels clicked on the marble floors, the sound echoing slightly as she walked down the long hallway. Piero Giuseppe Parodi, a Milan lawyer who had represented both Maurizio and Patrizia in the past, followed her. Franchini greeted the two visitors as they took their seats in one of Franchini's spacious meeting rooms. He knew Parodi, but not the woman, who identified herself as Signorina Parmigiani. Franchini doubted it was her real name.

"We can do something for your client, Maurizio Gucci," Parmigiani told Franchini, who leaned forward in disbelief. After months of trying to raise money for Maurizio, he couldn't believe his ears. Parmigiani explained that she represented an Italian businessman who operated a successful luxury goods distribution business in Japan. She referred to the businessman only as "Hagen" and explained he would be willing to lend Maurizio the money he needed to get his shares back. In exchange, he wanted an agreement to distribute Gucci products in the Far East.

Franchini met again with Signorina Parmigiani the next morning and again on Sunday at five in the evening, to review all the details of the transaction. In the process, Franchini learned that "Hagen" was an Italian named Delfo Zorzi who had fled to Japan in 1972, leaving behind a turbulent past and accusations of being a dangerous neofascist. Zorzi was wanted by Italian authorities for, among other things, the 1969 bombing of Milan's Piazza Fontana that killed sixteen people and wounded eighty-seven. The bombing kicked off a decade of violence known as *la strategia della tensione* that plagued Italy throughout the 1970s in an effort by an extreme and violent neofascist faction to push the country to the right. Zorzi, who has denied any involvement in the bombing, saying he was a twenty-two-year-old student at the University of Naples at the time, was accused by two convicted terrorists of driving with the bomb in the trunk of his car to the scene of the explosion. His trial was set for the year 2000 in the bunker courtroom under Milan's San Vittore prison.

In Japan, Zorzi had married the daughter of a leading politician in Okinawa and set up a business exporting kimonos to Europe. He quickly diversified into the import and export of luxury goods between Europe and the Far East and became well known to executives in the fashion industry who needed to get rid of old stock.

"Although nobody will admit it, Zorzi was seen as Santa Claus in the fashion business," said a Milan fashion industry consultant who declined to be identified. "He took all that old stock off your hands and paid good money for it," the source said.

After checking with Maurizio, Franchini learned that Gucci already knew about Zorzi. In 1990, when Italian authorities opened several investigations into the massive exports of designer counterfeits, including Gucci products, they discovered that Zorzi commanded a sophisticated commercial network that shipped both the designer fakes and the old stock from Italy to the Far

East through a network of Italian, Panamanian, Swiss, and English companies. In a few years, Zorzi became a millionaire, living his secret life in Tokyo in high style. When Maurizio quietly restarted the canvas business as a survival tactic to buy time with Investcorp, he made a deal to sell the merchandise through Zorzi's operation.

On Monday, May 10, Maurizio, Franchini, and Parmigiani met at 10 A.M. at the Lugano offices of Fidinam—the fiduciary company that held Maurizio's shares and, coincidentally, also handled transactions for Zorzi's operations. Fidinam executed a loan for Maurizio Gucci of 30 million Swiss francs, or about $40 million, at an interest payment of about $7 million and an agreement on paper to grant Zorzi distribution rights for Gucci in the Far East, though these were never formalized.

Before noon, Franchini handed over 30 million Swiss francs to Gian Zanotta, the Swiss judicial officer, and resumed possession of Maurizio Gucci's assets.

"It was an incredible adventure," said Franchini later, "but all in all, I have to say they were correct," he said, referring to Zorzi and his associates. "In the end, I only gave them a letter as collateral that promised them the shares in case of default, but I couldn't put up the shares themselves; that would have been a violation of the agreement with Investcorp."

Investcorp's Swiss lawyers who were following the auction procedures, immediately called London to report that Maurizio had paid off his personal debts and gotten his shares back.

Incredulous, Flanz and Swanson rushed to Milan. They waited for Maurizio in the gleaming wood-paneled conference room they knew so well. Maurizio, enjoying his moment, kept them waiting at least half an hour before he burst into the room, his old verve and enthusiasm back.

"Rick, Bill, how nice to see you!" Maurizio said in his most gregarious manner. "So you've heard the news?" Maurizio asked with a broad smile. "I know you guys have your spies everywhere!"

Maurizio called in Antonio, who poured out steaming cups of tea for the three of them. Finally, Flanz set down his porcelain teacup and took a deep breath.

"Maurizio," said Flanz, "where did you get the money?"

"Well, Bill, it's an incredible story!" Maurizio said with a twinkle in his eye. "I was trying to fall asleep in my home in Saint Moritz and I was worrying about everything and what I was going to do and I had a dream." Flanz and Swanson looked at him blankly, wondering what his dream possibly had to do with anything.

"And my father came to me in this dream and he said, 'Maurizio, you *bischero,* the solution to all your problems is in the parlor. Just look over there by the window, one of the floorboards is loose; pull it up, and underneath you will see.' So when I woke up, I got up and looked under the loose board and it was incredible! There was more money than I could possibly ever know what to do with there, under the floor! So I didn't want to be greedy, I took just enough to pay off my shares," Maurizio said, looking happily first from Swanson to Flanz and back again, pleased with his tale.

The two Investcorp executives slumped in their chairs. They knew that not only had they lost their leverage over Maurizio, but that he was thumbing his nose at them and relishing it. He had no intention of telling them where he got the money. The story was his humorous way of saying it was none of their business—and he didn't need any charitable loan offers from Investcorp.

"That's great, Maurizio," said Flanz, with a frozen smile on his face, his milky blue eyes blinking behind his glasses. "That's really great."

Flanz said later, "I felt as though I had been punched in the stomach. I thought we had finally found our opening, our window of opportunity to get some leverage over Maurizio, and instead I had to stand there and smile. That's the moment when I decided we were going to war."

Flanz and Swanson flew back to London, where they sat with Nemir in front of the fireplace and told him the story. The benevolent green eyes grew cold. This time, Kirdar—not Maurizio—turned off.

"He is making fun of us!" Kirdar said angrily. "He thinks we are weak and he doesn't respect us anymore."

"When Maurizio used up all his goodwill with Nemir, there was no turning back," said Bill Flanz later. "When Nemir decided he was closing down negotiations and using force, he could be one of the toughest and coldest warriors around."

Kirdar had already called Bob Glaser, the "devil with the red beard," to London from New York over the Labor Day weekend to head up an urgent, top-priority assignment: solve the Gucci problem.

"Bob," he had said, "you are the only person that Maurizio is afraid of. I need you to help me get him out!"

That Monday morning he called Glaser, Elias Hallak, Bill Flanz, Rick Swanson, and Larry Kessler, Investcorp's general counsel, and several corporate lawyers into his office and gave them strict instructions.

"You people have nothing, *nothing* better to do—twenty-four hours a day—until you solve this problem," Kirdar said, his green eyes intense. "We *must* rescue Gucci from Maurizio!"

Glaser looked back at his boss. "OK, Nemir, we'll do it, but you have to be willing to go to the brink and you have to be willing to back us up. Maurizio is going to sue us, he is going to embarrass us in the press, and he is going to push the company to the point of bankruptcy. We have to make him believe we will go to the edge. Otherwise you should not go down this path."

Nemir, pained and determined at the same time, nodded his consent.

The four men set up a "war room" in the basement of Investcorp's Brook Street offices, moving out people and desks and chairs and moving in long tables, chairs, boxes, and file cabinets full of legal and historical documents about Gucci. They hired top-notch lawyers and a high-priced investigative firm to find out where Maurizio had gotten the money.

While the "war team" pored through documents, on June 22, in a move that startled observers on both sides of the Atlantic, Maurizio fired the first shot in the new war. Franchini, worried that Guccio Gucci hadn't done all it should have to extract its credits from Gucci America, advised him to sue Gucci America for $63.9 million—the famous unpaid-for merchandise. Many thought Maurizio had gone crazy to sue his own company—but Franchini maintained that under Italian law, corporate administrators must do all they can to protect the interests of the company, even if it means suing a sister company.

Bob Glaser saw it a little differently. "I saw it as an effort to suck the assets out of the American company," Glaser said, explaining that if Gucci America hadn't been able to pay what it owed the Italian company, Maurizio would have been able to make a claim for Gucci America's assets—which primarily consisted of the Gucci trademark and the building on Fifth Avenue.

Glaser decided he had to get to the bottom of why Gucci America owed Guccio Gucci so much money and called for a meeting of the board of directors of Gucci America. "How can Gucci America owe Guccio Gucci so much money?" he queried the board, which included Maurizio, his four representatives, and four representatives of Investcorp. "This makes us look bad!" Glaser continued, noting that under U.S. corporate law, as a representative of the board of directors he had an obligation to Gucci's shareholders to protect their interests. "How can management be doing a good job?" he asked. "I demand an investigation!"

Maurizio stared at Glaser, dumbfounded. He never dreamed his toughest critic and worst adversary through the trying negotiations with Investcorp, the "devil with the red beard," could actually be taking his side. Glaser insisted and the board nominated him to a subcommittee to investigate the matter of the unpaid credits Gucci America owed the Italian company, which by then amounted to more than $50 million. That nomination gave Glaser full access to the company records. After completing his report, Glaser decided that the latest price structure Guccio Gucci had imposed on Gucci America in 1992 involved artificially inflated prices designed to sustain the dizzyingly high costs the Italian company had racked up over the past few years. "I did not see that money owed by Gucci America to Guccio Gucci as a legitimate debt," Glaser said. That the pricing policy had been intended as a scam to drain the resources from Gucci America—as Glaser believed—seems unlikely. More likely, it was another one of Maurizio's desperate efforts to keep the Italian company afloat. Regardless, Glaser's report provided plenty of material for Gucci America to defend itself from the lawsuit.

In the meantime, in his desperate quest for money to keep the company on its feet, Maurizio had hatched a deal with Severin Wunderman. Wunderman had agreed to give Gucci a lump sum for a long-term extension of his watch license, which was to expire on May 31, 1994. But to Investcorp's Gucci team, giving an extended license to Wunderman meant giving away the watch business, at that time the only moneymaker in the tattered Gucci empire.

Weeks before the upcoming meeting of the board of Gucci America at which Investcorp expected Maurizio to push through the Wunderman deal, Investcorp's Rick Swanson started calling Domenico De Sole to urge the Gucci America chief to change sides and vote against the agreement. If he changed sides, he could break Maurizio's control of the board.

"Domenico, this is Rick. We need to know. Can we trust you?"

"Listen, Rick," said De Sole from Gucci's offices in New York. "You are the only one who really understands. This company is being run by three-year-olds. This cannot go on or the company is going to collapse. You can trust me."

Swanson called again.

"Domenico, this is important. Can we trust you?"

"Yes," De Sole said. "Yes!"

The morning of July 3, 1993, Flanz called De Sole to a secret breakfast meeting in a private dining room downstairs at the Four Seasons Hotel in Milan. Bob Glaser, Elias Hallak, Rick Swanson, and Sencar Toker had gathered around the table.

They asked De Sole if he would vote with them against the agreement.

"Look, I truly feel that what is going on is destroying the company," De Sole said, scanning the tense faces of the Investcorp team. "If something isn't done, the company is going to go bust!"

"If you stand up to Maurizio, we will back you up all the way," said Hallak, looking De Sole in the eye.

"Maurizio is going to hate Domenico for this, if he doesn't already," Swanson interjected. Swanson explained to the group that De Sole had lent Maurizio $4 million of his own money in two separate installments during the past few years, in addition to the $800,000 of company funds he had paid back himself, and had little hope of ever getting that money back—especially if he sided with Investcorp.

"I give you my word of honor on behalf of Investcorp that we will do our best to include this in our negotiations and make sure you get paid," said Hallak.

A few hours later, the directors of the board of Gucci America settled into chairs in Maurizio's office, instead of the usual conference room. Maurizio had expected the meeting to be confrontational and he wanted to encourage a more intimate atmosphere but be able to preside from behind his own desk. He waved his butler, Antonio, in to take orders for cappuccino.

Mario Massetti, who had never met Glaser before, turned to De Sole to ask who the man with the red beard was.

"That's Bob Glaser," De Sole replied. "He is the only one at Investcorp Maurizio is really afraid of."

The meeting opened with a discussion of Gucci America's operations, which had a negative net worth of $17.4 million in 1992, when sales slumped to $70.2 million. Bob Glaser surprised De Sole by putting on his tough-guy hat and firing questions at him.

"Do you run a company called Gucci America?"

"Yes, I do," De Sole replied, taken aback.

"And what do you do when you get a product that in your view is over-priced?"

"There is nothing I can do," said De Sole. "I complain all the time. We are a captive company and you guys have never supported us," said De Sole, heatedly. "All you guys have ever done is just try to get along with Maurizio."

Maurizio grew incensed. "Are you saying that Gucci America overpays for the merchandise?" he shot over to De Sole.

"Yes, I have been saying that for years!" fired back De Sole. "You are overcharging Gucci America just to support your cost structure. Look at this building! What do we really need this building for?"

Maurizio, visibly upset at De Sole's allegations as well as Glaser's provocation, jumped up and paced the green carpet behind his desk as the other directors debated his proposed agreement with Wunderman, which would have secured Gucci some $20 million in exchange for renewing the watch license with Wunderman for some twenty years.

When it came time to vote, De Sole voted against the deal. Maurizio, angry and dismayed, spun around and looked straight at De Sole, his face white, his mouth set in a thin line. De Sole stared back at him and raised his hands, palms up, fingers spread.

"Look, Maurizio, this is what I have to do," De Sole said simply. "I am voting for the company, it is my duty. We can't just give away a license because we are running out of money . . ."

De Sole felt he had done the right thing for the company; Maurizio felt he had been stabbed in the back.

Once they had left Maurizio's office, Glaser took De Sole aside. "How are you planning to defend Gucci America from this lawsuit?" he asked.

De Sole looked at him skeptically. "I can't hire a law firm to represent the company without approval from the board of directors," De Sole protested, knowing full well that now Maurizio and his representatives—who had launched the lawsuit in the first place—would never approve the move. Glaser looked De Sole in the eye. "Oh, yes, you can!" he said, studying the executive's initially surprised reaction. Glaser, who had spent weeks hammering out the rules of corporate governance, had insisted on a clause in case of emergencies that would give the CEO the power to do whatever is in the interest of the company in the absence of a board meeting. De Sole understood in a flash what Glaser was telling him.

"You can't convene a board meeting without a quorum and we just couldn't ever seem to get our schedules together," Glaser recalled. "It just never happened!" he said glibly. "And that's how we hired a law firm to defend Gucci America."

Glaser was also aware that as a result of the vicious battle now raging between the two companies, Gucci America had no chance of receiving merchandise—and therefore had nothing to sell in its stores. He suggested something more to De Sole. "Why don't you go and commission your own product?" he asked.

"I can't do that without Maurizio's approval!" De Sole replied.

"Gucci America has the trademark, doesn't it? Your job is to do whatever is in the best interest of the company in the absence of a board meeting," Glaser reiterated. De Sole nodded—and went off to Italy to meet with leather goods manufacturers. Glaser's goal was to try to keep Gucci America autonomous and solvent despite the intensifying battle with Maurizio.

Meanwhile, Maurizio felt as though a conspiracy had closed around him.

He could not believe that De Sole had turned against him and voted against his proposal. He truly thought, despite their differences and their arguments, that De Sole was his firm ally—almost as though he were part of the family. In April he had approved a $200,000 bonus for De Sole. Without De Sole's vote, Maurizio knew, it was the beginning of the end for him. If he could no longer control the board, his power in Gucci was finished.

After the meeting, still pacing, Maurizio poured out his dismay to Franchini. "In the beginning, De Sole was nothing to anyone and I took him in. He had patches on the seat of his pants! Now he is going to ruin me!"

"Maurizio!" said Franchini seriously. "This is war! You have fifty percent of Gucci, which is now equal to zero. I can help you, but you must be ready to risk it all. You have to be ready to sink the ship and make them believe you will sink the ship, otherwise they will take it from you for nothing!"

Maurizio stopped pacing and looked at Franchini, then slumped in his chair, resting his hands on his knees.

"OK, *avvocato*, OK. Tell me what I should do."

The war intensified. Maurizio removed De Sole from Gucci America's board of directors, though he could not unseat him as CEO without a majority vote of the board. Flanz wrote a letter to Gucci's board of directors calling for the appointment of a competent CEO. The letter never mentioned Maurizio by name or title, but its meaning was clear to all. The document infuriated Maurizio so much he sued Investcorp and Flanz for 250 billion lire, or about $160 million, for libel in a Milan court and even asked a Florence prosecutor to bring criminal charges against Flanz for defamation of character. On July 22, Investcorp filed arbitration proceedings against Maurizio in New York in an effort to force him to step down as chairman, charging him with violating the shareholders' agreement and mismanaging the company. The court papers quoted Maurizio's story about finding the money under the floorboards after his father came to him in a dream, in an effort to further discredit him.

"We turned up the heat and pushed and pushed him," said Bill Flanz. "But Maurizio, being a sailor, said, 'I'm not going to surrender this company to the Arabs. I've lost everything, I've lost my fortune, I've lost my face, I've lost my respect in the business and I am going to take this ship down with me. We're going down together.'"

The war team truly feared he would.

"In most cases, you assume a stance like that is a bluff," said Rick Swanson. "But we were really worried. He seemed irrational enough that he just might do it."

The attacks continued hard and fast as De Sole sued Maurizio for the

$4.8 million he said he had lent him between April 1990 and July 1993. Maurizio then sought further action against Investcorp in the Milan courts, moving to expel Flanz, Hallak, and Toker from the Gucci board.

After weeks of trading blows, in a last-minute effort to salvage the relationship, Nemir Kirdar called to ask Maurizio to visit him in the south of France, where he habitually transferred his operations during the month of August. It had been more than a year since the two men had seen each other.

"Maurizio? This is Nemir Kirdar."

Maurizio held the phone in silent disbelief.

"I'm calling to see if we can get together," Kirdar said. "I like you, Maurizio, I want to put all this fighting behind us. I'd like to see you on a personal basis. Will you come and spend a day with me in the South of France? We can have lunch and go out on the boat and have some fun."

Maurizio, recovering from his surprise, had the presence of mind to crack a weak joke. "Are you sure I will be safe?" he said meekly.

"Maurizio, you are always safe with me," Kirdar answered warmly.

Maurizio, full of hope that Kirdar wanted to offer him a last-minute solution, traveled to the south of France the next day to meet the Investcorp chief for a poolside lunch on the balcony of the Hotel du Cap.

"Maurizio, I want you to understand, whatever has gone on between our two companies, I have never stopped respecting you or your vision. But I have a business to run and I have been under the gun. Who knows, someday, if we can turn this company around and stop the losses and start to put some value in it, we might be able to do something together again."

As Kirdar spoke, Maurizio realized that Investcorp would not budge. There would be no last-minute solution. They spent a pleasant afternoon— as far as appearances went. Maurizio returned to Milan, dejected and disillusioned.

That summer, Maurizio planned no vacation, but moved to the spacious apartment he had taken in Lugano, which offered cool breezes and a lake view from the shady green terrace. Maurizio commuted daily by car to his office in Milan.

In September, Gucci's *Collegio Sindacale,* or statutory supervisory board, notified Massetti that because Gucci's shareholders were unable to resolve their differences and hadn't approved any of the company's accounts since the beginning of the year, the board was obliged by law to turn the company books over to the courts. The courts would then sell the company's assets to pay off its creditors.

"They gave me twenty-four hours of time . . . then they were going to take in the books," said Massetti. He pleaded for a grace period of forty-eight hours, then called Maurizio and Fabio Franchini.

"Maurizio was stuck," Massetti said. "He was blocked on all sides. There was nothing he could do but strike an agreement."

"I can't imagine the kind of pressure he was under," added Swanson later. "As long as he had a lifeline, Maurizio was going to live through another day," Swanson said. "It wasn't until he was standing at the precipice—facing personal bankruptcy, company bankruptcy, losing everything—that he would face reality. And we were all wondering what was going to happen."

That afternoon, Maurizio drove to Florence and called a meeting of senior employees in the "Sala Dynasty" at 7:30 P.M.

"So *Dottore,* what's the upshot? Are we going to close down shop?" queried Degl'Innocenti with his usual gruff irony.

"I have done it!" responded Maurizio enthusiastically. "I have found the money. I am buying out Investcorp."

"Fantastic!" responded Degl'Innocenti and the others, who had been rooting for Maurizio in the battle, fearing that if Investcorp took over it would slash jobs, close down the factory, and turn Scandicci into a glorified buying office.

"The arrival of Investcorp had been painted to be the end of the world," said Degl'Innocenti.

While Maurizio rallied the Florence managers, the war team huddled in London, wondering what he was going to do.

"Somebody called us and said that he had gathered the staff and given this *bravissimo* speech in classic Maurizio fashion, saying he was going to beat the Arabs," recalled Swanson. "We were all wondering, 'Is he going to sink the ship or is he going to be rational and sell?' "

It turned out Maurizio's speech was the final act in his brinksmanship play. Late that evening, the phone call came in—Maurizio was ready to capitulate.

On Friday, September 23, 1993, Maurizio signed away his Gucci ownership in the offices of a Swiss bank in Lugano, surrounded by lawyers and financiers. That same morning, his secretary, Liliana Colombo, cleared his personal belongings out of his office on the fifth floor of the Piazza San Fedele building. The black-and-white photographs of Rodolfo and Sandra, the smiling faces of his daughters, the antique crystal and sterling ink set, the objects on his desk. Finally, with the help of two workmen, she had the painting of Venice that Rodolfo had given Maurizio taken down.

"That's what hit me when I next walked into his office on Monday morning," said Gucci's former administrative director, Mario Massetti. "Aside from his personal things, everything else was as it had been—except the painting from Rodolfo was no longer there," recalled Massetti.

That Friday night, Maurizio invited a small group of Gucci managers, including Massetti, to his apartment in Lugano for a private dinner.

As a single waiter moved discreetly around the table, Maurizio explained to them that he had sold his stake in Gucci. "I did what I had to do," he said simply. "I just wanted to let you know that I gave it everything I could, but they were too much for me. I had no choice."

When Maurizio's call came in with the message that he would agree to sell, Investcorp moved quickly. The documents had already been drafted, and Rick Swanson and another Investcorp executive flew to Switzerland for the closing. They had settled on a price of $120 million.

At the Swiss bank where the closing took place, "they had put me in a room and Maurizio was locked away in another conference room with all his lawyers and I wanted to see him," said Swanson. "He was also a friend of mine and nobody had seen him for months, so I kept going out into the hall to see if I could catch a glimpse of him."

Finally Swanson marched down to the door of the conference room, pushed it open, and saw four or five lawyers and Maurizio, pacing with his arms behind his back.

Maurizio stopped and his face lit up. "*Buongiorno,* Rick!" he said, walking over to Swanson and giving him a bear hug in perfect Gucci style.

"This is crazy! We are friends," Maurizio continued. "I am not sitting here with all these lawyers." They walked back down the hall together, chatting.

"Maurizio," Swanson finally said, taking a long look at the man he had worked so closely with for the past six years, "I am sorry about the way things turned out, but I want to let you know that we really believed in you and in your dream for Gucci and we will do our best to carry your vision forward."

"Rick," Maurizio said, shaking his head slowly. "What am I going to do now? Go sailing? I have nothing left to do!"

14

LUXURY

LIVING

On Monday morning, March 27, 1995, Maurizio Gucci woke up at around 7 A.M., as usual. He lay still for a few minutes, listening to the sound of Paola's breathing. She burrowed beside him in the massive Empire bed with its four neoclassical columns topped with a gold silk canopy and carved wooden eagle. It was a grand bed fit for a king, but then Maurizio loved being grand. He had scoured Paris with Toto Russo looking for the Empire furniture his friend had taught him to love, calling it "elegant, but not pompous."

The bed, along with other pieces he collected over the years, had been in storage until he and Paola Franchi, formerly Colombo, finally moved into the three-story apartment on Corso Venezia almost a year earlier. At the time, Maurizio and Paola had already been together more than four years, but it had taken more than two years to complete the renovations. In the meantime, Maurizio lived in a small bachelor apartment on Piazza Belgioiso, a quiet eighteenth-century square surrounded by imposing marble palazzi just behind the Duomo, and she stayed in a condominium owned by her ex-husband with their nine-year-old-son, Charly.

Stately nineteenth-century palazzi line Corso Venezia, a wide, treeless avenue that runs northeast from Piazza San Babila past the Giardini Pubblici. The palazzo where Maurizio and Paola lived at number 38 stands directly in front of the Palestro metro stop on Milan's red line and diagonally across the street from the Giardini Pubblici. Its classical facade, covered with an unusual, okra-colored stucco, is simple compared with the fronts of other buildings up and down the avenue.

Maurizio had met Paola in 1990 at a private party in a Saint Moritz dance club. Attracted by her handsome, blond beauty and lithe, lanky figure, he chatted with her at the bar. They realized they had known each other as teenagers, when they joined the same group of friends on the beaches of Santa Margherita. Maurizio liked Paola's relaxed manner and easy smile—she seemed the opposite of Patrizia in every way. Aside from his two-year liaison with Sheree, Maurizio hadn't had any other significant relationship since he had left Patrizia—who continued to occupy an important place in his life even though they lived apart. He and Patrizia talked frequently and argued often. He grew tired of their conflicts, but had little time or energy to pursue another relationship. Maurizio also had a deep fear of AIDS and had been known to ask his partners to take a blood test before he would go to bed with them.

"Maurizio was one of the most eligible men in Milan, but he was not a womanizer," added his friend and former consultant Carlo Bruno. "There were a lot of women interested in him, but he was not a playboy."

"Neither Maurizio nor Patrizia would ever find another partner of the same importance in their lives," said an astrologer whom Patrizia had asked to do all of their charts, "although Paola's chart had many of the same characteristics as Patrizia's—so it was understandable that Maurizio would feel attracted to her."

When Maurizio and Paola met, she was estranged from her husband, Giorgio, a leading industrialist who had made his money in copper. The first time Maurizio invited Paola out for a drink, they moved on to dinner and talked nonstop until one in the morning.

"He poured out the story of his life," said Paola later. "He needed to talk, as though he needed to lighten a load that he had in his heart and in his spirit. He may have seemed to take on the world, but in fact he was an extremely sensitive person, very fragile in the face of certain things. He wanted to defend himself and explain his side of all the scandals he and his family had been through. It was overwhelming. He told me he wanted to be like an eagle, flying on high—able to see and control everything, but never get entangled."

In the beginning, they met secretly in his small apartment on Piazza Belgioioso, where Paola discovered that nothing made Maurizio happier than simple dinners at home. He sliced the *salame* while she poured out the red wine and they nuzzled under the vaulted ceilings before moving to the wrought-iron double bed, painted Pompeian red, where Paola consolidated her hold over Maurizio.

"That apartment became our little love nest," she said later. While Maurizio and Paola cavorted, Patrizia seethed. Despite their efforts to be discreet, they could not escape the informal network of spies Patrizia commanded from her penthouse apartment in Galleria Passarella, where Maurizio still paid all the costs. From friends who reported back to her, she learned that Maurizio had been seen around town with a tall, thin blonde and it didn't take her long to discover Paola's identity. Patrizia, who had her own lovers, feigned indifference, but she watched Maurizio's every move.

Toto Russo had found the Corso Venezia apartment for Maurizio. Initially, Maurizio had hoped to find an entire villa—even if it meant moving out of town—that could become "Casa Gucci," a symbol of the same luxury and taste he had wanted the Gucci business to stand for. Maurizio never found his dream villa, but settled for the rental apartment on Corso Venezia.

When Russo first brought Maurizio in through the large wooden entry doors, past the graceful wrought iron gate, and into the hushed calm of the inner courtyard, Maurizio liked the stately feeling of the building instantly and its relative quiet. Inside the thick stone walls, noise from the busy avenue outside seemed muffled, distant. Maurizio admired the colorful Palladian mosaic floor and the grand marble staircase that rose to the apartment from the left of the courtyard. Beyond the marble staircase a modern elevator, enclosed by two large wooden doors with glass panes, also led upstairs.

Maurizio—still chairman of Gucci at the time—thought the prestigious location and luxurious setting was fitting for a person of his position. The apartment was on the first floor above the ground floor, or the *piano nobile,* so called in Italian because historically the noble families that once owned these grand palazzi always lived on that floor. At the top of the marble staircase, the front doors opened into a small entry hall. From there, two doors, side by side, led out to a long corridor. The kitchen and a large dining room were immediately to the right, then a series of parlors and reception rooms opened right and left off the long hall. At the end of it, the master bedroom suite overlooked a lush garden below, next to the Invernizzi garden. The apartment was so magnificent that its major drawback wasn't apparent at first—there was only one bedroom. When Maurizio first saw it, he was separated from Patrizia and living alone. After meeting Paola, he grew determined to rebuild his family life and wanted to have Alessandra and Allegra come live with them too, so the owners, the Marelli family agreed to rent him a second apartment upstairs that had become available in the meantime. By putting the two apartments together, there would be enough room for the girls as well as Paola's son, Charly. Maurizio rented both apartments and ordered an internal staircase built to connect them.

"This is going to be our new home," said Maurizio to Paola, putting his arm around her slim waist as their footsteps echoed through the empty rooms. Although it wasn't "Casa Gucci," the Corso Venezia apartment symbolized all he was working for: it was a fitting showpiece for Gucci's CEO that also held the possibility of a new, more serene family life. Maurizio liked the idea that all three of their children could sleep under the same roof with them and in their own rooms. He longed for his daughters to spend more time with him, and hoped they would once he and Paola were living together. Maurizio feared he would never have a healthy relationship with his daughters as long as Patrizia had so much control over them; even though it had been many years since he had moved out, the ongoing conflict between him and Patrizia had limited his ability to resurrect his relationship with the girls.

The renovation and decoration of the Corso Venezia apartment took more than two years and several million dollars. By the time it was finished, its grandiose style raised eyebrows and set tongues wagging all around Milan. The gossips longed to get a peek inside, but Maurizio rarely entertained and pictures of the apartment were never published. However, the endless crews of workmen and the deliveries of precious antiques, custom-made fixtures, fine wallpapers, and sumptuous silks didn't go unnoticed.

The combined space of the two apartments measured more than 13,000 square feet over three floors and the annual rent alone was more than 400 million lire, or some $250,000. Maurizio turned to Toto for the furnishings—and gave him no limits. Russo—thrilled to have such an enthusiastic and willing client—outdid himself. The entire apartment was gutted, the floors were torn up, and walls were removed and replaced. Russo ordered laser-cut wood inlaid floors copied from a palace in Saint Petersburg, designed custom-made paneling and light fixtures, and selected luxurious wallpaper and rich drapes. Specialists restored or re-created the ceiling frescoes. Maurizio loved boiserie, the decorative French carved wood paneling, and he bought an original set that once belonged to the former king of Italy, Vittorio Emmanuele di Savoia, for the long dining room. Bought at an auction in France, the boiserie was painted celadon green and delicately worked with gilded frames, flower and vase motifs, and stained glass insets. Russo and Maurizio commissioned a massive faux-marble dining table because they couldn't find one on the market that was long enough, and completed the room with pale gray curtains with a slight sheen and mirrors set into the walls. Designed for lavish banquets, that dining room also became the setting where the trio—Maurizio, Paola, and Charly—ate breakfast every morning.

Maurizio happily moved in the furniture he had been collecting. Two marble obelisks stood on the landing of the grand staircase, while a pair of prancing bronze centaurs graced the entryway, standing on either side of the door. His favorite piece—an antique billiard table dating from the mid-1800s—went in the last living room down the corridor to the right. It had expressive carved masks leering out from the rounded wooden legs and came with an original set of twin couches that stood against the walls. When workmen prepared to fit the room with custom paneling and bookshelves, to their surprise they discovered an elaborate carved plaster ceiling with a maze motif hidden under modern dropped panels. Maurizio agreed to restore the ceiling to its original state. When it came time to fill the yards of custom shelving, Maurizio—who had little time for reading himself—ordered old books by the pound.

Furnishing the Corso Venezia apartment put Russo on a collision course with Paola, who had worked as an interior designer and wanted to have her say. Each resented the other's influence over Maurizio.

Paola was subtle; Russo made no secret of the way he felt about her. A typical scene occurred one morning while the renovations were under way. Russo arrived at the apartment and called out at the top of his lungs, *"E' arrivata la troia?"* "Has the whore arrived yet?"

His assistant, Sergio Bassi, ran into the room, eyes wide behind round designer glasses, hushing him in vain. "Shhhhh! Toto! She's upstairs, she probably heard you!"

Russo didn't care. He had won a promise from Maurizio that Paola was limited to decorating the children's quarters upstairs and a game room downstairs.

"She was not allowed on our floor," recalled Bassi. "When Paola came into the picture, it changed the relationship between Maurizio and Toto, and in the end they fought bitterly. Toto was very Neapolitan, very possessive. He would pick fights with Paola and throw jealous fits."

Maurizio had asked Paola to transform a long, empty hall adjacent to the marble stairway off the main courtyard into a game and party room. It became Maurizio's personal playground.

"He was really a child at heart," Paola said years later. "His eyes would just light up at the thought of that room; he had all sorts of ideas for it."

The front of the room became a game hall, complete with video games, a pinball machine from the 1950s, and Maurizio's favorite toy, a virtual Formula One racing car driving game complete with helmet, steering wheel, and programmed courses. Farther back, Paola made the TV room look like a minicinema with velvet curtains, three rows of real movie theater seats, and a giant television screen. At the back of the long room she created a western saloon—Maurizio's inspiration.

"I had never done anything western before," Paola said, throwing up her hands with a smile, "so I got out the books and started doing research." She ordered a curved wooden bar, leather-topped bar stools, and studded leather couches. A trompe l'oeil desert with canyons, cacti, and rising smoke signals crept along the walls, and a painted cowboy swaggered fore and aft on the swinging wooden doors. Before the rest of the house was finished Maurizio and Paola inaugurated the game room with a costume party, to which the guests came dressed as cowboys and Indians.

Paola took particular care with the children's rooms upstairs, knowing how much it meant to Maurizio to have his daughters stay with them. For Alessandra and Allegra, she picked out girlish canopy beds and coordinating floral prints and wallpaper in beige, green, and rose. For Charly she chose more boyish colors and wallpaper with a cheerful book motif, since, she joked, he didn't love real books. The children had the entire second floor to themselves, including a den where they could entertain their friends, a small kitchen if they wanted to prepare a meal, a guest room, and a separate entrance so they could come and go as they pleased. Since Maurizio and Paola had moved into the apartment a year earlier, Charly had been the lone occupant of the children's suite; Alessandra and Allegra hadn't spent a single night in those dainty canopy beds.

As work on the house progressed, the tension between Toto and Maurizio over Paola finally exploded.

"The final showdown came when their two secretaries got together to do an inventory," recalled Bassi. "Toto's secretary told Liliana that Maurizio owed Toto a billion lire. Liliana said she was crazy, that Toto owed Maurizio money." Things got so bad that the two men stopped talking to each other. Paola had won.

Rumors circulated in Milan that Toto's cocaine habit was getting the better of him. Friends and clients once eager to be connected with him began to distance themselves. He lived apart from his wife and daughter, who were also in Milan, but he never sought a divorce. Later he developed health problems and underwent heart surgery to have three valves replaced. His doctors diagnosed him with endocarditis—*la morte bianca*—an infection common among cocaine users that attacks the lining of the heart. But affecting him more than his heart problems was impotence, another consequence of cocaine use.

"Toto was a true Don Giovanni," said Bassi. "He had a special magnetism over women, and probably over men as well. He could never accept the fact that he couldn't perform sexually anymore."

Toto's body was found in a Milan hotel room, a haunt to which he would habitually disappear for two- and three-day orgies. But this time, Russo had checked in alone. Hotel personnel tracing rivers of water gushing down from his room found him slumped over the sink, dead of a heart attack. To his friends, it looked like suicide.

Maurizio attended Toto's funeral and accompanied the coffin to Santa Margherita, the seaside resort where he was buried. During the final rites, the pallbearers discovered that Toto's coffin was bigger than his tomb and had to be refitted.

"Even in death you are over the top," thought Maurizio, smiling sadly at the memory of his friend and shaking his head. Another friend of theirs had died two months earlier. Maurizio turned to the small group of mourners and said, "Who knows who will be the third?"

As Paola gained importance in his life, Maurizio tried to cut the ties still linking him to Patrizia. Though he made generous monthly deposits into her Milan bank account—averaging between 180 and 160 million lire, ($100,000) each month—he forbade her to use the houses in Saint Moritz. He and Paola wanted to redecorate all three of those homes and turn L'Oiseau Bleu into their own retreat, designating the other two houses for the children, guests, servants, and entertaining. Patrizia went crazy. She considered L'Oiseau Bleu hers and pressured him to deed the small chalet to her and the other two to Alessandra and Allegra. The thought of Maurizio being there with Paola enraged her and she even threatened to burn the house down, going so far as to ask one of the servants to prepare two tanks of gasoline and leave them by the side of the house.

"Just put them near the house and I'll take care of the rest," she ordered the caretaker of the estate. When he didn't comply, Patrizia turned to one of her psychics, who went to work with potions and spells.

When Maurizio next came up to Saint Moritz, an intense wave of discomfort and unease overcame him as he entered the house. Ignoring the feeling, he unpacked and tried to settle in for the weekend, but the sense of rejection was so overwhelming that he left the same night and drove three hours back to Milan. The next day he called his psychic, Antonietta Cuomo, and explained the problem. A few days later, Cuomo went to Saint Moritz and lit candles in the house, freeing it of something she said "wasn't right." She later did the same for his apartments in Lugano and New York. Unrelenting, Patrizia held midnight séances in the kitchen of Galleria Passarella, so frightening the servants that they rushed to Piazza San Fedele to tell Maurizio of the strange events they had witnessed.

Through Gucci employees still loyal to her, Patrizia followed Maurizio's business moves, becoming convinced that he wasn't capable of running the company. One employee wrote her a letter, pleading with her to intervene.

"Signora Patrizia," the letter said. "He has become unrecognizable. We do not know how we are going to go forward. There is disorientation and insecurity. When we try to talk to him, we find a wall of indifference. A cold smile. Help us! Take the situation in hand!"

Through her spies—which included mutual friends as well as Adriana, Maurizio and Paola's cook—Patrizia knew all about the lavish restructuring of Corso Venezia, the *Creole,* the new Ferrari Testarossa in the garage, and about the private planes Maurizio chartered around the world. As his financial situation worsened, his payments to her grew erratic and she too found herself unable to pay all of her own bills. The grocer and the pharmacist stopped giving her credit. As her bank accounts ran short, she called Maurizio's secretary, Liliana, who learned a complex dance to keep Maurizio's creditors alternately satisfied or at bay.

"As the end of each month would come around, I used to worry how I was going to find enough money for Patrizia," Liliana recalled, saying she juggled Maurizio's creditors and prepared the money for Patrizia in installments. "I'll just bring you part of it tomorrow, and I'll try to get you the rest by the end of the week," Liliana would say, always gracious and accommodating.

"What?" Patrizia would cry indignantly. "He is spending money right and left on Corso Venezia and he can't find the money for his daughters?"

"No, no, signora, they've stopped the work on Corso Venezia," Liliana feigned.

"Okay, I'll wait," Patrizia groused. "If we must make sacrifices, we must."

One month, Maurizio became so desperate to find the money for Patrizia that his driver, Luigi, brought him 8 million lire, or about $6,500, he had taken from his son's piggy bank.

The fall of 1991, after Maurizio had confessed his personal problems to Franchini, he had asked Patrizia for a divorce. Paola, also with Franchini's help, asked her husband for a divorce, and she and Maurizio planned to move to Corso Venezia together. Patrizia felt everything she had achieved was slipping through her hands. Burning with rage and jealousy, Patrizia derided Paola as a superficial woman, hungry for money and status, who adeptly took advantage of Maurizio and ran down his fortune. Some thought she could have been describing herself.

Patrizia "had an almost obsessive fixation with his assets," recalled Piero Giuseppe Parodi, one of Maurizio's lawyers, whom Patrizia started calling regularly to determine her rights. "She felt she had a right to his assets—not on a legal basis, but on a romantic basis. She felt the boat was hers . . . the chalet in Saint Moritz . . . and she felt Gucci's success was due in large part to her advice. She was also very concerned about what she felt was his inability to run the company. She felt her husband was unable to control his spending in a normal way and she lived in a constant state of anxiety about his assets, which she felt belonged to her. She was concerned about the implications for herself and for her daughters."

Patrizia focused on Maurizio as the source of all her pain and suffering and vowed to destroy him before he destroyed the two girls.

"She wanted to see him on his knees," said Maddalena Anselmi, a friend of Patrizia's. "She wanted him to come crawling back to her." Patrizia gave up on the séances, spells, and strange powders.

"If it's the last thing I do, I want to see him dead," Patrizia said to her housekeeper, Alda Rizzi, while they were talking in her bedroom one day. "Why don't you ask your boyfriend if he can't find somebody to help me out?" Patrizia insistently repeated her requests until Rizzi and her boyfriend went to Maurizio in November 1991. He taped their report and handed the cassette over to Franchini.

Patrizia's headaches began that same fall. When she wasn't out shopping or ranting about Maurizio, Patrizia closed herself in her darkened bedroom for hours, incapacitated by the pain. At night, the headaches kept her awake. Her mother and daughters grew worried.

"*Mamma,*" said fifteen-year-old Alessandra one day. "I am tired of seeing you suffer. I am calling the doctor."

On May 19, 1992, Patrizia checked into Madonnina, a leading private clinic in Milan, the same one where Rodolfo Gucci had been treated for prostate cancer. Her doctors diagnosed a large tumor on the front left side of her brain. They had to operate immediately, they told her. Her chances of survival were not high.

"I felt my world was falling apart," Patrizia said. "I knew the tumor had been caused by him, by all the stress he had caused me. At one point I looked down at my hat and it was full of my own hair, hair that had fallen out of my head. I had a crisis. I wanted to destroy everything."

She turned bitterly to her diary.

"*BASTA!*" she wrote in large, angry letters across the page. "It isn't possible that a person like Maurizio Gucci can live his life among 60-meter yachts, private planes, and luxury apartments and Ferrari Testarossas without being judged as a low, base individual. Tuesday I was diagnosed with a tumor that is pressing on my brain, while Dr. Infuso looked at the X rays in dismay, fearing it is inoperable. Here I am, alone, with two daughters aged fifteen and eleven and an apprehensive mother, herself a widow, and a delinquent husband who has abandoned us because his continuous failures have made him realize that what is left of his assets suffices only for himself."

The next morning, worry gripped the faces of Alessandra and Patrizia's mother, Silvana, as they went to Maurizio's office in Piazza San Fedele to tell him the news. Behind the closed door of his office, Maurizio's secretary Liliana heard their low voices, then watched a shaken Maurizio usher them out, his face grave.

"Patrizia has been diagnosed with a brain tumor the size of a billiard ball," he told Liliana in a strained, low voice after Silvana and Alessandra had left. "Now I understand why she has been so aggressive," he said softly.

Silvana had asked Maurizio if he could take care of the two girls while she cared for Patrizia—he had told her it would be difficult; Corso Venezia wasn't ready yet, and he had no place for them to stay in his bachelor apartment. Furthermore, things were coming to a head with Investcorp and he traveled often. He said he would be happy to have lunch with them whenever he could. Patrizia felt even more disillusioned when she heard his response.

The morning of May 26, Patrizia lay on a hospital gurney, her dark hair completely shorn for the operation. She had kissed her daughters and squeezed her mother's hand; but until the orderlies wheeled her away, she kept a constant lookout for Maurizio. He didn't appear.

"There I was—I didn't know if I was going to come out of that room alive and he didn't even bother to show up," said Patrizia later. "Even though we were separated, I was still the mother of his daughters."

When Patrizia woke up in an anesthetic haze several hours later, she strained to focus on the faces around her bed. She saw her mother, Alessandra, and Allegra, but once again, Maurizio wasn't there. She didn't know that Silvana and the doctors had discouraged him from coming, for fear his presence would upset her.

Unable to concentrate, Maurizio had spent the entire morning pacing in his office. He finally told Liliana he was going out to send flowers to Patrizia. When she offered to order them, he declined. He knew exactly the orchids she loved, and wanted to pick them out himself. As he walked up Via Manzoni to Redaelli, the florist of the fashion set and the same shop where Tom Ford and Richard Buckley had bought the bouquet for Dawn Mello, Maurizio pondered what to write on the accompanying note. Afraid Patrizia might misinterpret any words, he finally decided to simply sign his own name: MAURIZIO GUCCI. When the flowers arrived in Patrizia's hospital room, she threw them angrily on the table, leaving them there unopened. The orchids Maurizio had so carefully selected were the same ones she had planted in front of L'Oiseau Bleu—a cruel reminder that she was no longer welcome there. When Patrizia came home a week later to more orchids and a note from Maurizio that said "get well soon," she burst into tears and threw herself on the bed.

"That *disgraziato* didn't even come to see me!" she cried.

Patrizia, who had been given only a few months to live, spurred her lawyers into action. They impounded her first divorce agreement with Maurizio, arguing that because of her illness she had been mentally unfit at the time she agreed to the terms, which had awarded her the Galleria Passarella apartment, one of the two Olympic Tower apartments, a lump sum of 4 billion lire (more than $3 million at the time), two weeks of paid vacation at a leading hotel in Saint Moritz for her and the girls, and 20 million lire, or about $16,000, a month for the girls. They renegotiated a new agreement with far more generous provisions, including 1.1 million Swiss francs a year, or about $846,000; a one-time payment in 1994 of 650,000 Swiss francs, or about $550,000; free use during her lifetime of the penthouse apartment in Galleria Passarella, which would be deeded to Alessandra and Allegra; and for Silvana, Patrizia's mother, an apartment in Monte Carlo and 1 million Swiss francs, slightly less than $850,000.

The tumor, initially feared to be malignant, was later diagnosed as benign. As Patrizia recuperated, she regained her energy and strength by thinking about her revenge on Maurizio Gucci.

"Vendetta," she wrote in her diary on June 2, quoting from Italian feminist writer Barbara Alberti. "I forgot that vendetta is not just for the downtrodden but also for the angels. Get your revenge because you are right. Be uncompromising because you have been offended. Superiority does not mean letting it all go but finding the best way to humiliate him and free yourself." A few days later she penned: "As soon as I am fit to talk to the press, if my doctors allow it, I want everyone to know who you really are. I will go on television, I will persecute you until death, until I have ruined you." She spit her fury out in a cassette tape and had it hand-delivered to Maurizio.

> Dear Maurizio, am I mistaken, or did you lose your mother as a young boy? Naturally, you did not know what it meant to have a father either, especially seeing how easy it was to weasel out of your responsibility to your daughters and my mother the day of my operation, without which they gave me a month to live. . . . I want to tell you that you are a monster, a monster that belongs on the front pages of all the papers, because I want everyone to know what you are really like. I will go on television, I will go to America, I will make them talk about you. . . .

Maurizio sat at his desk listening as the tape recorder played her sharp voice churning out the hate-filled words.

> Maurizio, I am not going to give you a minute of peace. Don't make up excuses, saying they wouldn't let you come visit me . . . my little darlings risked losing their mother and my mother risked losing her only daughter. You hoped. . . . You tried to crush me, but you couldn't. Now I have looked death in the face. . . . You drive around in a Ferrari, which you bought secretly because you had to appear to have no money, while here in the house the white couches have turned beige, the parquet has a hole in it, the carpeting needs to be replaced, and the walls need to be restored—you know that Pompeian stucco crumbles with time! But there is no money! Everything for *Signor Presidente,* but what about the others? . . . Maurizio, you have reached the limit—even your own daughters don't respect you and don't want to see you anymore to better forget the trauma. . . . You are a painful appendage that we all want to forget. . . . Maurizio, the inferno for you is yet to come.

Maurizio suddenly grabbed the tape recorder, tore the cassette out, and threw it across his office. He refused to listen to the rest and turned the cassette over to Franchini, who added it to his growing collection and advised Maurizio to hire a bodyguard. When he had calmed down, Maurizio decided to laugh it off. He didn't want to live obsessed with Patrizia's threats. That August he agreed to let Patrizia convalesce in Saint Moritz at her beloved L'Oiseau Bleu. She had a restful vacation—and renewed her claim to the estate.

"Desidero avere per sempre Oiseau Bleu," she penned in her diary; "I want my Oiseau Bleu forever."

Despite the generous revision in the terms of their agreement, true to her promise, Patrizia went to the press. She invited journalists to her Galleria Passarella apartment for interviews in which she smeared Maurizio as a businessman, husband, and father. Maurizio believed even the rumors that he had had homosexual affairs—by all accounts unfounded—could be traced back to Patrizia.

She appeared on a leading women's talk show, *Harem,* caked in makeup and dripping with jewels. She sat on the plump studio couch and complained to the audience that Maurizio Gucci had tried to wash his hands of her "with a plate of lentils," namely, the Milan penthouse, the New York apartment, and 4 billion lire.

"Something that is already mine shouldn't be part of the agreement," she protested as the other guests, not to mention viewers around the country, watched her, dumbfounded. "I have to think about our daughters, who find themselves without a future. . . . I must fight for the girls; if their father wants to go off on his *Creole* for six months at a time, well, let him go."

IN THE FALL OF 1993, when Patrizia realized that Maurizio risked losing control of the company, she intervened on his behalf; not because she wanted to help him, she explained later, but to save the Gucci company for his daughters. She said she acted as an intermediary with Investcorp, trying in vain—as so many others had—to persuade Maurizio to accept an honorary chairmanship and step back from management control. She tried to help him find money to get his shares back and claimed she sent the lawyer, Piero Giuseppe Parodi, who put Maurizio in touch with Zorzi for the last-minute financing that saved his Gucci shares from auction. When Maurizio lost his battle with Investcorp and was forced to sell his 50 percent stake in Gucci, Patrizia took it as a personal blow.

"Are you crazy?" she screamed at him. "That is the most demented thing you could have done!"

The loss of Gucci became another festering wound.

"For her, Gucci represented everything," said her former friend Pina Auriemma years later. "It was money, it was power, it was an identity for her and the girls."

15

PARADEISOS

Reaching over to the night table, Maurizio switched off the alarm clock before it sounded. Paola murmured and nuzzled her face deeper into the pillow. Maurizio put down the clock and looked across the room, past two green couches arranged intimately in front of the gas-burning fireplace to the large picture window that spanned the entire wall. The morning light had started to creep in softly through the blinds and gold silk drapes, which they always left slightly open in order to see the plant-covered balcony and garden below. Peacocks' screeching filtered up from the Invernizzi garden next door, while sounds of traffic starting to fill Corso Venezia were barely audible. Maurizio liked the sense of peace the apartment gave him, even though it was located in the heart of downtown Milan, a stone's throw from the elegant shops on Via Monte Napoleone and Via della Spiga that had once been the backdrop for the dream of his life.

For the first few months after he sold his stake in Gucci, Maurizio had lived in a daze, a state of shock, as though someone has died. He blamed Investcorp for not giving him enough time to achieve the turnaround, Dawn Mello for not sticking to his design concept, De Sole for betraying him. He felt he had been outmaneuvered.

"The big issue for Maurizio was that of betraying his father," said Paola, later. "His fear was of betraying all the work that had been done before him and that caused him a lot of anguish," she recalled. "Once he realized he had no choice but to sell, he relaxed. It was out of his hands."

With his debts paid off and more than $100 million left in the bank from the sale of his Gucci shares, for the first time in his life Maurizio Gucci had no battles to fight.

After the sale, Maurizio bought a bicycle, which he stored in the basement of the Corso Venezia building. Then he vanished from Milan. He sailed the *Creole* back to Saint-Tropez for the Nioularge, then he holed up by himself in Saint Moritz. As the weeks passed, the fog and depression started to lift. He realized that a huge burden had been taken from him.

"For the first time in his life, he could decide what he wanted to do for his own future," said Paola. "Maurizio hadn't had a carefree childhood; he had always felt the pressure of his name and all that the name brought with it. His father had thrown a lot at him and Maurizio had a strong sense that he was supposed to do what was 'right.' Then there was the jealousy of his cousins because he had inherited fifty percent without really doing anything, while it was their father who had built the Gucci name."

In early 1994, he came back to Milan, picked up his bicycle, and rode it back and forth from his Corso Venezia apartment to Fabio Franchini's offices on the other side of town, where he started drafting his ideas for new business ventures. "He didn't have anyplace to go and so he came here," recalled Franchini. "At eight o'clock in the morning, he was already here, a churning volcano of ideas."

During one of his early-morning rides, Maurizio stopped off in Piazza San Fedele. On that chilly, gray morning in early February 1994, Gucci's communications director, Pilar Crespi, had arrived early at the company's San Fedele headquarters and walked up the carpeted stairs to her second-floor office long before anyone else reported for work. As Crespi moved around her desk, sorting through piles of glossy fashion magazines, her chiseled features pulled tight in concentration, something suddenly caught her eye outside her window. Below, the recently cleaned chalky facades of the church and surrounding buildings in Piazza San Fedele shimmered in the pale, early-morning light, looking like a ghostly opera stage set in nearby La

Scala. Crespi put down her papers and moved to one side of the window to peer out without being seen. A silent, lone figure sat on one of the marble benches opposite the building, staring up at Gucci's offices. The man was wrapped in a camel overcoat, his dark blond hair just brushing his collar. His figure blended so well into the surrounding stone and marble that she almost didn't see him at first, but a familiar movement caught her eye as he brought one hand up to push his glasses higher on his nose. Crespi gasped—Maurizio Gucci sat looking up at the building. She hadn't seen him for nearly a year. For weeks before the sale he had been remote and inaccessible; after the sale he had dropped entirely out of sight. She watched him as he slowly scanned the Gucci building, as though he were trying to visualize what was going on inside. As she watched him sitting there, a wave of sorrow swept over Crespi. She thought about how patient and generous he had been with her in the beginning, letting her postpone her starting date until her son had finished school in New York and she could arrange a move to Milan. She recalled how energetic and enthusiastic he was—until desperation transformed him into a paranoid and unpredictable employer.

"There was an expression of such sadness on his face," Crespi said later. "San Fedele had been his dream. He just sat there and looked up."

"I am my own chairman now," Maurizio said later to Paola. He founded a new company, Viersee Italia, and rented offices opposite the park in Via Palestro, a few paces from their home. Paula helped him furnish the rooms with bright wallpaper and colorful Chinese lacquered wood pieces, and Antonietta gave him amulets and powders to ward off Patrizia's evil spells. He knew Paola frowned on his superstitions, but he liked Antonietta; she reassured him and gave him good advice. He turned to her the way other men might seek out a financial analyst or psychologist.

Maurizio earmarked $10 million and gave himself a year to develop new investment prospects in any sector but fashion. Particularly interested in tourism, Maurizio started looking at several projects. First, he had been asked to help sponsor a port for historic boats in Palma de Mallorca, the Spanish harbor where he kept the *Creole*. He also sent a team of scouts to Korea and Cambodia to explore new tourism prospects there. In addition, he thought about opening a chain of small luxury inns in picturesque European cities, and invested 60,000 Swiss francs—less than $50,000—in a hotel in Crans-Montana, the Swiss skiing resort. The hotel, a prototype for a larger chain, featured pinball games and other activities in the lobby, including slot machines.

"He was studying things very carefully," said Liliana, who continued as his secretary after Maurizio left Gucci. "He wasn't just throwing money at things the way he did at Gucci. Before taking on a new project, we worked very hard. He had finally grown up."

Maurizio's old charm and enthusiasm crept back. For the first time in his life, he lived for himself. He bought clothes for his new role, leaving the gray CEO suits in the closet unless he had a special business meeting. Cotton twill pants, corduroys, and sports shirts became his new uniform. His ties peeked out from under cashmere sweaters instead of jackets. Even though he had lost his company, he strove to hold on to his *bella figura*—Maurizio had the right style for every occasion. He loved doing simple things and when he jogged along the shady paths of the Giardini Pubblici, he did it with U.S.-bought running gear. When he rode his bike around town, he had the perfect touring bike and the right casual apparel. Maurizio also tried to spend more time with Alessandra and Allegra, though Patrizia still made it difficult for him to see them, especially when Paola was around.

Remembering how tightfisted his own father had been about giving him spending money, in June 1994 Maurizio gave Alessandra 150 million lire (about $93,000) for her eighteenth birthday, saying that the money was for her to manage, and should also cover the cost of her debutante party.

"I want you to be responsible for the money and to manage it as you like—you can choose to throw a big party or a small one, depending on how you want to spend your money," Maurizio said to his oldest daughter. Despite Maurizio's wishes, Patrizia immediately took over the party planning—and arranged plastic surgery for herself and her daughter "in order to look our best for the event." Patrizia had her nose done; Alessandra, her breasts.

The night of September 16, some four hundred guests made their way up the candlelit drive to Villa Borromeo di Cassano d'Adda outside Milan, which Patrizia had rented for the evening. The champagne continued to flow after a sumptuous dinner as the band tuned up and the guests squealed in delight to discover that the musicians were none other than the popular Gypsy Kings—whom Patrizia had hired at an exorbitant cost to surprise Alessandra.

Maurizio had failed to show up and Alessandra's godfather, Giovanni Valcavi, greeted the guests alongside Patrizia and Alessandra. During dinner, Patrizia turned to Cosimo Auletta, the lawyer who had handled her divorce settlement and was seated at the same table with her.

"*Avvocato,*" she said coyly as she seethed inside over Maurizio's absence, "what would happen if I decided to teach Maurizio a lesson?"

"What do you mean, 'teach Maurizio a lesson'?" the startled lawyer replied.

"I mean, what would happen to me if I got rid of him?" Patrizia specified more directly, batting her dark, mascara-covered eyelashes.

"I don't even want to joke about such a thing," muttered the shocked Auletta, who changed the subject. When she asked him the same thing a month later in his office, Auletta refused to represent her anymore. He wrote her a letter inviting her to stop such discourse and reported the conversations to Franchini and Patrizia's mother.

Several days after the party, Maurizio called Alessandra into his Via Palestro office. The bank had called to tell him her new bank account was 50 million lire overdrawn (about $30,000).

"Alessandra," Maurizio said sternly. "The bank tells me your account is overdrawn by fifty million lire. I don't intend to cover this amount and I want an explanation as to where the money went!"

Alessandra shifted uncomfortably under her father's gaze.

"I'm sorry, *Papà*, I know I have let you down," she said in a halting voice. "I don't know what it all went for; you know *Mamma* took over all the arrangements. I promise I will go over all the accounting. I promise it won't happen again."

When Alessandra came back with the accounts, it became clear that in addition to checks paid to the caterers and other services for the party, Patrizia had spent 43 million lire ($27,000) of Alessandra's money that couldn't be accounted for. Maurizio, exasperated, finally paid off the account. The financial lesson had failed.

On November 19, 1994, Maurizio's divorce from Patrizia became official. That Friday, he went home at lunchtime to surprise Paola, greeting her in the living room with a big smile and two martinis in his hands when she came home.

"Paola, starting today I am a free man!" he said as they clinked glasses and kissed. A month earlier, Paola had received her divorce from Colombo. Maurizio finally felt he could rebuild his life, free from the personal and business problems that had so absorbed him up to then. He ordered Patrizia to stop using the Gucci name and started the paperwork to seek custody of the two girls. According to those closest to him, Maurizio didn't want to remarry. However, he did ask Franchini to look into a relationship contract for Paola. Paola, of a different mind, told friends she and Maurizio were planning a Christmas wedding in the snow at Saint Moritz with a horse-drawn sleigh piled high with furs. That news flew back to Patrizia, who worried they might have a child together.

Patrizia vented her fury in a new project—a five-hundred-page manuscript, part fact, part fiction, called *Gucci vs. Gucci,* that she had started after Maurizio lost the company. She called her friend Pina to come up from Naples to help her finish the imaginative chronicle of her experiences in the Gucci family. Pina had grown destitute following the failure of a clothing boutique she had opened with a friend and was glad to flee Naples and her mounting debts. She confessed to Patrizia she had stolen 50 million lire, or about $30,000, from the cash box in her nephew's business where she had helped out for a time, and was eager to get out of town. Patrizia offered to put her up in a Milan hotel, but didn't invite her to stay in the house—Silvana and the girls didn't like Pina, finding her vulgar and unclean.

MAURIZIO SLIPPED QUIETLY out of bed so as not to wake Paola. He felt rested after spending a quiet weekend at home in Milan instead of going to Saint Moritz as they had originally planned. Charly had visited his father, leaving Maurizio and Paola to themselves. Maurizio had just returned Wednesday from New York, where he had settled an old debt with Citicorp that was still hanging over his head from his embattled days at Gucci. Every reminder of the trauma he had been through made Maurizio feel fatigued and depressed all over again.

That Friday, just before noon, Maurizio had decided he was too tired to make the three-hour drive to Saint Moritz. He called Paola, who canceled an appointment with the upholstery man in Saint Moritz, while Liliana notified the household staff in Saint Moritz and Milan of the change in plans. Most upper-class Milan families rarely spend weekends in the city, heading instead for the nearby Alps in the winter and the Ligurian seaside in the summer. Maurizio—in his new appreciation of a simpler life—enjoyed a weekend in Milan from time to time. As he left the office that Friday, his desk covered with a creative disarray of papers, pamphlets, and notes about his new projects, he taped his door closed with a note to the cleaning lady, asking her not to touch anything.

On Sunday, after sleeping late and enjoying a lazy breakfast on the terrace, Maurizio and Paola visited the antiques market in the Navigli neighborhood along the two canals that lead into the city, where once a month the sidewalks are filled with antiques dealers selling their wares. Maurizio's only disappointment that weekend was that he hadn't been able to see his daughters.

He had met Alessandra briefly on Friday at the driving school where she had gone to take her driver's test. The next day she called him elatedly to say she had passed.

"Fantastic!" Maurizio responded on the phone. "Next weekend, we'll go to Saint Moritz together, just you and me." That was the last time she spoke to her father.

On Sunday night, Maurizio agreed to a movie and dinner with a group of Paola's friends. At home together later that evening, he and Paola brainstormed for a name for the chain of small luxury hotels Maurizio wanted to open. His eye fell on a book of Chinese fairy tales on his night table entitled *Il Paradiso nella Giara,* or *Paradise in a Jar.*

"That's it," he thought, repeating the name over and over again before he fell asleep. " 'Paradise in a Jar'; it's perfect."

Maurizio showered the next morning in the spacious marble tiled bathroom next to their bedroom, thinking about the day ahead. His first appointment was at 9:30 A.M. in his office with Antonietta, whose opinion he wanted on some of his project ideas. Afterward he had a meeting with Franchini and a business lunch to which he had also invited Paola. However, he hoped to make it a short day—he had recently bought a new set of billiard sticks for his table and he wanted to get home early and give them a whirl.

Maurizio walked back into the bedroom after his shower just as Paola lifted her disheveled head off the pillow. Leaning over to give her a kiss, he picked up the remote control to open the automatic blinds covering the picture windows at the far end of their room. She blinked sleepily as the blinds lifted, flooding the room with morning light. An oasis of green foliage appeared outside their windows, creating the illusion that they were living in a garden paradise rather than downtown Milan.

Maurizio dressed, picking out a gray wool Prince of Wales suit, a crisp blue shirt, and a blue silk Gucci tie. Maurizio refused to give up Gucci ties after the sale of the company, and didn't see why he should. He sent Liliana into the shop from time to time to buy them for him—by that time, De Sole had graciously offered him a discount, although up to then, no members of the Gucci family were offered discounts in Gucci stores. He strapped on the brown leather band of his Tiffany watch and tucked a pocket diary in his jacket, along with some notes he had made for himself over the weekend. He slipped a coral and gold good luck charm into his right front pants pocket, a metal plaque with an enameled face of Jesus into the back pocket. Paola wriggled into a robe and they walked down the hall together, greeted by the smell of fresh coffee wafting out of the kitchen. Adriana, the cook, had prepared breakfast, which Paola's Somalian maid served them in the grand dining room. Maurizio picked up the paper and glanced at the day's headlines as he ate a breakfast roll and sipped his coffee. Paola—always careful about her waistline—spooned up a yogurt.

Maurizio put the paper down, drained his coffee cup, and looked over at her with a warm smile.

"You'll come over around twelve-thirty?" he asked, reaching over to cup her hand in his. She smiled and nodded. Maurizio got up, poked his head in the kitchen to say goodbye to Adriana, and walked out to the hallway, Paola behind him. He slipped on his camel overcoat because the morning air still had a nip to it. Putting his arms around Paola, he said to her, "Go back to bed if you like, sweetheart," he said. "There's plenty of time until lunch. Take your time, there's no need to rush."

He kissed her goodbye and walked quickly down the regal stone staircase, running his hand over the marble obelisks on the landing. Stepping through the great wooden doors and out onto the sidewalk, he glanced at his watch—just after 8:30 A.M. He waited at the corner for the light to change and crossed over Corso Venezia before walking briskly up the sidewalk along Via Palestro, in a hurry to put his papers in order before Antonietta arrived. He scanned the park across the street and counted his paces as he had so many times before: one hundred steps from door to door. Being able to walk to work was a true luxury, he mused as he neared the entryway at Via Palestro 20. He hardly noticed the dark-haired man standing on the sidewalk looking up at the number of the building as though checking the address.

Arms swinging, Maurizio walked in through the doorway of his building and greeted the doorman, Giuseppe Onorato, as he bounded up the stairs.

"*Buongiorno!*"

"*Buongiorno, Dottore,*" said Giuseppe Onorato, looking up from his sweeping.

ONLY THE MAID saw Patrizia Reggiani sobbing uncontrollably the morning of March 27, 1995, after she heard the news of Maurizio's death. Afterward, she dried her tears, pulled herself together, and penned a single word in her Cartier diary, all in capital letters: PARADEISOS, meaning "paradise" in Greek. With her pen, she slowly drew a bold black border around the date. At three o'clock that afternoon, Patrizia walked the few blocks from her apartment in Piazza San Babila to Corso Venezia 38, along with her lawyer,

Piero Giuseppe Parodi, and her oldest daughter, Alessandra. She rang the bell of Maurizio's apartment and asked for Paola Franchi, who was trying to take a nap.

That morning, a distraught Antonietta had come to the door shortly after Maurizio had left, asking for Paola. Antonietta said she had reported to Maurizio's office for their appointment, but had been unable to enter because of the growing crowd. She had rushed over immediately to tell Paola something was wrong. Paola had flung on some clothes and run across the street, pushing her way through the journalists crowding around the big doors.

"I'm the wife! I'm the wife!" she had cried breathlessly to the carabinieri who were restraining the journalists. They let her pass. Just as she was about to enter the wide wooden doors, Maurizio's friend, Carlo Bruno, came out of the crowd and pulled her away.

"Paola," he said gravely, "don't go in there. Come with me."

"Is it Maurizio?" she asked.

"Yes," he said.

"Is he hurt? I want to go to him," she whimpered, pressing back against Bruno's arm as they walked alongside the park. They had reached the intersection of Via Palestro with Corso Venezia.

"There's nothing more to be done," he said softly as she looked at him in disbelief. A few hours later, Paola went to see Maurizio in the city morgue.

"He was lying on the table, stomach-down, with his face turned to one side," Paola said. "He had a tiny little hole in his temple, but otherwise he was perfect. That was the incredible thing about him, when he traveled, when he slept, he was always perfect. He never seemed to wrinkle or look rumpled."

That afternoon, Milan magistrate Nocerino interrogated Paola about the murder, asking her if Maurizio had any enemies.

"The only thing I can tell you is that in the fall of 1994, Maurizio was worried because he learned from his lawyer, Franchini, that Patrizia had told her lawyer, Auletta, she wanted to have him killed," Paola said dully. "I remember that after those threats Franchini seemed more worried than Maurizio did, telling him to protect himself in some way. But Maurizio just let it roll off his back."

Nocerino raised his dark eyebrows skeptically. "And you, signora, were you protected in any way?" he asked.

"No, there was no piece of paper, no economic agreement between us, if that is what you want to know," said Paola stiffly, offended. "Our relationship was purely emotional."

Paola had gone back to Corso Venezia and was trying to sleep when Patrizia rang the bell and demanded to come up, saying they had important legal matters to discuss. When the servant said no, Paola was resting, Alessandra began to cry, asking if she could at least have a memento of her father, one of his cashmere sweaters. Paola refused to receive Patrizia, but instructed the servant to give Alessandra a sweater, which the girl received gratefully, burying her head in it to breath her father's scent.

Paola called Franchini to ask what she should do, but found little comfort. He told her she could only step aside. The relationship contract Maurizio had asked him to prepare was still an unsigned draft in Franchini's office. Paola had no legal claim to Maurizio's estate, which would go directly to his daughters. She should make arrangements to evacuate Corso Venezia as soon as possible.

The next morning, Patrizia came back—but not before a court official arrived to seal off the house based on a court sequester filed by "the heirs of Maurizio Gucci" at 11 A.M. the day before. Paola looked at the official, aghast.

"At eleven A.M. yesterday, Maurizio Gucci had only been dead a few hours," she protested. She persuaded the official to seal off only one room. "I live here with my son," she said. "How do you expect us to go so soon?"

Patrizia had moved quickly, but so had Paola—after her conversation with Franchini she made several phone calls and by late afternoon, a squad of movers loaded furniture, light fixtures, drapes, china, cutlery, and more into three moving vans parked in front of Corso Venezia 38. The next day, Patrizia's lawyers ordered Paola to return everything, although in the end she was permitted to keep pieces she said were hers, including a set of green silk living room draperies that Patrizia had hotly contested.

"I am here as a mother, not as a wife," Patrizia said coldly as she was ushered into the living room of Corso Venezia 38 the next morning. "You must leave as soon as possible," Patrizia explained. "This was Maurizio's house and now it will be the house of his heirs," she said, looking around the room. "What exactly do you plan to take with you?"

At 10 A.M. on Monday, April 3, a black Mercedes carrying Maurizio Gucci's coffin pulled up in Milan's Piazza San Babila in front of the church of San Carlo, whose yellow facade was in full view of the terrace of Patrizia's penthouse apartment. Four pallbearers got out and carried the coffin into the church, where few mourners had yet arrived. Liliana, standing outside with her husband, peeked inside the church and saw the coffin, draped in gray velvet with three large wreaths of gray and white flowers on top, standing alone in front of the altar. She put a hand on her husband's arm.

"Let's go inside with Maurizio," she said in a quavering voice. "I can't bear to see him there all alone."

Patrizia had made all the funeral arrangements. Paola stayed home. That morning, Patrizia played the perfect widow, wearing a black veil over dark black sunglasses, black suit, and black leather gloves. She didn't hide her true feelings, however.

"On a human level, I'm sorry; on a personal level, I can't say the same thing," Patrizia said flippantly to waiting journalists.

She took her place in the front row of mourners, alongside Alessandra and Allegra, who also wore large black sunglasses to hide their tears. No more than two hundred people showed up and of these, only a few friends, such as Beppe Diana, Rina Alemagna, Chicca Olivetti, names from the ranks of northern Italian industrial aristocracy. Many others had stayed home, fearing scandal surrounding Gucci's sinister death. For the same reason, many more refrained from placing the customary death announcements in the local newspapers in solidarity with the family of the deceased. The news stories were filled with speculation about Gucci's mafia-style execution and conjecture about shady business deals—infuriating Bruno and Franchini and others close to Maurizio who knew his affairs were above suspicion. Most of the people who came to the funeral were former employees who wanted to bid Maurizio goodbye, as well as journalists and curious onlookers. Giorgio Gucci flew up from Rome with his wife, Maria Pia, and their son Guccio Gucci, who had been named for his grandfather. They sat in a pew several rows behind Patrizia. Paolo's daughter Patrizia also came. Maurizio had taken pity on her despite his conflicts with her father and hired her to work in Gucci's public relations office in the years before he sold to Investcorp.

"Here we say goodbye to Maurizio Gucci and to all the Maurizios who lose their lives because of all the Cains of all time," said the priest, Don Mariano Merlo, as two undercover carabinieri secretly filmed and photographed the short ceremony and scrutinized the guest book, looking for possible clues leading to the killer. After the ceremony, the dark Mercedes pulled away and headed for Saint Moritz, where Patrizia had decided Maurizio would be buried, instead of with his family in Florence.

Afterward, Antonio, the sacristan, murmured sadly, "there were more television cameras and curious onlookers than friends."

"The atmosphere was more strange than sad," observed Lina Sotis, a society columnist for *Corriere della Sera,* speculating mischievously whether the murderer might have really been present at the funeral, as in the best mysteries. Sotis coolly remarked that despite his name and his wealth, Maurizio had never found a niche in Milan, Italy's financial and fashion capital.

"Maurizio Gucci, in this city, was in the shadows. Everybody knew his name, but few knew him," she wrote in her report the next day. " 'Milan is too tough for me,' he confided once to a friend. That blond-haired, blue-eyed boy could permit himself everything—everything except for a loving woman at his side and a tough city like Milan."

The next day, Paola organized her own mass for Maurizio in the San Bartolomeo Church near Via Moscova on the other side of the Giardini Pubblici from the Corso Venezia apartment.

"You knew how to win our hearts, but someone did not love you as much as we did," said Denis Le Cordeur, Paola's cousin and a friend of Maurizio's, reading a brief commemoration. "Someone who not only committed one crime, but ten, twenty, fifty crimes—as many as we are here today, because in every one of us who knew you, something has been killed."

A few months later, Patrizia triumphantly moved into Corso Venezia 38, where she had gotten rid of every trace of Paola, who returned to her ex-husband's condominium. In the girls' rooms, Patrizia had ordered the flow-ered wallpaper torn from the walls and the frilly canopy beds moved out. She redid the rooms in her own taste with polished Venetian furniture and printed fabrics and transformed the children's living room, which Paola had deco-rated with dark wine colors, into a television room for herself and the girls, painting the walls a bright salmon pink. She moved in her pink, blue, and yel-low floral couches and tassel-trimmed curtains to match from the Galleria Passarella penthouse. From one wall, she hung a larger-than-life oil portrait of herself, her face framed by the long gleaming locks of brown hair she had always desired.

Downstairs, she changed as little as possible, although she sold the bil-liard table and restyled the game room as a living room. At night, she slept in Maurizio's grand Empire bed, waking up to the sounds of peacocks squawk-ing in the Invernizzi gardens below. In the mornings, after her bath, she donned Maurizio's cozy terry cloth bathrobe.

"He may have died," she told a friend, "but I have just begun to live."

At the beginning of 1996 she penned a phrase on the inside cover of a new leather-bound Cartier diary: "Few women can truly capture the heart of a man—even fewer manage to own it."

16

TURNAROUND

On Monday morning, September 26, 1993, the first workday that Investcorp controlled 100 percent of Gucci, Bill Flanz and a small group of executives found themselves huddling outdoors in the courtyard of Piazza San Fedele: locked out of their own offices.

After closing the transaction with Maurizio and giving him the time to clear out his personal belongings, Flanz had given instructions to Massetti to secure the building during the weekend.

"I organized an airtight security service from Friday evening at nine P.M. to Monday morning at nine A.M.," recalled Massetti. "I gave strict orders that nobody, but nobody, would be allowed to enter the building before nine A.M."

Bill Flanz, Investcorp's man-in-charge, asked the top Gucci executives and managers to report to Piazza

San Fedele early Monday morning to tackle the most urgent financial and staffing problems immediately. But when they arrived at Gucci's double front doors at 8:00 A.M.—eager to get started—the guards refused to let them in. Even when Flanz explained that he was in charge, the guards just shook their heads and followed their orders. The group entered the building at 9:01 A.M.

"They didn't care if we were from Investcorp or not," Flanz recalled sheepishly. "They followed their orders—and we had to start our meeting out in the courtyard!"

Restructuring began that morning with an emergency transfer of $15 million from Investcorp to pay off the most urgent accounts. Rick Swanson calculated that the company would need a total of about $50 million, including the initial $15 million, to pay off its obligations and get up and running again, money that Investcorp quickly injected into the company.

"Each [Gucci] company had its own debt problem," Swanson recalled. "It was like having a bunch of little hungry birds that all had to eat at once."

Even though he had been a frequent visitor to the fifth floor of Piazza San Fedele, Flanz felt somewhat awed when he took over Maurizio's office. He sat in Maurizio's antique chair and ran his hands over the smooth, carved lion's heads on the front of the armrests and looked at his surroundings as though in disbelief. The professor's son who grew up in Yonkers and mowed lawns for pocket money was at the helm of one of the best-known luxury names in the world.

"I had worked at Chase Manhattan Bank, met often with David Rockefeller in his office, visited captains of industry and heads of state around the world, and I don't think I had ever seen a more elegant office than the one I inherited from Maurizio," Flanz said later.

That Monday, the first day Gucci opened its doors without a Gucci at its helm, Maurizio turned forty-five years old. The day before, Bill Flanz had turned forty-nine.

"It was a big birthday for each of us," Flanz said later. "Maurizio got $120 million and I got to run Gucci!"

The next day, Flanz took the train to Florence to soothe Gucci's angry workers as best he could, with the help of a translator. The disgruntled workers feared that Investcorp would scrap all in-house production and turn Gucci into a large buying office, sourcing all of its products from outside suppliers.

About a week later, Flanz asked Maurizio to attend a Gucci board meeting to formalize the change of leadership. Investcorp had appointed Flanz head of a committee composed of Gucci and Investcorp managers and given him all executive powers to handle the transition. They met on neutral territory, the offices of one of their lawyers in Milan. Again, Maurizio and his advisors were ushered into one room while Flanz and his colleagues sat in another. Flanz finally decided the separation was ridiculous and walked down the hall to greet Maurizio.

"Hello, Maurizio," Flanz said, with a soft smile. "There's no sense in us acting like strangers."

Maurizio looked Flanz in the eye as they shook hands. "Now you will see what it is like to pedal the bicycle," said Maurizio.

"Would you like to have lunch sometime?" Flanz asked him.

"First you pedal the bicycle for a while," Maurizio said evenly. "Then if you still want to, we'll have lunch."

Flanz never saw him again.

THE BATTLE MAURIZIO LOST could be seen on several different levels. He had inherited a difficult, if not impossible, legacy. His vision of a new future for Gucci was clouded by his inability to set his plans on an even keel, to marshal his resources for the task. His pattern of relationships—molded on that first, intense relationship with his father—further kept him from finding and keeping a steady shoulder to help him with his mission, whether in his personal or his professional life.

"Maurizio had this tremendous charisma and charm, the ability to sweep people away with him," recalled Alberta Ballerini, Gucci's longtime ready-to-wear coordinator. "But it was a shame because he lacked the base. He was like someone who built a house without making sure the foundation was there."

"Maurizio was a genius," agreed another longtime employee, Rita Cimino, "he had excellent ideas, but he wasn't able to carry them out. His big defect was that he couldn't find the right people to help him. He surrounded himself with people who weren't right. He would fall in love with them—because he was very sentimental—and then suddenly he would realize that they weren't right, but by then it would be too late," Cimino said. "I think he fell in love with them because he was attracted to their cynicism and because he realized that he could never be that tough—he looked to these kinds of people for support."

"It is very difficult to fall in love with the right person," ventured Massetti. "It happens rarely in life, and Maurizio was particularly unlucky. The people who had some sense never got close to him and those that did only lasted a little while before they got burned."

"What destroyed Maurizio was money," said Domenico De Sole. "Rodolfo had been thrifty and built a fortune—but he failed to teach thrift to his son. When Maurizio ran out of money, he became desperate."

Maurizio's fight was also a symbolic game of chicken that hundreds of

Italian family firms—both in and out of the fashion sector—were increasingly forced to play on the road to the global marketplace. They risked either being knocked off the road or overrun by giant multinationals. It is difficult for family-owned firms such as Gucci to attract and control the new capital and professional management resources they desperately need to stay in the race.

"In this industry there are so many companies with potential that never take off because the founder is still in control," said Mario Massetti, who continued to work for Gucci under Investcorp's ownership. "These are people who often have been geniuses at launching an idea, but their very presence holds it back. Maurizio set everything into motion, but at the same time, he blocked so many things."

On the other hand, Concetta Lanciaux, the powerful director of human resources for Bernard Arnault's luxury goods group LVMH, is sure that "Gucci would not be there today if it had not been for the vision of Maurizio Gucci." Maurizio had tried to woo Lanciaux, who is credited with spotting new talent and bringing it into the LVMH group, away from Arnault in 1989 when he was launching his dream for the new Gucci. She found his vision compelling.

"He had convinced Dawn Mello and he almost convinced me," admitted Lanciaux. "Like Arnault, he was a true visionary and the vision is the fundamental thing that moves a company forward."

Unlike Arnault, who had a loyal and competent deputy at his side in the figure of Pierre Godé, Maurizio had never found the strong, trusted deputy who could have given a practical foundation to his dreams. A strong relationship between the creative figure and the business manager had proven a winning formula at other leading Italian fashion houses. Valentino and Giancarlo Giammetti, Gianfranco Ferré and Gianfranco Mattioli, Giorgio Armani and Sergio Galeotti, and Gianni Versace and his brother Santo were just a few examples. Over the years at Gucci, many moved in and out of that role, but there was no single person who was able to give overriding continuity to Maurizio's grand plan. Andrea Morante paved Maurizio's way for a time in his various roles. Nemir Kirdar and his team at Investcorp partnered Maurizio and his dream—until it became financially unsustainable. Domenico De Sole lasted the longest, proved the most devastating to Maurizio, and would emerge as Gucci's true survivor.

Maurizio's lawyer, Fabio Franchini, still one of Maurizio's most passionate defenders, believes Investcorp cut Maurizio out too soon.

"They didn't even give him three years to put his dream in place," said Franchini, bitterly. "Maurizio's first results were approved in January 1991, and by September 1993, they had forced him to sell," he said, shaking his head. Franchini, who advised Maurizio step-by-step throughout the battle with Investcorp, grew close to him, although they always addressed each other with the formal *Lei*. Franchini still refers to Maurizio formally as *Dottore,* but his eyes light up and the wide mouth opens into a face-splitting smile at the mention of his name. Franchini now manages Maurizio's estate for his two daughters, Alessandra and Allegra.

"I want to save what's left of Maurizio Gucci for them," Franchini said. "He was an extraordinary man, but he was not prepared for the hard business world. He could never have been trained for it either, because he was a great gentleman—he wasn't thick-skinned. Maurizio Gucci was a correct person through and through."

"I tried to explain to him that it was better to have his cousins on the other side of the table, rather than a powerful financial institution. Maurizio Gucci was finished from the beginning because he was alone, completely and entirely alone with fifty percent—or the equivalent of zero." Franchini said.

Maurizio's inability to find a strong business partner may have cost him his dream, but it was also understandable given his past relationships and his position. So often, the people whom Maurizio Gucci grew close to wanted something from him. Rodolfo wanted utter obedience, Aldo wanted a successor, Patrizia wanted fame and fortune, and Investcorp wanted a calling card with Europe's business elite. As Maurizio fought to secure his hold over his family company, many of those who came forward to help him really sought their own place in the Gucci spotlight.

"When you are healthy, handsome, and have a highly visible last name and the most beautiful boat in the world, it is difficult to make real friends," said Morante. "You find yourself surrounded by people who are in desperate search for the indirect limelight, for easy money, and for the glamour of being associated with a well-known name."

Meanwhile, Flanz pedaled the Gucci bicycle. He hired a new human resources director, Renato Ricci, to help him repair the workers' broken trust in management, thin out excess personnel, streamline operations, and cut costs. In opening the San Fedele office, Maurizio had duplicated many jobs already done in Florence. Flanz asked fifteen out of twenty-two top managers in Milan to leave. He and Ricci tried to be open and fair with the unions in an effort to avoid antagonism. If angered, the unions could have exploded the entire situation onto the front pages of the newspapers—which could have been damaging for the restructuring. In Italy, which was grappling with unemployment and labor issues, the labor unions were powerful enough to topple the government and extract steep compromises from private industry.

"At that point, the one strength of Gucci was still its image," said Ricci. "The unions could have fought us tooth and nail and if we started getting a lot of bad press about firing people, it would really have been a disaster."

In the fall of 1993, to the astonishment of Gucci's management team—which had been focusing primarily on cutting costs—Flanz decided to double Gucci's advertising budget. At the time, Gucci's sales hadn't grown at all for some three years and the company was still losing money.

"We had good products and a good campaign and we had to get it out there and let people see what we had to sell," said Flanz.

In January 1994, Flanz announced Gucci would close the glamorous San Fedele headquarters by March—nearly four years after Maurizio had opened it full of excitement and hope—and move the company headquarters back to Florence.

The women's fashion show in March 1994 marked the end of Gucci's presence in San Fedele. Before the show, Tom Ford and one of the few remaining design assistants, a young Japanese man named Junichi Hakamaki, found themselves hanging the entire collection by themselves.

"No one wanted to help us because they all knew they were being fired," Junichi recalled. "We worked until two A.M. and then we had to be back in the office by five A.M. to bring all the clothes over to the Fiera," he said. The show, which featured a strong, masculine modster jacket and suit look, was well reviewed, though not overwhelmingly so. About a week later, Gucci closed its doors on San Fedele. Only a handful of people moved down to Florence.

There, the remaining managers sat in dingy offices that had never been updated or refurbished, firing angry memos at each other to defend their own positions—but doing little to help move the company forward.

"The workers were depressed," said Ricci. "They had lived for months with the fear of not being paid and that the company was going to go bankrupt. Then they were afraid of Investcorp and of being fired."

"The company was paralyzed," added De Sole, who had been shuttling back and forth between Florence and New York. "Management was completely balkanized, nobody was making decisions, and everybody was terrified of getting blamed. There was no merchandise, no pricing, no word processors, no bamboo handles. It was crazy! Dawn Mello had turned out some nice handbags, but the company couldn't produce them or deliver them."

In the fall of 1994, Flanz appointed Domenico De Sole as chief operating officer and asked him to stay in Florence full time.

De Sole was demoralized and depressed. He had been working for Gucci for ten years as CEO of Gucci America and for several years before that as a lawyer. Not even a year earlier, he had voted with Investcorp against the very man who had brought him into the company—a key move that had permitted the investment bank to take control. He hadn't asked Investcorp for anything in return. Furthermore, Maurizio, still hurt by De Sole's betrayal, balked at paying De Sole the money he owed him and Investcorp settled the deal anyway, without helping De Sole recover the loan.

"We had a responsibility to our investors," explained Elias Hallak later. "That was a personal matter between Maurizio and Domenico."

When Investcorp didn't name De Sole CEO and instead put Bill Flanz in charge of its so-called management committee for Gucci, De Sole called up Investcorp's Bob Glaser and threatened to quit.

"I should be running this company! I am resigning tomorrow!" blustered De Sole. "Everybody else on that committee is either incompetent or corrupt!"

Glaser, who admired and respected De Sole and what he had done, calmed him down—and then gave him some golden advice. "Domenico, I know you are frustrated and you should have that job—I recommended you for it. But let me tell you something as a friend. If it is true that everyone else on the committee is either incompetent or corrupt, stick with it. Eventually you will rise to the top, and others will see your value."

De Sole took Glaser's advice and moved himself and a close group of staff—people he trusted and knew how to work well with—from Gucci America to Florence. In Florence, De Sole and his team found themselves up against a group of angry, surly Florentine workers. Between his early, disparaging attitude toward De Sole and his later disillusionment, Maurizio had poisoned everybody's mind against De Sole—from Kirdar and the senior management at Investcorp down to the Florentine laborers.

"It looked as though we had brought in the American SWAT team and that was destabilizing to the Florentine staff," recalled Rick Swanson, "but it was the only way to fill the management hole."

More layoffs in Florence, and the Americans' new procedures, embittered Claudio Degl'Innocenti and the Florentine workers. They balked at De Sole's directives, earning the sobriquet the *"mafia fiorentina."*

"Maurizio had turned everybody against De Sole, they all hated him," said Ricci. But De Sole persevered. After coming close to a fistfight with Claudio Degl'Innocenti in the factory parking lot, De Sole came to terms with his opponent.

"I finally sat down with Claudio and asked him to explain to me: 'Why doesn't it work?' " De Sole said. "And I found out that it was mainly lack of projections and decision making. Do we need to buy black leather? OK, let's order it!" De Sole came to trust Degl'Innocenti and promoted him to director of production.

"First you were my enemy, now you are my friend," he would say later to Degl'Innocenti, who hid a sharp intelligence behind his bearlike exterior.

"De Sole was the company's biggest asset," said Severin Wunderman years later, even though he had not been De Sole's biggest fan. "He was like a willow tree in the wind—which bends but never breaks." De Sole took what Gucci dished out, first under the family—Rodolfo, Aldo and Maurizio—and later under Investcorp. He had been pushed, insulted, and gone unrecognized, but he didn't give up or go away.

"Domenico De Sole was really the only person who really understood the company, how it worked, and what it would take to get it up and running," Ricci said. "That was the turning point. De Sole was very effective in motivating people."

"He made things happen," agreed Massetti. "He worked from morning to night; he was a pain in the ass because he called everybody in the early mornings, at night, on Sundays—no time was sacred—that was all he did. He would hold two or three meetings simultaneously and run back and forth between all of them—there were never enough conference rooms for his liking!"

In the meantime, Flanz had ordered the renovation and enlargement of Gucci's Scandicci offices, which had grown shabby during years of neglect. He furnished new, more elegant executive offices. Support and secretarial staff were upgraded and retrained—many employees didn't have good administrative or language skills.

Flanz made a point of walking down from his executive office into the factory every day to talk to the workers and watch them work.

"I had spent so much of my career with intangible financial services," Flanz said, "that I loved watching a craftsman put a handbag together, the way he would roll the different layers of leather over a wooden form and place a few sheets of newspaper between the layers of leather to pad it slightly—nowadays there are synthetic materials that are probably far better—but the workers explained to me that they still used the newspaper because of tradition and nostalgia. They still had all these old stacks of Italian newspapers from which they would carefully cut out a few sheets to slip in the bags.

"Once I replaced Maurizio, I ceased being a member of Investcorp's management committee and I viewed my job as doing my best to make Gucci as successful as possible," Flanz recalled. "I became a great believer."

It didn't take Nemir Kirdar long to realize Investcorp had lost another man to Gucci—the following year he transferred Flanz to the Far East to explore new investment opportunities.

"Three casualties," Kirdar wryly said later, referring to Paul Dimitruk, Andrea Morante, and Bill Flanz. "*I* fell in love with Gucci," he admitted, "but I didn't want my people to. At Investcorp, we were doing dozens of transactions and if I lost a man to every deal, I'd be out of business!" Kirdar said.

After Gucci's human resources director Ricci finished handling all the layoffs—some 150 people—without a major uproar from the unions, he told Flanz he wanted to throw a party.

"A party?" Flanz gasped.

"Everybody made fun of me for this, but after we finished we threw a big party in Casellina and it was a frivolous thing, but it was a signal for everybody," Ricci said. He hired a caterer and ordered tables set up on the lawn behind the factory offices for the evening of June 28, 1994, invited some 1,750 people, including Gucci employees and suppliers, to a sumptuous buffet on the very lawns where once handbags had flown during the Gucci family wars.

"That party was tremendously important," said Alberta Ballerini. "It sent a signal; the signal that Gucci was coming back to Florence, that it was a Florentine company with Florentine roots."

In May 1994, Dawn Mello resigned as creative director of Gucci to return to Bergdorf Goodman as president, and Investcorp had to figure out how to replace her. Nemir Kirdar briefly caressed the notion of bringing in a big-name designer—he thought of someone like Gianfranco Ferré—but Investcorp's advisor and Gucci board member Sencar Toker quickly dashed his hopes.

"I explained that not only Gucci couldn't afford someone like Ferré, but that no designer of any fame would even contemplate going to Gucci in the state it was," Toker said. "No one would have risked ruining their reputation!"

Mello had recommended Tom Ford. Even though he was a young designer nobody had ever heard of, he had impressed Toker and the others as being bright, sensible, articulate, reliable, and capable—after all, he was already designing all of Gucci's eleven collections single-handedly!

"Tom Ford was *there*!" recalled Sencar Toker, who continued to help Investcorp through the transition. "Gucci was not a fashion house until Tom made it into a fashion house, and nobody realized he would do that," Toker said.

At the time, Tom, exhausted and demoralized, thought about resigning too. He felt frustrated and stifled—for four years he had designed collections for Gucci according to what Maurizio and Dawn told him. A heated debate exploded within the company: should Gucci maintain the "classic" style direction advocated by Maurizio, or should it try to pep up its look with more fashion-oriented design?

"Maurizio had a very strong viewpoint about what everything should look like," recalled Ford. "Gucci was round and brown and curved and soft for a woman to touch. I kept wanting to do black!"

"Everybody I had talked to said, 'Get out!' " Ford said.

On a trip to New York he even had his chart done by a fashionable astrologer who catered to several other designers. "Leave Gucci, there is nothing there for you!" she told Ford.

As the classic vs. fashion debate raged, De Sole and Ford quietly agreed to take the fashion route.

"It was a calculated risk, but the only way to go," said De Sole. "Nobody needs a new blue blazer."

Ford realized that for the first time in his life, he had total design freedom over all the products of an important—if tarnished—luxury name.

"Nobody was worried about what the product was going to be—the business was in such bad shape that nobody really gave the merchandise a thought. I was left with a completely open door," Ford said later.

He still cringes when he thinks about his first solo collection in October 1994, saying that it took him a season to shake off Mello's and Maurizio's influence and call up his own design aesthetic. The show, held once again in the Milan Fiera, featured feminine circle skirts with flowerpot motifs and tiny mohair sweaters, a sweet take on Audrey Hepburn in *Roman Holiday*—but a far cry from the hard-edged look of Gucci today.

"It was pretty awful," he admitted later.

And then, suddenly, in the midst of it all, the wind changed. Gucci store managers around the world noticed it immediately.

"Less than six months after Maurizio had packed his bags, the Japanese arrived," said Carlo Magello formerly of Gucci U.K. "They had revised their thinking on Gucci. Whereas for a year and a half before they had been buying Louis Vuitton, all of a sudden they started buying Gucci!"

"Demand bounced," agreed Johannes Huth, a young Investcorp executive who had recently joined the Gucci team. "All of a sudden they couldn't keep the bags on the shelves." Maurizio's conviction had proven true. The production logjam became dramatic.

De Sole, who had been bumping along dusty back roads outside Florence and climbing the Tuscan hills seeking out new and old suppliers for Gucci, knew he had to move fast. He persuaded disillusioned manufacturers who had dropped Gucci to come back and brought in new ones. He offered them incentives for quality, productivity, and exclusivity. He recast production and technical procedures to get the system running again through some simple planning, ordering ahead for some of Gucci's traditionally popular products that he knew would sell. In the meantime, Ford had given a new twist to some of Gucci's classic items. He shrank the backpack designed by Richard Lambertson, which was a roomy bag with backstraps, a bamboo carrying handle, and external pockets with bamboo closings. The new mini version was a smashing success. When De Sole received a phone call from Gucci's store in Hawaii saying that the new minibackpack was selling like hotcakes, he called Degl'Innocenti.

"Claudio, this is Domenico. I want to make a stock order. I want three thousand black minibackpacks!" When Degl'Innocenti protested, De Sole said, "Never mind, I am ordering them for myself. Do it!"

As bamboo supplies ran short for the signature handles, Gucci sought out new suppliers in addition to their traditional sources. The bamboo was still bent by hand into handles by artisans working downstairs in Scandicci with a blowtorch, holding the stick of bamboo over a hot flame and gradually shaping it into a graceful curve. At one point, an entire lot of bamboo handles sprang straight again—prompting a flood of complaints from customers and stores. The artisans fixed the bags, Gucci found better suppliers, and shortly afterward Gucci was producing minibackpacks at the rate of 25,000 a week.

"We were sending out a truckload of minibackpacks a day," recalled Claudio Degl'Innocenti. "We managed to do it, with the people that were there and a good mix of American method and Italian creativity and vice versa." He chuckled. "We hadn't become geniuses overnight, but perhaps we were a little less stupid than everybody thought we were!"

Since 1987, Investcorp had invested hundreds of millions of dollars in Gucci and hadn't yet delivered a return to its investors. What Investcorp had envisioned as its entrée into high-level European deal making had begun to feel like a seven-year curse! Feeling pressure to make a profit for its Gucci investors, Investcorp looked for ways to unload the business. Pressed to explore all solutions for a quick exit, in early 1994 Investcorp seriously considered merging Gucci with the watchmaking operations of the inimitable Severin Wunderman—but ultimately the two parties disagreed about the value of the companies and Wunderman's role, and a deal never came through. In the fall of 1994, Investcorp presented Gucci to two potential luxury goods buyers: Bernard Arnault's LVMH and the Rupert family's Compagnie Financière Richemont, which controlled the Vendôme Luxury Group, owner of Cartier, Alfred Dunhill, Piaget, and Baume & Mercier, among other labels. But despite forecasts of better sales—for the first time in three years, Gucci broke into the black by $380 thousand in 1994—the presentations to luxury goods firms did not attract sufficiently high offers. Investcorp wanted no less than $500 million for Gucci, but the offers came in much lower, between $300 million and $400 million.

"Then the prevailing psychology was, 'There might be some juice left in Gucci, but how hard do you have to squeeze to get it out?' " recalled Toker.

Kirdar even seriously thought of asking the Sultan of Brunei—who had bought the twenty-seven sets of matching luggage—if he wanted to buy the entire company, lock, stock, and barrel.

While Investcorp pondered Gucci's future, Tom Ford hit his stride as a designer and churned out some eye-catching designs. In addition to the fast-selling minibackpack, his Gucci clog captured attention and sold well. In October 1994, what *Harper's Bazaar* called his "toweringly wicked" stiletto generated waiting lists all over the world as customers clamored for the shoe.

"Tom knew how to keep a few hot things running," observed his former assistant, Junichi Hakamaki. "Every season he came up with two great shoes and two great bags. His antenna was always out, he always looked for the next thing," he said, recalling how Ford constantly fed his small design team with old movies, tear sheets from magazines, and objects from flea markets, showing colors, styles, and images he felt were right for Gucci. Ford would walk in and drop the clips onto their design tables with a flourish, saying, "Here! *This* is what we need for Gucci!"

"There were some flops," Junichi admitted. "He did the clog in fur and it looked like a hairy slipper—we all laughed so hard!

"He was extremely ambitious," Junichi continued. "You could just see he wanted to succeed. When we would have meetings, it would be as though he were on television—he would wear a suit, his voice was louder, you could tell he was promoting his image. When he is in front of people, he is *on!*"

Ford began to develop his own style, opening it up from the few hot items that had sparkled each season to an overall approach that could shape a complete collection across all product categories. He used films to inspire him and to communicate his ideas to his design assistants, sometimes watching the same film over and over again to immerse himself in the mood it projected. He began to ask himself and his design team the following questions:

"Who is the girl wearing this outfit? What does she do? Where is she going? What does her house look like? What kind of car does she drive? What kind of dog does she have?" This approach helped him create an entire world and make the hundreds of thousands of decisions he needed to make in order to shape Gucci's new image, a process he would find alternately exhilarating and exhausting.

Ford also traveled constantly, always on the lookout in every city he visited for the next new trend. He sent his staff to comb flea markets and directional shops in cities around the world. He would come home in the evenings to the Paris apartment on the Left Bank, where he and Richard Buckley had moved from Milan. Buckley, who continued working as a journalist in the fashion sector, provided Ford with a wealth of information and helped give Ford perspective on where the rest of the fashion houses were going. Buckley also clocked the celebrities and what they wore and spent hours at the FNAC listening posts on the Champs-Elysées, scouting great music for Ford's fashion shows.

"What happens next is here now," said Ford. "You have to be a part of your time and make it your job to sense it and then turn it into a *thing!*"

He rolled out his first solo men's collection during the seasonal Pitti Uomo menswear trade fair in Florence at a small, intimate fashion show in Gucci's historic Via delle Caldaie offices. As journalists sat in folding chairs under the frescoed ceilings in the upstairs room where Gucci artisans once stitched their bags, Ford sent muscular male models in skintight, brightly colored velvet suits down the carpeted runway, their metallic patent leather moccasins flashing in the lights. He knew he was onto something.

"I will never forget the look on Domenico's face when the man in the pink suit walked out on the runway," Ford said later. "He was shocked! The model wore a pink mohair sweater, really tight, and velvet pants and the metallic shoes. Domenico's mouth fell open. He was stunned."

As the press applauded enthusiastically, Ford saw his moment. For the first time in the four years he had been at Gucci, he walked out onto the runway and took a bow, a pert little smile on his face as though he had just thought of a joke to tell someone.

"I had so much pent-up energy," Ford recalled. "I had never been allowed to walk out on the runway when Maurizio and Dawn were still there—I just decided, this is my chance! I didn't ask anyone's permission, I had done the show, designed the clothes that I felt were right, and I just walked right out there. Sometimes in life you have to take things if you want to move forward!"

What shocked De Sole thrilled the fashion press. The next day De Sole, his wife, and his two daughters pored excitedly over the rave reviews as they traveled to Cortina D'Ampezzo in Italy's Dolomite mountains for a skiing holiday.

The momentum around Ford and what he was doing with Gucci began to build. When the press and buyers took their seats for Gucci's women's shows in March, they chatted and gossiped in excited expectation under the sparkling chandeliers of the Società dei Giardini, a Milan garden club, instead of within the gaping hall of the Fiera. The Società dei Giardini usually opened its doors to Milan's upper-crust social set, rather than the international fashion crowd. Twenty-three years earlier, *tutto Milano* had celebrated Maurizio's wedding to Patrizia in those very rooms. That evening, tension buzzed inside the tall French doors leading into the show hall. Everybody was curious to see what Ford would do. Ford had signed up fashion's most sought-after producer, Kevin Krier, and hired top models for the first time.

"Then, it was a big deal for us to be having a show, to have top models, to have a professional producer," Ford recalled.

As the room plunged into blackness, percussive, driving music beat out through the loudspeakers and a bold white spotlight focused on the runway. In that instant, model Amber Valletta stalked out. The audience gasped. She was a smashing young Julie Christie! Valletta wore a lime green satin shirt unbuttoned nearly to her navel and a pair of low-slung, skintight blue velvet jeans, with a lime green mohair coat. Her strutting feet wore the new cranberry patent leather pump with a stacked heel. Her tousled hair hung over her eyes, and her lips, slightly parted, gleamed pale pink.

"Ohhh, this is going to be fun," thought Gail Pisano, senior vice president and merchandise manager of Saks Fifth Avenue. The audience oohed and aahed as their chairs vibrated with the music and the girls stalked the runway under the glaring spotlight, each one more beautiful than the next.

"It was hot! It was sex!" said Joan Kaner, senior vice president and fashion director for Neiman Marcus. "The girls looked like they had just stepped off someone's private jet. You just knew that wearing those clothes would make you look like you were living on the edge—doing it and having it all!"

The sultry, wet-lipped look, velvet hip huggers, satin shirts, and mohair jackets charged onto the covers and inside spreads of fashion magazines around the world. "The effortless sexuality of it all had a chill factor that just froze the audience to their seats," *Harper's Bazaar* wrote, and *The New York Times*'s fashion critic Amy Spindler dubbed Ford "the new Karl Lagerfeld," referring to the German-born design director hired in 1983 to revamp Chanel.

"I knew the collection would be a hit from the moment I started working on it," said Ford later. "I put all my energy into it and I just knew that I had figured it out. It changed my career." But it wasn't until Ford went into the showroom the next day that he realized just *how* successful the show had been.

"You couldn't get through the door!" he said. "The showroom was mobbed. It was complete and total hysteria. Buyers were coming out of the woodwork, with no appointments; some of them hadn't even seen the show, but they had heard about it and wanted to come."

The jet set quickly wriggled into Gucci clothes—Elizabeth Hurley stepped out in Gucci's black patent leather boots and "bad girl" faux fur; in November 1995, Madonna wore Ford's silk-blouse-and-low-slung-pants ensemble to receive her MTV music video award; Gwyneth Paltrow made her fans swoon in his sleek red velvet pants suit. Pretty soon, Jennifer Tilly, Kate Winslet, and Julianne Moore were just some of the stars being spotted around town in head-to-toe Gucci. Even the top models were clamoring for Gucci off the set. Tom Ford had reached his target.

"Gucci's history is flashy," he said. "Film stars, jet-setters—I wanted to take that image and make a 1990s version."

After his first blockbuster collection, Ford ran through a heady round of press interviews and dinners, and went back home to Paris. He went immediately to bed.

"I came down with a fever and a sore throat, as I usually do after a show, and I lay in bed for a few days," Ford said. Then he called Domenico De Sole.

"Domenico? This is Tom. I need to talk to you. I need you to come to Paris." De Sole, worried, agreed.

Ford asked his secretary to book them a good table at an upscale, but not too trendy, restaurant—a place that would be appropriate for an important business conversation. He dragged himself out of bed and dressed formally— shirt, pants, jacket, even a tie—and went to meet De Sole at Le Bristol, the restaurant of the Bristol Hotel.

When De Sole arrived, Ford was already waiting for him at a table in the back of the formal restaurant located on the ground floor of the hotel. It wasn't the sort of place Ford usually patronized. "There was nobody else in the dining room," Ford recalled. "Fancy waiters were standing all around and there was candlelight, music playing, and flowers."

De Sole walked the length of the blue and red floral carpet, past rows of linen-covered tables, to the back of the dining room, where Ford rose to greet him. They chatted awkwardly at first. Ford, noticing De Sole's discomfort, smiled his pouting smile and said dramatically, "Well, Domenico, I guess you are wondering why I called you here tonight?"

"Yes, Tom, I am," De Sole replied, twisting his head to stretch the tension out of his neck with a nervous motion Ford would come to know well.

Ford mischievously reached over and put his hand on De Sole's.

"Domenico, will you marry me?"

De Sole stared back at him, speechless.

"He was shocked!" Ford recalled with a delighted chuckle. "He didn't really know my sense of humor yet, we had just started working together and he had no idea what I was up to."

Ford asked De Sole for a new contract and more money.

"I hit him up," Ford admitted. "I said, 'Look, things have changed, and I really want to stay here but this is what I need.'" Ford has not revealed the specifics, other than saying "it was a real change professionally in my relationship with the company."

JUST A FEW WEEKS LATER, Maurizio Gucci was shot. Rick Swanson learned the news from an Investcorp secretary as he walked into the office that morning.

"I was so stunned, I stopped in my tracks," Swanson said. It was tragic, as though a young boy had been killed in the prime of his life. To me, Maurizio was always that little kid on the way to the candy store."

When the news broke, Tom Ford sat in Florence, working on the spring '96 collection in his new design studio above the Gucci store in Via Tornabuoni. Bill Flanz and Domenico De Sole were working in their offices in Scandicci. Dawn Mello was sleeping in her penthouse apartment back in New York until a friend woke her up to tell her. Andrea Morante had just flown back to London from Milan, where he had been working on a new acquisition. Nemir Kirdar was at home in his London town house, getting ready to go to the office. Around the world, those who had known Maurizio were saddened and perplexed; the man who had given them the chance to shine had met a mysterious and violent death.

Gucci's public relations office struggled to distance the company from the news, explaining tirelessly to reporters that Maurizio hadn't been involved in the company for nearly two years, although Milan prosecutor Carlo Nocerino became a regular visitor to Gucci's Scandicci factory. Day after day, Gucci secretaries ushered him into the old "Sala Dynasty"—which was later dismantled—where he pored through files looking for answers to Maurizio's mysterious death—answers he never found there.

Investcorp hesitated, wondering if fallout from Maurizio's murder would scramble their plans to take the company public by selling shares on the stock market. But the furor over his death gradually subsided and Investcorp forged ahead with the listing.

Investcorp realized that if Gucci was going public, it needed its own chief executive officer. In 1994, Kirdar had initiated and then abandoned an executive search for an experienced luxury goods manager from outside. Not only had the right candidate been difficult to find—those who spoke Italian didn't have the breadth of skills he wanted—but he realized no right-minded executive would join a company that was up for sale. Kirdar started looking inside Gucci. At the recommendation of several Investcorp executives, who liked De Sole's hands-on, can-do attitude, his eyes settled on Domenico De Sole.

"By then, we saw Domenico's role in the turnaround," said Kirdar, "his determination, his capability, his relationship with Tom Ford. He was absolutely the right person."

In July 1995, Investcorp made Domenico De Sole CEO of Gucci—finally crowning his eleven-year Gucci career with the title he had earned. It wasn't long before Gucci's top businessman and Gucci's chief designer tested each other.

One day shortly after his promotion, De Sole dropped in on a design meeting in Scandicci where Ford and his assistants were developing a new line of handbags.

"Can you please leave us alone?" Ford said as De Sole looked at him, stunned. "We are working and I can't concentrate if you are here. I will speak to you later."

De Sole turned on his heel and left. When Ford came out of the meeting, a fuming De Sole called him upstairs to his office.

"How dare you throw me out of a meeting!" he shouted at the young Texan. "I am the CEO of this company! You cannot do that!"

"That's great that you are the CEO!" Ford fired back. "But by coming into that meeting you are undermining my authority with those people, and if you want me to design the collection, then do NOT get involved with the product!" Ford seethed.

The fight continued out into the parking lot as they left for the day.

"Fuck you!"

"No, fuck YOU!"

"FUCK you."

"FUCK YOU!"

Now Ford laughs about those early clashes and De Sole brushes them off, but those fights clarified their turf and laid the foundation for an airtight, trusting relationship unprecedented in the industry between a designer and an executive who hadn't started in business together or didn't have a previous personal relationship.

"After that, Domenico really respected me in terms of design," Ford commented. "He knew that I had a conviction about what I was doing and he could see that that conviction was paying off. He trusted me and I sensed that trust from him and in turn completely trusted him."

De Sole said he wasn't jealous of Ford's design territory. "I told Tom, 'Look, I am not going to design the collection; I am a manager, not a designer!'"

"The other reason that we make such a good team is that we are both obsessed," added Ford. "He cares about building the business, about making it solid. We are driven, driven, driven," said Ford, snapping off the words. "We are going to be successful and that's that! And we are not going to be second best. This is the other reason that I totally trust Domenico; I would rest my entire future with Domenico because I know that Domenico is not going to lose. In a business environment he is going to win."

Many observers criticized De Sole for giving so much power to Tom Ford, saying the designer risked overpowering the Gucci name and holding the company hostage to whatever decisions he might make about staying or leaving. But events would have an uncanny way of swinging the pendulum back and forth between De Sole's managerial power and Ford's creative power within the business. One story that kept the rumor mill busy for months was the costly renovation of Gucci's London flagship on Sloane Street with the new store concept developed by Tom Ford. Ford tolerated no interference in the project—but afterward the entire space had to be redone at well over the initial costs in order to comply with fire regulations, making Maurizio's once-criticized extravagances shrink in comparison.

By the summer of 1995, as Ford's blockbuster collection moved into stores, preparations for a fall stock market listing moved into high gear. Investcorp had picked two top merchant banks to lead the listing, Morgan Stanley and Crédit Suisse First Boston. Swanson oversaw the preparations, plowing through historical and financial information, and profiling the new management team.

Sales chugged ahead, jumping 87.1 percent in the first half of 1995 compared to the first half of 1994, higher than anybody's wildest expectations. By year-end, they would exceed $500 million, far exceeding the projections made to LVMH and Vendôme the year before.

"I remember Maurizio used to say to us, 'Just wait and see! Sales will explode!' and everybody used to laugh internally and say, 'Sales don't explode, businesses don't work that way,' " recalled Swanson. "Well, sales did just that: explode!"

In August, with the planned initial public offering (IPO) set for fall, Vendôme, one of the earlier low bidders, came back to Investcorp at the last minute and offered $850 million for Gucci, more than twice its initial bid a year before. Now Investcorp had a new dilemma: should it take the cash or go forward with the IPO?

Investcorp checked the offer with its advisors, who valued the company at more than $1 billion. "You can do better," they said.

A senior Investcorp executive leading the IPO process called Kirdar, who was vacationing on his yacht in the South of France. Kirdar listened, gazing out at the blue waters of the Côte d'Azur as the executive recapped the story. Although there were a lot of people within Investcorp who would have opted to sell to Vendôme and wash their hands of Gucci once and for all, Nemir stood his ground. He had never stopped believing in the potential of Gucci.

"Don't sell unless there is a 'one' out in front," Nemir said finally.

To draft the investors' prospectus, a detailed financial document required by the U.S. Securities and Exchange Commission (SEC) before it will approve an IPO, the Gucci team met in secret sessions away from the offices so employees would not learn about the plan.

"One of our sessions was in a cold, drafty old castle outside Florence, not an especially luxurious one," recalled Johannes Huth. While a fire burned cheerily in the fireplace to help warm the room as they worked, a sudden downdraft scattered glowing cinders into the room, starting a fire.

"There we were meeting with the most important investment bankers in the world and suddenly the room fills with smoke and everybody is coughing and swearing and we have to grab all our papers and leave," recalled Huth, laughing. One of the bankers turned up later at the Gucci IPO in a fireman's hat.

On September 5, Investcorp announced plans to take Gucci public, offering 30 percent of the company on international stock markets—which would still leave Investcorp with majority control at 70 percent. The next step was to prepare for the "road show," a mandatory marketing tour to sell the Gucci stock to European and American investment banks, who would in turn trade it on the open market once the company was listed.

Knowing that the international financial analysts would grill De Sole mercilessly, Investcorp managers hired a professional coach and prepared a speech De Sole had to memorize. "We didn't want any ad-libbing," Huth recalled.

Last-minute emergencies reduced De Sole's planned three weeks of rehearsal time to two days. The SEC unexpectedly asked Investcorp to rewrite part of the Gucci prospectus and then the Milan stock market commission refused to list Gucci, citing its recent losses. "It was important to have a listing in Europe," said Huth, who scrambled to find another European stock market that would accept Gucci. In the nick of time, he got a green light from the bourse of Amsterdam.

"It was like Italian opera," said Huth later. "Nothing was ready, nothing worked, everything was chaos. And it all came together at the last minute and everything worked beautifully."

De Sole—speech-perfect—and the others told their Gucci story across Europe, the Far East, and the United States, stimulating excitement about the listing as they went. So much so that Investcorp increased the offering to 48 percent. The night before the listing in New York, the executives worked late, settling the final details of the offering. The price was set at twenty-two dollars a share, the high end of the estimated range, and after logging all the orders, they realized that the Gucci offering was fourteen times oversubscribed—an outstanding success for a company on its knees just two years earlier.

On the morning of October 24, 1995, Domenico De Sole, Nemir Kirdar, and a team of Gucci and Investcorp executives and bankers walked through the doors of the majestic Renaissance facade of the New York Stock Exchange. An Italian flag hung outside next to the Stars and Stripes.

Inside, De Sole, amazed, saw a Gucci banner suspended above the trading floor and a large digital sign reading HOT STOCK TO WATCH: GUCCI flashing on and off. As trading opened on the exchange at the customary 9:30 A.M., pandemonium broke out as a flood of last-minute orders for Gucci stock came in. When trading finally resumed around 10:05 A.M., the stock price spiraled up instantly from $22 to $26. De Sole called the Gucci factory in Scandicci, where he had asked all the workers to assemble in the cafeteria. Over loudspeakers booming into the cafeteria, De Sole proudly announced a 1 million lire bonus (about $630) for every Gucci employee around the world, as a cheer went up.

Just a year earlier, top executives at LVMH and Vendôme had sniffed at projections that Gucci would reach $438 million in sales by 1998. Gucci closed its 1995 fiscal year with record revenues of $500 million.

In April 1996, Investcorp completed its sell-off in a secondary offering that was even more successful than the first, making Gucci a completely publicly traded company for the first time in its seventy-four-year history. It hadn't hurt that Ford had churned out another blockbuster collection in March, featuring simple white column dresses with sexy cutouts and flashing gold G Gucci belts that drove the fashion set wild. Now owned by large and small investors across the United States and Europe, Gucci was an anomaly in Italy, where even publicly traded companies were usually controlled by a shareholder syndicate, and in the fashion industry, where most companies were still privately owned.

De Sole, the naturalized American lawyer who had survived all the vicissitudes of Gucci family management to lead Gucci into the future, knew the years ahead would bring different challenges. Now he would have to answer to profit-oriented shareholders and the global stock market.

"This is real life, we have to perform," he said at the time. "I can be fired!"

Between the two public offerings, Investcorp took in a grand total of $2.1 billion, netting $1.7 billion after paying intermediary costs. The Gucci turnaround—albeit after nearly ten years since Investcorp had made its initial investment—had been the most spectacular, and most unexpected, success in Investcorp's fourteen-year history.

Gucci's remarkable turnaround and spectacular stock market listing soon paved the way for other luxury goods companies to go on the New York stock market, including Donna Karan, Ralph Lauren, and retailer Saks Fifth Avenue, also owned by Investcorp, while Italian designer clothing manufacturer Ittierre SpA went public in Milan.

Gucci's listing also coalesced into a sector the scattering of other luxury goods and apparel companies that were quoted on international stock markets. Before Gucci went public, the few companies already listed were a disparate group with little in common: LVMH was still viewed largely as a drinks business, Hermès had such a small float it hardly attracted attention, and the Italian jeweler Bulgari had recently been listed, but was also small—less than $100 million.

"Gucci created the sector," said Huth. "With between two billion and three billion dollars of stock out there, Gucci created a critical mass and people started to focus on it."

To promote Gucci's flotation, Investcorp had encouraged the big international investment banks to designate specific analysts to cover Gucci in the context of the wider luxury goods sector, just as they specialized in other sectors from airlines to automotive to engineering. Investcorp prepared training programs to help the analysts understand Gucci's strengths in comparison to its competitors'. Suddenly these analysts—many of whom had previously covered apparel manufacturers and retailers—found themselves with priority seats at Gucci fashion shows, tapping their feet to the music and struggling to integrate a critical eye for style into their expertise in financial analysis. They coined the term "fashion risk," meaning the implications a weak collection might have on business, and began to understand the business cycles of fashion companies, including sourcing, delivery, and sell-through as well as the importance of show reviews, glossy fashion spreads, and the style arbiters of Hollywood.

While the investment community studied Gucci's multiples, Tom Ford further streamlined Gucci's look into a modern, sexy image, restyling all eleven existing product categories and introducing a new home collection that even included a black leather dog bed and Lucite feeding bowls.

He strove to create a 1990s version of the flash bordering on vulgarity that Gucci had exhibited in the sixties and seventies; he felt that "too much good taste can be dull!" He continued to push that fine line between sexy and vulgar.

"I pushed Gucci as far as I could," Ford said later. "I couldn't have made the heels any higher, or the skirts any shorter." In 1997, *Vanity Fair* named Ford's double-G G-string one of the year's hottest fads. He had boldly brought it out during the men's show in January as an embarrassed murmur ran through the audience and brought it back for the women's show in March.

"Never have so few square millimeters of fabric generated so much hype," wrote the *Wall Street Journal* of the G-string, which sold out in stores worldwide and boosted sales of more conventional items.

Once he had the look just right, Ford wooed the Hollywood set. First he became an insider. He had already fallen in love with Los Angeles, which he called a "true twentieth-century city," for its architecture, lifestyle, and influence on contemporary culture. He bought a house there, photographed several Gucci ad campaigns there, and began rubbing shoulders with actors and actresses—some of whom also became his friends. He made his mark with an event that Hollywood will never forget: a sizzling fashion show, dinner, and all-night dance party in a private air hangar at the Santa Monica airport. Gucci sponsored the evening, which raised a record figure for the city's all-important AIDS Project Los Angeles benefit. Ford's guest list for the party read like the lineup at the Oscars, but the style of the party was all signature Tom Ford—especially the forty gyrating go-go dancers clad only in Gucci G-strings atop giant Lucite cubes.

Ford exerted tight control over every aspect of Gucci's image—not just the apparel and accessories collections, but also the new store concept, advertising, office layout and decor, staff dress, and even the flower arrangements at Gucci events. At the launch of Gucci's Envy perfume in Milan, Ford colored everything he could black—from the floor, ceiling, and walls of a huge hall that had been transformed into an elegant dining room for the occasion, to the entire menu: black pasta sauced with squid ink, black bread sticks, and even a black entrée! A medley of vegetables provided the only color on the transparent glass plates.

When he finally finished design work on Gucci's renovated 14,000-square-foot flagship store on London's Sloane Street—the model for Gucci stores around the world—he placed security men at the doors dressed head to toe in Gucci black and wearing headsets, a typical Ford touch. Outside, the sleek limestone and stainless steel facade was as imposing as a bank vault. Inside, travertine marble floors, acrylic columns, and hanging lightboxes created a stage set on which Ford's restyled Gucci products were the stars.

Even the format Ford developed for his fashion shows was all about control. At a time when other designers still offered several different themes within each show, thinking that the press, buyers, and customers alike wanted choice, Ford pared his collection down to about fifty outfits and sent the three most important looks down the runway first.

"I would have hundreds of outfits in the showroom and hundreds of Polaroids and twenty minutes to convince the world of my point of view," said Ford. He would edit and edit and edit, asking himself, "What is my message? What do I want to say?" Once he had decided his message, Ford used a white spotlight to focus the audience's attention during the show.

"You go to any other fashion show and they have just a little bit of light bouncing around and you can see people looking at their shoes or up and down and around at the other people in the audience. I wanted to get their complete attention," Ford explained. "I wanted that cinematic quality. When everybody is looking at exactly the same thing at the same time, I can control them and bring them in and up and down and get them going 'Ooohhh' and 'Aaahhh' all at the same time!"

Ford's clear, focused way of showing clothes made it easier for everybody—press, buyers, and customers alike—to make decisions because Ford had already done that work for them.

Just as determinedly, De Sole renegotiated Gucci's fragrance license with Wella after a notable fight and bought out Gucci's watch manufacturer, Severin Montres Ltd., from the craggy Severin Wunderman for $150 million after haggling long and hard over the deal. The new Ford–De Sole designer-businessman team was hailed as the second coming of Yves Saint-Laurent and his business partner, Pierre Bergé.

Despite all their success, it wasn't going to be a gentle, coasting ride for them. In September 1997—just a month after the *Wall Street Journal* held up Gucci as "the hottest name in luxury goods for fashion victims and fund managers alike"—two heady years of rising sales and stock prices at Gucci came to an abrupt halt. De Sole, recently back from a trip to Asia, didn't like what he had seen there. The best hotels and restaurants in Hong Kong, which for years had been a shopping haven for Japanese tourists, stood empty, while sales slumped in Hawaii—another stopover for traveling Japanese. Gucci did some 45 percent of its business in Asia and even more with Japanese tourists in other markets. Just as they had put the wind back in Gucci's sales in 1994, Japanese customers took it out three years later.

On September 24, 1997, De Sole, alarmed, predicted slower than expected growth in the second half of the year. He was the first luxury goods executive to warn of the Asian crisis that would roil international markets over the upcoming months. In response, Gucci's share price, which had soared to a high of $80.00 in November 1996, plunged some 60 percent over the following weeks to a low of $31.66.

Tom Ford—who by then had stock options worth millions of dollars—cringed as Gucci's stock plummeted, and berated De Sole behind closed doors for having been so explicit about the negative outlook, which had overpowered the good news about the Severin Montres acquisition. But De Sole's warning proved a bellwether for the entire industry—soon Prada, LVMH, and DFS, to name a few, were all struggling to contain their losses in Asia.

Gucci's low and trembling stock price meant that for the first time since its flotation Gucci could be snapped up for some $2 billion, sparking rumors that the other captains of the luxury goods industry such as LVMH's Bernard Arnault, already well known as a takeover baron, were considering a Gucci buyout. In November, despite intensive lobbying by De Sole, Gucci shareholders defeated an anti–hostile takeover measure that would have limited the voting power of a single shareholder to 20 percent, despite the size of the stake. This action left Gucci even more vulnerable—although for the moment all of the potential takeover kings in the business were busy shoring up their own empires in Asia.

"It's the shareholders' privilege to decide," said De Sole, trying to hide his disappointment at the defeat. "I've done my duty."

De Sole had survived the Gucci family wars as a champion leading Gucci into new territory. But like all conquerors, he would have to gird himself for new wars.

17

ARRESTS

Her dark, unbrushed hair wild around her head, Alessandra Gucci pushed her mother into the spacious master bathroom of the apartment on Corso Venezia without any of the police officers seeing her. Patrizia and her two daughters had moved into the magnificent apartment a few months after Maurizio's death, trading her penthouse in Galleria Passarella for Maurizio's extravagant rented apartment. Alessandra locked the door quickly behind them and pushed her mother into the far corner against the marble tile wall, where she thought no one could hear them.

"Mamma!" hissed Alessandra, holding her petite mother by the shoulders and staring into Patrizia's unblinking eyes. "I swear to you that whatever you tell me now will stay a secret between you and me.

"Tell me!" she said, her fingers digging into

Patrizia's shoulders. "Tell me if you did it! If you tell me, I promise you with all my heart, I won't tell Nonna Silvana or Allegra."

Patrizia looked back into the white face of her oldest daughter. For an instant she studied the troubled blue eyes, eyes that just minutes earlier had been peacefully closed in sleep.

At 4:30 A.M. on Friday, January 31, 1997, two police cars pulled up in front of the shuttered palazzo at Corso Venezia 38. Filippo Ninni, the dark-haired chief of Milan's Criminalpol police force, got out and rang the bell of the Gucci apartment, where Patrizia now lived with Alessandra, Allegra, and two servants, as well as Roana, a cocker spaniel, a chirpy, talkative mynah bird, two ducks, two turtles, and a cat.

"Polizia! Aprite!" he called into the intercom, to no response. The imposing arched wooden door remained shut. After buzzing several times with no results, Ninni, exasperated, dialed the Reggiani telephone number on his cellular phone. He knew Patrizia was home because his men had followed her back to the house after dinner. He also suspected she was awake because he knew from their wiretaps that she had been on the phone with her boyfriend, a local businessman named Renato Venona—Patrizia called him her teddy bear. They had talked until 3:30 A.M. Patrizia, who suffered from chronic insomnia, often spoke to friends on the telephone until dawn—and then slept until noon the next day. A groggy, foreign voice finally answered the buzzing doorbell and Ninni heard the bird squawking excitedly in the background.

"Listen, this is the police, you must open the door," Ninni said tersely. A few minutes later a sleepy Filipino maid swung open the heavy door and Ninni and his entourage of officers followed her through the stone courtyard and up the grand marble steps to the Gucci apartment, their footsteps ringing out in the early morning silence. As the officers ogled the plush furnishings, the maid ushered them down the hall into the living room and went to call Patrizia.

Calm and cool despite the dawn incursion, Patrizia entered the room a few minutes later, wearing a pale blue dressing gown. Of the officers gathered in her living room, she recognized only a tall blond carabiniere, Giancarlo Togliatti, from the interrogations after Maurizio was murdered. Two years had gone by since Maurizio's death and no suspects had been announced. Patrizia had a contact in the police department whom she called from time to time for updates on the investigation, but lately he had had nothing to report. She nodded to Togliatti and fixed her gaze blankly on Ninni, who was clearly in charge. He introduced himself and showed her the arrest warrant in his hands.

"Signora Reggiani, I must place you under arrest for murder," said Ninni, his voice like a deep rumble of thunder. Ninni, a seasoned investigator who had dedicated his career to fighting the ballooning drug trade in Milan, felt more at ease tracking mafia bosses and raiding abandoned warehouses than standing in Patrizia Reggiani's sumptuous living room. He looked into her clear, expressionless eyes.

"Yes, I see," she said vaguely, glancing disinterestedly at the document in Ninni's hands.

"Do you know why we are here?" Ninni asked, taken aback by her nonchalance.

"Yes," she said impassively, "it is about the death of my husband, isn't it?"

"I am sorry, signora," Ninni said. "You are under arrest. You must come with us."

Minutes later, upstairs in her bedroom, Alessandra woke in terror to find two policemen in her room. They explained that her mother had been placed under arrest and would be taken away with them.

"They went through everything in my room, my stuffed animals, my computer. Then we went downstairs." A startled and distraught Allegra joined them shortly with another investigator. As Allegra sobbed softly in the living room, Ninni ordered Patrizia to get dressed and come with him. That's when Alessandra followed her and pulled her mother into the bathroom. The mother and the daughter—the one a younger reflection of the other—stared at each other for an instant.

"I swear to you, Alessandra, I swear, I didn't do it," Patrizia said as one of the officers knocked on the door. While Patrizia dressed, supervised by a female officer, the other agents searched the apartment, sequestering papers and a stack of Patrizia's leather-bound diaries. When she emerged, they all stared at her in disbelief. Patrizia had donned gleaming gold and diamond jewelry and a floor-length mink coat. In her manicured hands she grasped a leather Gucci handbag.

"Well?" she said, surveying her astounded audience. "I'm ready!"

"I'll be back tonight," she said crisply, turning to kiss her daughters. As she walked out, she slipped a pair of black sunglasses over her eyes, which were unusually pale and vulnerable looking without their customary shield of heavy black liner and mascara.

Any compassion Ninni might have felt for Patrizia evaporated in that moment. "Where does she think we are going, to a masked ball?" he asked himself as he led the way down the marble steps and back out through the courtyard.

Thin and wiry, with piercing dark eyes and a severe mustache, Ninni had a reputation for being a determined, no-nonsense investigator, passionate about police work. His main adversaries were the southern Italian families that had migrated to Milan and taken advantage of the growing drug trade flowing out of the Balkans. Many of these families had lost out in clan wars back home or had simply come north in search of work and found quick, easy money in drugs.

As Ninni advanced through the ranks of the Milan police corps, he often thought of Modesto, a Sicilian who had come to Milan with a large family to maintain. In the early days, Modesto circled the city streets as an organ-grinder, sending his seven or eight children to beg for tips from passers-by. Soon Modesto traded in his barrel organ for more lucrative pursuits, becoming one of the most important drug lords in the Lombardy region surrounding Milan.

Ninni also came from southern Italy, from a small town outside Taranto in the Puglia region located on the heel of the boot of the Italian peninsula. As a boy, he devoured crime novels and police films, attentively studying all the techniques the investigators used. At family reunions, he peppered two of his relatives who worked for the police with questions about their work. Ninni even dropped out of a Rome university to enroll at the police academy, infuriating his father, a laborer at the naval shipyard.

"Are you crazy?" Ninni's father thundered at him. "Do you want to get yourself killed? Police work is dangerous," he fumed. But Ninni insisted—passionate about becoming a policeman, he also wanted financial independence. His father still supported his two teenage brothers at home and he hated asking for money for schoolbooks. His father finally agreed, accompanying him to Rome the day he entered the academy. At the end of the first week, Ninni's father went back to see how his son was faring. The minute he saw Ninni's drawn face he told him to pack his bags and come home. Ninni didn't hesitate.

"No," he said to his father, shaking his head. "I managed to get in here, I knew it was going to be rough and I'm going to leave when I graduate, unless they kick me out first."

Not only did Ninni survive the academy, he made his first arrest even before starting his first job—on the train north to Milan from Rome. A young Gypsy had just pickpocketed a carabiniere and kicked and screamed and carried on as the young officer tried in vain to arrest her and get his wallet back.

"I'll show you what to do," said Ninni curtly to the carabiniere as he yanked the Gypsy's bag out of her hand and tossed it onto the platform below. As the startled woman scrambled after her bag, Ninni arrested her and retrieved the wallet.

Not all of Ninni's arrests were so easy. In Milan he fought the warring factions of the *calabrese* mob—the clans of Salvatore Batti and Giuseppe Falchi—whose warfare had escalated into daily shootouts. But Ninni's hands-on approach, nerves of steel, and sense of ethics won him respect from colleagues and clan members alike. In 1991 alone, working with just four men, he made more than five hundred arrests. Ninni treated the people he arrested with dignity, believing that even criminals should be given respect. His humanity not only won him a compliment from one of Milan's most dangerous drug lords, it saved his life. During one trial, the Calabrian boss Salvatore Batti looked at him across the courtroom and said: *"Dotto' Ninni, se voi non fuste una persona onesta, avesse la morte,"* or "If you weren't an honest man, you'd have been killed already."

With Patrizia in the back seat, the police car sped through Milan's empty streets to the Criminalpol headquarters in Piazza San Sepolcro, a historic square behind the stock market that dates back to the Roman era. A police station was the last thing one might expect to be housed in the three-story Palazzo Castani, which rose around a central courtyard graced with a vaulted portico around three sides and dated in part back to the Renaissance.

Ninni and his squad ushered Patrizia in through the curving stone entryway between the sculpted profiles of Roman emperors Adriano and Nerva. High on the beam overhead a chiseled Latin inscription read *"Elegantiae publicae, commoditati privatae,"* or "For public elegance and private comfort," while another inscription in ancient Greek wished good luck to those who entered.

Ninni turned Patrizia over to his right-hand man, Inspector Carmine Gallo, a short, stocky man with dark, tender eyes. Gallo led Patrizia down a winding dark hallway and into an office furnished austerely with metal desks and file cabinets. She glanced at the heavily barred windows set high up in the wall as Gallo booked her. A photograph of murdered mafia-fighting judges Giovanni Falcone and Paolo Borsellino looked down on them. Shortly, Patrizia's mother, Silvana, arrived with Alessandra and Allegra, faces drawn. They too were ushered into Gallo's office as Ninni appeared in the doorway, staring at Patrizia, resplendent in gold and fur, sitting near Gallo's desk. He felt a wave of disgust.

"I have always tried to help the people I have arrested," said Ninni later, "but I looked at her and felt something that I had never felt before. I saw her as a woman with nothing inside, a woman who defined herself by the things around her, a woman who thought money could buy her everything. I'm not proud of this, but I couldn't bring myself to talk to her—something that has never happened to me in my career."

Ninni turned to Silvana, his dark mustache bristling with irritation.

"Signora, it's not a good idea to send your daughter to jail dressed like that, with all those valuables," Ninni said.

"They're hers; if she wants to take them it's up to her, nobody can stop her," retorted Silvana, frowning.

"Do as you like, but the prison authorities will confiscate them the minute she arrives. She won't be allowed to keep them with her," said Ninni as he turned heel and walked out the door.

"You'd better let me take these," clucked Silvana as she removed Patrizia's heavy gold earrings and chunky gold and diamond bracelets and slipped the mink coat off her daughter's shoulders and onto her own. Then she poked through the Gucci handbag.

"What in the world do you have in here?" she asked her daughter crossly, pulling out lip pencils, containers of makeup, and face cream.

"You won't be needing these," Silvana said as Patrizia started to shiver. Inspector Gallo looked up from his paperwork and offered her his jacket, a sporty green windbreaker, which she accepted willingly.

"I felt sorry for her," Gallo admitted later. Patrizia returned the coat after being admitted to jail. "She had come to the end of her road. She had done all that she could, she was at the end."

That same morning, four other people were arrested around Italy and charged with the Gucci murder. Patrizia's longtime friend Pina Auriemma was arrested in Somma Vesuviana near Naples by a squad of plainclothes policemen and later that day was transported to Milan. Ivano Savioni, a Milan hotel porter, and Benedetto Ceraulo, a mechanic, were also brought to the Criminalpol building in Piazza San Sepolcro. Orazio Cicala, a bankrupt restaurant manager who was already in jail in the Milan suburb of Monza on unrelated drug charges, was served his papers the next day. The startling news was splashed all over the press: after two years, Maurizio Gucci's ex-wife and four unlikely accomplices had been arrested for his murder.

Just two months earlier, the investigation into Maurizio's death had been going nowhere. Milan prosecutor Carlo Nocerino had asked for more time, but he grew despondent as the weeks went by and no serious leads emerged—until the evening of Wednesday, January 8, 1997. Filippo Ninni was working late, as he often did, when the night watchman rang saying there was a call for him.

"*Capo,* Boss, there's a guy on the line. He won't give his name, but he says it's urgent and he won't talk to anybody but you."

At that hour, all the other offices at the Criminalpol headquarters were dark. Ninni had turned on his desk lamp, which he preferred to the fluorescent lights overhead, and was poring through the stacks of files laid out on his large, glass-topped desk, amid computers he had fought to obtain from the police department in order to quickly execute cross-checks and otherwise speed up his work. Over the faded blue wallpaper, Ninni had carefully hung the more than twenty diplomas, certificates, and merit plaques he had earned throughout his career. In the center of the room stood a worn leather couch flanked by two armchairs arranged around a low coffee table where he had placed his prize possession: a hand-carved chess set made of soapstone. Ninni liked the way the smooth cream- and beige-colored chess pieces felt in his hands. He challenged his officers to a game from time to time, believing it kept his mind sharp.

That evening Ninni was reviewing the files of a drug case he had almost finished. Dubbed Operation Europe, the investigation had begun with a single Italian drug dealer who was at large. Instead of arresting him immediately, Ninni and his team tracked him. So far, their work had led to the arrests of more than twenty people across Europe and the confiscation of more than 360 kilos (792 pounds) of cocaine, 10 kilos (22 pounds) of heroin, and an arsenal of firearms. When they dug up the stash of drugs, which had been buried on the grounds of a small northern Italian business that operated earthmoving machinery, Ninni was stunned. A seemingly endless parade of tin containers filled with plastic bags of cocaine just kept on coming out of the ground.

He closed the Operation Europe file, curious to know who could be calling him so late. He told the night watchman to put the call through.

"Is this Ninni?" a low voice rasped, like the sound of a heavy metal gate being dragged over concrete.

"Yes, who is this?"

"I must speak with you face-to-face," said the scraping voice. Ninni sensed urgency, fear, and desperation. "I have important information I must give you. I will tell you everything I know," the voice insisted.

Ninni, at once intrigued and perplexed, asked, "Who are you? How do I know I can trust you? I have enemies out there—at least tell me what it is about!"

"Is it enough if I say it's about the Gucci murder?" The scraping voice had turned into a wheeze.

Ninni snapped to attention. His colleagues over at the carabinieri had been investigating the mysterious murder of the former businessman for almost two years with no breakthroughs. The magistrate, Carlo Nocerino, had returned the year before from Switzerland, where he had gone to investigate Gucci's business affairs, with no leads. Checking rumors that Gucci had invested in a string of gambling casinos, Nocerino discovered that the "casinos" were really a luxury hotel with a small game hall in the Swiss resort of Crans-Montana. Everything was aboveboard—no trace of sinister business dealings. All of Gucci's other business initiatives since he had sold his family company were only in the initial stages. Nocerino had also flown to Paris to interview Delfo Zorzi, who had agreed under strict conditions to answer prosecutors' questions about the Piazza Fontana bombing—and also agreed to speak with Nocerino about the Gucci loan. Zorzi confirmed that Gucci had paid back in full the famous $40 million he found "under the floorboards." Nocerino closed the "business" file on Gucci in May, but he had no other serious leads. That very morning, Ninni had read in the papers that Nocerino had gotten an extension to continue the investigation.

Ninni had followed the case with interest. The morning Gucci was killed, Ninni was passing through the neighborhood on his way to the office when he heard the murder report go out on his police radio. He asked his driver to swing by the scene of the crime on Via Palestro, only to find it crawling with carabinieri. Ninni stood to one side, observing the scene. Maurizio Gucci's body lay at the top of the steps as medics and investigators milled about. The commotion hushed as Nocerino entered the foyer, shooing everybody out except for the carabinieri. In the following weeks and months, Ninni ordered his men to ask for information about the Gucci murder whenever they arrested a member of Milan's criminal underground. If the assassin had been a professional killer, Ninni reasoned, then Milan's *malavita,* or criminal underworld, would know about it and sooner or later Ninni was bound to hear something. But time after time the person being questioned would shrug or shake his head. As the months went by, Ninni became convinced that the killer couldn't have been a professional. He felt sure the solution must be traced through Gucci's personal affairs.

"*Dottor* Ninni, I'm afraid," the voice grated. "I know who killed Maurizio Gucci."

"Can you come to my office?" Ninni asked.

"No, it's too dangerous. Meet me at the *gelateria* in Piazza Aspromonte," the caller said, indicating an ice cream bar in a square east of the city's central train station.

"I'm forty-nine years old, heavyset; I'll be wearing a red jacket. . . . Make sure you come alone."

Ninni hesitated, then agreed. "I'll be there in half an hour."

Ninni jumped into his car, his mind racing. As the car approached Piazza Aspromonte, he asked his driver to stop a few blocks away and he walked the rest of the way, through dark streets peppered with small, one-star hotels patronized by prostitutes and illegal immigrants trying to set up new lives. As he reached the *gelateria* the voice had indicated, Ninni saw a man standing outside, a bulging figure in a padded down jacket, tinged a garish green by the neon *gelateria* sign. The two men greeted each other cautiously and started walking around the small park in the center of Piazza Aspromonte. The man introduced himself as Gabriele Carpanese in the rasping voice Ninni recognized from the phone call. Overweight and in poor health, he walked slowly and breathed with difficulty. Ninni, a quick student of character, immediately sympathized with his mysterious caller, taking only a few minutes to decide he could trust him. He pointed to his car and driver down the street and invited Carpanese back to his office, where it was warm and safe from any curious onlookers hanging around the piazza.

Comfortably settled into the leather couches back in Ninni's office, Carpanese told his story as Ninni toyed with the smooth soapstone queen from his beloved chess set. Carpanese had moved back to Italy several months earlier with his wife after they gave up their efforts to operate an Italian trattoria abroad, first in Miami, Florida, later in Guatemala. Carpanese's wife was diagnosed with breast cancer, he developed diabetes, and their combined health problems forced them to come back to Italy where they could get treatment under the public health system. They had found cheap lodgings at a one-star hotel near Piazza Aspromonte until they could get settled. Carpanese made friends with the doorman, the hotel owner's forty-year-old nephew, Ivano Savioni. Savioni commanded a view of all who came and went from his post behind the desk in the narrow front hallway of the Hotel Adry, Carpanese explained. He could see visitors outside the one-way tinted glass door of the hotel, but they could not see him and with a flick of a finger on a buzzer under the desk he dictated whether or not visitors could come in. A stocky man with heavy jowls, a thick neck, and a head of dark, wavy hair he wore slicked back with gel, Savioni wore gold-rimmed glasses and dressed in cheap, dark suits and button-down shirts in pale pink and peach colors he thought made him look up-to-date. To Carpanese, Savioni seemed well-meaning, although he was constantly in debt and juggling multiple schemes to pay off a steady stream of creditors. Savioni scraped together extra cash by sneaking prostitutes into the Adry while his unknowing aunt was out running errands. Grateful that Carpanese never squealed on him, Savioni often gave him a break on the bill or sneaked him a bottle or two from the hotel bar.

As Carpanese's meager savings ran thin and his hopes of landing a job paled, his imagination came to life. He spun a lively tale for Savioni of big-time South American drug dealing, convincing Savioni he was a rich drug lord and was wanted by several countries' law enforcement agencies, including the FBI. Carpanese told Savioni he had millions of dollars in drug money stashed in U.S. bank accounts and that he would be able to pay for his lodgings as soon as he resolved his legal problems.

"As soon as my lawyers straighten things out, I'll be able to thank you properly and repay you—with interest—for your kind hospitality," Carpanese promised an awestruck Savioni, who convinced his aunt Luciana to let the unfortunate couple stay on, rent-free, for a few more months. Savioni, whose own small-time drug dealing never amounted to much, hoped that Carpanese could get him into the big time.

One hot August evening in 1996, Carpanese told Ninni, he and Savioni were relaxing together at a sidewalk café, smoking and drinking beer. Hardly a car passed on the street, tightly shuttered apartments silently awaited the return of their inhabitants from the traditional summer holiday. Even many of the neighborhood single-room-occupancy hotels had closed their doors for vacation. There was nothing much to do in the deserted city, but it was too hot to sleep or even be inside, the air was so heavy with heat and humidity. Savioni leaned back in his chair, took a long drag on his Marlboro, and looked over at Carpanese. He too had been involved in something really big, something that had been in all the papers, he said confidentially, studying Carpanese to gauge his reaction.

As the two men grew closer, Savioni told Carpanese snatches of the story, until he finally dropped the bombshell: he had lined up the killers of Maurizio Gucci. At first, Carpanese didn't believe him—he didn't think Savioni was particularly bright, and despite all his schemes and swaggering, Carpanese doubted he had connections with professional killers.

"What do you think you are, some kind of boss?"

"Think what you will," retorted Savioni, crestfallen at the skepticism of his new friend, whom he so badly wanted to impress. Over the next few weeks, Savioni told Carpanese every detail about the planning of the murder and the execution of Maurizio Gucci.

Carpanese was shocked. He couldn't believe Savioni had gotten himself into something so serious. After wrestling with his conscience for weeks, he decided to go to the authorities and report Savioni's story. He knew he and his wife would lose their lodgings, but he thought he might get some compensation for his information. Just before Christmas 1996 he walked to the pay phone in Piazza Aspromonte, dialed the number of the Milan court-house, and asked the operator for the magistrate handling the Gucci investigation. His heart pounded at the thought of what he was about to do. He fiddled nervously with the cold metal telephone cord as he listened to the pre-recorded message, but no one answered. After waiting nearly five minutes, he ran out of coins and hung up. When he tried the number again a few days later, the operator told him she didn't know who had the Gucci case. Carpanese then called the carabinieri, where the receptionist refused to put him through because he wouldn't leave his name or the reason for his call. One night in early January while idly flipping channels in the Hotel Adry's dank television room, he stopped to view a talk show about organized crime in which Ninni participated as a guest speaker. Carpanese liked Ninni's straightforward manner and sensible comments, and thought he was a man he could trust. He grabbed a phone book, looked up the number of the Criminalpol, and went back to the corner pay phone.

Carpanese told Ninni the story of the murder plot, rich with details that only an insider could have known. Ninni was sure Carpanese was telling him the truth.

Patrizia Reggiani had ordered the murder of Maurizio Gucci and paid 600 million lire, or about $375,000, for it, Carpanese told Ninni. Her long-standing friend Pina Auriemma had helped her and acted as intermediary, funneling money and information between Reggiani and the killers. Pina had gone to Savioni, an old friend, who in turn had involved Orazio Cicala, a fifty-six-year-old Sicilian who ran a pizzeria in Arcore, a suburb north of Milan. Savioni knew that Cicala, saddled with gambling debts that had ruined him and his family, needed the money. Cicala found the killer and drove the get-away car—his own son's green Renault Clio. The car Cicala had stolen for the job had disappeared—either stolen again or taken away by the police! The killer's name was Benedetto, a former mechanic who lived behind Cicala's restaurant. Benedetto had obtained the 7.65 caliber Beretta revolver used to kill Maurizio Gucci, constructed a silencer from a metal cylinder lined with felt, bought the bullets in Switzerland, and destroyed the weapon afterward.

As the months passed after the murder, Patrizia had taken up residence in Corso Venezia, enjoying all the benefits of Maurizio's multimillion-dollar estate—to which she had access by virtue of her control over their two daughters, Maurizio's heirs.

At the same time, the gang of accomplices had grown dissatisfied, Carpanese said. They had taken all the risks for a pittance while la Signora lived in luxury. Now they want to pressure her for more money.

Ninni listened, turning the soapstone queen in his fingers. As Carpanese talked, a plan started to take shape in his mind.

"Would you be willing to go back to the Hotel Adry with a microphone?" Ninni asked the wheezing man.

Carpanese, though he looked uncomfortable, nodded. Ninni, who had been touched by this man's honesty and sense of justice despite all of his misfortunes, vowed to help him if he could. Later he helped find Carpanese a new home, a job and clothing, and paid him regular visits to see how he and his wife were faring.

"WELL, NINNI, if you think you can get something out of it, go ahead," Carlo Nocerino said reluctantly to the Criminalpol chief as they sat in the prosecutor's cramped corner office on the fourth floor of Milan's labyrinthine courthouse. Ninni had just told the magistrate Carpanese's story and explained his plan: he wanted to send in an undercover detective to trap Savioni and his accomplices in their scheme. Ninni had found his man, a young detective named Carlo Collenghi, who spoke fluent Spanish because his mother was from Bogotá. Carlo would pose as "Carlos," a hardened killer from the Medellín drug cartel who was visiting Milan "on business." Carpanese would introduce Carlos to Savioni, proposing him as the ideal person to help "persuade" la Signora to give them more money. Milan's chief magistrate Borelli told Nocerino to authorize Ninni's plan. "If Ninni is behind it," he had told Nocerino, "you know it's serious."

Ninni's plan worked brilliantly. The next day, Carpanese invited Carlos to the Hotel Adry, where he introduced him to the swarthy Savioni. Savioni slowly looked him up and down, taking in the curly blond hair, ice blue eyes, black silk open-necked shirt, and the heavy gold chain around his neck.

"Buenos días," said Carlos, flashing a diamond pinky ring as he extended a hand to Savioni. Under the black silk shirt, two small microphones had been taped to his chest. A few blocks away, officers from Ninni's unit listened in a police van filled with recording equipment.

"Where are you staying?" Savioni asked Carlos as Carpanese translated.

"Tell your friend that I don't answer those kinds of questions," Carlos said, as Savioni stuttered an apology, looking at the cold-eyed "Colombian" with even greater respect.

The three men moved into the television room where they could talk more comfortably. Savioni brought them all coffee.

"How much sugar?" he asked Carlos, who pretended not to understand Italian as Carpanese translated.

Carpanese explained to Carlos in Spanish that Savioni wanted to ask for his help as Savioni strained to understand. When they had finished, Carpanese turned to the hotel porter.

"Savioni, don't worry," he said. "Carlos will solve all your problems. Even though he looks young, he is a professional killer, the best, used by the top dealers in the Medellín clan. He has killed more than one hundred people. He is the one who can teach a lesson to la Signora."

Savioni's jowls widened as a smile illuminated his face.

"Why don't you call Pina and talk it over with her?" Carpanese asked. "Now we must go; Carlos has some business he must attend to."

Savioni jumped up, elated, impressed, and eager to please.

"Of course, of course, I am sure Carlos is very busy. Why don't you take my car? And here, tonight dinner's on me," he said, pressing a hundred-thousand-lire bill into Carpanese's hand.

Carpanese drove Savioni's rusting red Cordoba four-door, a popular inexpensive model produced by the Spanish car maker Seat, down Via Lulli away from the Hotel Adry, checking in the rearview mirror to make sure they were followed only by the police intelligence van. Carlos cheered softly into the microphone taped to his chest. "*Ragazzi!* What luck!! Let's go fill this crate with bugs!!"

Back in the courtyard of Piazza San Sepulcro, Ninni's team placed hidden microphones on all sides of Savioni's car and inserted a chip behind the dashboard to track the car via satellite. The telephones of all the suspects had also been tapped, and Ninni's agents manned the central listening post in Piazza San Sepolcro night and day.

That afternoon, Savioni called Pina at her niece's house near Naples while the police reels turned. "Pina, you must come to Milan as soon as possible. I have a solution to our little problem. We need to talk."

The next evening, the double reels recorded another conversation—Pina from Naples calling Patrizia.

"*Ciao.* It's me. Did you see the news a few weeks ago?" Pina asked.

"Yes," answered Patrizia. "But it's better not to talk about it on the phone. We must see each other."

Pina arrived in Milan on January 27. Savioni drove the old, red Seat to pick her up at Milan's Linate airport as the police traced him on their Global Positioning Satellite screen. Although she had been pretty in her youth, Pina, now nearly fifty-one years old, showed her hard life in her face. Her streaked blond hair hung messily around her shoulders, and her basset hound eyes drooped into deep pockets. Her forehead seemed permanently pulled into long furrows. Savioni drove to a square near the Hotel Adry where he parked so they could talk. The police reels turned.

"*Gesummio,* Ivano," said Pina, invoking Jesus Christ in Neapolitan dialect, wringing her hands and pulling her thin gray raincoat more tightly around her. "When I read a few weeks ago that they had extended the investigation, I almost fainted on top of the newspaper. They already extended it once for six months and came up with nothing. What could they have? What are they thinking of?"

"*Dai, stai tranquilla,*" Savioni admonished her, telling her to stay calm and offering her a cigarette, which she accepted gratefully. "They don't have anything. It's just routine," he said as he lit her cigarette.

"I just stopped calling because I think my phone is tapped," Pina continued, wringing her hands. "I think *she* is being followed. If this whole thing starts to smell, tell me immediately—I'll go abroad, otherwise we'll all end up in jail. My friend Laura says they'll never find us—but we have to be very careful. One false step and it's *patatrac*! All hell is going to break loose!"

"*Ascoltami,* Pina, listen, I have something important to tell you," said Savioni as he lit himself a cigarette. "I met this Colombian, a really tough guy. You should see his eyes, they are like ice," said Savioni, exhaling. "He's killed more than a hundred people. Carpanese introduced us—you see, I always knew it would pay off to let him stay for free—anyway, this guy can help us with la Signora. He will make her pay up."

Pina looked sideways at Savioni as the smoke from her cigarette trailed out the window, which was open a crack.

"Are you sure? Maybe this isn't the best time. If they have extended the investigation—maybe we should just lie low for now. And what if they are following her?"

Savioni frowned and shook his head.

"Ohhhh, Pina, it's time to end this," exclaimed Savioni. "You're getting a monthly stipend, but what about the rest of us?"

"Yeah, a whopping three million lire [about sixteen hundred dollars] a month," Pina snapped back. "That's a whole lot to live on! And what happens if she changes her mind? I am finished. You know I see this thing the way you do—we take all the risks and she gets all the benefits. Maybe you're right. Maybe I should talk to her again, tell her, 'We did this thing together, and now you have to give us our due,' " Pina said.

"And if she says no," interjected Savioni, "we'll ask the *colombiano* with the eyes of ice to bring us her head on a silver platter!"

Over the next few days, the police reels whirred and recorded every conversation that Patrizia, Pina, and Savioni had. Ninni chuckled with pleasure. He had Savioni and Pina on tape talking about the plot. He had a conversation between Savioni and Benedetto Ceraulo, the alleged triggerman, and he had a conversation between Savioni and Pina talking about Cicala, the alleged driver of the getaway car. All he needed was la Signora, and his hand was closed with a full house. But la Signora was clever and although she talked on the phone constantly, she never discussed anything compromising. Ninni waited as the double reels turned. He had learned over the years the importance of not getting carried away with excitement over a breakthrough in an investigation.

"If you have a good lead, often the best thing to do is just play it out," Ninni said later. "I had everything set up: 'Carlos,' tapped telephones, bugs in the car—we knew who they all were and what they had done. All they had to do was talk."

Ninni didn't get all the time he wanted. On January 30, one of the agents at the listening post called him in.

"*Capo!* I think you should listen to this." He played a conversation that morning between Patrizia and one of her lawyers.

"There are dark clouds gathering over this family," the lawyer said ominously, although the subject of the call was an apparently innocuous debt Patrizia had run up with a local jeweler. After an emergency summit with Nocerino and his superiors, they decided they had enough evidence to cut the investigation short. They planned the arrests for dawn the following morning.

"We thought she was onto us," said Ninni later. "We were afraid she could slip out of Italy and then we'd never get her," said Ninni.

When the agents brought Savioni into the Criminalpol headquarters at Piazza San Sepolcro the morning of January 31, 1997, Ninni asked them to bring him into his office. Savioni slumped into the chair in front of Ninni's desk, his hands handcuffed in front of him. Ninni asked one of his officers to take off Savioni's handcuffs. He offered him a cigarette, which Savioni took.

"You lost this time," Ninni drawled. "We are one step ahead of you—we know everything. Your only hope is to confess, and if you do, things will go easier."

"I really thought he was a friend," said Savioni, shaking his head and puffing on the cigarette. He had figured out that Carpanese had gone to the police. "I'm sure it was him. He sold me out. He betrayed me."

At that moment, a knock sounded on the door. Ninni looked up and saw the blond, blue-eyed Inspector Collenghi.

"Ahhh, look who's here! Savioni, a friend of yours," said Ninni, smiling mischievously.

Savioni turned around and recognized "Carlos," the Colombian with the eyes of ice.

"No, Carlos, they got you too?" he blurted.

"*Ciao,* Savioni," said "Carlos," in perfect Italian. "I am *Ispettore* Collenghi."

Savioni brought his fist up to his forehead. "What an idiot I am," he murmured.

"As you can see, we played our hand well this time!" said Ninni. "Would you like to hear your own words? I can play them for you. Your only hope is to confess," repeated Ninni. "The court will be more lenient with you if you do."

18

TRIAL

J ust before 9:30 A.M. the morning of June 2, 1998, the door to the right of the judge's bench opened suddenly and five female prison guards wearing jaunty blue berets escorted Patrizia into a packed courtroom in the Milan courthouse. A murmur rippled through the crowd. Photographers and television camera operators surged forward as she walked in, wearing the startled look of a deer frozen in car headlights. Her lawyers, in sweeping, tassel-trimmed black robes and ruffled white bibs, rose from their seats in the front row to greet her.

The trial for the murder of Maurizio Gucci had already been in session for several days, but that gray Tuesday morning marked Patrizia's first appearance in court. She had preferred to sit out the preliminaries in her San Vittore jail cell, as was her right. Patrizia consulted briefly with her lawyers, two high-profile criminal defense attorneys. The distinguished, white-haired Gaetano Pecorella would be elected a *deputato* to the Italian parliament before the trial was over, while the perpetually suntanned Gianni Dedola defended leading industrialists, including television magnate and former prime minister Silvio Berlusconi. Both attorneys had urged her to come to court well before she would take the stand in her own defense in order to become comfortable with the courtroom atmosphere.

Patrizia walked straight past prosecutor Carlo Nocerino and the rows of lawyers and journalists behind him to take a seat on the last bench. Behind her, curious onlookers strained to get a good view, pressing against the waist-high wooden barrier that separated the trial's participants from the general public. To her left and peering in at her between the blue-capped guards surrounding her, journalists scribbled every detail of her appearance in their notepads. Gone were all traces of the society queen dripping in jewels and self-confidence. At nearly fifty years old, pale and unkempt, the Patrizia who entered the courtroom that day had lost her bearings. Never had she been so on display, yet nothing had prepared her for what she must face. Her short, dark hair lay uncombed around her face, which was puffy from medications. She looked down at her hands, avoiding the staring eyes, twirling around her right wrist a string of pale green rosary beads given to her by the popular healing priest Monsignor Miligno. On her left, she wore a blue plastic Swatch watch. Though her closets back in Corso Venezia overflowed with designer suits, with shelves full of matching handbags and pumps, that morning Patrizia wore simple blue cotton slacks, a polo shirt, and a blue-and-white striped cotton sweater wrapped around her shoulders. Ever conscious of her diminutive height, on her tiny feet she wore pointy white leather mules, size four, with four-inch heels.

Outside, television trucks, motors humming, parked in front of the courthouse, ready to broadcast live. Faced in white marble with the inscription IVSTITIA marching across its façade, the hulking building had been designed by Marcello Piacentini, a leading architect during the Mussolini regime. Churches, gardens, and two convents had been razed to build the courthouse, which occupied an entire city block on the east side of Milan. Each day, a teeming rush of people swarmed to the courthouse, parking fleets of bicycles, scooters, and cars outside and flooding up the concrete steps to deal with the more unpleasant aspects of life. Inside, kilometers of corridors wound around a main foyer whose high columns reached up several stories. From there, winding halls linked some sixty-five courtrooms and twelve hundred offices in a kafkaesque maze. Directly behind the courthouse stood

Santa Maria della Pace, the basilica where Maurizio had married Patrizia twenty-six years before.

For weeks before the trial, the Italian papers and television stations had produced scintillating accounts of the pending face-off between the "Black Widow," as they called Patrizia, and the "Black Witch," as they dubbed Pina, despite Auriemma's protests that she had no real occult powers. In March, two months before the trial started, Pina broke her stony, fifteen-month silence and confessed. She said Patrizia had delivered a secret message to her cell via another inmate, offering to "shower her cell with gold" if she took all the blame for Maurizio's murder. Pina, offended and angry, said she told Patrizia to go to hell—and told her lawyer to call Nocerino.

"I'm an old woman and I'm going to be here a long time! What good is two billion lire [or about $1.5 million] to me in jail?" fumed Pina, who had turned fifty-two in March.

Both Pina and Patrizia were held in the women's section of the San Vittore prison, located on the western edge of central Milan. Savioni, the hotel doorman, and Ceraulo, the alleged triggerman, were also detained there, while Cicala, the former pizzeria owner, was locked up in Monza, just outside Milan. San Vittore held nearly two thousand people within its gray walls; it had been built in 1879 to house just eight hundred inmates. Copied from the Philadelphia model, long famous among penal experts, the facility consisted of a central tower from which four stone wings emanated in a star shape. Only about a hundred of all the inmates were women. They were housed separately in a low, concrete building that faced the main entrance, running between the two front wings. Armed guards paced the tops of the high external walls that enclosed the prison and others manned control towers at each corner. The guards watched as the inmates streamed into the courtyards for exercise every morning and afternoon while just a few yards away, on the other side of the walls, Milan's residents motored back and forth on the city's busy streets. The entrance to San Vittore looked like the gateway to a medieval fortress. Rose-colored stones bordered the high arched door and upstairs windows, while forked battlements flourished along the top of the main building.

San Vittore had become the symbol of *Tangentopoli,* the Clean Hands corruption cleanup scandal. Crusading magistrates had had leading politicians and captains of industry arrested and jailed to pressure them to confess to having paid and received kickbacks worth millions of dollars. However, their pretrial detention in this forbidding place alongside convicted drug dealers and mafiosi stirred up a heated civil rights controversy. And protesters charged that pretrial detention had caused two suicides among the incarcerated politicians and industrialists.

As Patrizia's lawyers battled in vain to have her released to house arrest for medical and psychological reasons, citing periodic epileptic attacks following the brain tumor operation, each day at San Vittore took Patrizia further away from the gilded world she had conquered and lost.

In the beginning, Patrizia had clashed with the other inmates. "They think I am privileged, spoiled, and have had everything in life, so it is right that I must pay," she said. She asked for permission to stay alone during recess in a separate garden after the other women had jeered and spit at her and tossed a volleyball onto her head during the group exercise breaks in the main courtyard. San Vittore's director, an understanding man who tried to keep morale high despite the crowded conditions, agreed. But when Patrizia asked permission to install a refrigerator in her cell to store the homemade meatloaf and other delicacies her mother, Silvana, brought her on Fridays, he refused. When she offered to donate a refrigerator for every cell, he refused again. Patrizia sighed, resigned herself to the bland prison fare, and watched television late into the night inside the gray walls of cell number 12, a non-smoking cell.

Her third-floor cell measured no more than six square meters, hardly seventy square feet. Two bunk beds, two single beds, a table, two chairs, and two closets lined the walls, leaving a skinny passageway in the middle. A small doorway at the far end opened into a tiny room with a sink and toilet in the far corner. In the other corner stood a table and chairs for meals delivered on trays by prison personnel three times a day through an opening in the iron cell door. Patrizia curled up in her bottom bunk where she had taped up a photograph of Padre Pio, a celebrated priest destined for beatification whose image had become highly commercialized.

In the beginning, she refused to socialize with her cellmates—Daniela, another Italian woman who had been jailed on charges of fraudulent bankruptcy, and Maria, a Romanian girl accused of prostitution. She isolated herself in the lower bunk on the right, flipping through magazines and tearing out pictures of outfits she liked. Silvana did all she could to pamper her, bringing her nightgowns and lingerie in chiffon and silk that became the envy of her cellmates. Silvana also brought lipsticks, face creams, and Patrizia's favorite perfume, Paloma Picasso. Patrizia wrote loving letters to her daughters, sealing the envelopes with stickers bearing hearts and flowers and the name Patrizia Reggiani Gucci—which she refused to drop. She prohibited Alessandra and Allegra from visiting her except at Christmas and Easter, saying jail wasn't the right place for two young girls to visit their mother.

Twice a week, prison guards walked her down the long hallway so she could call home from the orange pay phones at one end. In addition to a library, sewing workshop, and chapel, San Vittore boasted a hair salon, where Patrizia went once a month. There, with authorization from the prison director, famed Italian hair guru Cesare Ragazzi tended to the hair implant that covered Patrizia's scar from her brain surgery. At night, suffering from insomnia, she read comic books to help herself fall asleep. The entire time she thought about her upcoming trial.

Pina, afraid that Patrizia had decided to blame her, broke their pact of silence and told the entire sordid story to Nocerino, pointing her finger at Patrizia as the instigator of the murder plan. Pina's confession confirmed what Savioni had said in police inspector Ninni's office the day of his arrest. Nocerino was delighted. Despite his futile two-year foray into Maurizio's business affairs, by the time the trial opened in May 1998, he had accumulated a staggering amount of evidence against Patrizia in forty-three bulging cardboard filing boxes. The defense attorneys had had to pay a small fortune to photocopy the contents and the court clerks repeatedly had to wheel the boxes in and out of the courtroom on metal carts. In addition to the confessions of Pina and Savioni, Nocerino had thousands of pages of transcripts from telephone conversations, including Patrizia's and those of her codefendants, as well as depositions from friends, servants, psychics, and professionals who had known the Gucci couple. In the fall of 1997, investigators had even raided Patrizia's jail cell, finding a statement from her Monte Carlo bank account, code-named "Lotus B," that showed withdrawals corresponding to the sums Pina and Savioni said they received. In the margin next to the figures, Patrizia had written "P" for Pina. Nocerino even had Patrizia's leatherbound diaries, which police had confiscated when they arrested her. But he had no direct admission of involvement from Patrizia, and this troubled him.

From her seat at the back of the courtroom, Patrizia blankly scanned the brown steel cage—a standard feature in Italian courtrooms—that ran along the right side of the high-ceilinged room. Even though in Italy, as in the United States, defendants are considered innocent until proven guilty, people charged with violent crimes must sit out their trials in the cage. Inside, Benedetto Ceraulo, the accused triggerman, and Orazio Cicala, the alleged driver of the getaway car, hung their arms on the bars and scanned the sea of journalists, attorneys, and curious onlookers. Ceraulo, forty-six, dressed neatly in button-down shirt and jacket, his dark hair recently clipped and combed, scowled proudly out at the crowd with an unsettling stare. He had declared himself innocent—and there was no direct proof of his role in the murder, though Nocerino was confident he had enough circumstantial evidence for a conviction, including Savioni's confession naming Benedetto as the killer. The balding, fifty-nine-year-old Cicala stooped next to him, his oversize jacket hanging from his shoulders as though on a hanger; after two years in jail, the bankrupt pizza man had lost more than thirty pounds and most of his hair. A series of frosted, louvered windows above the cage provided the only ventilation in the room. Black marble tile reached up the walls about eight feet, giving way to dingy white stucco covering the rest of the walls and ceiling.

Patrizia refused to look at Pina, who sat on a bench a few rows in front of her sporting a new red hairstyle and a cotton sweater with a tiger motif. From time to time, Pina leaned over to whisper with her lawyer, Paolo Traini, a portly, smiling man who punctuated his speech by waving his bright blue reading glasses, which started a fashion trend among other lawyers in the Milan courthouse. Ivano Savioni, the doorman of the Hotel Adry, his face sullen and his hair gleaming with gel, slumped silently on the back bench to Patrizia's right, wearing a black suit and pink shirt and surrounded by male guards.

A buzzer sounded and the murmur hushed as Judge Renato Ludovici Samek swept into the courtroom followed by his assistant magistrate, both wearing the customary black robes and white bibs of the judiciary. After the two magistrates came six civilian jurors and two alternates, dressed in business clothes and each wearing a ceremonial sash draped from one shoulder across the chest, striped in the white, red, and green of the Italian flag. They all filed in behind the wooden podium that curved around the raised platform in the front of the courtroom. Samek sat down and the jurors took their seats on either side of him and his assistant. Samek looked out sternly over the reading glasses perched on the tip of his nose, as courtroom guards ushered out television camera operators and photographers who had been banned from the actual proceedings.

"If I hear another *telefonino* ringing, the owner will be asked to leave," Samek said, glaring out at the assembly after unsuccessfully trying to open the hearing over the rings of a cellular telephone. A trim man with a slightly receding hairline and unflappable, thin-lipped expression, Samek had become famous in Milan's judicial community for the day when gunshots broke out in the high-security bunker courtroom under San Vittore as he presided over the 1988 trial of mafia boss Angelo Epaminonda—a dangerous man with a long string of homicides on his record. As terrified attorneys and legal assistants dove for cover under tables and chairs, Samek jumped to his feet, shouting for order—the only person left standing in the entire room. The shooting, a settling of accounts among clansmen, left two carabinieri seriously wounded. To show that the state would not be shaken by such violence, Samek suspended the trial only momentarily and resumed the hearing that same afternoon.

During the Gucci murder trial, Samek proved a demanding taskmaster, holding the court to an intensive three-day-a-week hearing schedule and meeting with the jury during off days to review the evidence. Samek, who would decide the case along with the jurors, as is the practice in the Italian court system, pushed for clarity throughout the trial. Intolerant of lazy questions or evasive answers, he often took over the interrogation of witnesses himself—something unheard of in a U.S. courtroom. The defense attorneys compared Samek under their breath with the unyielding, larger-than-life marble bas-relief of Sant' Ambrogio, Milan's patron saint, that looms high on the wall behind the podium. In his right hand, Sant' Ambrogio raises a leather whip with seven knotted strands, sending two oafish figures tumbling with his blows.

In the following weeks and months, Italians did not miss a detail of the Gucci trial in newspapers and on television as reports of the testimony unfolded into an epic story of love, disillusionment, power, wealth, luxury, jealousy, and greed.

The Gucci murder trial became the Italian equivalent of the O. J. Simpson case in the United States. "This is not a murder case," muttered Patrizia's attorney, Dedola, "this story makes a Greek tragedy look like a children's story."

The trial spotlighted the passionate, excessive lives of Maurizio and Patrizia in stark contrast to the gray squalor in which Pina and her three accomplices lived. And like the O. J. Simpson trial, which underscored divisive racial attitudes in American society, the Gucci trial highlighted the chasm separating wealthy from poor in Italy.

Thus millions of Italians were watching their televisions in fascination a few days earlier as prosecution and defense delivered their opening arguments. Nocerino, the darkly handsome prosecutor, stood on the left-hand side of the courtroom, facing the judge's podium and the adjacent television camera—which Samek had approved for the opening and the closing of the trial—and painted Patrizia as an obsessed, hate-filled divorcée who coldly and determinedly orchestrated the murder of her husband to gain control of his multimillion-dollar estate.

"I intend to prove that Patrizia Martinelli Reggiani negotiated the fee she would pay for the organization and execution of the murder of Maurizio Gucci and made the payments in several installments, including a down payment and final balance," Nocerino said, his voice echoing in the high courtroom.

Patrizia's defense attorneys, Pecorella and Dedola, standing on the right-hand side of the courtroom, didn't deny Patrizia's obsessive hatred for Maurizio, which they admitted she had broadcast widely. But they painted her as a rich, sick woman who had become the puppet of her long-standing friend, Pina Auriemma. Pina, not Patrizia, they said, arranged the murder and then blackmailed and threatened Patrizia for her silence. The 150 million lire (about $93,000) Patrizia paid out before the murder was a generous loan to a friend in need, the attorneys said. The 450 million lire (about $276,000) she paid afterward had been cruelly extorted from her by that same friend with threats to Patrizia and her daughters. The proof, said Dedola dramatically in his resonant, baritone voice, was a three-line letter Patrizia wrote, signed, and deposited with a Milan notary in 1996 that read: "I have been forced to pay hundreds of millions of lire for the safety of myself and my family. If anything should happen to me, it will be because I know the name of the person who killed my husband: Pina Auriemma."

Dedola's elegant oratory and Patrizia's apparently desperate letter couldn't counter the sharp blow her defense received that gray Tuesday morning—a surprise confession by Orazio Cicala, the driver of the getaway car. The defense strategy paled against the bizarre story Cicala told in the simple, ungrammatical speech of an uneducated man in his Sicilian dialect; the story of a vengeful princess, Patrizia, and a pauper, himself.

The blue-capped prison guards had released Cicala from the cage, allowing him to stand next to his lawyer, a young woman in her early forties. They made an odd pair—the glamorous, accomplished lawyer who captivated the courtroom with her rich voice, dark-haired good looks, and tight suits, and the hunched, gaunt Cicala who had destroyed his family, first with gambling debts and now with a murder charge.

His toothless mouth gaping at the court, Cicala described the day Savioni had come to him saying he knew about a woman who wanted to kill her husband. "At first I said I wasn't interested, but the next day he asked me again and that time I said yes, but it was going to be expensive. When he said 'How much?' I told him, 'Half a billion lire!' [about $310,000]" Cicala said, warming to his task and beginning to enjoy the attention he was getting. "They came back to me and said OK. I said I wanted half up front, half after the fact."

Besieged by usurers, Cicala said he happily received 150 million lire ($93,000) from Pina and Savioni in sealed yellow envelopes in several installments during the fall of 1994, but did nothing to organize the murder. When Pina and Savioni began to pressure him, he lied to buy more time, saying that the killers he had hired had been arrested; the car he had stolen for the job had disappeared.

"When they asked me for the money back, I told them I had already given it to the people and I couldn't get it back," Cicala said, his oversized jacket swinging loosely around his emaciated frame as he gestured.

Patrizia, who had been listening impassively on the last bench of the courtroom, suddenly appeared ill and a white-capped nurse bustled to her side with a small leather bag and a syringe, asking her if she wanted an injection. Patrizia had been taking prescription medicine to control seizures following her brain surgery. Her lawyers had arranged for the nurse to attend Patrizia during the trial in case of a medical emergency, also hoping that the presence of the white-uniformed aide might help sway the court in Patrizia's favor.

Patrizia, used to playing the role of the strong woman, refused the injection. "No, no," whispered Patrizia, leaning over and holding a tissue to her face. "Just some water, please."

Cicala also described an encounter with Patrizia herself that shifted the murder plot into overdrive. Up until the end of 1994, Patrizia dealt only with Pina, who in turn, he said, funneled information and money to Savioni and Cicala. But in early 1995, frustrated by the lack of action and concerned that she was being defrauded, Patrizia cut out Pina and took matters into her own hands, Cicala said.

"One afternoon—it must have been late January, early February, because it was cold—I was at home and the doorbell rang and it was Savioni," said Cicala. "So I came downstairs with him and he whispered, 'She's in the car!' "

"And did you ask him what she was doing there?" asked Nocerino, sitting in his chair at the front left side of the courtroom.

"No, I didn't say anything. I just got into the backseat of Savioni's car and there was a lady with sunglasses sitting in the front seat who introduced herself as Patrizia Reggiani," Cicala told the prosecutor, adding that by then he knew she was the one who wanted to kill her ex-husband, Maurizio Gucci. "I got into the backseat and she turned around and asked me how much money I had received, what had happened to the money, and what point I was at," he said.

"I told her that I had received 150 million lire [$93,000], that I had found the people but they had been arrested, and I needed more money and more time. At that point she said, 'If I give you more money, you must guarantee that this thing gets done because time is running out. He is about to leave on a cruise and when he does he'll be gone for months.' "

Cicala took a deep breath and asked for water. "And here we come to the main point," he said, looking around the courtroom for confirmation.

"Please, please, continue," said Nocerino with a wave of his hand, leaning back comfortably in his chair.

"She said that it wasn't a question of money, but of a job well done," continued Cicala. "And I asked her, 'If I do this thing myself and something should happen to me, what is my situation?' She said, 'Look, Cicala, if you leave me out of this, and they find out about you, the walls of your cell will be papered with gold,' and I said, 'I have five children, five children who I have ruined; I have left them in the middle of the street,' and she said, 'There will be enough for you, your children, and your children's children,' she told me."

Cicala looked up and begged the court, the prosecutor, and his lawyer to excuse him for what he had to say next.

"I finally saw the chance," Cicala continued, speaking slowly, "once and for all, to fix things for my family, for my children, who I had ruined. From that moment on I became determined that I was going to do this thing," he said, opening his hands wide. "I didn't know how or when, but I was determined I was going to do it!"

In the following weeks, Pina telephoned him daily with an overwhelming stream of information about Maurizio Gucci's whereabouts, Cicala said. "Maurizio Gucci became the topic of the day," he said, rolling his eyes at the memory.

Not sure that he could carry out the murder himself, Cicala decided to hire a killer, a man he described as a small-time drug dealer he knew. As Samek peered down at him skeptically and Nocerino watched in consternation, Cicala denied the killer was Benedetto Ceraulo—the scowling man in the cage with him—saying he was afraid to pronounce the real gunman's name because he was still on the loose. Nobody believed him, but there was nothing to be done: in Italy a defendant who takes the stand in his own defense is not obliged to tell the truth, the whole truth, or nothing but the truth.

The night of Sunday, March 26, Pina, who knew that Maurizio had returned from a business trip to New York, called Cicala with a cryptic message: *"Il pacco è arrivato,"* "The package has arrived."

The next morning, Cicala picked up the killer and they drove together to Via Palestro to wait for Maurizio.

"We waited about forty-five minutes, and then we saw him cross the street at Corso Venezia and start walking up the sidewalk." Cicala said he glanced at his watch, which read 8:40 A.M.

"The killer asked me, 'Is that the guy?' "

Cicala recognized the man walking jauntily up the street from the photograph of Maurizio Pina had given him.

"I said, 'Yes, it's him.'

"At that point, the killer got out of the car and went over to stand by the doorway, pretending to look at the address number. I moved the car and—that's when it happened," said Cicala, looking out at the silent courtroom. "I didn't see anything or hear anything; I was moving the car. Then the killer jumped back in the car and I drove the escape route we had studied that weekend back to Arcore. He said he thought he had killed the *portinaio* too. I dropped him off and by nine A.M. I was home."

When Pina took the stand a few weeks later, she explained in her sardonic, Neapolitan drawl, how Patrizia had asked her to organize Maurizio's murder.

"We were like sisters, she told me everything," said Pina, who had exchanged the tiger-motif sweater for one with large roses. "She wanted to do it herself, but she didn't have the courage. Because of her super–northern Italian mentality, she assumed that all of us southern Italians must have ties to the *camorra*," said Pina, rolling her eyes, referring to the Neapolitan mafia. The only other person Pina knew in Milan was Savioni, the husband of a friend. Pina, who was in Milan helping Patrizia with her manuscript, described the unrelenting pressure Patrizia put on her.

"Every day that passed for her was a day lost," Pina said. "She tortured me, day after day, and in turn I tortured Savioni, who in turn tortured Cicala. I couldn't stand it anymore!"

Pina said that after Maurizio was killed, she fell apart emotionally, growing depressed, nervous, and paranoid. A few days before Maurizio's funeral, she gathered her composure and called Patrizia.

"So, you've had good news?" Pina said.

"Yes, I am fine, 'Fine' with a capital 'F,' " Patrizia said emphatically. "I am finally at peace with myself, I am serene and the girls are serene. This thing has given me tremendous tranquillity and joy."

Pina told Patrizia she was so troubled and depressed she was taking tranquilizers and contemplating suicide.

"Pull yourself together, Pina, don't exaggerate!" said Patrizia coolly. "It's all over now, just stay calm, behave yourself, and don't disappear." Pina moved to Rome and lived on the three million lire, or about $1,600, a month that Patrizia sent her. At one point, Pina said she broke down and confided in a mutual friend.

"Patrizia has bought my misery," she said, as the friend listened, horrified. That phrase became a theme of the trial in the papers and the courtroom alike.

Pina often grew angry during the trial at Patrizia's efforts to pin the blame on her—and at one point retaliated, asking to make a spontaneous statement to the court. Samek consented and Pina stood up and accused Patrizia's mother, Silvana, of knowing about her daughter's murder plan, adding that months before Maurizio's murder, Silvana had contacted an Italian named Marcello who had links to the Chinese gangs proliferating in Milan, but that they had disagreed on the price and so nothing happened. In the months after Patrizia's arrest, Nocerino had also received a memorandum from Patrizia's stepbrother, Enzo, who had long since moved to Santo Domingo, in which he not only accused Silvana of being an accomplice to Patrizia, he also accused Silvana of having years ago hastened the death of *Papà* Reggiani to secure his estate. Enzo, who had chronic financial problems, had sued Silvana for a larger share of the Reggiani estate—and lost. Silvana vigorously denied her stepson's sinister allegations, saying she had kept her late husband alive for months beyond the period of life expectancy predicted by his doctors. As the Italian papers jumped on the "Mother-Daughter Predator Team" story, prosecutors opened a formal investigation into the accusations against Silvana—though nothing ever came of Pina's charges and Silvana vigorously denied any involvement in both cases.

Some of the witnesses moved the entire courtroom, which became a small community of lawyers, journalists, legal assistants, and curious onlookers who came back day after day as the trial unfolded. Onorato, the observant doorman displaced from his Sicilian homeland, chilled everyone with his firsthand account of the murder, his own shooting, and incredible survival. Alda Rizzi, the Guccis' former housekeeper, amazed everyone when she described her anguished call to Patrizia the morning Maurizio was murdered only to hear classical music playing loudly in the background and find Patrizia serene and indifferent on the telephone. Antonietta Cuomo, Maurizio's psychic, described how she tried to protect him from evil spirits and reassure him in his business plans. Paola Franchi—who had failed in her efforts to get a settlement from Maurizio's estate—entertained the court with details of their love affair and wedding plans, never once in four hours glancing at Patrizia, who stared at her blankly from her new post at the front bench between her lawyers. During the trial, both Paola and Patrizia referred to Maurizio as their "husband," although he was married to neither at the moment he died. Tiny diamonds flashed discreetly from Paola's earlobes and fingers. Dressed in a richly embroidered linen suit, she crossed and uncrossed her long suntanned legs as she spoke, while all the eyes in the courtroom followed the gold ankle bracelet that dangled provocatively from one svelte leg.

"The best thing that can happen to Patrizia now," Paola said to journalists outside the courtroom after her testimony, "is for her to sink into total oblivion."

As the hearings wore on into the summer, policemen and investigators recreated the crime, the misguided hunt for the killer among Maurizio's business contacts, and the unexpected breakthrough two years later thanks to Carpanese and Inspector Ninni. Then Patrizia's gray-suited banker from Monte Carlo described the packets of cash he personally delivered to her Milan apartment, cash Patrizia subsequently said was a loan to her good friend Pina.

"If the money was a loan, why didn't you just order a bank transfer?" boomed one of Pina's two lawyers, Paolo Trofino, a lanky Neapolitan with oily, shoulder-length hair and an open smile.

"I don't even know what a bank transfer is," rebutted Patrizia nonchalantly when she testified afterward, "I do all my banking in cash."

Doctors told the story of Patrizia's illness. Lawyers itemized the terms of her divorce settlements. Friends recounted the vengeful tirades against Maurizio. As the witnesses paraded to the witness chair, Patrizia, in court during much of their testimony, listened silently and gathered her strength.

In July, hair freshly coiffed and toenails polished at the San Vittore salon, she took the stand in a smart, pistachio green designer suit and delivered a composed, three-day defense, nimbly refuting all the charges against her. She seemed to be almost her old self—proud, cutting, arrogant, and uncompromising. Observed by a court-ordered panel of three psychiatrists—who later declared her perfectly sane—she appeared at times more lucid than Nocerino himself. The psychiatrists subsequently diagnosed her as having a narcissistic personality disorder, saying she was egocentric, was easily offended, and exaggerated her problems with an inflated sense of her own importance. Had she perhaps also washed herself of her guilt? Was she loath to confess the truth to her two daughters: that she had killed their father? Or was she telling the truth? Had Pina taken the situation out of her hands? The psychiatrists quickly made up their minds.

"We can comprehend her actions," said one of the psychiatrists, who testified, "but we cannot condone them. Just because someone goes around with her nose out of joint doesn't mean she can be allowed to kill people!"

On the stand, Patrizia described the first thirteen years of marriage with Maurizio as perfect bliss—which she said broke down when he became more influenced by a series of business advisors than by his own wife.

"People said we were the most beautiful couple in the world," Patrizia recalled. "But after Rodolfo died and Maurizio went from executing his father's decisions to making them himself, he turned to a series of advisors for support."

"He became like a seat cushion that takes the shape of the last person to sit on it!" Patrizia said in disgust.

She described their separation and divorce agreements, in which he gave her hundreds of millions of lire a month, but no title to the assets she coveted. "He gave me the bones so he didn't have to give me the chicken," Patrizia added cuttingly.

One day, before they were divorced, Patrizia said, she arrived at the Saint Moritz estate with the two girls only to find the doors to the houses closed and the locks changed.

"I was just a *little* bit upset, so I called the police," she told the courtroom. "They let me in and I changed the locks. Then I called Maurizio. 'What is this all about?' I asked him. He said, 'Didn't you know that when a couple separates, the locks change?' I said, 'Well, now I have changed the locks too, so we'll just have to see who changes them next!'"

Patrizia acknowledged that over the years, her hatred of Maurizio ballooned into an obsession.

"Why?" asked Nocerino. "Because he had left you, because he was with another woman?"

"I didn't respect him anymore," she said softly after a brief silence. "He wasn't the man I had married, he didn't have the same ideals anymore," said Patrizia, describing how shocked she had been at Maurizio's treatment of Aldo, his leaving home, his business failures.

"Then why did you write down his every phone call, every meeting with your daughters in your diary?" asked Nocerino, reciting examples for the court. "July 18: Mau calls and then disappears; July 23: Mau calls; July 27: Mau calls; September 10: Mau shows up; September 11: Mau calls, he meets the girls, we talk; September 12: Mau goes to the movies; September 16: Mau calls; September 17: Mau meets the girls at school."

"Perhaps—perhaps I didn't have anything better to do," answered Patrizia limply.

"It doesn't seem, from these diary entries at least, that Maurizio had abandoned the family, the girls," Nocerino said.

"He would have moments of tremendous interest," Patrizia explained, "and he would call the girls and say, 'OK, I'm taking you to the movies this afternoon,' and they would go there and wait for him and he wouldn't show up and he would call at night and say, 'Oh, *amore*, I'm so sorry, I forgot. How about tomorrow?' And it would go on like that," Patrizia said.

"What about the phrases—'PARADEISOS,' on the day Maurizio died; 'There is no crime which cannot be bought,' ten days before the murder—how can you explain these?" Nocerino asked.

"Ever since I started working on my manuscript," Patrizia answered coolly, "I wrote down quotations and turns of phrase that attracted me or intrigued me, nothing more," she answered.

"And the threats written in your diaries, the cassette you sent him in which you say you won't give him a minute of peace?" Nocerino asked.

Patrizia's dark eyes narrowed.

"How would you feel if you were in a clinic and the doctors gave you only a few days to live and your mother took your children to your husband and said, 'Your wife is dying,' and he said, 'I'm too busy, I don't have time,' and the girls had to watch you being wheeled away and they didn't know if you were going to come out of that room alive? How would you feel?"

"And the relationship with Paola Franchi?" Nocerino pressed on.

"Every time we spoke, Maurizio would tell me, 'Say, did you know that I'm seeing a woman who is the complete opposite of you? She's tall, blond, green-eyed, and always walks three steps behind me!' " Patrizia said. "From what I could tell, he had had other blond women who walked three steps behind him. I was different."

"And were you worried that they might get married?"

"No, because Maurizio told me, 'The day we get divorced, I don't want to have another woman at my side, not even by mistake!' "

Patrizia said the first she knew about the plot to murder Maurizio was from Pina, a few days after he died. Out walking, the two women had stopped in front of the Invernizzi gardens, behind the Corso Venezia apartment, to watch the pink flamingos walking daintily across the manicured lawn. Patrizia described their conversation to the court.

"So, are you happy about the nice present we gave you?" Pina said. "Maurizio is gone, you are free. Savioni and I don't have a lira—you are the goose with the golden eggs." Pina—her friend of more than twenty-five years, the woman who had been at her side at Allegra's birth, who had helped her through Maurizio's departure and her brain surgery—became "arrogant, rough, and vulgar," threatening her and her daughters if she didn't pay five hundred million lire for the death of Maurizio.

"I felt sick, I asked her if she had gone crazy, I said I would go to the police. She said if I did, she would accuse me. 'Everybody knows you went around talking about finding a killer for Maurizio Gucci.' She told me, 'Don't forget—there has been one death, but there could easily be three [meaning Patrizia and the two girls].' She said she wanted five hundred million lire," Patrizia said as Pina, seated a few rows back, snorted and spread her arms wide, shaking her head in disgust at Patrizia's words.

"Why didn't you rebel?" asked Nocerino. "Why didn't you go to the police?"

Patrizia looked at him as though the answer were obvious. "Because I was afraid of the scandal that would explode, just as it did," she answered. "Besides," she added nonchalantly, "Maurizio's death was something I had wanted for so many years—it seemed to me a *fair price to pay* for his death." (Italics added.)

Nocerino reminded Patrizia that in the months after Maurizio's death she and Pina had talked on the phone almost daily, taken a cruise together on the *Creole*, and gone to Marrakesh on vacation.

"Your relationship was the picture of an intimate friendship between two women, rather than of a victim being blackmailed," Nocerino pointed out.

"Pina warned me that the phones were almost certainly tapped and told me that I should not betray any tension in my voice or words. She said our behavior had to seem as normal as it had always been," Patrizia retorted without batting an eyelash.

In September, Silvana took the stand to defend her daughter. Dressed simply in brown slacks and matching checked jacket, her red hair teased and smoothed back from her forehead, she described Patrizia as "putty in Pina's hands—Pina decided everything, from what they would have for dinner to where they would go on vacation." Her gnarled fingers resting on a silver-tipped cane and dark brown eyes dense and dull, she said, "Pina had drunk her brain." Silvana also admitted that Patrizia talked openly about finding a killer for Maurizio—and that she, Silvana, had thought nothing of it.

"She would say it the way she would have said, 'Would you like to go have tea at Sant' Ambroeus?' I never gave much weight to her words, unfortunately. . . ."

Samek raised his eyes over his spectacles to peer down at Silvana.

" 'Unfortunately,' why?" he asked her.

"Because I should have made her stop saying such stupid things," Silvana replied.

"Hmmmm," mused Samek out loud. "That 'unfortunately' doesn't convince me."

In late October, Nocerino launched into his closing arguments, which lasted two days and spared no detail of the complex trial. Samek took off his reading glasses and settled into his high-backed leather chair. The witness chair sat empty at the front of the courtroom, and the single television camera had returned, trained on Nocerino.

"Patrizia Martinelli Reggiani has categorically rejected the accusation that she ordered the murder of Maurizio Gucci," Nocerino said, his words ringing in the lofty courtroom. "She has offered us her version of the facts, saying that Pina Auriemma gave her a present and threatened her to make her pay for it. This is her defense.

"But her defense is not credible," Nocerino said softly, before raising his voice again.

"Patrizia Martinelli Reggiani was a woman of high society whose pride had been deeply wounded at the hands of her husband. *Only his death could cauterize those wounds!*" he cried to the court. "And after his death she talks of the serenity she finally feels, she writes the word 'PARADEISOS' in her diary—this tells us about her spirit," Nocerino said. In closing he asked the court for life sentences—the severest punishment under Italian law—for all five defendants. Patrizia promptly announced a hunger strike in protest.

Patrizia's daughters, Alessandra and Allegra, came to court for the first time the day her defenders stood up to deliver their closing arguments. The two girls huddled on the back bench with Silvana, while Patrizia remained up front in between her lawyers.

When Patrizia's lawyer, Dedola, began to speak, he filled the high room with his trembling baritone.

"There was a *thief* who stole Patrizia's desire to see her husband dead!" Dedola intoned. "A *thief* who took things into her own hands! That *thief* is in this courtroom. The *thief* is Pina Auriemma!"

During breaks in Dedola's closing oratory, Patrizia moved back to hug and kiss her daughters—whom she had seen only a few times since her dawn arrest. As she embraced the girls, they were surrounded by the flashing strobe lights of the paparazzi who crowded into the courtroom. The girls stroked Patrizia's cheeks and handed over a bag of carrots they had brought for her so she could eat something despite her hunger strike. They chatted awk-wardly in undertones, pretending to ignore the crowd of onlookers who were robbing them of any privacy they might have hoped for.

On November 3, the last day of the trial, the sky, the buildings, and the streets all seemed the same shade of dirty gray, a not-so-uncommon phenom-enon of Milan winters. Samek opened proceedings promptly at 9:30 A.M. and announced that the verdict would be handed down that afternoon. Reporters rushed out of the courtroom to notify their head offices. Samek then allowed each of the defendants to make a statement.

Patrizia, wearing a black pin-striped Yves Saint Laurent suit and black vinyl hooded jacket lined with silvery fabric, stood up first. She had discarded a statement prepared by her lawyers, preferring to use her own words.

"I have been naive to the point of stupidity," she said. "I found myself involved against my will and I deny categorically that I was an accomplice." Then she repeated an old adage she attributed to Aldo Gucci: "Never let even a friendly wolf into your chicken coop; sooner or later it will get hungry." Silvana clucked her tongue at her daughter's willfulness and refusal to read the lawyer's statement.

Roberto and Giorgio Gucci, each watching her on the news separately that night—Roberto in Florence, Giorgio in Rome—exploded in fury that she had invoked their father's name in the sordid story she had set into motion.

By late afternoon, the sky had thickened with fog and a steady drizzle. A stream of journalists, cameramen, and television trucks made their way to the courthouse, where Sant' Ambrogio's marble eyes stared grimly down on the packed courtroom. The room filled with murmurs as the blue-bereted guards brought in Patrizia and her four codefendants. She settled into the bench between her lawyers, her eyes wide, her skin pale and waxy. As journalists and cameramen jostled for space, Nocerino put a hand on the arm of Togliatti, the young carabiniere who had worked by his side during the past three years. For an instant, the dark head moved close to the blond one as Nocerino whis-pered in Togliatti's ear.

"*Mi raccomando,* whatever happens, control yourself. Don't let yourself go," said Nocerino, knowing that Togliatti, who could be emotional, had invested the past three years of his life in searching for the solution to the Gucci murder—Nocerino didn't want any unseemly reactions, either in joy or despair.

All eyes followed Samek's clerk as she moved back and forth between the packed courtroom and the judge's chambers. Only Silvana, Alessandra, and Allegra were missing. That morning, after the defendants' final statements, they had gone to Santa Maria delle Grazie, the church that draws hundreds of tourists each year to view the modern restoration of *The Last Supper*. They lit three candles: the first one for Sant' Espedito—the saint of quick forgiveness—as Patrizia had begged them to do. Then they lighted two more—one for Patrizia and one for Maurizio. Alessandra left for Lugano, where she had her own apartment and studied business at a branch of Milan's prestigious Bocconi University, preferring to be by herself. She slipped three sacred images into her sleeve—Sant' Espedito, the Madonna of Lourdes, and Sant' Antonio—and tried to attend class, but the courtroom images of her mother, the lawyers, the jury, and the judge flowed through her head and she couldn't concentrate. She went back to her apartment, watched her favorite videotape—Walt Disney's *Beauty and the Beast*—and prayed.

At 5:10 P.M., after nearly seven hours of deliberations, the buzzer sounded and Samek swept into the room, followed by the assistant magistrate and the six jurors. Photographers and television camera operators strained forward. For a few seconds, the shutters snapping furiously were the only sounds in the room.

Samek looked up momentarily from the sheet of white paper in his hands to scan the crowd before he began to read.

"In the name of the Italian people . . ."

Patrizia Martinelli Reggiani and all four accomplices were found guilty of the murder of Maurizio Gucci. Samek read out the sentences, which in Italian courts are issued at the moment of the verdict: Patrizia Reggiani, twenty-nine years; Orazio Cicala, twenty-nine years; Ivano Savioni, twenty-six years; and Pina Auriemma, twenty-five years. Despite Nocerino's request, only Benedetto Ceraulo, the killer, received a life sentence. The crowd murmured.

As television cameras trained on Patrizia, she stood, immobile, her eyes glued to Samek's face. As he read out her sentence, her eyes fluttered. She looked down for an instant, then up again, impassive as Samek finished reading. He looked out at the courtroom again, folded his sheet of paper, and swept out. It was 5:20 P.M.

The crowd in the courtroom surged forward as the door closed behind Samek and the jurors. Journalists and cameras pressed around Patrizia, who huddled between the dark robes of her lawyers.

"Truth is the daughter of time," she said, and closed her mouth firmly, refusing to say more. Dedola raised a cellular phone to his ear and dialed the number of Corso Venezia 38, where Silvana and Allegra had gone to await the verdict.

As Samek read the verdict, blood rushed to Togliatti's head. He had never heard of a person who commissioned a murder receiving less than the killer. He looked at Nocerino, choked back his anger, and fled the courtroom, running a quick calculation in his head—twenty-nine years? That meant Patrizia Reggiani could be out in twelve to fifteen years' time. She would be sixty-two to sixty-five years old. Togliatti, after all the murder cases he had handled, felt sick.

In the cage, the surly Benedetto Ceraulo jumped up high on the bench, clinging to the bars, looking down on the crowd for his young wife in the crowd. She, the mother of their new baby, had collapsed in tears.

"I knew it would end like this," Ceraulo shouted out over the crowd. "They think they have discovered hot water! Other than cry out my innocence, there is nothing I can do. I am just a monkey in a cage!"

Despite their stiff prison terms, Pina, Savioni, and Cicala sighed in relief. It was all over; they had avoided life imprisonment. They leaned toward their lawyers for whispered consultations. With time off for good behavior, they might be out in fifteen years or less.

Samek would later issue his written opinion, in which he explained the reasoning behind each sentence. In Patrizia's case, he reiterated the seriousness of her crime, though he acknowledged the impact of her "narcissistic" personality disorder as diagnosed by the panel of psychiatrists, thus justifying the twenty-nine-year jail penalty instead of a full life sentence.

"Maurizio Gucci was sentenced to death by his ex-wife, who found the people who were willing to satisfy her hatred in exchange for money," Samek wrote. "Her hatred had been cultivated, day after day, with no mercy for a man—the father of her daughters—who was young, healthy, finally serene and whom she had once loved. Maurizio Gucci certainly had his defects—perhaps he wasn't the most present of fathers, nor the most attentive of ex-husbands, but in his wife's eyes he had committed an unpardonable wrong: Maurizio Gucci had stripped her, through their divorce, of a formidable patrimony and an internationally recognized name—and the accompanying status, benefits, luxuries, and prerogatives. Patrizia Reggiani did not intend to give these up."

Samek said that Patrizia's behavior was especially serious in view of the gravity of the crime, the lengthy planning, the economic motive, the disregard for the emotional ties that united Maurizio with her and still do via their daughters, and the sense of liberation and serenity she admitted feeling after his death.

Patrizia's personality disorder emerged when her life twisted away from her dreams and expectations, Samek pointed out. "During the long stretches in which life was generous with Reggiani, she didn't manifest any signs of disturbance," pointed out Samek. "But the instant this mechanism was broken, her feelings and her behavior went far beyond acceptable standards, manifesting signs of disturbance," Samek said. "Patrizia Reggiani cannot underestimate the seriousness of what she did: an act of extreme violence only because someone didn't respect her wishes, deliver her ambitions, or fulfill her expectations."

Maurizio Gucci had died for what he had—his name and his fortune—and not for who he was.

Back in the pink-walled living room of the apartment on Corso Venezia, Silvana rocked herself back and forth on the overstuffed couch in front of the wall-sized oil portrait of Patrizia, whose liquid brown eyes stared out over her mother's head.

"Twenty-nine years, twenty-nine years," Silvana said over and over, as though repeating the words could somehow cancel their meaning. Allegra hugged her grandmother to console her and then called Alessandra in Lugano to give her the news. After she hung up, the telephone rang constantly as friends, relatives, and Patrizia's social worker from San Vittore called to console them.

"I don't have twenty-nine years to wait," Silvana said forcefully, hugging Allegra again. "It's time to stop crying. Tomorrow morning at nine-thirty we have to go to Patrizia. We have to get her out."

The week Patrizia was convicted, Gucci stores around the world displayed a gleaming pair of sterling silver handcuffs in their windows—although a spokeswoman assured callers the timing of the display was a "coincidence."

19

TAKEOVER

Domenico De Sole had just settled into bed with his wife, Eleanore, in their Knightsbridge town house to steal a mid-morning nap after making the transatlantic flight back to London overnight from New York. It was Wednesday morning, January 6, 1999, and they had just returned from a skiing vacation in Colorado with their two daughters, who by this time were in their teens.

The previous fall, De Sole and Ford had moved Gucci's corporate offices to London, although the company's production operations remained in Scandicci and the group's legal headquarters in Amsterdam as before. The move came five years after Bill Flanz had closed San Fedele and moved Gucci's headquarters back to Florence saying it was important to unite the company's head with its heart. But a lot had happened in five years, and both De Sole and Ford felt the move would be positive for Gucci. Having a

London corporate headquarters would help Gucci recruit top-level international managers; it was difficult to find qualified people willing to move to Florence. Furthermore, Ford had set his heart on moving to London—flourishing, fashionable, and a hotbed of new trends. Though Paris was ever-chic, he hadn't found the city welcoming. "I was ready to live somewhere that I spoke the language!" he admitted. De Sole's wife, Eleanore, was thrilled. She had been longing to move away from Florence. The London move had caused some concern and controversy within the firm at first, but that seemed to have dissipated. De Sole traveled frequently to Florence, where he kept an office. The move also enabled Ford to unite his creative staff in London. Previously he and his assistants had shuttled between Florence and Paris, an inconvenient and inefficient arrangement. Ford ordered video conferencing equipment installed at several of his homes and in Gucci's main offices and around the world so he could conduct fittings and design meetings wherever he was. Though he acknowledged the equipment was expensive, he felt the savings in time, energy, and travel were well worth the investment.

That morning, De Sole uncharacteristically wanted to get a little sleep before going to the office, which was in temporary quarters Gucci had rented on Grafton Street, a few paces from Gucci's Old Bond Street store. He expected the day to be a quiet one, especially since businesses were closed in Italy and France for Epiphany. For the first time since last June, when rival fashion company Prada had announced it had bought a 9.5 percent stake in Gucci, the largest held by a single shareholder, De Sole felt relaxed. Prada had apparently stopped buying below 10 percent and its representative had voted with management at the latest shareholders meeting. De Sole thought Gucci was in the clear.

Prada had rocked the fashion industry and stunned De Sole when it first announced having acquired the Gucci stake the summer before. Some thought that Prada, smaller than Gucci and inexperienced in takeover raids, might have been an advance runner for a larger group. But as the months passed with no new developments, De Sole reasoned that Prada had neither the financial muscle nor the larger alliances needed to take over Gucci, which at that point was valued at more than $3 billion.

In little more than ten years, Patrizio Bertelli, the crusty, volatile Tuscan married to Mario Prada's descendant and chief designer, Miuccia Prada, had ingeniously transformed Prada from a sleepy, unknown luggage manufacturer into a global fashion and accessories powerhouse that had become one of Gucci's toughest rivals. Bertelli, steeped in Tuscany's leatherworking traditions and a former Gucci supplier himself, bristled at Gucci's expansion under new management and its growing control over the regional manufacturers. Prada consolidated its business and design headquarters in Milan and its production operations in Terranova, near Arezzo, about an hour from Florence. Both Gucci and Prada had begun to demand exclusive contracts from their suppliers, to ensure production capacity and discourage copies and fakes. Bertelli felt the encroachment and didn't like it. An explosive man known for his violent outbursts, he was often the subject of outrageous tales in fashion circles. The story that he smashed the windshields of cars irregularly parked in Prada's reserved spaces became lore in Milan. Another episode even splashed into the papers. One day a handbag suddenly flew out of an overhead window and struck a woman walking down the sidewalk outside Prada's offices. Bertelli, rushed out, apologizing profusely. He admitted to the woman he had thrown the bag in a fit of rage.

As Gucci recovered, Bertelli criticized everything he could about his Florentine competitor. He dismissed Dawn Mello as arrogant, accused Ford of copying the looks that had brought Prada success; granted, Prada did pioneer the black nylon handbag, but soon everybody produced it, Gucci included. Bertelli, an admirer of LVMH's Bernard Arnault, dreamed of expanding Prada's reach through acquisitions in the fashion and luxury goods sector.

"Arnault has built a luxury goods empire with financial logic. I don't see why it can't be done with hands-on industrial logic," he said. When Bertelli decided to make his first move, he lunged at Gucci, taking mischievous delight in De Sole's discomfort about his new shareholder. Bertelli called up De Sole, suggesting the two groups could exploit their "synergies" in areas such as finding prime store locations at competitive prices or media buying.

De Sole spurned Bertelli. "Patrizio, this is not my company. I have to talk to my board. We can't make this pizza together," De Sole told Bertelli.

The Gucci camp downplayed their discomfort over the attack and code-named Prada "Pizza." One Gucci employee sent De Sole a large geriatric bandage, commonly sold in Italian pharmacies for arthritis and rheumatism under the brand name Bertelli. He glued the bandage onto a giant-sized hand-lettered keep-your-chin-up card that read: "The ONLY Bertelli we fear is THIS one." This card was displayed in his Scandicci executive office, which he visited regularly.

Through the fall, the Gucci stock price slipped and slid to the $35 range due to fallout from the Asian financial crisis. A disgruntled Bertelli watched his investment dwindle, but didn't buy more. In January, as prospects for Asia improved and analysts forecast heady earnings for Gucci, its stock charged back up to more than $55 a share. De Sole reasoned the price was then high enough to send bargain hunters elsewhere and breathed a sigh of relief. The threat, it seemed, had passed.

Minutes after the De Sole couple had settled down for their nap, the phone rang. Constance Klein, De Sole's London assistant, was on the other end, her voice tense. "Mr. De Sole, I am sorry to disturb you, it's urgent," she clipped.

"Excuse me, honey," De Sole said to Eleanore, moving into another room as his wife rolled her eyes. "I'll just take this call and I'll be right back," he said as she shook her head in disbelief and turned over to get some sleep herself, knowing her husband's work habits only too well.

Eleanore didn't see her husband again until nearly midnight that evening, when an exhausted and overwhelmed De Sole dragged himself back home after one of the most sobering days in his fourteen-year career at Gucci.

Klein had called to say that De Sole had an urgent call from Yves Carcelle, the president of Louis Vuitton and a trusted aide of Bernard Arnault, the clever, fifty-year-old chairman of the LVMH luxury goods group. De Sole and Carcelle had a cordial relationship and often consulted each other about trends in the industry. But something about the urgency of the call on a French national holiday tripped an alarm in De Sole's head. He knew instantly Carcelle wasn't calling to chat.

From the next room, De Sole called Carcelle back. He had been right. The French executive told De Sole that LVMH had acquired more than 5 percent of Gucci's common stock and would make an official announcement later that afternoon. In a reassuring voice, Carcelle told De Sole that Arnault, impressed with all that Gucci had accomplished in the past few years, had decided to make a "passive" acquisition in Gucci with purely "friendly" intent.

De Sole hung up the phone, stunned. The moment he had dreaded for months had arrived. Not only was LVMH the largest luxury goods conglomerate in the world, its profitable Louis Vuitton division was one of Gucci's most direct competitors. In the past few years, Louis Vuitton had also adopted many of the same strategies as Gucci. It had hired a young, hip designer—American Marc Jacobs—to create a new ready-to-wear line, and it had opened a gleaming new flagship store on the Champs-Elysées to give those clothes a grand showcase.

That afternoon, from his third-floor office in the cream-colored town house on Grafton Street Gucci rented until the building it had bought could be renovated, De Sole spoke to Arnault's second in command, Pierre Godé, a towering French lawyer with elegant manners, piercing blue eyes, and a shock of white hair. From LVMH's headquarters—a honeycomb of hushed, gray-carpeted offices on Avenue Hoche just a stone's throw from the Arc de Triomphe—Godé reiterated Carcelle's message: "This is a *passive* investment."

"Excuse me, Pierre," De Sole finally said into the telephone, "but exactly how many shares do you have?"

When Godé claimed not to know the exact amount, De Sole knew he was in trouble. "Okay," he said to himself, "here we go."

De Sole called Morgan Stanley, only to find that his trusted banker, James McArthur, to whom he had turned over the Prada problem the summer before, was leaving the following week for a yearlong sabbatical in Australia. De Sole, whose problem-solving method hinged on working with loyal people he knew and trusted, felt a pang of despair. McArthur called his boss, a forty-two-year-old Frenchman named Michael Zaoui. In minutes, Zaoui rang the bell at Gucci's Grafton Street office.

De Sole greeted Zaoui, trying to hide his nervousness. The handsome, polished investment banker, whose bread and butter was hostile takeover battles, slid into one of the Charles Eames chairs that Tom Ford had picked out for De Sole's office. Zaoui began to tell De Sole what he knew about Arnault.

Arnault, born in the provinces to a building tycoon, had abandoned a career as a concert pianist as a young man and attended the elite French military and engineering institute École Polytechnique before moving to the United States in 1981 to help expand his family's real estate business. His U.S. move, prompted by the election of Socialist president François Mitterrand, gave him a new perspective and taught him a different, more efficient way of doing business. When he returned to France in 1984, he took $15 million of his family's money and bought a failing, state-owned textiles company called Boussac, which contained a jewel—Christian Dior. From there, in the short span of a decade, he became an icon in the world of luxury goods, amassing an impressive stable of designer names including Givenchy, Louis Vuitton, and Christian Lacroix, not to mention the vintners Veuve Clicquot, Hennessy, and Château d'Yquem, the perfume house Guerlain, and the cosmetics emporium Sephora.

"LVMH is his creation, and he runs it," said Zaoui. "There is no question that he is the boss."

But the devastated families, smear campaigns, and forced retirements he left in his wake earned him unflattering nicknames in the French press. His critics dubbed him "The Terminator" and "The Wolf in Cashmere" for bringing American hardball tactics to the genteel world of French business. A trim, long-limbed man with graying hair, an aquiline nose, and a thin line of a mouth, Arnault also had been dubbed "Tin Tin" after the Belgian cartoon character for his dark, circumflex-shaped eyebrows. Although he could appear boyish and whimsical at times, his image had remained ruthless rather than kind. Although he shunned politics, Arnault's growing power brought him acceptance from the Parisian social and business set, who fawned over him and his second wife, a pretty Canadian concert pianist named Hélène Mercier, whom Arnault married in 1991. She had read the reports about her allegedly ruthless husband with perplexity; to her he was charming, affectionate, and an attentive father who often made time to put at least one of their three children to bed at night.

Zaoui didn't describe a conscientious father figure to De Sole. "He is smart, quick and has a strategic mind, like a chess player who thinks twenty moves ahead," Zaoui said, explaining that Arnault's style was to keep building his stake in a "creeping takeover" until he could control the company. Zaoui felt sure that was Arnault's design with Gucci. Though he might make reassuring overtures to existing managers in companies he had set his sights on, after he moved in, he usually moved them out. At Louis Vuitton, he allied with, then expelled the former chairman and family member Henri Racamier in a battle so vitriolic then–French president François Mitterrand chided both sides in a nationally televised speech and called on the French stock market agency to investigate. At Christian Dior, Arnault fired six senior executives in four years, further shaking up the French fashion business establishment.

Zaoui had closely observed Arnault's tactics during another highly publicized European corporate battle. In 1997 the Guinness brewery, in which LVMH had a significant stake, fought Arnault over a merger with U.K. beverage and food conglomerate Grand Met. At the time, the French press speculated that if Arnault couldn't block the merger, he could sell his stake in Guinness for some $7 billion and use it to buy another brand.

"That would be enough to buy Italian luxury house Gucci, the grand rival of Vuitton," *Le Monde* wrote, generating a flurry of then-unfounded rumors. Arnault ultimately backed down about Grand Met and the two companies merged to become a mega drinks group called Diageo, in which LVMH started out as the largest single shareholder with 11 percent, although it later reduced its holding.

A tenacious fight for control of the Duty Free Shops (DFS) chain followed Arnault's wrestling match with Guinness, further fueling the image of Arnault as a heartless conqueror. In all his campaigns, Godé played

Talleyrand to Arnault's Napoléon. "Arnault came up with the ideas and Godé brought him the ammunition," said Marie-France Pochna, author of the recently published *Bernard Arnault: Tout le Monde en Parle,* and a biographer of Christian Dior.

Arnault had been kicking himself ever since he walked away from Gucci back in 1994, saying it was worth nothing. At the time, he had been immersed in digesting his 1990 acquisition of LVMH, which had involved significant financial implications.

"We had other priorities," admitted Godé during an interview in one of LVMH's tiny, mirrored, top-floor conference rooms. "Now everybody says Gucci is wonderful, but at the time it was a mess!" he added. "The turnaround could have failed, nobody knew."

Concentrating on reviving his brands, Arnault had successfully generated attention for Christian Dior, Givenchy, and Louis Vuitton, among others, with a new generation of younger, high-profile designers and powerful advertising campaigns—further shaking up the French fashion and business establishment. Of all the brands, Louis Vuitton became the most commercially successful. With LVMH's dominant position in France, it made sense for Arnault to start extending his reach to other countries. Up to then, the French luxury industry had always looked down its nose at Italy as merely a supplier country. But with the return of Gucci, the meteoric rise of Prada, and the continuing success of others such as Giorgio Armani, Arnault began to view Italy as a ripe field for potential acquisitions and alliances.

"Italy is a place we should have ties with," insisted Concetta Lanciaux, Arnault's influential director of human resources—the same person Maurizio Gucci had tried to hire—who fingered most of the new design talent Arnault has hired for LVMH in the past few years. "It's written on the wall. This is not just about Gucci, but about the leadership of the European luxury goods industry," said the blond-haired, brown-eyed LVMH executive, who is Italian-born, though she has spent most of her professional life in the United States and France.

Arnault didn't move on Gucci in the fall of 1997, when everyone expected him to, because he was preoccupied with the Guinness–Grand Met battle and struggling with newly acquired DFS, hard hit by the Asian financial crisis.

As the Asian market slowly regained stable footing in 1998, Arnault finally set his sights on Gucci. A phantom corporation with LVMH's Paris address quietly began buying up Gucci shares in 1998, accumulating nearly 3 million shares.

"If he wants the company he can have it!" De Sole exploded, pacing agitatedly in front of Zaoui. "I'll just go sailing. My wife is sick of all this. I want to spend more time with my daughters."

De Sole, the Gucci survivor, realized all too well he was at the brink of a new battle. He wasn't sure he wanted it.

Zaoui looked De Sole in the eye. "Domenico," he breathed. "This is war. I have been through these fights. It takes incredible determination and there are no guarantees. You really have to want to win."

De Sole slumped in another Charles Eames chair across from Zaoui. He knew he had no choice. He couldn't just walk away.

"OK, Michael, what do we do?" said De Sole, palms out, fingers spread. "I have never done a takeover corporate battle before, but I certainly know how to fight."

Zaoui asked for a pad of paper and a pen. "Tell me, Domenico, what are the company's defenses?"

As De Sole talked, Zaoui realized there wasn't much. The most Gucci had were golden parachute provisions for Tom Ford and Domenico De Sole—Gucci's two most precious employees—in the event of a change in control. The Morgan Stanley team had nicknamed the provisions the "Dom-Tom Bomb," or the "human poison pill." The clauses allowed Ford to flee Gucci, cashing in his considerable stock options, if a shareholder accumulated 35 percent of the company's stock. Ford also had the right to follow De Sole out the door; he could leave a year later if De Sole walked out. De Sole's clause was more open to interpretation; the Gucci CEO could bail out if any single shareholder assumed "effective control" of the company.

Two days later, the third-floor conference room of Gucci's Grafton Street town house was inaugurated as the latest Gucci war room. De Sole had rallied a small group of Gucci's senior executives. Over the weeks and months ahead, they would become his war team. One of them was De Sole's old friend and Gucci's general counsel Allan Tuttle, the same man Rodolfo had given his overcoat to in Venice sixteen years earlier. De Sole had brought Tuttle over from Patton & Boggs in Washington, D.C., hiring him to work for Gucci full time. Another was the company's chief financial officer Bob Singer; De Sole had stumped alongside him on the Gucci IPO road show four years earlier. Rick Swanson, the man who had supported De Sole within Investcorp, was also there. Tuttle, Singer, and Swanson, as well as the others, were not only talented professionals but also loyal soldiers; De Sole knew he could count on them. Zaoui outlined Gucci's meager options in front of the worried Gucci executives: either negotiate with Arnault or find a white knight with whom they could merge to fend him off.

The ensuing fight for control of Gucci riveted the attention of the international fashion and business community as De Sole and a small team of executives, lawyers, and bankers marshaled the most determined, surprising, and successful defense Arnault had ever come up against in his fifteen years in the business.

Though the faceoff between Gucci and Arnault was just one corporate takeover battle in a wave of corporate consolidation sweeping Europe—and a relatively small one at that—for Gucci, it marked a new frontier. Gucci had fully evolved from a Florentine mom-and-pop handbag shop to a global fashion corporation that had whetted the appetite of the sector's most feared and respected takeover lord. In 1998, Gucci's sales pierced the $1 billion mark— just five years after it had reported losses in the tens of millions.

That Wednesday in January, as far as De Sole was concerned, Arnault had thrown down the gauntlet at his feet, challenging his leadership of one of the world's most successful luxury goods groups. De Sole really had started thinking about retirement, wanting to spend more time with his family and sailing his sleek new 63-foot sailboat, *Slingshot*. But in just a few hours, Arnault's advance had snapped him back to attention.

"I was ready to retire," De Sole admitted, "but I wasn't going to let anybody push me out," he said. "I don't go around starting fights, but if you pick a fight with me, I am going to fight back just as hard as you do." And he did.

De Sole had survived all the Gucci wars—first as the foot soldier for the family factions, later as the linchpin that allowed Investcorp to strike down Maurizio. In the process, he had made his own enemies and detractors. His critics painted him as ruthless, mercenary, and self-serving, with an uncanny ability to marry his own interests with those of the company so as to appear selfless. At the same time, De Sole was the one figure in Gucci's history who had changed the most. Over the years he had transformed himself from a subservient, awkward, and badly dressed lieutenant into a commanding, articulate CEO. *Forbes* magazine put a steely-eyed portrait of De Sole—his beard now impeccably trimmed—on the cover of its February 1999 Global edition for a cover story entitled "Brand Builder."

De Sole had led Rodolfo's fight against Aldo, Aldo's fight against Paolo, and Maurizio's fight against Aldo and his cousins. He had acted decisively in Investcorp's fight against Maurizio. After years of hard work and scant recognition, Investcorp had finally handed him his prize. Now the campaign to fend off Arnault's challenge would engage LVMH on De Sole's turf, where his best weapon would be his sophisticated legal knowledge. He dug in his heels with relish for the fight. "The guy [Arnault] just asked himself over for dinner without calling first!" De Sole said indignantly.

As Zaoui and a team of lawyers pored over Gucci's bylaws, they discovered that the company's statute had actually been written to facilitate a takeover; when Investcorp was looking for an exit back in 1995, a takeover would have been an easy way out. But those same provisions had left Gucci's front door wide open to intruders.

In 1996, De Sole had instituted Project Massimo (Italian for maximum) to examine every possible defense that could lock out potential invaders. Gucci's bankers and lawyers turned over every stone—defensive stock restructuring, partial and total mergers with companies including Revlon—but came up with little. After shareholders defeated the proposed 20 percent voting limitation in 1997, there wasn't much else to do. There weren't any more tricks in the bag.

"We were just sitting there, waiting for someone to take us over," Tom Ford recalled. "It was so frustrating."

In the summer of 1998, after Prada took its stake, De Sole and Ford even met with leveraged-buyout king Henry Kravis, and looked at buying the company themselves. But they soon realized that a leveraged buyout would be too expensive and risky, possibly igniting a bidding war with a strategic buyer from the industry who could afford to pay more than a financial one.

At Gucci's men's show in January, Tom Ford had sent white-faced models with bloodred lips striding aggressively down the runway to the theme song from *Psycho*, baring their teeth like Dracula as though to say "Back off!" to Arnault. The next day, Zaoui called an LVMH banker in London. "This is an official message," he said. "Stop now!"

To everyone's surprise, on January 12, Arnault turned up in Milan as the surprise guest at Giorgio Armani's men's fashion show, where he was thronged by journalists and paparazzi in an appearance that symbolized the dramatic changes going on in the fashion and luxury goods business, where the businessmen had become stars and the stars—at least for an instant—had become passé. At the time, both Arnault and Armani stunned the fashion world once again by acknowledging their two groups were in talks, further consolidating Arnault's image as a great white shark, strong enough to tackle even the largest prey. Nothing would ultimately come of their discussions. Nothing had come either of earlier, little-known conversations between Ford, De Sole, and Giorgio Armani. An idea to merge the two companies into one giant fashion powerhouse equally strong in apparel and accessories was stillborn.

In the following weeks of January, the fashion and business community watched in awe as Arnault moved forward in lightning strikes, snapping up large blocks of Gucci shares from private institutional investors and on the open market. In mid-January, Bertelli sold Arnault his 9.5 percent stake, cheerfully grossing $140 million on the deal, calling the proceeds a *simpatica plusvalenza,* a "delightful profit." Overnight, "Pizza"'s chief executive became a genius in the eyes of his peers.

During the next nine months, Bertelli went on to lay the cornerstones of his dream—emerging at the helm of the first Italian industrial-based luxury goods group. He bought controlling stakes in German designer Jil Sander, known for her high-quality, minimalist styles, and Austrian designer Helmut Lang. In the fall of 1999, he would join forces with LVMH to snap up a majority in Rome-based accessories house Fendi out from under Gucci's nose in what had become a furious bidding war. The luxury goods business was no longer just about quality, style, communication, and stores, but also about ruthless corporate fights that underscored just how high the stakes had become.

By the end of January 1999, Arnault had accumulated a startling 34.4 percent in Gucci, for an estimated $1.44 billion. In the three weeks since LVMH had announced its initial stake, Gucci shares had shot up nearly 30 percent, while the international press hung on every move. Even the *New York Times,* which has seen many a corporate fight, called the affair "the most riveting cliffhanger to transfix the fashion industry in some time."

Arnault hoped to soften his aggressive moves through back channels—not only through Yves Carcelle, who had broken the news to De Sole, but also through De Sole's old friend from Harvard, Bill McGurn, who worked in Paris for the New York law firm Cleary, Gottlieb, Steen & Hamilton, one of the firms that represented LVMH. From frequent conversations with McGurn, Godé felt confident that a friendly deal was possible.

In the meantime, De Sole desperately looked for a white knight, another company that could come in as a partner and stave off LVMH's advance. He spoke to at least nine possible rescuers, but none came through. No potential buyer in his right mind wanted to step into a company that seemed poised to come under LVMH control. Furthermore, it seemed every time a hopeful De Sole contacted a potential new partner, Arnault snapped up another block of shares.

"This is David against Goliath," De Sole said wearily at one point during the struggle, wishing he hadn't turned a cold shoulder to Bertelli. Arnault smiled. From his austere, glassed-in headquarters on Paris's Avenue Hoche, he knew De Sole's every move. "The people who refused him called us." He grinned.

At night, De Sole talked over the problem with his wife, Eleanore, who well remembered the ways of the business world from her days as an IBM executive but had retained her highly developed moral sensibility. She urged him to do not what was "best" for De Sole, but what was "right" by Gucci.

Resigned and angry, De Sole agreed to meet with Arnault, but he didn't feel friendly about it. The two sides bandied about times and locations for nearly a week. Arnault had proposed a meal to keep the meeting personal; De Sole opted for a business setting.

"I asked him to lunch," Arnault quipped later, "and he asked me to Morgan Stanley!"

The meeting, on January 22 in Morgan Stanley's Paris office, was a stiff, scripted encounter, for which both men had rehearsed their parts. The two CEOs used the time to study each other. Arnault, the brilliant, French-educated takeover baron; De Sole, the determined, Rome-born, and Harvard-educated quick study.

"They were total opposites," said Zaoui, who attended the meeting. "Arnault was formal and ill at ease; De Sole was natural, straightforward, and talkative."

Arnault lavished praise on De Sole and Ford, saying his interest in Gucci was not hostile. He urged De Sole to consider that Gucci could benefit from LVMH control and pressed for representation on the board. De Sole demurred, citing a conflict of interest. He cringed to think that LVMH could maneuver its own executive onto Gucci's board and have full access to confidential information ranging from sales, marketing, and distribution data to potential acquisitions and new strategies. He asked Arnault either to stop buying Gucci stock or to make a bid for the entire company.

De Sole's fear was that Arnault could buy up enough Gucci shares to effectively control the company without making a fair offer to all of its shareholders for 100 percent of stock. Although New York Stock Exchange regulations do not set a threshold over which a bidder must make a full offer to all the shareholders in a company it has accumulated a significant stake in—called a public tender offer—most companies quoted in the United States already have antitakeover measures in their corporate charters. The same is true for the Amsterdam stock exchange, where Gucci was also quoted. Stock markets in other European countries, such as the United Kingdom, Germany, France, and Italy had all passed antitakeover laws setting specific levels after which a public tender offer is required. Gucci found itself in a no-man's-land: its statute had no built-in defenses—its effort to institute one had been voted down by its own shareholders—and it was listed on two stock markets that had chosen not to set specific takeover limitations, putting the onus back on the companies themselves.

De Sole tried to get Arnault to agree to stop his advance.

"There was goodwill in the beginning," recalled Zaoui. "De Sole even showed up at the next meeting with a Gucci handbag for Arnault's wife." He offered Arnault two seats on Gucci's board in exchange for reducing his voting rights to 20 percent, from 34.4 percent. But by their third meeting, Arnault rejected the offer and threatened to sue De Sole and members of the board personally if they didn't acquiesce. Both sides grew frustrated. On February 10, citing its rights as a shareholder, Arnault sent Gucci a letter requesting an extraordinary shareholders meeting to appoint an LVMH representative to Gucci's board. That move sent De Sole into a rage.

"We were convinced the proposal would be well received!" said Godé later, saying that LVMH had proposed an outside candidate with no ties to LVMH and had asked for only one representative instead of three. "We thought it was a sign of good faith," he said.

But De Sole's blood was boiling over a report that had quietly made its way back to him: an LVMH executive had told one of Gucci's institutional shareholders it wanted to have its own "eyes and ears" on the board to pave the way for acquiring complete control. De Sole wasn't about to let the wolf into his chicken coop.

"I became convinced that they never intended to make a full and fair offer for the company," De Sole said.

On Sunday, February 14, Gucci executives and bankers mustered their forces in the small Grafton Street conference room. In the months since Prada first bought its Gucci stake, a lawyer named Scott Simpson, who worked in the London office of the high-powered New York law firm Skadden, Arps, Slate, Meagher & Flom—famous for its work on corporate takeover battles—had been studying a far-fetched and risky ploy that he thought just might work. So far untested in court, the defensive ploy focused on a loophole in New York Stock Exchange regulations. The idea was an ESOP, an employee stock ownership plan, that would allow Gucci to issue a huge block of stock to company workers—and thereby dilute Arnault's percentage. The ESOP wouldn't make Arnault disappear, but it would neutralize his voting power. De Sole held the ESOP card up his sleeve and tried one last time to get Arnault either to agree to a written "standstill" agreement that would legally prohibit him from buying more shares or to make a fair and full offer for the entire company. Arnault's answer crept through Gucci's fax machine the afternoon of February 17 in the form of a letter asking Gucci to provide the LVMH board with "a valid reason" to accept a standstill. De Sole, initially reluctant to put up a fight, but now hard and determined, hit the roof.

"A reason for a standstill? He wants a reason?" De Sole shouted. "Tonight, I'll give him a reason!"

The next morning, February 18, Gucci announced it had issued an ESOP, consisting of 37 million new common shares, to Gucci employees. The block of new shares immediately diluted Arnault's stake to 25.6 percent and neutralized his voting power. De Sole had fired his opening shot.

"He started to enjoy the game as we moved on," Zaoui said. "He became determined to win."

When news of the ESOP broke, neither Arnault nor Godé knew exactly what an ESOP was. Godé did a double take as the surprising news scrolled across the Reuters screen on his desk; Arnault received the news via fax in a New York hotel room. Arnault ordered an immediate report from Godé, who told both his boss and the flood of reporters calling for comment that the ESOP was a clear violation of NYSE regulations. Before making its move on Gucci, Arnault had been assured by LVMH's New York lawyers that no company quoted on the New York Stock Exchange could issue new shares amounting to more than 20 percent of its capital. Only later, after urgent phone calls to stock exchange officials, did LVMH learn what Gucci's lawyers already knew: the veto against issuing the new shares didn't apply to foreign companies, which were regulated instead by laws in their own countries. Gucci, with corporate headquarters in Amsterdam, had no such restrictions under Dutch law.

"We were very surprised when we saw that horrible measure," admitted Godé later. "They were phantom shares that suddenly appeared, were owned by no one, and financed by the company. It was no coincidence that the number of shares matched exactly the number of shares we owned."

Another surprise for LVMH came on the heels of the ESOP—in a filing with the SEC, Gucci had revealed the clauses that would allow Tom Ford and Domenico De Sole to bail out in the event of a change in control. By then, the De Sole/Ford team was considered one of Gucci's most valuable assets. If they left, Gucci would be much less attractive as a takeover prize. Gucci maintained its lawyers had informed LVMH of the measures long before; LVMH claimed it knew nothing of the golden parachutes that allowed Gucci's "dream team" to bolt, collecting millions of dollars in stock options.

Arnault fired back, suing Gucci to block the ESOP and accusing the Gucci management of dirty tricks. De Sole's claim that an LVMH director represented a conflict of interest was simply a pretext to keep the company to himself, LVMH officials charged. A week later, an Amsterdam court froze both LVMH's shares in Gucci and the ESOP shares. Once again, Gucci's future lay in the hands of a court, its shares frozen, its management under siege. Although the Dutch judge had ordered both sides to negotiate in good faith, both camps felt bruised and angry. De Sole charged James Lieber, an American lawyer and senior aide to Arnault, with calling him a fascist in the French press and stopped believing anything Arnault said.

"It became intensely personal," recalled Zaoui.

The tension rose. De Sole ordered regular security sweeps of Gucci's Grafton Street offices to ensure that no hidden microphones had been planted. Tom Ford noticed a man sleeping in a car outside the apartment he and Buckley maintained in Paris and believed he was a private detective from the New York investigative firm Kroll Associates, which Arnault had reportedly hired to snoop on him—the stuff of a crime movie.

Undaunted, Arnault began to lace his offensive with sugar, sending conciliatory messages directed at Tom Ford in an effort to drive a wedge between him and De Sole and lure the Texan over to the LVMH camp. If De Sole bolted under the change of control clause, Arnault could find another manager to replace him, but if Ford left, Gucci's entire image went with him.

"Businessmen, there are a lot of them, but designers, there are few," an LVMH executive commented pointedly in a conference call with journalists.

Then Arnault sent a French journalist, a friend of Ford's, to meet the designer for dinner in Milan. Ford found out halfway through the meal that she was really there on behalf of Arnault and had agreed to call him after their meal.

"He approached me through every channel except the right one—the direct one." Ford finally agreed to lunch with Arnault several weeks later at Mosimann's, the exclusive London club where ten years earlier an exiled Maurizio Gucci had furnished the Gucci room with his signature green fabric and stately Empire furniture. On the day of their appointment, news of the supposedly secret meeting blared from the apricot-colored pages of the *Financial Times*—along with details of Ford's stock option plan revealing that he had options on some two million shares on which he stood to make some $80 million based on the stock price at that time. Ford promptly blamed LVMH for the leak—and canceled lunch. The effort to separate Ford from De Sole had only driven the two men closer together.

Meanwhile, although the ESOP had bought Gucci time, it hadn't changed the company's fundamental vulnerability to a takeover and the outcome of the move was still in the hands of the Dutch court. Gucci still needed to find its white knight.

Domenico De Sole had never heard of François Pinault, even though he was one of the richest men in France. In June 1998, *Forbes* had ranked Pinault as the thirty-fifth richest man in the world with an estimated net worth of $6.6 billion. Born in Normandy, the sixty-two-year-old Pinault had over the years transformed a small family-owned sawmill into Europe's largest nonfood retail group, Pinault Printemps Redoute SA (PPR), becoming a household name in France. His holdings included the Printemps department stores, the FNAC electronics outlets, and the Redoute mail-order catalog. His better-known assets outside France included Christie's auction house, Converse shoes, and Samsonite luggage. During a routine chat with one of his Morgan Stanley bankers, Pinault's ears had perked up at the mention of Gucci. He had been attracted for some time by the luxury goods business. After a quick trip to New York, where he dropped in on Gucci's Fifth Avenue store—which at the time still sported the dark marble and glass decor from Aldo Gucci's days—he asked for a meeting with Domenico De Sole. They met in Morgan Stanley's London Mayfair town house on March 8. De Sole gave his speech—which he had polished to perfection collecting no-thank-yous from other potential partners—about how he and Tom Ford had taken Gucci in five years from a company with sales of $200 million to one with sales of $1 billion. Both he and Ford knew that what took Gucci to the $1 billion mark wasn't going to get it to the $2 billion mark, De Sole said, telling Pinault their dream of turning Gucci into a multibrand company. It was exactly what Pinault wanted to hear.

"I like building things," said the smiling, blue-eyed Pinault, with a nod to his lumber mill past. "This is a chance to create a global group."

Pinault, a high school dropout, had acquired all the traditional French symbols of success, wineries, media, and political ties. He was a close friend of French president Jacques Chirac. Now he wanted to move strongly into Arnault's territory and Gucci gave him that opportunity.

"There is room for two in this business," said Pinault. "Gucci had a rope around its neck, the noose was tied, and the countdown had begun: it was only a question of time before they would become a division of LVMH."

Pinault invited De Sole and Ford to lunch at his sixth arrondissement Paris town house on March 12 along with his senior executives, PPR CEO Serge Weinberg and top aide Patricia Barbizet. The small group dined on baked fish in Pinault's lavishly furnished apartment amid a stunning modern art collection that included paintings by Mark Rothko, Jackson Pollock, and Andy Warhol and sculptures by Henry Moore and Pablo Picasso. De Sole and Ford warmed to Pinault's direct, no-nonsense, open-minded style—a far cry, they felt, from Arnault's feints and parries.

"I liked his eyes, there was instant rapport," recalled Ford, who watched in admiration the way Pinault listened to and respected the opinions of his senior aides without losing his authority. "One even corrected him."

"There was instant personal chemistry," agreed Weinberg, a tall, clear-eyed executive who had traded a promising public sector career to help meld Pinault's diverse acquisitions into a smoothly running group nearly ten years earlier.

"I felt we all spoke the same language," said Weinberg. "It wasn't about diplomas, but about personalities."

That feeling carried one of the fastest and toughest negotiations bankers on both sides had ever seen. Time was short: Pinault set a deadline, March 19, the date on which court-ordered negotiations between Gucci and LVMH were to resume. If Gucci and Pinault couldn't reach an agreement in a week, there would be no deal.

By that evening, a squadron of lawyers and investment bankers for both sides got to work hammering out the nuts and bolts of the Gucci-Pinault alliance. As usual in such top secret deals, the players were dealt code names: "Gold" for Gucci, "Platinum" for Pinault, "Black" for Arnault.

A SMALL, discreet businessman's hotel on Rue de Miromesnil with no room service and no coffee bar became one of their unlikely meeting places, the executives coming and going secretively through back exits. De Sole drove a hard bargain on issues of price and control, fearing as he did that Pinault would back away. But on the contrary, Pinault had yet another card to play. He called De Sole and Ford to a private meeting at London's Dorchester Hotel. If De Sole and Ford agreed, he wanted to buy Sanofi Beauté, which owned the famed Yves Saint Laurent (YSL) design house and a stable of designer fragrances, and turn it over to Gucci to run. Arnault himself had rejected buying Sanofi before Christmas, saying it was too expensive.

"Do we want it!" exclaimed Ford as De Sole shot him a long "what are we getting ourselves into?" look. "Yes!" Ford said. "YSL is the number one brand in the world!"

Ford himself had looked to Yves Saint Laurent's work—especially from the seventies—as inspiration for his sexy mannish suits, tuxedo looks, and Bohemian touches. The thought of the magic Ford and De Sole could work for YSL excited everyone in the room.

In one week, Gucci had gone from narrowly escaping the devouring jaws of LVMH to commanding a deal that valued the company at $7.5 billion and gave it $3 billion in the bank along with the first pearl in the campaign to build Gucci into a multibrand luxury goods group.

The morning of March 19, as cameras flashed, Pinault and Gucci announced their unexpected new alliance: François Pinault had agreed to invest $3 billion for a 40 percent (later raised to 42 percent) share in Gucci in addition to turning over the Sanofi business Pinault had just bought for $1 billion. The agreement valued Gucci stock at $75 a share—a 13 percent premium over the average price during the past ten days of trading—and called for Gucci to issue 39 million new shares to Pinault. The megadeal effectively reduced Arnault's 34.4 stake to 21 percent and shouldered him out of any decision making. Gucci agreed to increase its board of directors from eight to nine members and give Pinault's group four representatives, in addition to three out of five seats on a new strategic committee to evaluate future acquisitions. De Sole and Ford happily described their newfound partnership as a "dream come true." They explained to reporters that they had been willing to give Pinault what they refused Arnault because PPR was not a direct competitor and Gucci would become the cornerstone of a new strategy in luxury goods instead of being folded into a larger group, such as LVMH, as just a division. Pinault had also agreed to all of their conditions and signed a standstill agreement, promising that he wouldn't increase his shareholding beyond the 42 percent.

When news of the Gucci-PPR deal hit the newswires, Arnault was outside Paris delivering a speech to a group of LVMH managers at Euro Disneyland. He cut short his engagement and sped back to Paris, less than an hour away. His senior aides, the white-haired, blue-eyed Godé and hardjawed Lieber, learned about the massive deal in Amsterdam's Hotel Krasnapolsky, where they were awaiting an 11:00 A.M. meeting with Gucci's general counsel Allan Tuttle.

"What do we do now?" Lieber asked Godé helplessly.

"We keep our appointments," said Godé through his teeth.

When Tuttle met Godé and Lieber in a downstairs conference room, the Gucci executive politely declined to give the men additional details of the Pinault deal, further infuriating the LVMH duo.

"To have a successful meeting, three things are required: courtesy, transparency, and politeness," said Godé sternly. "I regret that this morning you have shown none of these," he fired as the LVMH executives turned on their heels and left. By early afternoon, they reunited with Arnault in LVMH's top-floor Avenue Hoche conference room. Just the day before, at an LVMH analysts' conference in Paris, Arnault had insisted he had no intention of launching a full bid for Gucci. In the light of the Pinault alliance, Arnault realized he had two options: stay as a powerless minority shareholder in a company controlled by hostile management or try to buy Gucci outright. That afternoon, Arnault made a $81 per share bid for Gucci, valuing the company at more than $8 billion—a remarkable figure considering that just six years earlier, Gucci had teetered on the edge of bankruptcy.

De Sole was on the telephone in a conference room at his Paris hotel, explaining the Pinault agreement to a reporter, when he heard the news. He cut the interview short and began to shout: "I rest my case! I rest my case! I rest my case!" Finally, it seemed, Arnault had done what De Sole had asked for all along: made an offer for all of Gucci.

Arnault's bid never went anywhere. The offer was contingent on the abolition of Gucci's agreement with Pinault. But the Gucci team had played its cards well and made sure that the agreement with Pinault was an unshakable, cash-in-the-bank transaction. Subsequent offers from Arnault, in which he raised the price to $85 per share, and, according to some reports, as high as $91 per share—valuing Gucci at nearly $9 million—also went nowhere. Gucci's board of directors examined and then rejected each one for not being full and unconditional. Arnault filed a new round of lawsuits to block the Pinault deal. On May 27, in a green-walled room of the Enterprise Chamber of Amsterdam, five black-robed judges, presiding under a photograph of Queen Beatrix, upheld Gucci's agreement with PPR. Although the court struck down the ESOP, the unprecedented poison pill had served its purpose by buying Gucci time to find its white knight. De Sole immediately called Tom Ford, who was in Los Angeles to pick up an award, with the good news. Then he instructed his staff to make plans for a party. That night the tired, overjoyed, and relieved Gucci team members celebrated on a barge floating down the canals of Amsterdam, toasting each other merrily with non-LVMH champagne.

Licking their wounds, Arnault and Godé retreated to their glass and marble Avenue Hoche tower, sheepishly admitting that perhaps they had gone wrong. But they refused to go away. Although common wisdom might have dictated Arnault quietly sell his Gucci shares, he stubbornly maintained his position in the belief that in the long run he would have his way.

"We are going to stay right here," said Godé at the time. "It isn't every day we get to sit back and watch other people working for us. But if things don't turn out to be as easy as announced, we will be there in the first row." He smiled, implying that LVMH would be ready to swoop in to protect its interests. By mid-2000, however, LVMH appeared ready to unwind its Gucci shareholding.

For Domenico De Sole, the true end of the battle with LVMH didn't come until July 1999, when a series of routine Gucci board appointments were approved despite LVMH opposition at Gucci's annual general shareholders meeting in Amsterdam.

"All of the independent shareholders voted in our favor," De Sole said. "For me that was the real end of the battle. Arnault thought he was the master of the universe! Well, he got beaten!"

In the meantime, as Godé promised, LVMH continued to breathe down De Sole's neck, attacking first the Pinault agreement, then the planned acquisition of Yves Saint Laurent through Sanofi Beauté. Arnault mounted technical challenges to the way the Gucci-PPR alliance had been concluded, charging that the Gucci-PPR alliance had failed to pay the $30 million corporate tax on the transaction. Gucci defended its actions, saying its lawyers had determined they weren't obliged to pay the tax and that they had saved their shareholders money in the process. Gucci otherwise shrugged off the allegation, saying that even if they were required to pay, it was a minor issue with respect to the $3 billion deal they had secured. Still, Arnault had made his point: he was watching De Sole's every move. Arnault also announced that he believed the 6-billion-franc (about $1 billion) price tag for Sanofi Beauté—the fragrance group that controlled YSL—was too steep. As Gucci's second-largest single shareholder, he could threaten the transaction if he could prove it wasn't in the interests of Gucci shareholders. Arnault had walked away from buying Sanofi himself in December, saying it was too expensive.

In addition to Arnault, De Sole had two other Frenchmen to contend with. The first was Pierre Bergé, YSL's feisty, sixty-eight-year-old chairman and cofounder. Bergé, who had an airtight contract through 2006 that gave him veto power over creative decisions taken at the house, wasn't about to be elbowed aside. Nor was he willing to allow newcomers into the hallowed inner sanctum of Yves Saint Laurent, a rarefied, Proustian mansion on Paris's Avenue Marceau with spacious salons hung with green curtains and chandeliers, design studios, and offices.

"This building and these offices are untouchable!" Bergé had intoned. "This is the reign of haute couture."

On the other side of the negotiating table, Domenico De Sole was equally uncompromising. He and Tom Ford had to have complete control or there would be no deal.

The other Frenchman De Sole had to deal with was his own savior and newfound partner—François Pinault, who had acquired YSL through his private holding company Artemis SA, but was anxious to complete the transfer to Gucci.

"I was negotiating very hard against my largest shareholder!" De Sole said. "We had to find a formula that would give Gucci total control. The deal had to win the compliance of the independent members of the board."

"The strong point of the Tom Ford–Domenico De Sole team was their ability to exert control over the art and value of a brand through product design, communications image, and store concepts," observed a Milan-based luxury goods consultant, Armando Branchini, senior vice president of Intercorporate. "It would have been a shame if they couldn't have gotten the freedom to do that."

Just when it seemed there was no solution to the problem, Pinault himself came forward with a graceful compromise: he would buy the haute couture operation through his own investment company, Artemis, and Gucci would get the rest. In addition to the YSL business, Sanofi contained the Roger & Gallet brand and a stable of fragrance licenses including Van Cleef & Arpels, Oscar de la Renta, Krizia, and Fendi. At YSL, there was already a division between the haute couture—which was still designed by Yves Saint-Laurent himself—and the Rive Gauche women's and men's ready-to-wear collections, which were designed by young designers Alber Elbaz and Hedi Slimane, respectively. The formal separation of the business into two distinct companies seemed both natural and feasible. Pinault's eleventh-hour solution gave everybody what they wanted. Yves Saint-Laurent and Pierre Bergé signed over full control of the Yves Saint Laurent brand to De Sole and Ford for a princely payoff of $70 million, while they retained artistic and executive control of the haute couture operation, which employs some 130 people, registers sales of some 40 million French francs—and operates chronically in the red. Pinault agreed to swallow that pill in the interests of moving on with the larger transaction.

"I am very low key, but some very stubborn people have misread that as being soft," De Sole said. "I'm not soft. It was very simple. I knew what I needed."

De Sole had showed his negotiating fiber during the past few months when a lively bidding war exploded over the Rome-based accessories label Fendi, the darling of the accessories market for its so-called baguette handbag, a versatile model created in 1997 that had flown out of stores faster than it could be restocked. Fendi was controlled by five spirited sisters, the daughters of the company's founder, Adele Fendi, and their families. As a gaggle of suitors circled, offer prices began to spiral far beyond average values for luxury brands being quoted in the industry at the time. As the price rose, early bidders, including Rome-based jeweler Bulgari and U.S. buyout fund Texas Pacific Group, dropped out. De Sole, who had made an offer for a controlling stake that valued the entire company at about 1.3 trillion lire, or an estimated $680 million, watched the others walk away, thinking he had the deal in the bag. Then Prada's Patrizio Bertelli—who had been a long-ago supplier of leather goods to Fendi—bounded on the scene with an offer of 1.6 trillion lire, or the equivalent of about $840 million. De Sole really wanted to buy Fendi. He felt he and Ford could do wonders with the Italian fur, leather, and accessories firm, whose roots were not unlike Gucci's. De Sole topped Bertelli's offer at 1.65 trillion lire, or about $870 million. Then Bertelli delivered his bombshell: he teamed up with LVMH in an unprecedented alliance, beating out Gucci with an offer that valued the entire company at more than $900 million, more than 33 times Fendi's bottom line. At that time in the industry, a multiple of 25 for a sale price was already considered high. The Fendi deal hit established values right out of the ballpark and made De Sole feel as though his two worst enemies had ganged up on him. Nonetheless, De Sole marched back to his board of directors.

"We can beat the Prada-LVMH bid," he told them, "but in my view it's too much." He had also balked at some of the Fendi family's conditions, including ensuring jobs for the younger family members and their spouses. "I can treat people well, but I cannot promise anybody a job," De Sole said. "It isn't about family anymore. You have to perform."

The Fendi transaction, even though Gucci lost it, helped De Sole in two ways: it established him as a tough negotiator who could walk away from the table if he didn't get what he wanted and it deflated Arnault's argument that Gucci was paying too much for Sanofi, relieving some of the pressure surrounding that transaction.

On November 15, 1999, Gucci finally announced it had acquired Sanofi Beauté, and with it the historic Yves Saint Laurent name, which veteran fashion journalist Suzy Menkes at the *International Herald Tribune* dubbed "fashion's shiniest trophy." In the process, Gucci had even managed to elicit remarkably conciliatory remarks from Bergé, well known in the business for his barbed tongue: "The only thing that I wanted to protect was M. Yves Saint-Laurent. If others want to come and apply their marketing and communication techniques, let them come. We don't know how to do those things. We created the greatest maison of haute couture, but we don't know about marketing."

With the YSL acquisition, Gucci had not only taken its first step toward becoming a multibrand group, it had also done so with one of the golden names of the industry. On November 19, Gucci further announced it had bought control of a small, luxury shoemaker in Bologna called Sergio Rossi, paying 179 billion lire (about $100 million) for 70 percent of the company, leaving the Rossi family with 30 percent. More acquisitions would follow, including the purchase of fine French jeweler Boucheron in May 2000.

By January 2000, Tom Ford was appointed creative director of Yves Saint Laurent, as expected, in addition to his duties at Gucci. The announcement came just in time for Ford to attend the YSL haute couture show in Paris and followed news the previous November that Gucci had appointed one of its rising young stars, thirty-six-year-old Gucci sales director Mark Lee, as the new managing director of Yves Saint Laurent Couture, as the company is now called. When Lee's appointment was announced, many in the industry didn't even know who the shy, soft-spoken Lee was. Gucci itself didn't even have a prepared bio for him. Lee had worked at Saks Fifth Avenue, Valentino, Armani, and Jil Sander, before joining Gucci, and was well respected by his colleagues for his low-key, conscientious style. While Ford's job will be to refresh YSL's faded glory, Lee's job will be to run the day-to-day business of the brand's ready-to-wear, fragrances, and accessories, which includes overseeing some 187 licenses.

As the quakes and tremors in the luxury goods business continue to turn established relationships upside down, two sharp young Americans have taken charge of two of the most visible—and previously sacred—jobs in French fashion. The next question in everyone's mind was: who would Ford bring in to design the YSL ready-to-wear, or would he keep it for himself, and if so, would he continue designing for Gucci? Though on all counts a bright and talented young man who had brought a new perspective to the industry, one that melded fashion, design, lifestyle, and business into one overarching concept, could he really have it and do it all?

Gucci had ridden the crest of the wave of consolidation sweeping the luxury goods industry and still had an active wish list of companies it would like to bring within its orbit. However, De Sole maintained that the real issue was still creativity, not size.

"Tom and I look at our job as fixing and mending," De Sole said. "We are really brand managers. When we look at a company, it's not 'Let's buy it,' but 'What do we do with it?' We aren't investment bankers, after all." Indeed, Ford and De Sole weren't investment bankers and they didn't come from the tough Florentine merchant stock that had engendered Gucci, but they brought their own brand of spirit, determination, and drive that continued to propel Gucci into stardom as an international enterprise.

* * *

IN ITS EIGHTY-YEAR HISTORY, Gucci had plowed new ground at crucial moments. It gained attention both for the unprecedented litigious antics of its second and third generations as it drew back the curtain on the ups and downs of a privately held family business and as it logged achievements in the world of Italian luxury goods. In the 1950s, Aldo brought Gucci to New York, one of the first Italian names to land there. By the sixties and seventies, Gucci meant style and status. In the eighties, Maurizio invited a sophisticated financial partner into Gucci's private share capital and signed off on a joint business plan. He was among the first in the industry to do this. In the early nineties, again leading the industry, Maurizio imported American design and marketing talent into the heart of European luxury by hiring Dawn Mello and Tom Ford. Steered by Investcorp in the late nineties, Gucci brought off one of the first and most successful IPOs ever staged in the fashion and luxury goods industry. By the end of the decade, with De Sole in control, Gucci first warned of the economic hardships coming to roil Asian markets and then weathered one of the fiercest takeover challenges in the business, winning against all odds with a previously untested takeover defense and a remark-able new partnership. Following the Gucci-LVMH battle, the European Community established community-wide regulations governing takeovers and tender offers, a project that had been in the works but never completed. Now as a new century rolls in, the Harvard Business School plans to conduct a case study of Gucci's achievements.

"I was interested in an Italian company that had wide appeal beyond an individual sector or country, a company in which there had been dramatic change and which had a broadly recognized consumer brand," said Professor David Yoffie, who is heading up the study.

Tolstoy wrote in *Anna Karenina,* "All happy families resemble one another, but each unhappy family is unhappy in its own way." The Guccis' own peculiar vintage unhappiness played out dramatically in boardrooms and courtrooms and newspaper headlines for the world to see. "The Gucci story is the perfect example of what a family should not do," mused Severin Wunderman. "The amount of blood spilled was tragic, and a lesson in how not to end a dynasty." What if things had turned out differently? If the Gucci family had been more united, would Gucci today be a quiet, predictable family firm happily churning out plastic-coated GG shopping bags with the red and green stripe or brown, bamboo-handled handbags? If Maurizio

Gucci had achieved his vision—already radically different from that of his relatives—would Gucci be more like Hermès, a safe, respectable luxury firm with beautiful products and no fireworks? The Gucci family was mortified as each new blowup blazed across newspaper headlines. But who can say if their dysfunction and the attendant publicity didn't help ignite that inexplicable magic that infused the Gucci name with desirability and style, raising the stakes of the business so high it ultimately tore the family apart? It was that magic, combined with the style and high quality of Gucci's goods, that made Gucci products special in the customers' eyes. After all, at its previous peak in the sixties and seventies, Gucci was still just selling black and brown handbags, Italian penny loafers, and status luggage. Today, despite all the magic Tom Ford works on the runway, in Hollywood and in Gucci's glossy ad campaigns, black shoes and handbags are still the number one sellers in Gucci stores around the world.

When asked where that magic came from in the past, Roberto Gucci answered without hesitation. *"L'azienda era la famiglia e la famiglia era l'azienda!* The company was the family and the family was the company! The issues that created the splits were company issues, not family issues," mused Roberto, referring to clashes first over Paolo's desire to create and license less expensive lines for younger buyers, and later to Maurizio's ambitious mission to take Gucci upmarket and the sacrifices that entailed. "When you have a company where the managers and the family are one, then it is more difficult," Roberto said. In a grotesque twist where blood ran thicker than company politics, Aldo Gucci had even tided his son Paolo over financially when the latter ran out of money after taking Gucci to court.

While Gucci's products became status symbols, the company and the family won the hearts of its workers, workers who remained loyal through the years despite the ups and downs of the market and family strife. "It was something that got into your blood bit by bit, like a drug," said one long-time employee. "You began to understand the product, to know the artisans, and you began to see the potential and feel it inside you. You were proud to work for this company. It's hard to explain. Either you believe in it or you don't."

And the notion that there was a real flesh-and-blood Gucci family behind the signature luggage and handbags also captivated consumers.

The Gucci story symbolizes the struggles faced by many families and individuals in Europe who have created and grown their own businesses. Now they face a classic catch-22: the price they must pay for their success is often letting go of their companies. As global competition accelerates industry consolidations, family and individual owners must surrender their autonomy by bringing in professional management, joining new business combinations, or selling out entirely, if they hope to survive financially.

Others have contended with destiny more quietly. Valentino's decision in 1998 to sell his Rome fashion house to Italian investment company HdP was accompanied by a few elegant tears during the press conference announcing the sale. Emanuel Ungaro's decision to sell his Paris-based maison to Florence's Ferragamo family in 1997 was sealed with warm handshakes. More recently, German designer Jil Sander stoically relinquished control to Italian label Prada in hopes of helping her business grow far beyond what she could achieve on her own. Rome's Fendi family successfully kept the curtain down on its internal rifts while it artfully choreographed the orbits of its circling suitors until agreeing to sell control to the alliance between Prada and LVMH.

Gucci's family wars evolved into a struggle between family management and professional, financial management as Maurizio failed to marry his vision for Gucci with a strong, pragmatic program. Sadly, the strong, pragmatic woman Maurizio did marry led him to his own violent fate. Driven by his vision but shackled by his temperament, Maurizio Gucci couldn't do what ultimately needed to be done because he failed to lay a strong financial foundation for his dream. Nonetheless, he paved the way for Domenico De Sole and Tom Ford to move in their winning blend of business sense and style—and the right mix of power, ego, and image to bring the magic back. Following the transition, Gucci reappeared as a leader in the luxury goods market.

In retrospect, the formula appears clear, but can it be copied? "I don't think so," said Suzy Menkes, the respected fashion critic of the *International Herald Tribune*. "There must be a magic ingredient. It's like making a Hollywood film: you can have a great script and get all the right stars, but it's not always a hit at the box office. Sometimes it works and sometimes it doesn't."

Now the Gucci family, well compensated, watches from the sidelines—with mixed sadness and bitterness—as the company that bears their name continues to dominate business and fashion news. Giorgio Gucci still lives in Rome with Maria Pia and travels frequently to Florence, where he acquired a respected Florentine leather goods manufacturer, Limberti, today one of Gucci's suppliers, and where he works alongside his oldest son, Guccio. Guccio, who married into a wealthy textile manufacturing family from Prato, a medium-sized city near Florence, has been the most entrepreneurial of the fourth generation, trying to start first a leather goods business under his own name in 1990 and subsequently a collection of ties under the name Esperienza in 1997. He currently works full time with Limberti. Guccio has had various legal diatribes with the Gucci company over the years on issues ranging from the use of his name to real estate.

The rest of the family, most of which lives in relative obscurity between Milan and Rome, finds Gucci's continuing success hard to swallow. "Does the bitterness ever fade?" Alessandro, Giorgio's youngest son, said to his mother, Orietta, once.

Roberto Gucci still lives in Florence, where he founded his own leather goods business, House of Florence, just one month after Maurizio sold out to Investcorp. House of Florence produces handcrafted leather bags and accessories in the old tradition, operates a shop on Via Tornabuoni not far from Gucci's, and has offices in Tokyo and Osaka as well. Roberto's wife, Drusilla, and five of his six children—Cosimo, Filippo, Uberto, Domitilla, and Francesco—also work in the firm. The sixth, Maria-Olympia, is a nun. Roberto's eyes still light up when he talks of handcrafted leather bags and the artisans that make them.

"I do no more and no less than what I was taught—that is all I know how to do," said Roberto Gucci. "I learned this trade and no one will take it from me and I will continue down this path."

The remaining Guccis have withdrawn into private life. Aldo and Bruna's daughter, Patricia, who has homes in Palm Beach and California, often visits her mother, who lives quietly in Rome. Paolo's youngest daughter, Patrizia, who worked for Gucci from 1987 to 1992 under Maurizio, lives on the outskirts of Florence in a tree-shaded villa where she pursues a career as a painter. Her older sister Elisabetta, the mother of two children, is a housewife.

In Milan, Patrizia, having lost her appeal, passes the days in her San Vittore jail cell, trying to forget the past and unable to imagine a future. Her mother, Silvana, lives in the vast apartment on Corso Venezia and visits Patrizia regularly, still bringing her favorite meatloaf every Friday. In February 2000, prosecutor Carlo Nocerino quietly closed the file of reports that Silvana had hastened the death of her husband, Fernando Reggiani, and had known about, or assisted in, Patrizia's plan to murder Maurizio. Now Silvana takes care of Patrizia and Maurizio's daughters, checking in regularly with Alessandra, who is completing her third year of business school in Lugano, and Allegra, who lives in the Corso Venezia apartment with her grandmother and studies law in Milan—as her father did. Despite the cost, the girls have maintained Maurizio's magnificent yacht, the *Creole,* which they enter in Saint-Tropez's Nioularge each year in memory of their father. They have also enjoyed idyllic vacation cruises on the *Creole* and visits onboard from members of the European elite—Prince Albert of Monaco, for example. Today, Alessandra and Allegra think of their father as Peter Pan, the boy who never wanted to grow up.

"He loved to play," recalled Alessandra. "He and Allegra would play soccer for hours, then they would come home exhausted and start with the video games. He was passionate for Ferrari, Formula One, Michael Jackson, and stuffed animals. One Christmas he came home with a giant red parrot for me, rang the bell, and talked with a funny parrot voice. He always delivered his presents in person."

But he wasn't always there for the girls.

"For months at a time we would speak up to six times a day," Alessandra recalled. "Then he would disappear and reemerge four or five months later. He could be alternately tender or like ice. But I was convinced that one day, despite all the fights, sooner or later he and my mother would get back together again." The most important thing parents can do for their children, it is said, is love each other.

A few blocks north of Corso Venezia, Paola Franchi lives with her son, Charly, in the twelfth-floor apartment deeded to her by her second husband. In a sumptuous living room decorated with plush upholstery, fine antiques, and hung with the famous green silk drapes she and Patrizia had argued about, pictures of Maurizio Gucci adorn every table and shelf.

Perhaps of all the people Maurizio left behind, the one whose life is emptiest without him is Luigi Pirovano, his faithful driver. Now retired and a widower, Luigi spends his days retracing his memories of Maurizio. Each day he drives into Milan from his home in Monza in the city's northern suburbs and tours their old haunts—the tenth-floor apartment on Corso Monforte where Maurizio and Rodolfo lived; and Via Monte Napoleone, where in 1951 Rodolfo opened Milan's original Gucci store, still operating up the street from Gucci's sleek new flagship store. Luigi drives past the Bonaparte residence in Via Cusani where Maurizio once lived and down Via Palestro, where on sunny days he parks to walk along the sandy paths of the Giardini Pubblici opposite the windows where Maurizio had his office and the doorway where he died. Four years passed before Luigi could bring himself to lunch at Bebel's, a family-style trattoria that served Maurizio's favorite *fiorentina* steaks. Maurizio brought Alessandra and Allegra here for lunch the week before he was shot.

As he ate and chatted with the owners at Bebel's, Luigi pushed his tortoiseshell glasses higher up on his nose, just as Maurizio used to do with his own glasses. In fact, Luigi's were Maurizio's glasses. A river of memories cascaded through Luigi's head—recollections of Maurizio as a boy, his first car, the early sweethearts, his relationship with Patrizia, the beginning of the troubles, *il periodo sbagliato.* There were times when Luigi brought a feverish Maurizio homemade chicken soup from his own kitchen, nursing his boss back to health in Maurizio's lonely pied-à-terre; regular evenings spent sharing roast chicken Luigi would pick up at a local delicatessen; constant traveling—Florence, Saint Moritz, Monte Carlo, Rome, and beyond.

"Maurizio was alone. Completely, entirely, fundamentally alone. For him there was only Luigi. Night after night I left my wife and my son to go to him," Luigi recalled. "It was too much, too much to ask of a person—but who wants to hear these things?"

At Maurizio's funeral, Luigi sobbed uncontrollably. His son looked accusingly at his father and said, "*Papà,* you didn't cry like that when *Mamma* died."

Luigi still goes to Maurizio regularly, visiting his tomb in the little Swiss cemetery on the hill of Suvretta, just below the Saint Moritz estate he so loved and the place where Patrizia and the girls decided he should be buried. Luigi also visits Rodolfo, who is buried with the rest of his family—Aldo, Vasco, Rodolfo, Alessandra, Grimalda, Guccio, and Aida—in the cemetery of Soffiano, just outside Florence.

Back in Florence, in his high-ceilinged office overlooking the Arno, Roberto still blames Maurizio for the loss of Gucci and he points a finger at Patrizia without ever mentioning her name. It is outsiders marrying into a family, according to Roberto, who disrupt the subtle balance of power the family has carefully achieved. "What is the spark that lights the fire of ambition, the fire that burns out reason, moral principles, respect, and attentiveness, in the pursuit of unchecked riches? If one already has that ambition and beside him has one who blows the flicker into a flame—rather than dousing it with water—this is how!

"The Guccis were a great family," intones Roberto. "I ask forgiveness for all their mistakes—who doesn't make mistakes? I don't want to criticize their mistakes and I don't want to accept them, but I can't forget them. Life is a giant book with many pages. My father taught me to turn the page. As he used to say, 'Turn the page! Cry if you must, but shoot!' "

The Guccis were forced to turn the page when desire failed to keep step with reality. From the moment the family and the company split apart, the family set out on its bitter and tragic path, while the company began climbing from disarray to unprecedented success. Today, as Gucci develops its luxury goods group, the Gucci story continues to unfold as new players, captivated, commit themselves to perpetuating the magic. The challenge now is to move from hands-on management of a single brand to bringing along the new talent needed to handle multiple brands—while remembering that the Gucci legacy has a double edge.

Bibliographical Notes

: HISTORICAL RECONSTRUCTIONS :

I reconstructed some of the historical conversations and events surrounding the Gucci family by checking published accounts with first-person sources with either direct memory of the episode or a recollection of what others had said at the time. References to what a person was thinking are based on extensive research into the situation and the person's frame of mind at the time according to people close to him or her or other reliable accounts. In dramatizing contemporary conversations, I have based dialogue on conversations with one or more of the participants.

: HISTORICAL BACKGROUND :

For the historical reconstruction of the Gucci family and business, I worked from two existing books and numerous news articles, checking information with family members, current and former employees, and specialized historians. The fullest account of Guccio Gucci's early years appears in Gerald McNight, *Gucci: A House Divided,* London, Sidgwick & Jackson, 1987, and New York, Donald I. Fine, Inc., 1987. An Italian work by Angelo Pergolini and Maurizio Tortorella, *L'Ultimo dei Gucci,* Milan, Marco Tropea Editore, 1997, was also a helpful resource. Another valuable document about the Gucci family and history is Rodolfo Gucci's own documentary film: *Il Cinema nella Mia Vita,* directed and produced by Rodolfo Gucci and currently held in the archives of Cinecittà in Rome.

Fashion historian Aurora Fiorentini has done invaluable work to help reconstruct the Gucci Archive. Fiorentini has located some key documents, including one held in the Florence Chamber of Commerce that attests to the founding of the first Gucci company. Previous corporate biographies and press reports had dated the start of the Gucci business much earlier, in or around 1908. As the Gucci company evolved over the years, it became Azienda Individuale Guccio Gucci, a sole proprietorship, which was transformed into a *Società Anonima* in 1939, a family proprietorship, when for the first time Aldo, Ugo, and Vasco became co-owners. Ugo would later sell his shares at Guccio's insistence and Rodolfo would be invited into the company ownership. After the war, the company became a *Società di Responsabilità Limitata,* or S.r.l., a small corporation that has lighter capitalization requirements and more reporting flexibility than a *Società per Azioni,* or SpA, which is equivalent to a C-class corporation in the United States. Guccio Gucci didn't become an SpA until 1982. Information on establishments operating in historic Florence is available in the volume Confcommercio di Firenze, *I Negozi Storici a Firenze,* Firenze, Edizioni Demomedia, Nuova Grafica Fiorentina, November 1995.

Precise documentation about the exact dates, order of openings, and locations of the Gucci stores opened in Florence on Via del Parione and Via della Vigna Nuova is no longer available. Roberto Gucci recalls that the first shop was on Via del Parione, followed a few years later by a shop at Via della Vigna Nuova. However, according to Fiorentini, the first important Gucci shop was probably at Via della Vigna Nuova 7, where it held various locations over the years before moving to its final location at number 47–49, where the Valentino and Armani boutiques are currently located. Fiorentini believes the Via del Parione location identified at number 11 or 11-A, was probably a small workshop that the Gucci family opened briefly in the early period and later closed. Gucci's Via Condotti store in Rome was moved to its current location at number 8 in 1961.

: PATRIZIA REGGIANI MARTINELLI :

Patrizia's story is based in part on the author's personal correspondence with Patrizia Reggiani, as well as author interviews with her mother, Silvana Reggiani, friends of Patrizia and Maurizio's, and Liliana Colombo, Maurizio's former secretary who went to work as Patrizia's personal assistant after he died. The psychiatric report ordered by the Judge Renato Samek during Patrizia's trial, *Corte Di Assise Di Milano, Relazione di Perizia Collegiale Sullo Stato di Mente di Patrizia Reggiani Martinelli,* also provided rich insight into her childhood as she recounted it to the panel of psychiatrists. Excerpts from Patrizia's manuscript, *Gucci vs. Gucci,* were published in the Italian daily *Corriere della Sera* between March 25 and 28, 1998, describing her experiences with the Gucci family. The manuscript was widely circulated among Italian publishers but was never published.

: THE PAOLO CASES :

The numerous "Paolo Cases" were nicely summed up with an internal brief by Patton, Boggs & Blow in Washington, D.C., where George Borababy was very helpful in locating material and providing information on the key issues of each case. Rich material on the conflict with Paolo can be found in published court opinions, including: Paolo Gucci, Plaintiff, v. Gucci Shops Inc., Defendant, No. 83, Civ. 4453 (WCC) United States District Court, S.D. New York, June 17, 1988 in *Federal Supplement 688,* pp. 916–928, and Paolo Gucci, Plaintiff, v. Gucci Shops Inc., Guccio Gucci SpA, Maurizio Gucci, and Domenico De Sole, Defendants, No. 86, Civ. 6374 (WCC) United States District Court, S.D. New York, Dec. 1986, in *Federal Supplement 651,* pp. 194–198.

: FINANCIAL AND CORPORATE HISTORY :

Investcorp published its own "Detailed Information Memorandum" on Gucci in 1991, complete with historical background, schedules, and charts. The most complete sources of financial and business information about Gucci from 1991 to 1995 are the financial prospectuses prepared for Gucci's initial public offering in 1995 and the secondary issue in 1996.

: SELECTED ARTICLES :

Lisa Anderson, "Born-again Status: Dawn Mello Brings Back Passion and Prestige to the Crumbling House of Gucci," *Chicago Tribune,* January 15, 1992, 7:5.

Lisa Armstrong, "The High-Class Match-Maker," *The Times,* April 12, 1999.

Judy Bachrach, "A Gucci Knockoff," *Vanity Fair,* July 1995, pp. 78–128.

Isadore Barmash, "Gucci Shops Spread Amid a Family Image," *The New York Times,* April 19, 1971, 57:4, p. 59.

Amy Barrett, "Fashion Model: Gucci Revival Sets Standard in Managing Trend-Heavy Sector," *The Wall Street Journal,* August 25, 1997, p. 1.

Logan Bentley, "Aldo Gucci: The Mark That Made Gucci Millions," *Signature,* February 1971, p. 50.

Nancy Marx Better, "A New Dawn for Gucci," *Manhattan Inc.,* March 1990, pp. 76–83.

Katherine Betts, "Ford in Gear," *Vogue,* March 1999.

Nan Birmingham, "The Gift Bearers: Merchant Aldo Gucci," *Town & Country,* December 1977.

Carlo Bonini, "I Segreti dei Gucci," *Sette,* no. 45, 1998, p. 22.

"Brand Builder: How Domenico De Sole Turned Gucci into a Takeover Play," *Forbes Global,* February 8, 1999.

Holly Brandon, "G Force," *GQ,* February, 2000, p. 138.

Holly Brubach, "And Luxury for All," *The New York Times Magazine,* July 12, 1998.

Brian Burroughs, "Gucci and Goliath," *Vanity Fair,* July 1999.

Marian Christy, "The Guru of Gucci," *The Boston Globe,* May 19, 1984, "Living," p. 7.

Ron Cohen, "Retailing Is an Art at New Gucci 5th Ave. Unit," *Women's Wear Daily,* June 2, 1980, p. 23.

Glynis Costin, "Dawn Mello: Revamping Gucci," *Women's Wear Daily,* May 29, 1992, p. 2.

Ann Crittenden, "Knock-Offs Aside, Gucci's Blooming," *The New York Times,* June 25, 1978, III, 1:5.

Spencer Davidson, "Design," *Avenue,* October 1980, pp. 99–101.

Ian Dear, "200 Years of Yachting History," *Camper & Nicholson's Ltd. 1782–1982,* as reprinted in *Yachting Monthly,* August 1982.

Denise Demong, "Gucci: The Poetic Approach to Business," *Women's Wear Daily,* December 22, 1972, p. 1.

E. J. Dionne, "Repairing the House of Gucci," *The New York Times,* August 11, 1985, III, 5:1.

Carrie Donovan, "Fashion's Leading Edge: Bergdorf Goodman, Resplendent in Crystal and Cloaked with Tradition, Strikes a New and Unexpected Pose as the Fashionable Women's Mecca," *The New York Times Magazine,* September 14, 1986, p. 103.

Hebe Dorsey, "Gucci Seeking a New Image," *International Herald Tribune,* October 21, 1982, p. 7.

——, "Gucci Puts an Even Better Foot Forward—in New Moccasin," *International Herald Tribune,* July 26, 1968, p. 6.

Victoria Everett, "Move over Dallas: Behind the Glittering Facade, a Family Feud Rocks the House of Gucci," *People,* September 6, 1982, pp. 36–38.

Camilla Fiorina, "Sergio Bassi," *YD Yacht Design* by Yacht Capital, December 1988, pp. 82–86.

Bridget Foley, "Gucci's Mod Age," *W,* May 1995, p. 106.

——, "Ford Drives," *W,* August, 1996, p. 162.

Sara Gay Forden, "Gucci Is Expecting Break-Even Results Despite Sales Drop," *The Wall Street Journal,* November, 14, 1991, second section, p. 2.

———, "Banks Putting Big Squeeze on Gucci Chief," *Women's Wear Daily*, April 26, 1993, p. 1.

———, "Gucci Denies Financial Straits," *Women's Wear Daily*, April 27, 1993, p. 2.

———, "Bringing Back Gucci," *Women's Wear Daily*, December 12, 1994, p. 24.

———, "Gucci on Wall Street: Launching Pad for Worldwide Growth," *Women's Wear Daily*, November 2, 1995, p. 11.

———, "Gucci's Turnaround: From the Precipice to the Peak in 3 Years," *Women's Wear Daily*, May 2, 1996, p. 1.

———, "Prada Using Star Status to Expand on the Global Stage," *Women's Wear Daily*, February 15, 1996, p. 1.

Robin Givhan, "Gucci's Strong Suit," *The Washington Post*, May 5, 1999, C1.

Lauren Goldstein, "Prada Goes Shopping," *Fortune*, September 27, 1999, pp. 83–85.

Adriana Grassi, "The Gucci Look," *Footwear News*, April 28, 1966.

Robert Heller, "Gucci's $4 Billion Man," *Forbes Global*, February 8, 1999, pp. 36–39.

Lynn Hirschberg, "Next. Next. What's Next?" *The New York Times Magazine*, April 7, 1996, pp. 22–25.

Thomas Kamm, "Art of the Deal: François Pinault Snatches Away Gucci from Rival LVMH," *The Wall Street Journal*, March 2, 1999, p. 1.

Sarah Laurenedie, "Le Grand Seigneur," *W*, January 2000.

Suzy Menkes, "Fashion's Shiniest Trophy, Gucci Buys House of YSL for $1 Billion," *International Herald Tribune*, November 16, 1999, p. 1.

Russell Miller, "Gucci Coup," *The Sunday Times*, p. 16.

Sarah Mower, "Give Me Gucci," *Harper's Bazaar*, May 1995, p. 142.

John Rossant, "At Gucci, *La Vita* Is No Longer So *Dolce*," *Business Week*, November 23, 1992, p. 60.

Barbara Rudolph, "Makeover in Milan," *Time*, December 3, 1990, p. 56.

Galeazzo Santini, "Come Salire al Trono di Famiglia," *Capital*, December 1982, pp. 12–20.

Eugenia Sheppard, "Sporting the Gucci Look," *International Herald Tribune*, July 25, 1969, p. 12.

Mimi Sheraton, "The Rudest Store in New York," *New York*, November 10, 1975, pp. 44–47.

Michael Shnayerson, "The Ford That Drives Gucci," *Vanity Fair*, March 1998, pp. 136–52.

Amy Spindler "A Retreat from Retro Glamour," *The New York Times*, March 7, 1995, p. B9.

Angela Taylor, "But at Gucci You'd Think People Had Money to Burn," *The New York Times,* December 21, 1974, 12:1.

Lucia van der Post, "Is This the Most Delicious Man in the World?" *How to Spend It, The Financial Times,* issue 35, April 1999, p. 6.

Constance C. R. White, "Patterns: How LVMH May Make Its Presence Felt at Gucci, Now That It Controls 34.4% of the Stock," *The New York Times,* January 26, 1999, fashion section, p. 1.

:   SELECTED READINGS   :

Teri Agins. *The End of Fashion: The Mass Marketing of the Clothing Business.* New York: William Morrow and Company, Inc., 1999.

Salvatore Ferragamo. *Salvatore Ferragamo, Shoemaker of Dreams.* Florence: Centro Della Edifini Srl.,1985 (from original publication, 1957).

Nadège Forestier and Nazanine Ravai. *Bernard Arnault: Ou le gout du Pouvoir.* Paris: Olivier Orban, 1990.

Gerald McKnight. *Gucci: A House Divided.* London: Sidgwick & Jackson, 1987, and New York: Donald I. Fine, Inc., 1987.

Angelo Pergolini and Maurizio Tortorella. *L'Ultimo dei Gucci: Splendori e Miserie di una Grande Famiglia Fiorentina.* Milan: Marco Tropea Editore, 1997.

Marie-France Pochna. *Christian Dior.* New York: Arcade Publishing, 1996; Bernard Arnault. *Tout le Monde An Parle,* Paris: Millafford, 2000.

Stefania Ricci. "Firenze Anni Cinquanta: Nasce La Moda Italiana," in *La Stanza delle Meraviglie: L'Arte del Commercio a Firenze dagli sporti medioevali al negozio virtuale.* Florence: Le Lettere, 1998, pp. 78–87.

Hugh Sebag-Montefiore. *Kings of the Catwalk: The Louis Vuitton and Moët Hennessy Affair.* London: Chapman, 1992.

:   OTHER SOURCES   :

Britain's Channel Five documentary produced by Studio Zeta: *Fashion Victim: The Last of the Guccis,* November 1998.

Charlie Rose interview with Tom Ford on December 28, 1999.

60 Minutes, "Gucci," May 22, 1988.

Today, "Gucci Murder," NBC Network, June 24, 1998.

Robert Gucci, *"Il Cinema nella Mia Vita."* Private documentary production, November, 1982.

Index